And Then Your Soul is Gone

And Then Your Soul is Gone

Moral Injury and U.S. War-culture

Kelly Denton-Borhaug

equinox

SHEFFIELD UK   BRISTOL CT

Published by Equinox Publishing Ltd.

UK   Office 415, The Workstation, 15 Paternoster Row, Sheffield,
      South Yorkshire S1 2BX
USA   ISD, 70 Enterprise Drive, Bristol, CT 06010

www.equinoxpub.com

First published 2021

British Library Cataloguing-in-Publication Data

A catalogue record for this book is available from the British Library.

ISBN-13   978 1 80050 103 4   (hardback)
          978 1 80050 104 1   (paperback)
          978 1 80050 105 8   (ePDF)
          978 1 80050 124 9   (ePub)

Library of Congress Cataloging-in-Publication Data

Names: Denton-Borhaug, Kelly, author.
Title: And then your soul is gone : moral injury and U.S. war-culture /
  Kelly Denton-Borhaug.
Description: Sheffield, South Yorkshire : Equinox Publishing Ltd, 2021. |
  Includes bibliographical references and index. | Summary: "This book
  exposes the threads of violence that tie together the naturalized
  dynamics of U.S. ways of war and militarization with collective
  practices of national distraction and self-deception. It shows how these
  same threads of violence are also tightly woven and sacralized in the
  tapestry of U.S. national identity, tragically concealing moral injury
  from greater consciousness, and sourcing its toxic growth - ironically -
  in the very lives of those the nation claims it most highly esteems, our
  military service members and veterans"-- Provided by publisher.
Identifiers: LCCN 2021004439 (print) | LCCN 2021004440 (ebook) | ISBN
  9781800501034 (hardback) | ISBN 9781800501041 (paperback) | ISBN
  9781800501058 (pdf) | ISBN 9781800501249 (epub)
Subjects: LCSH: War and society--United States. | War--Moral and ethical
  aspects--United States. | War--Psychological aspects. | Violence--Moral
  and ethical aspects--United States. | Violence--Psychological aspects. |
  Militarization--United States. | Militarism--United States. | National
  characteristics, American.
Classification: LCC HM554 .D466 2021 (print) | LCC HM554 (ebook) | DDC
  303.60973--dc23
LC record available at https://lccn.loc.gov/2021004439
LC ebook record available at https://lccn.loc.gov/2021004440

Typeset by Sparks – www.sparkspublishing.com

For Eric, Claude AnShin, Alex, Andy, and all the truth tellers

Contents

Preface

For almost twenty years I've been puzzling, researching, writing, teaching and learning about "U.S. war-culture." I'm not the first to use this term, but along the way of this journey I developed my own definition: U.S. war-culture is the interpenetration of the ethos, institutions and practices of war with (supposed) civilian sites of culture and life, including the economy, politics, education, religion, the arts, entertainment and popular culture, sports and media, corporate and consumer practices, and the list does not end there.

This was not a focus I randomly chose; the changing nature of U.S. culture and life following the events of September 11, 2001, compelled and motivated me. The United States was going to war, and everywhere around me I heard this war was a "necessary sacrifice." As a religious studies scholar already deep into research of *soteriology* in Christianity (the study of the many diverse theories, images and metaphors of salvation in Christian tradition and history), my attention was riveted. What was this relationship between the surging of war, the justification of violence, and frameworks of sacrifice? Eventually I came to see that the intertwining of war-culture and sacrifice has a very long history, and not only in the United States. Excavating this confusing tangle led me to the nature of war-culture itself, the related need to explore and analyze this monolith in the U.S. context, and the overwhelming impact it has on people of the United States individually and collectively, as well as far beyond in the world. My first book, *U.S. War-culture, Sacrifice and Salvation,* explores these relationships. I found this challenging and often provocative work, because of the widespread legitimation of war-culture in the United States, including thick practices of concealment that shield the truths about war-culture from common awareness. It was not easy to get traction on the dangers of sacrificial war-culture when its presence and impact were mostly absent from the general population's horizon of concern. Eventually I came to see how the very process of sacralization in sacrificial war-culture acts as a protective mechanism that disables criticism.

About ten years ago my attention again shifted after hearing Jonathan Shay speak about moral injury at the *Truth Commission on Conscience in War to Protect and Honor Freedom of Conscience for Our Nation's Service Members*, at the Riverside Church in New York. Also present were veterans and journalists who gave testimony to their own painful experiences of war and its aftermath in their lives, families and communities. This book traces and develops the impact of this gathering on the continuing path of my work as a scholar and teacher. I knew that I needed to better understand and analyze where moral injury fits within the larger framework of sacrificial U.S. war-culture. The process of disentangling all this has taken many years.

Like so many in the United States, my family history includes many links to branches of the U.S. military. I am a civilian through and through, but my family tree includes forebears who fought on both sides of the U.S. Civil War. More recently, uncles saw combat in World War II, and cousins in Vietnam. My father was drafted and served in the U.S. Army in Korea. He avoided combat by raising his hand in formation one day, when a military superior came through looking for any servicemembers able to type and help with needed office work. I often have thought about how different his and my own life might be but for his instinctive reaction. Among the many stories he told about his deployment to Korea, in his later years my father talked about the military commander he worked for as a driver. This man had been a civilian medical doctor before being drafted, and resented and disliked the military. But he liked my father, and recommended generous promotions and leaves for him. My father took the opportunity multiple times to take leave in Japan. He and his buddy traveled all over the country, climbing Mount Fuji, visiting Japanese guesthouses. He traveled to Hiroshima when the city was still under control and censorship of the U.S. military, and recovering from the atomic bombing. Again, now in his later years, my father shared his reaction of being haunted by seeing the shadows of human beings who were carbonized by the blast, reduced to dark outlines on concrete.

When teaching courses touching upon ethics, war and war-culture, I ask students to share their own histories and links with the U.S. armed forces. In the Lehigh Valley of Pennsylvania, I find that almost every student raises his or her hand, and has their own stories to share. I'm deeply grateful for the student veterans who have taken my courses; and also grateful for colleagues and friends who are veterans, who have taught me so much along the way. My encounters with military servicemembers over many years leave me with the distinct impression of these fellow citizens as among the most morally centered, impressive individuals I could ever hope to meet.

The work of analyzing U.S. war-culture, and critically examining its relationship to the phenomenon of moral injury, is not without its critics. This book also explores why the analysis I have undertaken over these years engenders different and powerful reactions. Some people (both civilian and servicemember/veteran) express relief at being assisted to better explore and understand their own confusing reality; others find themselves unsettled and angry because ideals that they deeply cherish and consider sacred are being held up to the light of examination and criticism. I have sympathy for all these reactions along this spectrum.

So many wonderful investigative works on moral injury have been published since I first heard Shay in 2010; and in addition to scholarship there have been important centers established to promote better understanding and support. This book in particular focuses on the Moral Injury Group at the Michael J. Crescenz Veteran Affairs Medical Center in Philadelphia, led by Chaplain Chris J. Antal and Psychologist Peter Yeomans. I cannot express sufficient thanks for Chris' outreach to me, and opportunities to teach and learn with him in diverse contexts in recent years. The individuals in the Moral Injury Leadership Group from Crescenz VAMC similarly are teaching all of us who are willing to listen.

The book also builds on some of my earlier publications. I offer thanks to publishers for permission to draw on some of this writing, including from my chapter, "'Like Acid Seeping into Your Soul': Religio-cultural Violence in Moral Injury," in *Exploring Moral Injury in Sacred Texts,* ed. Joseph Mc-Donald (London: Jessica Kingsley Publishers, 2017) 111–134; "Martyrdom Discourse in Contemporary U.S. War-culture," in *Wiley Blackwell Companion to Christian Martyrdom,* ed. Paul Middleton (Hoboken, New Jersey: Wiley-Blackwell, 2020), 417–484; and "Moral Injury and the 'U.S. War-culture Bible,'" in *Moral Injury: A Guidebook for Understanding and Engagement,* ed. Brad Kelle (New York: Lexington Books, 2020), 173–188.

I also wish to express my thanks to Albert György, the artist of the work featured on the book cover, *Mélancolie.* The phrase, "And then your soul is gone," comes from Iraq veteran and author Kevin Powers, and his novel, *The Yellow Birds.* Following his deployment as a private in the Iraq war, protagonist John Bartle is back home, and disintegrating and disappearing into an overwhelming pain arising from his experiences of war, and his own conscience. A long stream-of-consciousness passage describes and brings the reader into Bartle's inner world of isolation, confusion, and looming self-destruction, "It's like acid seeping down into your soul, and then your soul is gone."[1]

In addition to defining war-culture in this preface, readers will note the regular use of the terms, "militarism" and "militarization" in the pages that follow. I follow Catherine Lutz's definition of these terms. "Militarism" refers to the prevalence of war-like values in society, and the dominance of the military in centers of authority; whereas "militarization" bears similarity to the way I define "war-culture." Lutz defines militarization as "a discursive process ... [defined by] an intensification of the labor and resources allocated to military purposes, including the shaping of other institutions in synchrony with military goals."[2] I use "interpenetration" to describe the mutually reverberating impacts in the shaping process Lutz outlines.

I hope this book will be read by servicemembers and veterans; civilians, medical, psychological and religious caregivers and congregations; and the family, friends and communities that support these individuals and groups. I also hope it will be read by students and researchers. Because the ideas here challenge practices of U.S. nationalism, and the status quo of U.S. war-culture, I suggest that a reading community of support, dialogue and critical analysis will help create the sanctuary needed for the work of introspection about the meaning of U.S. citizenship and U.S. war-culture. And all of us should be alert to and concerned about supporting people whose experiences of war have resulted in continued mental and spiritual anguish in their lives. Please consider contacting the Veterans Crisis Line if you are in crisis, or concerned about someone else: https://www.veteranscrisisline.net/.

I keep hoping I'll find a way to "finish" working on war-culture, and perhaps take up other questions and themes that are less provocative. But U.S. war-culture is not diminishing, nor are its many destructive consequences. Some years ago John Lewis, the civil rights icon and congressperson, visited the college where I teach and delivered a public lecture, in which he admonished all of us to "get into good trouble." Whatever "trouble" U.S. citizens like me experience with regard to challenging war-culture, it is nothing in comparison with what the morally injured deal with every day, and their friends, families and communities. It also bears no comparison to the struggles faced by refugees of war across the world. I hope this effort helps to move the needle toward greater peacebuilding, and away from war and war-culture. When and wherever we accomplish such movement, in ways both small and large, it's worth the trouble.

December, 2020

Introduction: Moral Injury and the Triangle of Violence

Hearing their voices

Too many servicemembers in different branches of the United States military, and too many veterans, journalists and other witnesses of war, find themselves facing a deep internal moral clash, existential disappointment, shame and grief, and resulting invisible and sometimes immobilizing injuries and disabilities. Others, unable to bear this suffering, are taking their lives.

A rare few are finding their voices, telling their stories, and seeking an audience with the courage to listen and respond.

One collection of these voices comes from *The Moral Injury of War Study and Art Installation.* These individuals agreed to be interviewed, share their stories and have their voices counted. The lead creator of the project, Jack Saul, developed an exhibit space that invites visitors to hear, and then talk about, what they have absorbed from this listening. Those who visit the art installation are confronted with voices like these below:

– I felt I needed to do something for my country …

– There's three rules you need to follow to survive in the military. The first thing you need to do is you need to do as you're told; the second thing you need to do is do as you're told. The third thing, the most important thing out of all these that you need to do, do what you're told …

– The military just teaches you, don't ask questions, and if you figure it out, it really isn't your business anyway. That part, that probably is the biggest thing, is having to do things you wonder about, but you can't ask a question …

– No matter what now, I always think that there's room for diplomacy. I think that war altogether is absolutely unnecessary, so I've just become more cynical about all the conflict around the world. The cynical part of me wants the public to understand that it's your fault; we are all complicit in all of this horror. I don't need other people to experience my pain, I need other people to understand that they are complicit in my pain. I can hold my pain myself; but other people need to understand that they have part in causing it.

– I signed up for the Marine Corps in the Delayed Entry Program my junior year in high school ... a recruiter came and talked to us during my freshman year ... September 11 happened my first day of boot camp ... we lost guys, they got killed ... their blood is still there, there's parts of us still there ... the underlying story is – you don't get to be right, you don't get to have your feelings, you don't get to grieve ... the rest of the time it's suck it the fuck up, do your job ... it's insanity ... the message that I would have for somebody who is in a place of wanting to relate ... is to recognize the trauma ... like being at the bottom of a well ... the hypervigilance ... the whole human experience condensed into a six month deployment cycle ... people want to say thank you for your service, wave a flag ... but you're left with these experiences that leave you feeling deeply shameful ... I burned through any relationship in my life with anybody who loved me ... I have this feeling in my gut that something really bad is going to happen ... the ceiling to fall in ... God's shoe was going to fall on me, I can't breathe ... your life hanging by a thread ... it's my responsibility to address the root of those feelings.[1]

Hearing these words, and taking in the intensity of these voices, compels a person to stop, listen, and be still. But the *Art Installation* is not an aberrant collection representing the experience of inexplicable outliers. Others are sharing their stories through their own writing, such as Eric Fair.

Fair served in the U.S. Army as an Arabic linguist, then later worked in Iraq as a contract interrogator in early 2004; but coming to terms with his wartime experiences is a lifelong process. He writes,

In April 2004 I was stationed at a detention facility in Fallujah. Inside the detention facility was an office. Inside the office was a small chair made of plywood and two-by-fours. The chair was two feet tall. The rear legs were taller than the front legs. The seat and chair back leaned forward. Plastic zip ties were used to force a detainee into a crouched position from which he could not recover. It caused muscle failure of the quads, hamstrings and calves. It was torture ...

The detainees in Fallujah were the hardest set of men I've ever come upon. Many killed with a sickening enthusiasm. They often butchered what remained of their victims. It is easy to argue that they deserved far worse than what we delivered ...

Still, those tactics stained my soul in an irrevocable way, maybe justifiably so. But as members of our government and its agencies continue to defend our use of torture, and as the American people continue to ignore their obligation to uncover this sordid chapter, the stain isn't mine alone.[2]

There is so much in the above narratives that demands attention. For instance, what does it mean when a veteran declares to the U.S. public, "we are all complicit in this horror"? What does Eric Fair mean by his sense of being "stained" by these acts? What is it like to feel as though you can't breathe, as though "God's shoe is going to fall on me"? These questions are at the very heart of this book's investigation. And all these voices confront hearers not only with the *personal impact* of these experiences, but also consideration of a much wider and deeper landscape. Fair's story, for example, stops one short by his honest description of being conscripted to participate in torture on behalf of the United States. The expert scholar on torture, Darius Rejali, would categorize Fair's acts as "clean torture."[3] This begs further explanation.

Beginning in the 1960s and 70s, as non-governmental agencies such as Amnesty International began to track and more widely publicize practices of torture (both state and non-state torture), torturers gradually shifted their practices to methods that would leave no marks on the body, making it harder to "read" the torture that had occurred. The type of torture described by Eric Fair falls into this category. Rejali further classifies this as "The National Security Model" of torture. In other words, torture performed by citizens like Eric in U.S. wars persists in democracies like the United States, due to being justified (and in this case, legalized) by the state as a reasonable response to a perceived national emergency, or because the national security bureaucracy overwhelms other democratic systems that have been put into place for restraint.[4]

Clearly, the need for continued investigation of the use of torture by the U.S. remains paramount. But the moral pain Eric Fair expresses is not unique to these experiences. This is not the result of "a bad apple." No, Eric's experience of pain and shame is shared by servicemembers and veterans of the U.S. Armed Forces who have performed many different sorts of labor in their military roles. It is shared also by civilian witnesses of war. Learning

about Fair's actions in Iraq, some readers might wish to set his case apart
from others, and categorize his experiences as somehow distinct, beyond the
scope of what war requires. Torture, even legalized torture, is *not* what the
United States asks of its military servicemembers. War, when fought "the
right way," may be withstood morally and psychologically, especially with
the right kinds of training and support. But are such neat dividing lines really
possible? Consider the case of Claude AnShin Thomas, a decorated veteran
of the Vietnam War. He writes,

> My job in Vietnam was to kill people. By the time I was first injured in
> combat (two or three months into my tour), I had already been directly
> responsible for the deaths of several hundred people. And today, I can
> still see many of their faces.[5]

Claude AnShin was very good at his job, receiving many medals and com-
mendations over the course of his military service. According to international and U.S. law, nothing he did was 'illegal' (and, at least to date, Eric's
participation in what he admits was "torture" has never been officially prosecuted). Yet Claude emerged from this formation and experience equally as
conflicted and troubled as Eric:

> Vietnam was not just in my head; it was all through me. I had talked
> intellectually about Vietnam, but I had never fully opened myself to
> the totality of this experience. Now the pain reached a point where it
> was so great I wanted only to hide from it, to run from it yet again. My
> first thought, of course, was to get drunk. When I drink, it covers the
> pain like a blanket. But under the blanket, inside me, is full of barbed
> wire; every time I move, it cuts at me, tears my skin. When I drink,
> I have the illusion that I have put a buffer between my skin and the
> barbed wire, but this is not the truth; when I am anesthetized, I am just
> not so aware of the ripping and tearing.[6]

In his novel about the Iraq war, writer and veteran Kevin Powers puts it this
way, "… if there is any true thing in this world, it is that war is only like itself."[7] The world of war is not like the world at all: it thrusts basic bedrock
moral guideposts that people trust in to be able to *live*, into confusion, dissonance and conflict.

While it is well known that suffering widely exists among U.S. military
servicemembers and veterans, and that it somehow is connected to the perpetuation of war and war-readiness, at the same time, questions – such as

how many people are affected, and why they are so deeply impacted – have not yet been answered to anyone's satisfaction. Suicide rates among servicemembers and veterans of the U.S. have been growing since they began to be tracked in 2001. The suicide rate for veterans in 2018 was determined to be 1.5 times that of non-veteran adults, with over 17 veteran suicides taking place every day in the United States, and the rate of suicide among active-duty U.S. troops also rising, despite serious and committed efforts to alleviate its causes.[8]

In fact, a multitude of experiences intrinsic to war, militarism and militarization have laid the ground for the growth of a specific injury of war, now called *military moral injury*, which may be the unspeakable origin of the current suicide epidemic. But at the same time, military moral injury remains a puzzle for researchers trying to understand it. Simultaneously, until recently *consciousness* about this epidemic among servicemembers, veterans, and citizens at large, much less any demand that the nation *act* to address its causal factors, largely has been absent in the lives and minds of most people in the United States.

How can this be? Part of the problem has to do with how difficult it is for U.S. citizens to face what has happened, what we have done, and who we have become. As Fair writes, instead of "opening the book" on U.S. practices of war, and in place of trying to understand what occurred in the lives of citizens such as Eric, the United States over the last two decades largely persisted in "… denying, ignoring or defending our use of interrogation practices that manipulated and abused the emotional, mental and physical well-being of thousands of foreign detainees."[9] Again, Fair's description of the response of the nation goes beyond the specific acts he now deplores.

U.S. citizens don't really want to know what has gone on in our name, with our money, and our tacit permission with regard to a host of practices of U.S. violence around the world. For Eric, and many other military servicemembers, *not only* experiences of "enhanced interrogation," but many diverse acts of war, as well as the sheer witnessing of the devastation, suffering, cruelty and death of war, have resulted in an overwhelming barrier in their lives, and division with a willfully ignorant public. Despite their private accounting, they often can't fully deal with the impact of this devastation, are unable to adapt, and find themselves disabled. As Fair wrote about his experience, "I'm dealing with my own burdens now. My marriage is struggling. My effectiveness as a parent is deteriorating. My son is suffering. I am no longer the person I once was. I try to repent. I work to confess. I hope for atonement."[10]

The problems this book addresses are much bigger than torture alone, as heinous as that is. For the consequences of the longest ongoing wars in U.S. history emphasized in Eric Fair's struggles, borne witness in Claude AnShin's pain more than forty years after the Vietnam war, and intensely given voice in the *Moral Injury of War Study and Art Installation,* are widely shared by a significant number of veterans and military servicemembers. Meanwhile, most U.S. citizens enjoy the privilege of proximity. They are geographically far removed from war zones, and have the choice to remain untouched. It's easy to avoid and distance ourselves systematically (and unconsciously) from the impact of this phenomenon, a deep suffering that arises from war, and that haunts, plagues and debilitates an untold number of servicemembers, veterans, other witnesses of war and, secondarily, their friends, families and communities. The very war-culture we live in encourages and facilitates citizens' ignorance, denial and withdrawal. But adequate understanding and response to military moral injury means breaking through the practices of concealment in U.S. war-culture that block moral vision.

Understanding military moral injury

An expanding group of psychological researchers, ethicists and other professionals might identify Eric's struggle as "moral injury." This term, "moral injury," was coined by psychologist and writer Jonathan Shay, in 1994; this was his attempt to articulate an adequate terminology that could put words to an experience of a wound of war never addressed satisfactorily by physiological or psychological terminologies alone.[11] Shay's early insights spurred an avalanche of investigation, such that moral injury now is identified with a host of diverse contexts. I follow others who use "military moral injury" in conjunction with research focusing on moral injury in the context of military service, war and war-culture.

While many of its symptoms overlap with the pain experienced by people who suffer from Post-Traumatic Stress Disorder (PTSD), military moral injury stems from a different cause. Put most simply, moral injury is a consequence of assault to one's moral center of being. Making matters more complex, the resentment toward others, self-judgment and hatred-of-self often experienced by military servicemembers and/or veterans who are morally injured, may be entirely consistent, appropriate and accurate with regard to ethical frameworks for judgment on human actions. In other words, this is not an injury that stems from a distorted view of the world, such as PTSD; *moral injury results from participation in the moral distortion of the world that is created by war.* Chaplain Chris Antal crystalizes this insight, "Moral injury is best understood as the inevitable outcome of moral engagement with the harsh reality of war and killing."[12]

A team of psychological researchers, led by Brett T. Litz, defined moral injury in the following way: "… someone perpetrates, fails to prevent or bears witness to acts that transgress deeply held moral beliefs and expectations."[13] While psychologists link military moral injury most specifically to the act of killing, or witnessing others who kill in the context of war, increasing numbers of diverse researchers are widening the scope of investigation, trying to better understand what military moral injury is, how it is caused, and what may be done to address it.

Military moral injury involves "morality." Moral codes are fundamental to the way we human beings make our way in the world, live as people in relationship with others, and make sense of the world. They derive from diverse sources, such as culture, family, legal systems, religion, and more. Moral codes both cut across different cultures and also are culture-specific. For instance, different cultures may have contrasting ideas about the appropriate age for marriage, but ethicists debate about cross-cultural principles that may protect and honor women's human rights across diverging cultural practices of marriage. Or to imagine another example, there exist many different cultural standards about what is proper with regard to economic practices (and within and between cultures there is debate about these issues as well), but the notion that it is wrong to steal is ubiquitous (though people still find ways to mask and justify stealing).

However, the context of war is peculiar with respect to moral codes, moral formation and functioning. For if moral codes play that central and fundamental role of helping human beings to understand, navigate and live in their worlds, it also is true that the actual experience of war turns human expectations about moral experience upside down; in essence, as far as moral codes go, war all too frequently is world-destroying. Not only this book, but any investigation of military moral injury reveals this truth. But here one arrives at a curious juncture, because military moral injury research has yet to focus on the *social context* that enables military moral injury to take root and grow. The purpose of this book is to address this missing piece of the puzzle.

Moral injury cannot be limited to the injury of one person; investigating, thinking about, or witnessing military moral injury, means running headlong into a complex dynamic of violence, with tentacles that reach deeply into social structures, and cultural assumptions and practices. This demands a more comprehensive investigation. But simultaneously, military moral injury *also* involves a very personal sense of damage done to one's very "soul," mixed up with what Eric describes as his "failures" and "the need to confess." I argue the following: *military moral injury not only is an individual phenomenon, but also inevitably grows from the sedimentary layers of war's institutions, and U.S. war-culture.* The urgent need for a deeper social analysis of this context, the morally injured individual in the U.S. landscape of war-culture, is the reason for this book.

According to Albert Bandura, moral standards include the interplay of conscience, moral prescripts and principles. But he writes,

> People often face pressures to engage in harmful activities that provide desired benefits but violate their moral standards. To engage in those activities and live with themselves, they have to strip morality from their actions or invest them with worthy purposes. Disengagement of moral self-sanctions enables people to compromise their moral standards and still retain their sense of moral integrity.[14]

Bandura well describes the moral conundrum experienced by people in the context of war and war-culture, and the methods through which they attempt to address the dissonance they feel. Being asked (or required) to engage in activities that violate one's moral center of being is destructive to the self, creating a dissonance, or moral chasm within a person. According to Bandera, in such a situation, people either will divest themselves of their actions of morality altogether, or try to find a way to justify such actions morally. But as the phenomenon of military moral injury reveals, sometimes the internal sense of harm people experience in these moral black holes seems impossible to escape. A lasting disintegration of the person him/herself rots away the individual from the inside out. These are such painful, terrible realities to experience or witness. Bandura's analysis begins to explain how and why U.S. society at large ignores or distances itself from facing the destructive consequences of its actions with regard to war-culture and war. A deeper investigation of U.S. avoidance of this pain is part of the goal of this book.

Edward Tick, the psychotherapist who spent over twenty-five years working with war veterans, understands the powerful dissonance in the lives of servicemembers and veterans. Tick uses the language of "soul wound" and describes its consequence as "the undoing of character."[15] What does this mean, and what does it look like? Tick stresses that those who are wounded in this way lose the ability to trust themselves, others and their society; in essence, they may lose their very identity. And deprivation of this basic human capacity results in a host of "downstream secondary complications," such as alcohol and drug abuse, suicide, criminal involvements, relationship dysfunction and danger seeking.[16] Specifically, what is at stake in understanding "military moral injury" is that at its root, the "pathology" involved, ironically, is the strength of conscience at the center of human experience and self-understanding. Moral injury occurs as that core systematically is violated and vitiated through witnessing, experiencing and enacting the demands of war and war-culture.

But herein lies the paradox: while there is little disagreement about the devastation that war brings, including its very erasure of a world in which a person/people can *live*, at the same time, since time immemorial, war has been surrounded by rituals and rhetoric based in heroicizing, even divinizing narratives. Yes, Mars is war. But more must be said. For, on the one hand, Mars is war due to war's incomprehensible capacity for destruction of everything needed for life, and everything that is life-giving. On the other hand, Mars *also* is war because of the human tendency across time and cultures to glorify war and wrap it in a sheath of sacred cloth. This practice helps humans to justify war, as well as legitimate the assumption that war is inevitable, a "fact of human nature," while people simultaneously lurch to shield themselves from its horrors.

As Bandura underscores, war is one preeminent experience in which people are acculturated, trained and pressured to "engage in harmful activities" that they are *told* "provide desired benefits," while potential violations of moral standards that will be required, are both sublimated and justified. For instance, we hear that war, when fought the "right way," may be absorbed, tolerated, withstood. There even are those who argue that war "develops character." But people like Eric and Claude Anshin have lost the luxury of believing that war may be survived and successfully assimilated by those who perpetuate it. The "compromise of their moral standards" cannot be so easily mitigated.

The religio-cultural aspects of "war-culture" will be examined later in this book. But first, deeper thinking is required about the nature and cause of military moral injury. What kind of injury is this?

According to military psychological researchers, moral injury is "… a state of loss of trust in previously deeply held beliefs about one's own or others' ability to keep our shared moral covenant."[17] Deeply held beliefs that one trusted in to be able to live in a shared world, have been shattered. What is most important about the definition above is its stress on the *cause* of moral injury. In other words, the moral injuries sustained by servicemembers reveal *not* individual pathological deficiencies or weaknesses, but *a deeper question about whether it is possible to successfully accommodate human beings and their morality to war.* The belief that such accommodation is not only possible, but necessary, lies at the heart of all just war theory. However, the experiences of an untold number of military servicemembers, veterans and others suggest something different. Ongoing research about the moral injuries among servicemembers from the United States' wars in Iraq and Afghanistan shows that many have been impacted. One 2017 study, using data from the National Health and Resilience in Veterans Study, indicated deeply troubling reports of "PMIEs" (potentially morally injurious events) from a population-based sample of U.S. veterans. As they summarized, "A total of 10.8% of combat veterans acknowledged transgressions by self, 25.5% endorsed transgressions by others, and 25.5% endorsed betrayal." The experience of moral injury among individual veterans, left unaddressed by effective intervention, may result in a legacy of long-term anguish and dysfunction resulting from participation in and exposure to war.[18]

In the last decade, research on military moral injury has grown and widened, now including not only psychology and psychiatry, but also social work, philosophy and religious/spiritual studies.[19] But no single consensus yet has emerged regarding a singular definition of military moral injury. Researchers and scholars have developed lists of "PMIEs" – potential military injurious events – but have yet to develop the "gold-standard, theoretically grounded, content-valid measure" that will clearly indicate just how and why a broad range of activities associated with perpetrating war lead to "associated subjective distress, interfering symptoms and behaviors, and resulting functional impairment."[20]

Nevertheless, experts agree that "moral injury generally is assumed to result from exposure to events that involve either perpetrating or witnessing actions that violate one's core beliefs, or betrayal by a leader or trusted authority."[21] And these two prongs have been identified as needing further research: 1) the way that "individuals appraise themselves as having committed moral violations;" as well as 2) moral injury that arises through victimization by another's "transgressive behavior."[22]

Most important, leading analyses of military moral injury are limited by yet another gap in existing research on military moral injury: researchers have yet to mount a more thorough examination of *the wider context* of military moral injury. As leading researchers emphasize, "Future work should examine the range of social, cultural, and political factors that may contribute to the occurrence of PMIEs (e.g., placing men and women in positions where they must compromise shared moral values or violate their own sense of justice to accomplish a conflicting social imperative)."[23] In other words, a deeper social and cultural analysis of the phenomenon of military moral injury is urgently needed; such precisely is the aim of this book.

A social and contextual phenomenon

As investigations of moral injury took off in the last decade, the methods used to analyze military moral injury branched beyond the purely psychological. In 2009 Brett T. Litz and a group of psychologists were instrumental in identifying moral injury and suggesting a beginning definition; but it is clear that this type of injury cannot be understood or addressed *only* from within psychological disciplinary frameworks. Theological ethicist Warren Kinghorn asserts that "… moral injury is an irreducibly social and contextual phenomenon."[24] Rita Nakashima Brock, founder of "The Soul Repair Center," and since 2017, director of the "Shay Moral Injury Center," agrees on the importance of a wider communal analysis; focus only on the "individual trees" in the forest is not sufficient to understand what is going on; adequate understanding of moral injury may be compared to "a complex forest, in which we must move past monocrop knowledge to explore food forest knowledge."[25]

Addressing moral injury from *only* an individual therapeutic perspective, risks the danger of reductionism. Then the focus of investigation centers on determining a therapeutic method to best address and ameliorate the disabling consequences moral injury causes in individual lives. But this is too narrow. The problem with *primarily* utilizing psychological modalities is that these methods, while possibly helpful, and in some cases harmful, as a whole do not address the heart of the problem. They may address the suffering that is being experienced in the life of one person, but fail to get to the root of this experience. In other words, the symptoms are treated, but not the disease itself; what is left intact and untouched are all the social systems and structures, assumptions and cultural values and practices that enable, encourage, aggravate and exacerbate the phenomena of moral injury in individual veterans. As Antal and Winings write, "the guilt and shame they [veterans] may be experiencing is not confined just to them. They are part of a larger social contract and system that had a hand in the decision to deploy the troops in the first place either directly or indirectly."[26]

Some are calling for different strategies to address this problem. For instance, Kinghorn draws on his Christian background to call for wider and deeper practices of reconciliation and restoration of the soldier – to God, to restored participation in the Christian community for whom he writes, even

reconciliation with the creation itself. Kinghorn believes this will require "…
interlocking practices of patience, of confession and of forgiveness."[27] This
framework involves a communal aspect to address complicity and responsibility for harm. But additional investigation is needed to dig to the bottom of
what is happening in this world human beings have built, the world of war
and war-culture, of which military moral injury is a critical symptom that
something is drastically wrong.

Moral injury is not a new phenomenon; in fact, it is as old as war itself. Among other scholars, Robert Meagher has traced its roots to ancient
Greece, and explored its presence through the centuries of Christian Europe
all the way to the contemporary U.S.[28] Various analyses of moral injury have
pointed out how in earlier historical epochs, societies required returning
warriors to undergo practices of penance before re-entering society.[29] These
cultures recognized the moral and spiritual distance warriors would need to
travel, in addition to geographical travel, in the return home from the fields
of war. Today's U.S. Army refers to this transition as "out-processing," and
requires a minimum of five days for servicemembers to complete a long series of steps, including passing through the station of "Behavioral Health."
One wonders about the sufficiency of this process, given the enormous leap
involving so many factors, that soldiers or contractors are required to make
in the return to civilian society.[30]

Veteran and writer Tyler Boudreau pushes the questions raised by moral
injury beyond an individual focus, expanding the scope to include broader structural realities. "A man might wring his hands and say in anguish, 'I
killed!' But it's not as though he thought it up and did it on his own. There
were other factors and other agents involved … Even war crimes can't be
owned exclusively by the perpetrators."[31] Boudreau tells the story of awak-
ening to his own sense of complicity while deployed in Iraq, becoming
aware of "… the grave reality of American foreign policy and the extent of
what it means to be a superpower on earth. It means that nothing can stop us
from going anywhere and doing anything we want to do … at that point in
the deployment I'd already begun to sense what I was doing to myself and
what I was quietly standing by allowing my country to do to others."[32] This
veteran writer knows that soldiers' and veterans' individual experiences may
not be separated from structural realities. We see the same awareness in Eric
Fair's writing; it is impossible for him to adequately come to terms with his
own actions and their aftermath in a national atmosphere of insistent avoidance, self-deception, and failure of collective self-examination with respect
to twenty years of war.

Meanwhile, research based in pastoral psychology also is addressing a wider scope of concern beyond the individual, such as Nancy Ramsay indicated:

> … the ethical importance of bearing witness to the stories of moral injury among soldiers is echoed by veterans such as Michael Yandell, who remind us that moral injury not only shapes the life stories of those who served in combat, it also has consequences for all civilians on whose behalf these veterans served.[33]

Moral injury: An insult?

Despite voices such as these above that have called for a wider analysis of moral injury, and despite growing recognition of moral injury among leaders in the branches of the U.S. military, there still is a long way to go to adequately acknowledge and respond to this phenomenon. In 2019 the U.S. Special Operations Command held a "Moral Injury Symposium." Designed to "educate, train and equip," the symposium hoped to improve upon the building of "readiness and resilience." Attended by about 130 mostly military chaplains and mental-health specialists, one attendee, a journalist, came away with a sense of deep discomfort, as he wrote,

> I was a civilian journalist, not a soldier. I went to Vietnam to report, not to fight. I didn't come home with any trauma symptoms. But I have all the feelings that Chaplain Orris [one of the symposium presenters] listed as identifying markers for moral injury: sorrow, grief, regret, shame, and alienation. Those emotions come from what I learned about war, not from anything I did, and that makes me believe it may not be wrong to think that what we call moral injury might not be just one person's response to particularly troubling events, but a symptom of something larger, of seeing war individually and collectively for what it truly is.[34]

If, in 2014, journalist David Wood wrote, "The Pentagon does not formally recognize moral injury," today the military response to moral injury is more complex. Wood's queries to the Defense Department were met with a statement from spokesperson Joy Crabaugh, saying that "… moral injury is 'not clinically defined' and ... there is no 'formal diagnosis' for it."[35] However, today, increasing numbers of military researchers are better understanding moral injury. For instance, Captain William P. Nash and his team of military psychological researchers agree with Meagher, "the phenomenon of moral injury appears to be ancient."[36] In a study of twenty three Department of Defense and Veterans Affairs healthcare and religious ministry professionals, it was "… universally agreed that the concept of moral injury was needed to inform their work with combat veterans."[37] The 2014 Fort Leavenworth Ethics Symposium, sponsored by the U.S. Army Command, included analysis of moral injury as a key topic.[38] Nevertheless, both the Navy and the Marine Corps refused to use the term: "… only the term 'inner conflict'" could be used because "… the potential synonym moral injury was perceived to be pejorative."[39] This was the official reaction, in contradiction with other views, such as Captain Nash, who told the *Huffington Post*, "… definitely a majority of returning veterans bear some kind of moral injury."[40]

Meanwhile, in 2014, at a Navy and Marine Corps annual conference on combat and operational stress control, with moral injury a leading topic of discussion, one Marine commander went so far as to say that he was "insulted" by the phrase, declaring that moral injury implied "… that the Marines were stressed as a result of immorality." In contrast, he stressed, Marines are trained to have "… the skill and the will to kill … it's based on an ethical standard."[41]

Colleagues in the military or closely associated with it, upon learning of the commander's rejection of the term, "moral injury," tend not to be surprised by such a reaction. Military culture, they emphasize, is behind this response. According to Lieutenant Colonel Douglas A. Pryer, the official military rationale behind rejecting moral injury is that the terminology has not yet been officially recognized as a psychological disorder in the *DSM* (The Diagnostic and Statistical Manual of the American Psychiatric Association). However, Pryer continues, this is something of a ruse used by the military to cover a deeper problem. For acknowledging that war requires servicemembers to "… do things that seriously trouble them" is in direct conflict with notions of American exceptionalism that portray soldiers "… as exceptional, not because of what they do but because of who they are."[42]

Psychotherapist Edward Tick further explains that mythic notions about U.S. American innocence and goodness run counter to the realities of wartime experiences. "We believe that our young men and women should be able to go to war, get the job done, and return home blameless and well … we deny that war changes its participants forever, promoting instead the belief … that vets and survivors can resume an ordinary civilian identity."[43]

Diverse researchers, both civilian and from the U.S. military, *are* searching for ways to describe, understand and address the deep distress connected to moral experience that many servicemembers and veterans are experiencing. But the programs being developed by the military to address this reality often mirror the reaction of the Marine commander above. In other words, while moral and spiritual injury are recognized as a result of wartime experiences, the necessity and morality of war itself will not be questioned. Here is where one begins to arrive at the nub of the problem raised by the phenomenon of moral injury.

The difficult questions

Especially in military contexts, and also across much civilian society in the United States, certain questions may be raised, but others evoke a strong negative reaction. Questioning how we may psychologically ameliorate the destructive consequences of war that are experienced by individual military servicemembers is deemed appropriate, but digging deeper to examine the social and cultural systems that give rise to moral injury, forces uncomfortable questions that are less socially acceptable. Simply put, questioning the connections between moral injury and standard assumptions and practices in U.S. culture raises hackles. Further investigation that raises suspicion about the links between moral injury and just war thinking is to stand on even more tenuous ground. Examining U.S. "ethical standards" for war that provide justification for violence, destruction and death, and that are intrinsically involved in the evolution of moral injury, is deemed "pejorative" and "insulting." Why?

Clearly, these questions challenge deeply held beliefs. People want to believe that it is possible to conduct war justly and rightly; we want to believe that we can control and manage the violence war unleashes, and protect servicemembers from being permanently damaged by it; we want to believe, as Lieutenant Colonel Pryer puts it, "… when American troops kill or otherwise inflict violence, the violence that they inflict is moral."[44]

But in addition to Pryer's words above, it must be said that the situation is even more complex and confusing, because the same belief he identifies, that U.S. violence is *moral,* shapes the identities of U.S. citizens. Through years of researching U.S. war-culture and moral injury, I have come to recognize that the deepest and most salient threads of U.S. national identity, especially in the post-9/11 era, are linked to a commitment of military supremacy: the intrinsic expectation of U.S. as the biggest, most highly developed, influential and feared military power on the planet. Simultaneously, the sharp and unforgiving edges of this national identity are softened, and find pseudo-moral justification, as they work hand in glove with the resonant ideology of "the necessity of war-as-sacrifice." This book explores both sides of our confusing context.

Examining war through the lens of moral injury casts doubt on what U.S. citizens have believed, and how they have understood themselves and the nation. Satisfactorily trying to understand moral injury takes one down a rabbit hole. New questions emerge that require a reexamination of assumptions, values and beliefs. Not only the *structural* realities of the military/security/war/surveillance machine of the U.S., investigation of moral injury *also* forces questions that probe *cultural* violence, including U.S. forms of national self-identity, an identity that is dear to citizens even as it remains largely critically unexplored. Exploring moral injury all the way to its base compels a person to revisit and rethink the purpose and meaning of the military, the nation, even citizenship, and especially the (civil) religious underpinnings of U.S. national identity.

"Resilience" is not enough

Some have imagined that moral injury perhaps may be forestalled or ameliorated through increased resilience. In 2020 a "Spiritual and Moral Resiliency Course," developed by the Joint Special Operations University on MacDill Air Force Base, Florida, drew international and domestic participants with the goal to "create a holistic model of well-being for the Special Operations Forces (SOF) warrior."[45] An earlier editorial in the journal, *Military Medicine*, explained the new emphasis that was initiated by the U.S. military in 2010 to address enormous disabling dysfunctions affecting many returning servicemembers. These self-destructive behaviors and disorders had become impossible to ignore or deny, such as epidemic suicides, incidence of mental illness, substance abuse, relationship dysfunction, domestic and other forms of violence committed by servicemembers, etc. The response from the Department of Defense (DoD), called "Total Force Fitness," was described as "a new paradigm for maintaining health, readiness and performance in the Department of Defense." The editors continued,

> We are in an age of sustained conflict. Wars and threats to our security are no longer episodic, but require continuous optimal performance, resilience and recovery. Injury from these conflicts may be physical

and mental, social and spiritual … If we are to protect the freedom and security of our nation, we must move beyond simply having a sound body to a holistic view of health that includes both mind and body.[46]

The philosophy behind this and "resiliency" programs overall in branches of the U.S. military reveals significant values at work regarding human moral accommodation to war. First, the claim is made that a constant threat to "security" makes war a seemingly permanent function of the state. Second, the editorial explains the military's chosen way forward, defending the idea that it is possible, with the proper preparation and training, guidance and support, for human beings to develop the strength and resilience that will withstand the distortions of humanity, morality and life experienced in war. This is one pathway to address the devastation of moral injury.

But another, different subtext has emerged in the debate about moral injury, its proper disciplinary parameters, and whether and how comprehensively the U.S. branches of the military, and U.S. society in general, will address it. I suspect that the sense of "insult" articulated by the Marine commander was more revealing than he knew. Tracing the distress of moral injury to its roots stirs up questions that unsettle the status quo. This distress unseats and challenges a host of assumptions – about the nature and purpose of human resilience, the place war occupies in U.S. nationalism, the institutions of war and militarization humans have constructed, and how humans best may achieve security. Facing all this is uncomfortable indeed. Pryer advocates for a change that would challenge the dominant focus on "what is legal" in military culture, to a focus on "what is moral." Then, he writes, perhaps "The 'good' conscience of an individual soldier could be reinforced through education rather than smothered in blanket 'resiliency' programs."[47]

Moral injury as a "flashpoint": The violence triangle

Rather than treat moral injury as an unfortunate byproduct of war to be treated on an individual basis with appropriate therapeutic methods, or to be forestalled or withstood through resiliency or other training programs designed to prevent or withstand it, this book takes a different tack: what would happen if we considered moral injury as a flashpoint, a lens through which to *see* and morally *assess* war and war-culture? Moral injury then would become a starting point to better understand what war actually is, and what it does to human beings and societies.

However, this beginning point requires a different sort of investigation, something broader and deeper than the investigations primarily focused on methods that explore individual experience and psychology. Kinghorn is right: emphasis on the individual, and techniques to reduce individual guilt and ameliorate psychological pain is far too thin an approach; these initiatives may address the symptoms, but never touch the actual causes and deep dynamics of the phenomenon itself. Moreover, a psychological response alone is captive to potential colonization of the military goal to return damaged and wounded soldiers to the war zone as quickly as possible. In addition, stress on building resilience among servicemembers is vulnerable to an even more insidious development. Pryer writes, "The last thing we want is for soldiers to feel that they can suppress their consciences whenever they please."[48] No, a much thicker description and ethical analysis of moral injury is needed, including its roots, outgrowth, inner workings, and interactions across a wide social landscape.

To achieve this thicker social analysis of moral injury, I use Johan Galtung's theoretical development of "the violence triangle." This tool clarifies not only the individual experience of "direct violence," but goes further, providing a framework that shows how structural and cultural forces and patterns also shape the reality of moral injury.[49] First, however, a working definition of "violence" is needed.

According to Galtung, violence is best defined as "avoidable insults to basic human needs, and more generally to *life*, lowering the real level of needs satisfaction below what is potentially possible."[50] Think about the vectors of moral injury that Galtung's definition spotlights. First, as he emphasizes, some experiences of violence in human experience are *unavoidable*, especially events outside human control and agency. Earthquakes and tsunamis cause enormous violence and destruction to human communities. Human beings can't stop such incidents from taking place – this is unavoidable violence – but they can avoid or lessen certain aspects of violence that come with these natural events through careful building codes, emergency alert systems and preparations, thoughtful city planning, etc. At the same time, seemingly "natural disasters" such as large scale wildfires, or massive flooding and destruction from storms, increasingly scientifically linked to the climate crisis, cannot be labeled "avoidable violence;" people *could* make different choices to address what is happening with the climate, and mitigate these events. Critical thought helps sort out what may be avoidable through thoughtful human agency, or not. An individual hiking the Pacific Coast Trail who encounters a bear may avoid a violent response if she knows how to properly respect and behave within this environment. But even in such cases hikers still may experience a happenstance encounter with possible violence. This is mostly "unavoidable," and no one bears any culpability for it. We also could speak of the violence of a heart attack that comes about not because of unjust public healthcare systems, poor healthcare, or diet and health management, but because of a history of heart disease in one's family that may have little to do with environment or behavior. Some experiences of violence are unavoidable.

However, second, and in contrast to these examples of "natural violence," or other unavoidable violence in human experience, Galtung's main point regards violence that humans *could prevent*; this *avoidable* violence disables human agency, and diminishes human flourishing. Avoidable violence negatively impacts human needs that are associated with physical survival and human well-being; avoidable violence also eviscerates the creation of meaningful identities and communities, and human capacity for positive action with others. Chapter 5 addresses the global pandemic of 2020 as one example of avoidable violence on a worldwide scale.

With this definition of violence, Galtung further developed the "violence triangle," a typology of different, but interconnected forms of *avoidable violence* that lessen and distort the potentiality and well-being of the human person, communities and world. Galtung's first prong of the triangle, *direct violence,* refers to those acts of violence that are most visible. Direct violence involves some sort of event or outbreak of violence, such as the direct events of violence in war, including the experience of moral injury among servicemembers and veterans. It is the violence one *sees* taking place. But *direct violence* is only the beginning of the story; the violence triangle also compels investigation of deeper and less visible vectors of violence that bring to the surface the other two points of the violence triangle, *structural* violence, and *cultural* violence.

The three prongs of violence all played a strong role in the life of Freddy Gray, who died in Baltimore, Maryland, on April 19, 2015, a week after sustaining a severe spinal injury.[51] In Freddy's case, the event of direct violence occurred when he was pursued on foot by police and arrested, handcuffed and placed without a seatbelt in a police van, in the neighborhood of Sandtown-Winchester on Baltimore's west side. He sustained a mortal injury as he was thrown about, without the ability to protect himself from injury inside the van. But this is only one prong of the "violence triangle," just the tip of the iceberg above the ocean concealing a much larger frozen structure below. Beneath the iceberg tip of visible violence, the second prong addresses *structural violence*, in other words the humanly created structures and systems that inevitably give rise to direct forms of violence. Structural violence also may be compared to a kind of sediment that creates the fertile ground needed for direct violence to spring forth. Galtung notes that exploitation and repression are at the heart of structural forms of violence, "the unequal exchange," as he calls it.[52] Social structures *hide* or *mask* various types of violence, even as they ready the ground for incidences of direct violence. They normalize inequalities and repress protest, and inequitably distribute costs exacted by structural violence.

In Freddy Gray's case, the sediment of structural violence leading to his death included many different elements. Understanding this structural violence shows how the interlinking systems of police, government, economy, and education, in Sandtown-Winchester, Baltimore, and more broadly, the U.S., are implicated in the direct violence that took his life. Freddy lived in an impoverished section of Baltimore where the drug economy thrives, in dilapidated housing impacted by lead pollution. Exposure to toxins and lack of adequate support and education diminished growth opportunities; court depositions claimed that his mother was a heroin addict and illiterate; his reading level remained four years behind the standard.

In addition, the unjust structural violence in police systems also have come under question. While the Baltimore police admitted to significant errors in this case, including neglecting to put a seatbelt on him in the van, and refusing to respond to his pleas for medical assistance, this event co-occurred with so many others locally and across the country, many of which are being brought to greater public attention as a result of being captured by cell phone video. The violent events could not be denied, were highlighted in the media, and protested by groups such as *Black Lives Matter,* igniting renewed attention and anger regarding systemic practices of police brutality across the country that destructively impact Black lives. The case of Freddy Gray illustrates the importance of attending to what is going on beneath the surface, and direct acts of violence, to see how human systems and structures create the conditions for direct violence to erupt.

But investigation of the sources of violence may be pushed even further. For looking past specific experiences or outbreaks of violence, and beyond the structures that promote, undergird and inequitably distribute the costs of direct violence, one discovers the seabed of *cultural forms of violence*, the third prong of the triangle. Cultural values, rituals, language, methods of education and disciplinary worldviews and norms socialize and prepare people to accept, internalize and participate in the systems and structures that rationalize and support direct violence. This third prong, cultural violence, is "a substratum from which the other two can derive their nutrients." Galtung further writes, "Good weeding presupposes getting at the roots [of violence], in this case at the structural and cultural roots..."[53]

Returning to Freddy Gray's case one last time, and exploring the cultural violence that contributed to his death, new questions arise: What beliefs and attitudes led to the decision not to seatbelt him? What kind of justifications enabled the force used, such that he sustained a mortal injury in his arrest? Perhaps most important, why was he apprehended and chased in the first place? Was there reasonable cause to pursue him? This final question has been one of the most troubling about Freddy's death. Early that morning, as he stood on a corner and caught the eye of police officers patrolling nearby, his reaction was to run away. Then police pursued and apprehended him, handcuffed and searched him.

As investigative reports indicated, running away is not in and of itself probable cause for apprehension and search; questioning the beliefs, attitudes and norms that stereotype and demonize Black and poor citizens sheds light on how this cultural landscape contributed to the harsh reactions of police in this context, compared to very different reactions in other settings. A *Frontline* investigation also revealed the impossible role of police officers in these structures and culture:

> Officers were sometimes explicitly ordered to target Blacks. One lieutenant, for example, ordered all officers patrolling one district to "lock up all the black hoodies" in a neighborhood. When one sergeant objected, she was given a poor performance review and transferred to another unit.[54]

The growing ubiquity of cellphones ties Freddy's case to other examples of the deaths of Black, brown, and poor citizens at the hands of police. For the renewed wave of anger and protest, as well as new court cases across the country holding police officers and departments to more vigorous standards of accountability, grow from the fact that many of these incidents have been filmed by bystanders. Does this mean that before the rise of cell phone video, such incidents happened with less frequency? Of course not; the impact of the videos now means that it is harder to dismiss or disbelieve victims' testimony in such cases, less easy to deny institutionalized police violence, and cultural patterns of discrimination. Galtung would point us to the cultural production of racist ideology that dehumanizes or criminalizes certain "underdogs" while elevating other "topdogs."

The student in my course who dismissed Freddy Gray's case, saying police force was justified because "there is so much violence in poor Black communities," demonstrates cultural violence in action. This ideology dismisses or excuses structural and direct violence, and provides important cover to conceal it. As Galtung writes, "After some time, direct violence is forgotten, slavery is forgotten, and only two labels show up, pale enough for college textbooks: 'discrimination' for massive structural violence and 'prejudice' for massive cultural violence. Sanitation of language: itself cultural violence."[55]

In the case of Freddy Gray, Galtung's "violence triangle" increases honesty about the dynamics of violence that led to Freddy's death, as well as clarity about effective possible change. Addressing only direct violence will not get us very far; in fact, addressing only the direct violence involved in Freddy's death might have the unintended consequence of concealing and providing ground for further incidents of violence to develop unheeded.

Much the same may be said about the use of Galtung's insights to assist this investigation regarding moral injury. There is need for increased investigation that goes beyond the first prong of the triangle, "direct violence." A primary focus on direct violence is akin to the way that *The Titanic* attempted to bypass the iceberg; it may have missed the bit of ice poking above the ocean's surface, only to be devastated beneath the waters by the sharp ice cutting through the ship's hull. Yes, the direct violence of moral injury in the lives of individual servicemembers is compelling and awful. The mother of one young man who killed himself after multiple tours in Iraq described the direct violence of moral injury in the following way, as "killing a person from the inside out."[56] But focusing either primarily or only on this one aspect, the direct and most visible vector of violence embedded in the phenomenon of moral injury, seriously limits both a deep understanding of this experience of violence, and capacity to discern methods for redress. The acute need to address this glaring gap is the rationale for writing this book.

Chapter overview

Chapter 1 explores the phenomenon of moral injury within the wider context of "U.S. war-culture." War-culture takes on a different appearance when it is explored as a consequence of human world-building, as opposed to being accepted as an inevitable human condition. Different questions come into view that challenge dominant assumptions in the U.S., and some scholars' assertions, such as Ian Morris, that war is a "social good," "necessary" and "inevitable."[57] Steady looking and unflinching investigation of the phenomenon of moral injury makes it impossible to remain undisturbed with U.S. ways of war.

From the macro to the micro context, the chapter takes up the case study of a personal communication I received from a veteran, and his honest narration about his struggle to shine light on what I have come to call, "sacrificial war-culture." Structures, social practices, and dynamics of U.S. war-culture, intermix with the ideology of "the necessity of war-as-sacrifice." This process promotes concealment of the destructiveness and costs of U.S. war, and muddles awareness of moral injury's devastation in the consciousness of most U.S. citizens. Chapter 1 also draws on two recent novels that highlight a more personal and descriptive portrayal of moral injury, *The Yellow Birds,* a National Book Award finalist, by Iraq veteran and author Kevin Powers; and *Billy Lynn's Halftime Walk,* by Ben Fountain. Literature offers a rich resource to push past concealment to a deeper understanding of the inner dynamics of moral injury, and how it is sourced by diverse structural and cultural factors of violence in the war-culture that lie at its roots.

Chapter 2, "Moral Injury and Structural Violence," draws on the second prong of Galtung's theoretical triangle of violence, to explore three pillars of *structural violence* in the war-culture of the United States, and their role in the development of military moral injury: 1) the permanent war economy, 2) the U.S. "empire of bases," and 3) the reverberations of "interpenetration," as the structures of militarization continuously interact with and influence countless sites of supposed "civilian" life in the United States. Many scholars have written with compelling urgency about the destructive forces of structural violence in U.S. war-culture, yet seemingly paradoxically, most U.S. citizens appear to be unconcerned and/or unaware.[58] I draw from Latin American liberation theologian, Jon Sobrino of El Salvador, who characterizes the contemporary world by way not only of its structural and cultural violence, but also its practices of *concealment* of both injustice and violence.[59] One of the most significant concealers of the devastation of war-culture involves the role of religion; Chapter 2 explores the sacrificial rhetoric and cognitive patterns in war-culture that rely on religious and civil-religious sources. These patterns mask and distort the truth about violence. Lastly, the concept of "the grey zone" from writer Primo Levi is introduced as a tool to increase understanding of the ambiguity faced by servicemembers and veterans in the world-turned-upside-down of structural violence in both war and war-culture.

Chapter 3, "Moral Injury and Cultural Violence," turns to Galtung's final tip of the violence triangle, the role of *culture* at the deepest roots of the phenomenon of military moral injury. Three vectors of cultural violence sourcing military moral injury are investigated here: 1) ideologies of military masculinity, 2) the role of religion, and 3) the interplay of national identity.

This exploration of culture and violence, at the deepest levels of military moral injury, thrusts the least visible, but perhaps most deeply impacting interactions of violence into view. Different exposés of "military masculinities," reveal the deep ambiguities and conflict between stated military values, such as those from the U.S. Army, "loyalty, duty, respect, selfless service, honor, integrity, and personal courage," and the actual realities of military acculturation in the U.S. armed services. Religion also comes into play, because training in "expendability," as Kathleen Barry describes it, is both undergirded and justified by way of (civil) religious patterns that extol "the ultimate sacrifice." Exploring these deep veins of cultural violence uncovers patterns of interpenetration that tie religious centers of experience together with sites of U.S. nationalism, such as the 2016 Democratic Convention.

Zeroing in on the factors of shame and power, sacrificial norms, and diverse constructions of masculinity, this chapter investigates how multiple cultural frameworks work in tandem; they derive from both structural and cultural sources, contribute to the development of moral injury, and *both mask and rationalize* the resulting inequitable distribution of suffering and loss.

Chapter 3 concludes with the case of one veteran, "Mr. Jones," a military convoy driver, who was ordered to commandeer his military vehicle to crush an Iraqi boy who did not get out of the middle of the road. Tracing the myriad causes leading to this particular case of military moral injury, I ask what went wrong with regard to the professional treatment of his suffering, following his return to the United States and discharge from military service.

Chapter 4, "Moral Injury and Atrocity," gathers together the insights from the preceding chapters, to reconsider the entirety of the triangle of violence and phenomenon of military moral injury, against the backdrop of the theory of philosopher Claudia Card. I make a challenging claim: moral injury is an atrocity, as described by Card, a "foreseeable intolerable harm produced by culpable wrongdoing."[60]

If the earlier chapters of this book forge insight about the causes and development of military moral injury, Card's theory of atrocity pushes the analysis an important step further. For if moral injury is named "an atrocity," it then follows that human beings will need to do something about this grave injustice. In this way, Card's framework raises questions about a common drop-off in critical thinking regarding war and its consequences. Many people assume that war (and moral injury) are inevitable – they are "givens" to be endured, costs that must be borne, human realities that some always will bear, or phenomena that human beings may never change. But Card's un- wavering moral analysis pierces through this passive acceptance. Moral in- jury as an atrocity requires a response of justice, and to arrive at this, human beings must better understand and address the deeper forces and dynamics of cultural and structural violence that give rise to it.

In contrast to various fatalistic or unquestioning attitudes, Card writes, "We need a theoretical account of what makes wrongdoing serious enough to count as evil or in what ways it is serious. 'Evil' is a heavy judgment."[61] Card's paradigm of evil as "atrocity," as a theoretical framework, forces a host of uncomfortable questions: Does moral injury count as an "atrocity"? If so, what should human beings do about it? Why would calling moral inju- ry "an atrocity" provide stronger grist for moral deliberation to comprehend it, and strategies to address its harm? I argue that Card's theoretical distinc- tions provide a pathway to sift through the many ambiguities and complexi- ties involved in the "evil" of moral injury. This ethical deliberation advances *thought* about moral injury, and leaves people in a better place, as Card hopes, to better know what to do about this evil, and how to transform it.

In addition, Chapter 4 connects theory to reflection in one last case study, the suffering experienced by "Andy," a veteran whose moral injury led him to the brink of self-destruction. I explore his story, and reflect on it with help from both Galtung and Card. Andy's experience shows how and why the macro phenomenon of military moral injury as a whole, should be under- stood as "atrocity." But going further, the chapter also explores the gradual transformation that is taking place in his life, involving Andy's leadership in a relatively new Moral Injury Program that has been developed at the Corporal Michael J. Crescenz VA Medical Center in Philadelphia. The labor undertaken by Andy, other veterans, and the professional caregivers in this program, shows why there is an indispensable need and role for a deeper social analysis of military moral injury, for people like Andy, their families and care providers, everyday citizens, and people across the world whose lives are affected by U.S. wars.

Chapter 5 concludes with reconstructive imagination and a call to action to address the complex dynamics of violence, atrocity, healing and hope that are intertwined in the phenomenon of moral injury and society. Is a cultural swerve possible in the United States? Seeing war through the lens of moral injury could lead to increased collective awareness and social change. What about the religio-cultural dynamics of violence in the seabed of this phe- nomenon? These questions invoke exploration of U.S. American self-iden- tity and sovereignty with respect to war and militarism; they push toward new ways of self-understanding that have yet to be imagined. Moreover, exploration of religious identities also is urgent. What may be said is that a (re)newed U.S. identity will dethrone war and militarism in the national imaginary; and Christian settings will need to explore their complicity in this cultural arrangement. A renewed identity will involve effort to *refuse* the dominant mode of perceiving war as "the necessary sacrifice for human/ national security and wellbeing." It also will demonstrate the urgency of re-thinking the national imaginary and its (civil) religious foundations. For an honest accounting pulls the curtain back from widespread cognitive frames that perceive moral injury as an unfortunate and inescapable byproduct of "war-as-sacrifice;" and unsettling this ground leads to further doubt about the ways we have conceived conflict, security, militarism and war. Finally, this reevaluation faces human beings with the senselessness of today's world-building of war-culture, and human identification with it.

Does an honest accounting of moral injury lead to the conclusion that it is impossible to accommodate human morality with war? The claim of this book, first, is that investigating violence in the flashpoint of moral injury will result in a more truthful seeing of the reality of war, especially in the 21st century U.S., and most particularly with regard to the ways human beings, especially those whose lives are more protected from the direct violence of the fields of war, have concealed the actual consequences of war and war-culture from their vision. For ultimately, as many of those who are dealing with military moral injury intuitively understand, addressing moral injury only from an individual perspective will fail to illuminate the place where the deepest engine of assault to life persists and swirls, in the structural and cultural architecture of the nation.

And second, an honest investigation of moral injury, all the way down, not only gives voice to the depth and breadth of moral injury's devastation in individuals, families and communities; it ethically sharpens reexamination of citizenship and national identity. Different possibilities for collective self-understanding emerge on the horizon, and wider pathways for human imagination and responsibility. In the end, this investigation underscores the continuing project facing human beings: to re-envision human morality and well-being apart from U.S. war-culture, as citizens and leaders alike shoulder the urgent need to forge a different way of life, altogether.

1 Moral Injury and U.S. War-culture

"Every society is engaged in the never completed enterprise of building a humanly meaningful world."

Peter Berger[1]

Human world-building and war-culture

Human beings are "world builders." Sociologist Peter Berger's characterization of humans is truly a beautiful one. He emphasizes that it is in human
beings' very nature to *pour ourselves* into the creation of social worlds.[2] We
continually produce and reproduce human society, "culture," as a collective
enterprise. This social activity of human beings is understood by Berger to
be rooted in our very biology. We can't help ourselves, and we seemingly
can't live without such externalization. Yet simultaneously these humanly
constructed worlds come to appear to us as given, objective, and in and
of themselves they act upon and shape us. Humans are curiously forget-
ful of their own role in their creative outpouring, as Berger puts it, "men
[sic] forget."[3] Perhaps even more curious, humans inevitably participate in
unending practices of legitimation that further present our social creations
not only as given, but as natural and inevitable, and finally, even divinely
ordered. There is a reason for this defensive activity, however, for according to Berger, the deepest fear facing human beings is the disintegration of
their social worlds. And humans rightly have this fear, for as he puts it, "All
socially constructed worlds are inherently precarious."[4] Of course, those
with prestige, social power and material well-being have further reason to
legitimate the human arrangements that benefit them. Experiences of marginalization, especially potential and actual death, pull away the proverbial
curtain to reveal the dubious and vulnerable nature of those "plausibility
structures" at the seabed of our social worlds that help us to live from day
to day, "business as usual."[5]

The social worlds that we build as human beings appear to us as independent and autonomous, though they have arisen through our very outpouring. Berger describes a kind of dialectic that occurs as human beings
co-produce themselves through the building of worlds that then turn about
to face humans and shape them in distinctive ways. Each generation faces

the challenge of communicating and handing on "a meaningful order," to the next, to protect against the terror of meaninglessness.

Berger's sociological insight helps explain a vexing problem related to moral injury. For by and large, not only laypeople, but many researchers and experts also approach moral injury as a "given." Rarely is moral injury considered as a human consequence of a larger social and cultural world that has been humanly constructed. Even less frequently has it been asked whether moral injury might reveal something important to us about the social worlds we humans have created, or whether the phenomenon of moral injury may suggest something drastically off-kilter with the world-building human beings have wrought. This chapter investigates the importance of questioning how and why the roots of moral injury are firmly embedded in "U.S. war-culture." In other words, the curtain is pulled back to better reveal how moral injury is related to wider and deeper cultural forces and practices.

In the United States, "war-culture" is at the center of "the meaningful order" humans have created, in particular their social construction of the nation itself, the national "imaginary." "U.S. war-culture" may be defined as the ethos, institutions and practices of war that interpenetrate with vast and diverse cultural sites. War's ethos, values and practices interact with, influence and seep into the economy and education, labor and practices of consumption, business and corporate activity, religion and popular entertainment, government, and on and on.[6]

The ethos of war and militarism provides a deep, mostly unexamined and fundamental nucleus of national identity formation in the United States. This identity stands out in prized national symbols, such as the national anthem and flag, and national festivals like the Fourth of July and Memorial Day. Additionally, less visibly, militarism and war in the United States play a decisive role in the self-and-collective understanding of citizens; and war influences everyday lives in all kinds of ways, far more than many tend to imagine.

Countless cultural examples of these dynamics abound. For instance, a Google search of "halftime military appreciation," results in a long list of YouTube video links that chronicle the deep links between war-culture, sports and education in the U.S. Not only in professional sports, but also in high school, college and university stadiums across the country, the structures and activities of war are lauded and ritualized. We might look, for instance, at the "Penn State Blue Band Military Appreciation" halftime show, dedicated to celebrating all the various branches of the military at a football game. Video of the show highlights songs affiliated with different branches of the military, while band members smartly shift from one complex formation on the field to another, outlining the shapes of various military weapons, war-machines and symbols associated with those branches, including a tank, submarine, anchor, war-ship, eagle, and fighter jet. Near the end of the performance, the voice of an announcer is projected over the music, as if this were some sort of commercial, declaring all military forces "a global force for good," that ensure American citizens' "unparalleled freedom." Meanwhile, as the show closes with a rendition of "America the Beautiful," huge American flags twirl, and red, white and blue streamers unravel across on the field, as the announcer declares the need for spectators in the stands to be "grateful" for everything the military does for citizens.[7] A very specific legitimation of militarization seamlessly interpenetrates with the institutions of education and college sports, not to mention the arts and popular entertainment.

That many citizens may balk at the idea that this amounts to little more than a form of propaganda only further reveals how deeply embedded such legitimation of militarization is in the U.S. national self-conception. Not only is it "forgotten" that the war-culture in the U.S. was created by human beings, the naturalization of war-culture has become so profoundly buried in the common imagination that one must struggle to consciously see it. Meanwhile, the actual extent and consequences of U.S. militarization and war contradict people's imagined vision of themselves as citizens and as a nation. Like Berger says, people have "forgotten" our own cultural creation. But U.S. war-culture has distinct consequences in people's lives. In the United States, we are "easy with war," as one scholar puts it; or, as another writes, "War has become our national posture and we are more or less comfortable with it."[8] Fifty years ago President Eisenhower understood and expressed concern about the destructive consequences for the culture, freedom and even spirituality of people in the United States, resulting from deepening links between the corporate manufacturing for war, government and Pentagon military institutions. In his final speech to the nation, he coined the terminology of "the military-industrial complex" of the United States. But today, sociological researchers see that the permutations of war-culture in the United States now thread their way into exponentially far reaches of culture at large. As sociologist Nick Turse describes, U.S. citizens live in a "military-industrial-technological-entertainment-academic-scientific-media-intelligence-homeland-security-surveillance-national-security-corporate complex."[9] And in addition to this long list, at least one additional site needs to be included: religion.

Meanwhile, cognitive dissonance characterizes life in the United States with respect to "war-culture." For instance, many U.S. American citizens strongly believe themselves to be a nation that intends good to the rest of the world. But how does this square with the reality of U.S. military spending? In 2019 the United States dedicated $732 billion for military expenditures; it was reported that in 2014 the U.S. spent *more than the **total** of the next ten highest national military spenders in the world.* This was in excess of 53% of the total discretionary U.S. federal budget overall.[10] Some citizens rise to the defense of this structural reality with the argument that the rest of the world depends upon American protection. Military might ensures security. This is related to Ian Morris' argument, in *War! What Is It Good For?* According to Morris, "… war *has* been good for something: over the long run, it has made humanity safer and richer."[11] War may be "… the worst imaginable way to create larger, more peaceful societies" – but Morris claims that humans have never found any better way. As he writes, "… the creation of a bigger society tends to make *everyone*, the descendants of victors and vanquished alike, better off."[12] War led to the development of larger and more complex societies, according to Morris, and these benefits justify the negative consequences of war. Morris' thinking no doubt mirrors that of many, even a majority of American citizens. How else may we explain the relative lack of distress regarding the amount of money, labor, creative thought, time and unending resources dedicated to militarization and war in the U.S.? This book takes up and deconstructs these arguments about the supposed necessity, benefits, inevitability, and ultimately, the assumed sacred nature of war.

For instance, what if Morris' logic is applied to, say, the beginnings of U.S. American history? One historical artifact from this early era that rarely makes it into high school history courses is the Oct. 18, 1861 letter written by William Penn to the Delaware Indians. Though he was considered a troublemaker in England for his Quaker beliefs, and arrested and jailed more than once, nevertheless Penn was given the land that would become "Pennsylvania" as a proprietary province. He set sail soon thereafter from England, but even more quickly deputized commissioners to sail before him with a letter to share with the indigenous people already occupying the land. Addressing the ongoing injustices emerging from the colonization of what was termed, "the new world," and specifically addressing the settlers' relationship with the Delaware Indians, in his letter Penn took care to emphasize the intention to "… live justly, peaceably and friendly" with them, and to provide "a full and speedy satisfaction" for any wrongs that had been committed.[13]

Penn's letter remained within the dominant colonial frame; it failed to raise any questions regarding the justice of this new arrangement imposed upon First Peoples without their consent. They already were long established in the land. Nevertheless, articulating intentions of justice and equity, Penn signed his letter, "I am your loving friend." Though never verified by documentary evidence, historical tradition is replete with narratives and artwork that depict and celebrate Penn and the Lenni Lenape Indians in Shackamaxon beneath a huge elm tree, exchanging promises of friendship.[14] However, looking back over the more than three hundred years of history since this letter, what might have been different for First Peoples of Pennsylvania and the U.S., had Penn's written intentions taken precedence, not only for a few decades, but permanently? Penn and others' lack of awareness regarding the structural and cultural violence of colonization would trump any wishes, however well-meaning, for a different and more equitable relationship, however much desired by Penn. The main point here regards the devastating genocidal consequences of colonialism, including legitimated armed violence against First Peoples in what would become the United States, leading us back to Morris' assertions about the benefits of war to ask, were these "vanquished" "better off" in the end?

War and war-culture should be considered a public health crisis; war "… damages human health through multiple routes, both during and after conflict," write the editors of *War and Health*.[15] Between 2004 and 2007, malnutrition, infectious disease, food shortages, unsanitary living conditions, all commonplace consequences of war, led to the deaths of an additional four individuals for every person who died violently in the context of war. The "syndemics of war" refers to the intermixing multiple interactions of war's morbidity and mortality:

> War, by causing physical and emotional trauma in populations, destroying healthcare systems and social infrastructure, despoiling the environment, intentionally or unintentionally causing or exacerbating food insecurity and malnutrition, creating refugee populations, and spreading infections … touches the lives of those who fight wars (e.g., combatants, including soldiers, militia members, and increasingly, military contractors); refugees and internally displaced persons; healthcare professionals and those in or fleeing the war zones.

But not only is war a disaster for public health, contrasting with Morris' optimistic view; the assessment of Mark Pilisuk and Jennifer Rountree raises further questions. According to their investigation, far from providing widespread benefit or evolutionary gain across the board for human beings, in the global era in particular war has proved disastrous and destructive. Military and economic violence both are linked to the concentration of power and economic gain within a small elite. In contrast to frequent promises about wars – that they protect the innocent, reduce violence and increase peaceful outcomes – Pilisuk and Rountree describe the U.S. as "the largest beneficiary of global inequality," and "the world's specialist in weapons."[16] Given "the over 639 million small arms and light weapons" across the world today, one for every ten people on the planet; and given U.S. responsibility for approximately half of all weapons sold worldwide, perhaps it will not surprise readers to learn about the response of the American leadership elite to a resolution from the U.N. General Assembly in 2006 that proposed a global arms trade treaty. Out of 154 votes, the U.S. was the single dissenting vote.[17]

Analysis of U.S. national policy reveals a consistent pattern: according to Pilisuk and Rountree, the U.S. repeatedly and insistently refuses and undermines cooperative international efforts to reduce armed structural violence in the world. For instance, in 2001 the U.S. withdrew from the 1972 Anti-ballistic Missile Treaty, and retreated from the 1972 Biological and Toxic Weapons Convention, formerly ratified by 144 nations, including the United States. The list continues with opposition to the United Nations Program of Action to Prevent, Combat and Eradicate the Illicit Trade in Small Arms and Light Weapons, and refusal up to the present to sign the Anti-Personnel Mine Ban Convention, signed by 122 nations in 1997, but refused in 2001 by the United States, though 123 other nations made this commitment.[18]

The U.S. spends over $100 million *each day* maintaining its nuclear weapons, and dedicates more resources to their development and testing than at the height of the Cold War. During the second term of his administration, though he visited Hiroshima, and spoke about the need for a moral reawakening to address nuclearism, President Obama simultaneously launched plans to rebuild the U.S. nuclear stockpile, focusing on the creation of small nuclear weapons.[19] Some analysts concluded that the focus on small nuclear bombs makes their potential use more likely.[20] As fifty countries of the United Nations ratified the U.N. Treaty for the Prohibition of Nuclear Weapons in 2020, the United States was putting pressure on them to withdraw their support for a nuclear weapons ban, in contrast to U.N. Secretary-General Antonio Guterres, who called the nuclear weapons ban treaty "a very welcome initiative."[21]

It is important to emphasize that these are not incidental or accidental decisions, as Pilisuk and Rountree write, "[Wars] are products of a social order that plans for them and then accepts this planning as natural."[22] The structural violence of U.S. war-culture is taken up in greater depth in the next chapter.

Exploring U.S. war-culture creates cognitive dissonance. One might think that a rash of governmental actions to reject so many international collaborations to reduce structural militarized violence in the world would ignite political protest, but in the U.S., the reaction mostly is the opposite. Collective consciousness of war-culture remains out of reach, and those who do protest make little impact. Why is this the case? Facing the reality of war-culture is not in accord with the way U.S. citizens understand themselves. And the powerful tool of political rhetoric legitimates a careful depiction of war-culture in the national imaginary. This rhetoric conceals the beneficiaries of U.S.-led war, minimizes the nature of public health devastation due to war, and discourages awareness of other damaging consequences of U.S. militarization. The carefully worded speech of President Obama to the troops returning from the Iraq war in 2011 is just one example showing how dominant political rhetoric conceals reality and fosters a false consciousness.

Notice, first, how President Obama defines the national character of citizenship: "the most important lesson we can take from you," he told the returning soldiers, "is not about military strategy – it's a lesson about *our national character*." He continued,

> Because of you – because you sacrificed so much for a people that you had never met, Iraqis have a chance to forge their own destiny. That's part of what makes us special as Americans. Unlike the old empires, we don't make these sacrifices for territory or for resources. We do it because it's right. There can be no fuller expression of America's support for self-determination than our leaving Iraq to its people. That says something about who we are. And let us never forget the source of American leadership: our commitment to the values that are written into our founding documents, and a unique willingness among nations to pay a great price for the progress of human freedom and dignity. This is who we are. That's what we do as Americans, together ...
>
> The war in Iraq will soon belong to history. Your service belongs to the ages. Never forget that you are part of an unbroken line of heroes spanning two centuries – from the colonists who overthrew an empire, to your grandparents and parents who faced down fascism and communism, to you – men and women who fought for the same principles in Fallujah and Kandahar, and delivered justice to those who attacked us on 9/11.[23]

Coming at a pivotal moment in the Iraq War, President Obama missed an important opportunity for greater honesty about the very war he had opposed as a senator. Think about the claims that are cleverly suggested here. First, American citizenship and character are conflated with military service, defined as "sacrifice." The problematic association between tropes of "sacrifice" and ways of collective national identity are explored further on in this chapter. This language erects a sacred canopy that mystifies and conceals the destructive realities of war and militarism.

In addition, President Obama suggests that the U.S. scaled down the number of troops in Iraq "to leave Iraq to its people," in other words, as an act of respect for Iraq's "self-determination" and national sovereignty. But this is little more than a distraction from troubling realities related to the decision to draw down troops. For despite approximately 20 years of direct violence, enormous amounts of money, the death and disabling injury of tens of thousands of U.S. Americans, and deaths of perhaps a million Iraqis, the war could not be "ended" with a clear U.S. "victory." The actual outcome is more troubling. At the time of this writing Iraq is considered to be a quagmire of sectarian violence, a state that is mostly "failed." If anything is clear about the Iraq war, it is that this war *has not* better enabled Iraqis "to forge their destiny." Though more than $25 billion dollars was spent over ten years to "train, equip and sustain" Iraqi security forces, by 2014, the U.S.-trained Iraqi force mostly had "spectacularly collapsed." Andrew Bacevich, retired Army Colonel and Professor Emeritus at Boston University doubted that self-determination was in any way possible, "I don't think it's self-evident that Iraq exists, except in the most nominal sense. If that's true, then further efforts – a second decade's worth of efforts to build an Iraqi army – simply are not likely to pan out."[24]

Moreover, President Obama's characterization of U.S. intentions in Iraq as "a delivery of justice" in response to those who attacked the U.S. on 9/11, also demands further examination. Seven years before this speech, the analysts of the 9/11 Commission, whose mission it was to examine the factors that laid the ground for 9/11, concluded that there were no connections between the 9/11 terrorists and Iraq.[25] At the very least, this is a disingenuous rhetorical connection. Finally, what about the speech's claims regarding U.S. principles undergirding all the different wars and military actions undertaken by the United States over its history? Can U.S. military action really be so simply summed up, as "an unbroken line of heroes spanning two centuries"? Such language frankly is dishonest. It is indeed troubling to hear such a celebratory and misleading accounting of the role of militarization and war of the U.S. in Iraq, much less U.S. history overall.

This book investigates the phenomenon of moral injury as an inevitable consequence of the wider reality of U.S. war-culture. I argue that a conscious contextualizing of moral injury within culture at large has important implications, both for moral deliberation about the nature of this debilitating wound of war, and also for more honest vision regarding U.S. ways of war. Approaching and treating moral injury mostly as an individual phenomenon is inadequate; a deeper investigation takes into account all the structures, cultural forces, practices and mindsets that lay the ground for it to take root in people's lives. But few researchers of moral injury are making these connections. However, this vacuum in thought is not accidental; the very war-culture that permeates life in the United States at all points, also shapes the boundaries of collective (un)awareness. People are encouraged to think about moral injury in this way, primarily through individualistic and de-contextualized terms (if they are aware of moral injury at all). In the end, understanding war-culture through the flashpoint of moral injury clarifies and unsettles the U.S. "easy way with war." But in order to set the stage, further disentangling of the interpenetrations of war-culture is necessary.

Untangling the knot of sacrificial war-culture

Those European colonists who first set foot on what would eventually become "the United States," brought with them a host of religious images, commitments and practices. But though this is well known and celebrated, less attention is given to the intertwining of religion with the machinery of violence in the history of the U.S., including practices of armed force, militarism and war. From its beginnings, the intermixing of religion and violence has played a strong role in the formation of U.S. national identity.[26] Moreover, during times of potential or actual war, this enmeshed relationship rises to the surface and impacts U.S. culture with greater power and urgency. Such most definitely was the case in the years following 9/11. As this book was in preparation, Alex, a former Navy corpsman, who had come across my first book and analysis of "war-culture" in the United States, sent me an email about his own experience during these years. He details the strange and uncomfortable interweaving of the cultural dynamics of religion, militarism and war with dominant assumptions in the nation regarding what it means to be a citizen, and his own painfully won development of a new consciousness. He writes,

> I could tell you had us in mind, there aren't many of us. Putting it in perspective, in the book you said that recruiters had to talk to 150 people to get 1 person to sign up in 2005 ... I was that person. They

didn't even need to talk to me because I came to them. Ready to give my life. Right after high school in 2005 I wanted to "save lives" and be a superhero. I was a Navy corpsman from 2005–2008 during the Bush years. I heard a couple chaplains use sacrificial rhetoric, one of them describing how the faith of "those animals" "over there" who behead Americans and hate "our way of life," is not a true faith in God, and our sacrifices show that; as if our "ultimate sacrifice" was more pure. Homophobia, Islamophobia, misogyny, rape culture, the general devaluing of human life was all okay in the U.S. military; a military that I remember would have us recite in cadence on our morning runs through the hills of Camp Pendleton: "we're going to rape, kill, pillage and burn, we're going to rape kill pillage and burn AND eat their babies."

Hearing and repeating this was just <u>one</u> of many "I didn't sign up for this" moments.

I tried many ways to get out, but it usually was a dead end. I especially wanted to leave after I found out that American oil companies (Texaco and Chevron) had been in Ecuador destroying people's lives and land. My father is from Ecuador, and served in the U.S. army for eight years during the Carter and Reagan administrations' dabble in Latin and South America (he went in at 18, from Yonkers, NY, he could barely speak English). I looked at the irony at the time: I'm training to kill and fight people over there for oil, and my father was in his time too … It made me angry. I never deployed, I just got to sit back and observe; while working as personnel support in internal medicine I checked in some Marines returning from deployment with psychological traumas and physical handicaps, I felt and heard their pain and confusion, only to walk them down the hall to a Navy doctor who assured them all is well and they should take this pill. It'll make them stop choking their wives in the middle of the night during a nightmare. Get my drift?

I wrestled my way out after they denied honoring my contract, I didn't care what type of discharge they threatened to give me. I did find a way out eventually, albeit I put my reputation on the line, in that they threatened me with a general discharge if I went AWOL. I walked away during the reserves when that rhetoric you cover in your book started to be supplemented with outrageous historical claims (e.g., "The Japanese praise us for dropping nuclear bombs on them" like they were "grateful") by high ranking officers and enlisted personnel. They also kept changing the conditions of my contract. Long story short they allowed me to walk away with an honorable discharge, but not as many educational benefits. I got to keep my hands clean from combat, but I struggled to recalibrate my moral compass after it had been manipulated. As my own mother said, "I gave the Navy a sweet boy and they gave me back an angry drunk." I would have taken a general or dishonorable anyhow, as I see no honor in killing civilians, women and children.

I came across your book after I left the VA hospital in Ann Arbor, Michigan. I was hospitalized for 13 days in the oncology wing in December of 2014 (last year), eventually being diagnosed with a form of Ulcerative Colitis, pancolitis. While I was there I (and the other veterans) would get Christmas cards from kids thanking us for our "sacrifice." Volunteers would come in repeating the same thing, offering religious comfort via books on veterans who "found God" after their time in combat. After I left the hospital I asked myself, "what sacrifice did I make? I didn't go anywhere, give my life or take another's. The kid down the hall was 26 and paralyzed, cursing the majority of the time he was there in pain, is this the culmination of his sacrifice, then?" I felt as if I needed to support my claims and lived experience with the work of religious studies scholars, mostly because my college history courses were whitewashed and portrayed essentialist and elementary versions of Christianity and America – founded on love, morality and principles. I needed more insight to legitimate my experience while I was being socially alienated (by the community, friends, family, academic peers), legally punished (by "veteran treatment," courts and civilian courts; with the latter being more harsh) and politically ignored (by federal, state and VA representatives with pleas for holistic, integrated community care) everywhere else during my assimilation back to civilian life.[27]

Alex's email excruciatingly outlines the weaving interpenetrations of (civil) religion, militarism and militarization in the monolith of U.S. war-culture. First, consider the nature of the "irony" that he details. The son of an immigrant from Ecuador, he and his father both served in branches of the U.S. military. He was acculturated to believe that the apotheosis of citizenship in the United States would be to become a corpsman, "to save lives" and become a hero through risk to his own life. In other words, he assumed that the highest meaning of citizenship involved self-sacrifice for the survival or well-being of the nation. Remember the same cognitive configuration in President Obama's speech to the returning troops; this remains the common national imaginary absorbed and assumed unquestioningly by most U.S. Americans. But quickly the question surfaces: what happened to so disappoint this young man? What was behind his sense of betrayal? The consciousness he eventually developed was not easily constructed; it took him a long time to understand and analyze what happened not only in his own life, but with fellow sailors and marines, and indeed, the country itself.

Chapter 3 explores the interpenetration of war with the economy of the United States, resulting in what scholars call "a permanent war economy;" but already in Alex's story there is reference to the interpenetration of corporate structures in the pursuit of oil, with the systems of militarization and war; this relationship has impacted many generations in the United States. Alex thought he was joining the military "to save lives," only later to learn of the geopolitical complexities of militarized violence in the U.S. used to pursue, protect and develop the flow of oil, and the profits of corporations. In a double bitter irony, he notes that not only he but his father participated in branches of the military that were instrumental in the despoiling and commodifying of their native homeland.

Chapter 3 investigates the colliding masculinities embedded in the culture of war of the United States, but again, Alex's email foreshadows this relationship. Relaying his dismay about Basic Training, he describes an unabashed process of acculturation into a form of masculinized identity that normalized unthinkable violence (think about the military cadence he and others were forced to chant). He had his "I didn't sign up for this" moment, clear that his moral code could never be accommodated to rape, burning, and the killing (and *eating*) of babies. How can such acculturation be rationalized or explained?

Think further, about the deep confusion that results as his experiences clashed with the rhetoric of military clergy. He was encouraged to interpret his experience as the necessary *sacrifice* one makes for the well-being of the nation. Betrayal takes root here, as deep bedrock moral principles are twisted and undermined. But not only was religion commodified to suit military goals and purposes; this specifically religious advocacy of sacrifice melded with civil recommendations of the same, legitimating "the sacred canopy over war and militarism" in the U.S. This canopy mystifies clear accounting of the consequences of militarized violence, and labels those who might protest as "heretics" or traitors. Religion can be exploited as a powerful form of concealment that sacralizes U.S. identity centered on an overpowering military as the foundation of what it means to be a "strong nation."

Alex's disgust regarding perceived exploitation and manipulation is evident in his reflection about the systems of the Veterans Affairs assigned to provide healthcare for devastated and injured returning warriors. Not only in Basic Training or in deployment, but also here in the healthcare setting, Alex claims that volunteers, clergy, civilians and other veterans heaped on religious and sacrificial justifications, while he witnessed unmitigated suffering and loss. Journalist Ann Jones, who interviews and writes about the profound struggles confronting servicemembers, comments, "America's soldiers return with enough troubles to last the rest of their lives … But all through these wars we've heard the patriotic tales of heroism and sacrifice, refashioning the suffering of soldiers and their families into the national narrative we know so well – the one about the greatest nation, the greatest military force, the greatest generation the world has ever known."[28]

Alex's sarcasm is not difficult to understand. His experiences left him angry, bitter and also confused. For the actual context of his life as a servicemember and veteran was in contradiction to the rationalizations and legitimations surrounding him at every point in the culture. Eventually, Alex turned to the work of religious studies scholars for help; he hoped to disentangle the mystifying knot of all these tightly interwoven dynamics.

Alex's confusion parallels my own as a religious studies scholar in the years following the devastating events of 9/11 in the United States. For in those months and years, I frankly was shocked to hear the surging of sacrificial religious rhetoric tied to war. I heard it in political and military contexts, in the realm of popular culture and entertainment, in religious and educational settings, in the business of commerce and national commemoration, and beyond. Suddenly language of "the necessity of war-as-sacrifice," such as in President Obama's speech above, was everywhere, and in countless contexts, this rhetoric of war consistently referenced Christian sacrificial constructions buried deep in the U.S. (civil) religious psyche. Having recently completed a dissertation that focused on the mapping of women's writing about the theological locus of *soteriology* (the diverse flowering of understandings of Christian "salvation" throughout history), I was sensitized to the rhetoric of sacrifice. At least since the 1970s, a growing body of theological scholarship has identified and criticized dominant sacrificial formulations in Christian theology, and deconstructed how these frameworks justify violence, mask its destruction, and inequitably distribute its costs.[29]

Berger's theory of human world-building also helps explain *why* sacrificial rhetoric surged as the nation descended into war. War is one of those marginal experiences that presents a potential threat to the given order of any social world. Suddenly the world appears more precarious; its "taken for granted" reality seems less formidable and inevitable, and the legitimations propping up the world face more intense questioning. In these contexts,

Berger writes, "… religious legitimations almost invariably come to the front."[30]

The conflation of sacrifice and war after 9/11 could and still can be found everywhere, in political commercials, State of the Union addresses, Nobel Peace Prize speeches, Facebook messages, veterans' websites, commercial advertisements of all sorts, commemorations of national holidays, educational settings, and of course, in a huge variety of entertainment venues.[31] For instance, one memorable example came from the highly acclaimed popular TV series, *House of Cards*, featuring actor Kevin Stacey as a fictitious villainous president of the United States. Watching this president and his equally heartless and ambitious first lady, played by Robin Wright, ruthlessly climb the ladder of power in U.S. politics, is an exercise in guilty pleasure for the television viewer. Occasionally the series ventures into the realm of religion, and in one striking episode, the president travels to Arlington Cemetery to attend a funeral for soldiers who died as a result of the president's order to deploy troops in a conflict abroad. Viewers observe the president standing uneasily on the lawn during the graveside service, his glance rotating between the open grave and the distraught spouse of one of the dead. Then the clergyperson intones the following graveside homily:

> And God said to Abraham, "Take your son, your only son who you love, Isaac, and sacrifice him." Abraham was willing, but when he raised his knife above Isaac on the altar, God stopped him, for Abraham had proven his devotion to God. Then God, to prove his own devotion to us, made his own sacrifice. For God so loved the world, that he gave his only son. Devotion. Sacrifice. Love. This is what the Lord teaches us, what these young men have exemplified. We shall forever honor them, and in heaven they will have eternal life. Amen.[32]

Perhaps Alex heard words similar to these above, for the conflation of "a nonviolent messiah" with the loss and death of servicemembers is widespread as a meme in U.S. culture.[33] The cognitive/religious frame is repeated and enacted endlessly in Christian settings, but also in military, political, educational and many other cultural sites. Sacrificial mechanisms justify violence through providing the glue that binds the death and destruction of war to the claim of ultimate meaning. Sacrifice surges to the surface, providing legitimation in response to these unspeakable losses. Berger would describe this as the process of "alienation;" religion flows as the ultimate legitimating force, squelching serious questioning that might threaten the social order in the face of marginalization. Nevertheless, as sacrifice surges, cynicism blossoms. Think of the tone in Alex's email. Along these lines, in the same episode of *House of Cards*, the president later seeks out the clergyperson to ask him about his homily on sacrifice, only to hear the following: "Between you and me, that's the same sermon I always give at Arlington. You put enough soldiers in the ground, you get tired of writing new ones."[34]

Popular culture does not grow out of a vacuum; buried in its roots are the legitimations, assumptions and unquestioned values of a wider culture and nation. And these patterns are not limited to the imaginary world of fictitious TV series. To more clearly *see* the contours of the U.S. national sacrificial sacred canopy, I turn to another example from one of the latest memorial additions to the National Mall in Washington D.C.

This memorial project was approved unanimously in Congress, and appears to have easily met every requirement for its construction. Money flowed in to support it, and few if any questions or criticisms were raised about the message it conveys. "The American Veterans Disabled For Life Memorial in Washington," is dedicated to veterans whose war-time experiences have left them with life-changing injuries, and was planned and prepared for over sixteen years. Its dedication day was Oct. 5. 2014.[35]

One of the veterans whose picture appears in the memorial's structures is Army Lt. Dawn Halfaker, who lost her right arm in an explosion while serving in Iraq. As Chairwoman of the Wounded Warriors Project, in an interview with *The Associated Press*, Halfaker was asked why the memorial is important: "I think it will bring it home for visitors. I think it will give people a better understanding of how somebody's life is forever changed and really help them understand the sacrifice a little bit more." Others involved with the project described its purpose with the same sacrificial language, such as Arthur Wilson, another disabled veteran from the Vietnam era, and co-founder of the foundation tasked with building the memorial: "Who could take issue with honoring those who have given a life sacrifice?" Yet another young veteran of the U.S. recent wars, whose photograph in the memorial structure portrays him at his Purple Heart ceremony in a wheelchair, had this to say, when interviewed about his experience: "It's a blessing to be wounded in the name of my country."[36]

The language, logic and emotion of "sacrifice" urgently rise as people try to explain and respond to the drastic aftermath of war's losses. Developers of this memorial, and citizens who donated to help it come into being, bear witness to the meaning of these losses, and servicemembers' selflessness and dedication. People draw on the language of "sacrifice" to give voice to the enormity of what has been lost, they hope, not in vain, but for a greater purpose. The memorial, and the voices and faces of those depicted in it, underscore the impossibility of ever adequately measuring either the costs, or the depth of the losses that have been experienced.

A true disequilibrium takes shape as I dare to pose the question, what is the impact of these sacrificial expressions? For once the theme of sacrifice is raised, there follows a resounding lack of further critical appraisal. The longstanding saying, "it is sweet to die (or be wounded) for one's country," leads to a deafening silence.

Think about Alex's perplexity, and mine. In U.S. war-culture, sacrificial language surges in any attempt to speak about the wounds of war. But this language and framework have a much longer history. So many writers and poets have struggled to find words adequate to the losses of war; they also have wrestled with the language of sacrifice so tied to the ways human beings understand and make sense of war. One unforgettable example regards the World War I era poet Wilfred Owen, and his piercing poem about the death of a young soldier who dies horrifically as a result of exposure to poison gas on the battlefield.[37] Owen shows how hard it is to deal with the meaning of this loss and destruction. In the poem he too is on the battlefield, where the poisoned soldier "plunges" at him, "guttering, choking, drowning." He cannot stop dreaming about this, it would seem, long after it has taken place, seeing "the white eyes writhing in his face," and "the blood come gargling from the froth-corrupted lungs." Is there any way to stop this dream, any way to explain or respond to this loss, this horror?

But in the end, the soldier's gut-wrenching death is no dream, it is reality; and Owen wants people to *see this.* Such vision cannot but wake people up from the sweet dream that he calls "the old Lie": *Dulce et decorum est; Pro patria mori* – the exact words we hear from those featured in the American Veterans Disabled for Life Memorial – it is sweet and proper to die for the fatherland. The familiar adage goes back much further than the World War I era, to the poet Horace in the era of the Roman Empire.[38]

Sacrificial language rises to the surface in the face of war's horror, but not only in the United States, and not only in the present time. This is part of a longstanding and understandable deep-seated human need to try to come to terms, try to find an explanation, or somehow distract, lessen, or soften war's harsh realities.

But why does Owen call this a "lie"? On the one hand, deeper thinking about the surge of sacrifice helps underscore how truly terrible, threatening and life-extinguishing war really is. The need to make sense, and to reach for ultimate meaning, is a very human response to the unmitigated destruction and loss of war. There are families, individuals and communities, for whom just getting up and getting through the day, in this morass of grief and loss, reach for this frame of meaning: *He/she made the ultimate sacrifice.* Especially in military cultures, but in other circles too, the language of sacrifice connotes honor, respect and remembrance, even a link to eternity. This book explores the way that human beings intertwine religious resources in sacrificial language and rituals to conserve memory, honor and give voice to unthinkable grief.

But on the other hand, as Owen powerfully communicates in his poem, sacrificial frameworks *hide* war's true nature. The logic in *Dulce et decorum est* perpetuates the idea that this destruction is "sweet," because it is the necessary, "proper" way to protect, maintain and honor the nation – and such logic is a lie. In contrast, Owen was sharply aware of the ways that sacrificial explanations may be used to manipulate people, especially young people. As he insists in the poem, people should stop to look at this gurgling, choking, dying young soldier – after all, he's really not much more than a child. Owen cries out, perhaps, if they really saw this, people would not so easily recommend "the old Lie" to "children ardent for some distant glory."

There are additional important arguments to be taken into account, as to the danger and deformation of sacrificial frameworks and patterns of thought. Sacrificial frameworks encourage what Judith Butler calls "derealizing narratives."[39] In other words, placing war into a framework of sacrifice leads to the emphasis on certain storylines, while burying others. For instance, think about how commonly people use the language of "the ultimate sacrifice," to try to put words to the terrible losses of U.S. military servicemembers and veterans. But the rituals of grieving war's losses in the U.S. only rarely take into account even much greater and more terrible losses abroad as a result of U.S. wars. These are "enemies" that "must be sacrificed" for the protection of the U.S. Delving into the logic of sacrifice, it's easy to become confused. And the process is more difficult still, because the all-important task of approaching war and war-culture with suspicion and analysis is interrupted and discouraged, if not extinguished altogether, once sacrificial frameworks are applied. For sacrifice is not to be questioned, but held in awe. As sociologist Hans Mohl discovered, "sacrifice" leads to an aura of "untouchability;" thus the silence.[40]

Bridging from Owen's era to the current time, not only the image of the poisoned soldier, the phenomenon of moral injury *also* slices through collective lack of awareness, sharpening conflict with "the old Lie," and puncturing a false consciousness that is bolstered through sacrificial frameworks. This is a painful process, most especially for people on the front lines of these losses. I have sympathy and appreciation for the strength, character and ideals of those whose faces are depicted in the American Veterans

Disabled for Life Memorial on the National Mall, and those who support them.

At the same time, the common interpretive framework of moral injury as one more "necessary sacrifice of war" should be attended with deep suspicion. Berger describes cultural frameworks such as "the old Lie" as "plausibility structures" in the humanly constructed world. These collective thought patterns arise out of a deep human need to provide explanation and justification in the face of unbearable grief and fear of the loss of their worlds; people turn to these ideas to live in the worlds they have constructed. How else can people bear this pain and these costs? But the "old Lie" also has been utilized and commodified to stir up feelings of patriotism and commitment, to drive "children ardent for some distant glory" to war; and it squelches critical thought about the structure and nature of war-culture.

The most devastating deception involved in sacrificial constructions has to do their undermining of serious challenges to any status quo. They conceal even as they justify the destructiveness and costs of U.S. war, and distract people from seeing how and why moral injury indelibly results from the humanly constructed world of war-culture. I am not alone in arriving at the conclusion that this plausibility structure, in the end, has to be faced, and morally addressed. The literary examples below illustrate cognitive dissonance involved in the transcendentalization of war. *Is war really sacred?* The "old Lie" conflates too much along the way. Yes, the immeasurable losses, injury and death of servicemembers demand citizens' response. The question is, what should that response be? Should it be to continue uncritically, with the ways of war-culture that led to these losses? To defend war and its losses as the only way to maintain the sacred nation? It would seem that the sacralization of the national imaginary grows in ratio to the unbearable losses war always exacts.

An alternative response could be to say, "this loss is unacceptable"![41] People could question the world they have created, and insist on something different. A deeper examination of the phenomenon of moral injury breaks through the wall of deception and illusion that this world, the world of war-culture, is the only world possible.

While it may be hardest for those whose livelihoods and sense of identity are deeply tied to the countless sites of war-culture, some of those most profoundly impacted by moral injury are pointing a way forward. These individuals are building capacity to question the cognitive constructions that mask and justify the world of war-culture, showing the way forward for all citizens. They are modeling for all of us a more thorough understanding of our reality, and the moral imperative to build a different world. Readers are encouraged to attend to the stories of servicemembers and veterans, such as "Andy," in later chapters of this book. They are demonstrating how and why all citizens must build greater capacity to hold painful truths, be open to multiple and conflicting perspectives, and find a different path.

"U.S. war-culture" is shorthand for the overwhelming and unending interpenetration of the ethos, institutions and practices of war with an unending array of supposedly "civilian" cultural sites in the United States. This system undergirds and encourages dominant assumptions in the U.S., and some scholars' assertions, such as Ian Morris, that war is a "social good," "necessary" and "inevitable."[42] These assumptions find further concealment through the rhetoric and logic of sacrifice. *But the nation is not sacred.* Chapter 5 explores alternatives to these ways of valuing, grieving, and world-building.

The final section of this chapter continues to attend to the reality of moral injury by turning to two recent novels about the longest wars of the United States. In *The Yellow Birds*, a National Book Award finalist, Iraq veteran and author Kevin Powers explores the inner world of protagonist John Bartle, a private serving in Iraq.[43] We enter into Bartle's moral injury imaginatively through his eyes, emotions, and inner conflict. In this way readers understand more viscerally the internal devastation of this wound of war. Additionally, a second novel, *Billy Lynn's Halftime Walk,* provides an opportunity to begin to demonstrate the validity of using Galtung's theory of violence to explore the wider structural and cultural context of moral injury.[44] Written by Ben Fountain, the novel tells the story of a platoon of soldiers on leave from duty in Iraq to advance "the military brand" of the United States through an appearance at a NFL halftime show with the Texas Cowboys. Fountain's satirical portrayal opens the way to a profound literary exploration of structural and cultural forms of violence at the root of moral injury, including the structures of the defense/war establishment in the United States, and religio-cultural dynamics of sacrificial war-culture combined with dominant frameworks of masculinity. Thus, both novels serve as guideposts to understand the inner dynamics of moral injury as well as the religio-cultural factors of a war-culture that lie at its roots.

Moral injury: Literary depictions

The Yellow Birds tells the story of fictional soldier, John Bartle. Following his deployment to Iraq in 2004, he has returned to his childhood home in Virginia, and is spiraling down into a dark void.

One day Bartle walks off the back porch of his mother's house and without a plan heads toward the woods. An "all-encompassing type of ache" moves through his body, "… like my whole skin was made out of a fat lip." He numbly follows the railroad tracks through the woods toward the city, "… not so much of a decision as it was a product of trying to turn off my mind." Discovering a rough campsite looking out over a river, from a remote spot he watches young people his own age, including at least one who used to be his friend. They have come to the river for an afternoon of listening to music and playing in the water. "They were beautiful. I had to resist the urge to hate them."

Bartle remains hidden, observing this innocent scene, but his quiet physical posture belies his internal turmoil. Powers gives the reader the opportunity to listen to Bartle's agonized thinking in an extended stream of consciousness that continues for over two pages of the novel. A portion of this intimate portrayal of the internal dynamics of moral injury is excerpted below:

> I had become a kind of cripple. They were my friends, right? Why didn't I just wade out to them? What would I say? 'Hey, how are you?' they'd say. And I'd answer 'I feel like I'm being eaten from the inside out and I can't tell anyone what's going on because everyone is so grateful to me all the time and I'll feel like I'm ungrateful or something. Or like I'll give away that I'm ungrateful or something. Or like I'll give away that I don't deserve anyone's gratitude and really they should all hate me for what I've done but everyone loves me for it and it's driving me crazy.' Right.
>
> Or should I have said that I wanted to die, not in the sense of wanting to throw myself off that train bridge over there, but more like wanting to be asleep forever because there isn't any making up for killing women or even watching women get killed, or for that matter killing men and shooting them in the back and shooting them more times than necessary to actually kill them and it was like just trying to kill everything you saw sometimes because it felt like there was acid seeping down into your soul and then your soul is gone and knowing from being taught your whole life that there is no making up for what you are doing, you're taught that your whole life, but then even your mother is so happy and proud because you lined up your sight posts and made people crumple and they were not getting up ever and yeah they might have been trying to kill you too, so you say, What are you gonna do?, but really it doesn't matter …

... like you have bottomed out in your spirit but yet a deeper hole is being dug because everybody is so fucking happy to see you, the murderer, the fucking accomplice, the at-bare-minimum bearer of some fucking responsibility, and everyone wants to slap you on the back and you start to want to burn the whole goddamn country down, you want to burn every goddamn yellow ribbon in sight, and you can't explain it but it's just, like, Fuck you, but then you signed up to go so it's all your fault, really, because you went on purpose, so you are in the end doubly fucked, so why not just find a spot and curl up and die ...

"What was it like over there?" In his "Author's Note," Powers tells us that this question, more than anything else, was what he hoped to be able to answer by the end of this writing. All in all, he says, "... the answer could be known to each of us if we'd only allow ourselves to be reminded of it."[45] The book ends with this mysterious and not fully fleshed out statement of Powers' own conclusions.

Nevertheless, Bartle's stream of consciousness provides a burning entry to the inner conflict and pain associated with the experience of moral injury. We hear the impossible moral crisis in his words. He can't live with himself and the memory of his own actions; he blames himself, especially since he volunteered for this service. The requirements of deployment, and the person he has become through being trained to do these things and enact these deeds, crashes against a deeper set of morals and meaning, the deepest part of his identity, such that he doesn't know what to make of anything anymore.

But this is not Bartle's crisis alone. For as the reader attends carefully to his words, the landscape of ethical morass expands, and begins to stretch into a wider field. For instance, what should we make of the following?

... even then your mother is so happy and proud because you lined up your sight posts and made people crumple and they were not getting up ever ... a deeper hole is being dug because everybody is so fucking happy to see you ... you start to want to burn the whole goddamn country down ...

This crisis involves more than Bartle's individual identity, set of values, experiences, and pain. As Powers illustrates in this novel, Bartle's reality also collides with broader structural realities, and cultural norms and practices in the development of this wound.

If Powers' novel suggests the internal experience of moral injury, and begins to raise wider questions, a second and very different novel about the Iraq War moves well past the internal and individual. *Billy Lynn's Long Halftime Walk*, by Ben Fountain, opens as Bravo Company nears the end of a national tour in the U.S. through which their recent military "victory" in Iraq has been trumpeted and cashed in on in every possible way.[46] Unlike Powers, Fountain is not a veteran of any war, but his satirical novel has been acclaimed not only for its depiction of dilemmas faced by soldiers, but also for the way it skewers the excesses and deformities of contemporary American culture, especially those aspects of culture related to violence, masculinity, money and war.

Just a few weeks earlier, the military company was part of a gruesome battle in Iraq that happened to be caught on film by Fox News. The protagonist of the novel, a 19-year-old soldier, Billy, appears in the footage "… firing with one hand and working on Shroom [a dying soldier] with the other … pulling the release on his IBA [Interceptor Body Armor] to get at his wounds."[47]

The film footage from the battlefield goes viral. The video has electrified a bizarre chord in American culture; and before anyone can blink, the entire military company has been brought back to the U.S. for a victory lap in various media venues, ending with an appearance at a halftime performance featuring Beyoncé and Destiny's Child, at none other than a Cowboy's football game on their home turf in Texas. If that wasn't bad enough, along with Bravo's surreal experience of the football game, a Hollywood agent throughout is working to sell their story to a film company for a feature movie they hope will include the film star Hillary Swank. Readers of the novel have to laugh even as they also groan throughout this narrative.

Meanwhile, with the laughter there is a sense of dread, because Billy's experience motivates consideration of the structural and cultural forces at play. In a passage relaying Billy's own internal thoughts near the end of the novel, Fountain writes,

> For the past two weeks he's been feeling so superior and smart because of all the things he knows from the war, but forget it, they are the ones in charge, these saps, these innocents, their homeland dream is the dominant force. His reality is their reality's bitch; what they don't know is more powerful than all the things he knows … To learn what you have to learn at the war, to do what you have to do, does this make you the enemy of all that sent you to the war?[48]

What does Billy mean by "the homeland dream"? His encounters with the U.S. citizens who have come to see Bravo Company *and* the Cowboys really tell the story. In these passages, readers are confronted with the devastating simplistic style of U.S. Americans who fawn over Billy, placing him into the iconic role of "hero." It's as if, for many of these citizens, any difference between the sports team and the military company has been mostly erased. Fountain describes the dynamic: "After two solid weeks of public events Billy continues to be amazed at the public response, the raw wavering voices and frenzied speech patterns, the gibberish spilled from the mouths of seemingly well-adjusted citizens."[49] Their "verbal arabesques ... spark and snap in Billy's ears like bugs impacting an electric bug zapper:"

terrRr

    Eye-rack,

        Eaaaar-*rock*,

    Sod'm

freedoms

    nina leven,

        nina leven,

           nina leven

hero

    sacrifice,

   soooh-preeeeme sacrifice

Bush

                Osama

        values

            di-mock-cruh-see[50]

These passages, constructed intentionally so that the reader *also hears* what Billy is audibly processing in these encounters with "grateful citizens," litter the pages of Fountain's novel, and illuminate the meaning of "the homeland dream." In this dream complex geopolitical realities have been boiled down to easy-to-understand tropes that are free from any danger of U.S. self-implication or examination. Iraq easily is conflated with terror; war with "freedom;" "nina leven" is chanted like a mantra, or a football stadium cheer; and soldiers are those who make "sooh-preeeeme sacrifice" for the sake of values and "di-**mock**-cruh-see" (I intentionally place into boldface the one word through which Fountain implies that the foundational value of democracy in the U.S. has become little more than a sham).

Most significant, the trope of "sacrificial hero" creates a useful distance for these U.S. "fans" from the actual realities of war. They love the viral footage – it looks like any number of Hollywood movies they have seen – and the sacrificial language they use in their encounters with Billy works as a protective cloak, demonstrating how loathe they are to listen openly to the conflicted and painful internal jumble of these soldiers' lives. Billy has put it well; the reality of his own experience is so at odds with this "dream," it is as though he has become an enemy to the working assumptions and cultural norms at the heart of the nation that sent him to war.

Billy finds himself flummoxed, cut to the heart, disgusted, sympathetic to the ignorance and superficiality of it all, laughing at the absurdity, but also deeply confused by these cultural realities. Earlier in the novel he wondered, when he saw himself in the viral video, "Is this what they mean by courage? Simply doing all the things you were trained to do, albeit everything at once and very fast. He remembers the whole front of his body being covered in blood and half-wondering if any of it was his, his bloody hands so slick he finally had to tear open the compression bandage with his teeth ...".[51]

Karl Marlantes, the Vietnam veteran famous for writing *What it is Like to Go to War*, has described this novel as "... a funny, yet totally sobering, dissection of the American way of watching war ... Fountain applies the heat of his wicked sense of humor while you face the truth of who we have become."[52]

Conclusion

The impacts of U.S. militarism (the ethos and culture of war) and militarization (the social structures and practical material readiness for war) go far beyond the actual production of war. The institutions, practices and ethos of war simultaneously infuse a host of supposedly civilian institutions. These institutions include the government, economy, educational systems, religious institutions, the realms of art and popular culture (especially youth culture), patterns of labor and consumption, the list goes on. The result of this intermixing is not innocent, because the depth and breadth of interpenetration ultimately reaches into the human capacity for imagination. U.S. war-culture thus dominates the self-understanding of citizens, as individuals, and as a people, a nation. On Memorial Day in 2014, at Arlington Cemetery, Vice President Joe Biden's words perfectly illustrated the contour of the U.S. national imaginary, "You are the veterans of America, the most trusted among us, and the most tested of all Americans ... who have served and sacrificed for all of us. You are not only the heart and soul, but you are the very spine of this nation."[53]

The systems and structures of U.S. war-culture *are* the scaffolding beneath the inevitable occurrence of direct violence in moral injury. And deeper still lie the vectors of U.S. *culture* that are the bedrock of this phenomenon. All three of the points of the "violence triangle" outlined by Galtung, and their interrelationships, have to be part of the investigation of moral injury, to make sense of it.

In U.S. society the experience of moral injury is defining and debilitating an unknown percentage of this generation's servicemembers and veterans, not to mention the impact this has on their family, friends, communities and society at large. Simultaneously, awareness about the vast streams of destruction internationally, linked to U.S. systems and culture of war, is muted. Yet an inclusive examination regarding what has enabled this situation to develop, and what citizens should do about it, has yet to occur. Most people remain passive, uninformed and inactive. Few protest the response that places further burdens on servicemembers (not to mention the impact on the world at large) through the false claim that with sufficient grit and training, military servicemembers can develop the "resilience" to withstand the war's deformations and destruction. According to Galtung, we should not be surprised: "... structure and culture are usually not included in 'arms control' studies, both being highly sensitive areas. These taboos have to be broken."[54] In the end, a multitude of structural and cultural facets of war-culture influence and give shape to the eventual violent "event" of moral injury and citizens' (lack of) response.

Reflection on moral injury in this way invariably leads to many questions. A re-evaluation is called for, seeing that moral injury is concretely tied to both human structure and culture. How should this moral and social ill be addressed? For example, is it sufficient to say that the problem of moral injury is due to a "lack of sufficient resiliency" among U.S. military servicemembers?

Will Eric Fair, Claude AnShin Thomas and others benefit from primarily individualistic treatments? Do current treatments enable the process of concealment of the structural and cultural forms of violence at moral injury's root? Finally, how will these same forms of redress take up important questions of communal complicity for moral injury? And all these questions relate to one more: *can human morality really be accommodated to war?*

Traditionally, just war thinking, and analysis of the costs of war, especially are focused on war's devastating impacts on noncombatants and the environment. One important way just war theories measure these negative outcomes is through various types of calculus that weigh the supposed benefits of war in ratio to the destruction it wreaks. Underscoring such destructive consequences is all-important ethically. But the dynamics of moral injury suggest that war not only is destructive to others; it *also* is deeply destructive to those who perpetrate it, individually and collectively.

This is not a new idea. For example, Martin Luther King Jr. prophetically anticipated the destructive blowback to those who enact war, not only servicemembers, but all citizens.[55] He declared in his speech, "Beyond Vietnam," "If America's soul becomes totally poisoned, part of the autopsy must read Vietnam" (Chapter 5 further addresses this important speech). The moral assault of war applies not only to individuals, not only to those who are servicemembers or noncombatant victims of war, and not only to the natural world. Moral degradation of the nation as a whole also must be addressed. To say this is to underscore that moral injury is more than an individual or mainly psychological problem; no, this injury begins in vast structural systems, and cultural norms that shape the way people understand themselves; it begins in their world-building and shapes collective understanding of life's meaning. Moral injury naturally grows out of U.S. war-culture.

2 Moral Injury and Structural Violence

Introduction

After 30 years of working in television and print news media, veteran reporter William Arkin decided to leave NBC. He loved his work investigating U.S. wars and national systems of surveillance, militarism and security, and he became a well-known expert in these areas. But in his resignation letter he said that he was more and more "out of sync," and "a lone voice."[1] After the terrorist attacks of 9/11, his questions increasingly were out of step, even unwelcome in his workplace and with the wider U.S. public. He found himself struggling in a media landscape that was becoming more tightly controlled, as he wrote, a "new martial environment where only one war cry was sanctioned."

So for a time he left NBC and worked elsewhere, but eventually Arkin was invited back to the network, during the 2016 campaign cycle. He agreed, hoping this might be the opportunity "to break through the machine of perpetual war acceptance and conventional wisdom." But he would be disappointed. For the culture of the media in the post-9/11 era, not only at NBC but more broadly, only had grown more cynical: "NBC just began emulating the national security state itself – busy and profitable. No wars won but the ball is kept in play."

One wonders who is paying attention to Arkin's analysis of the war-culture of the United States in this resignation letter. Not only this veteran reporter, but a diverse trove of scholars in recent years has attempted to communicate to the U.S. American public the seriousness of our reality in the United States and world. Arkin summarized the situation, "There is not one country in the Middle East that is safer today than it was 18 years ago. Indeed the world becomes ever more polarized and dangerous."[2]

But U.S. Americans mostly turn away. While some "fawn over" the military and government protagonists of the longest wars in U.S. history, who cycle in as news analysts, by the time of the Trump era, Arkin assessed the situation: "... the national security establishment not only hasn't missed a beat but indeed has gained dangerous strength. Now it is ever more autonomous and practically impervious to criticism." And meanwhile, the news media became ever more distracted, retreating from urgent questions: How can the U.S. "defeat terrorism" without understanding why they are fighting? What are the consequences of the unparalleled growth of the national security–surveillance complex for the U.S. and world? Finally, and most important – why has the United States been unable to solve any of the violent conflicts it waded into and/or created during the last 20 years?

Instead of focusing on questions like the ones above, the approach to the Global War on Terror in the post-9/11 era was covered by the media as if it was a horse race, Arkin claims. It was "… Rumsfeld vs. the Generals" or "Wofowitz vs. Shinseki" or "the CIA vs. Cheney." It's not hard to imagine the result: increased cynicism, detachment and ignorance.

What does moral injury have to do with this? I argue that systemic militarism and war nurture the roots of direct violence of individual moral injury. Why investigate this ground? *Moral injury may not be fully understood, much less addressed ethically or practically without a social analysis of moral injury's anchor in U.S. war-culture.* Ergo, this critical examination is needed.

Remember that one of the distinguishing features of war-culture regards the dynamic of "interpenetration;" that is, different sites of civil life (social, political, economic, religious, etc.) are shaped as they intertwine with the institutions, ethos and practices of war. Arkin's story provides a good example of this, as he describes how news media were influenced by the growing culture of war in the post-9/11 period. Media outlets like NBC were swayed by the increasing presence of the institutions (and their officials) of war, and began to subvert, dismiss or criticize his analysis; his voice didn't mix well with this martial environment. Arkin's narrative also shows how "concealment" of the same reality takes place. Through subtle and not-so-subtle mechanisms, the media shifted away from the hard, driving questions he raised, to the "horse race" strategy. This undermined the urgency of what is at stake – not human lives, not unimaginable destruction, and overwhelming financial costs – but one seemingly arbitrary political thrust or another, take your pick. To be clear, frameworks such as this never will squarely face citizens with the sharp realities of death and destruction, to ask how all this came to be, and what should be done about it.

Pulitzer-prize-winning historian John W. Dower also highlights "the mass media's addiction to sensationalism and catastrophe" in the post-9/11 period. Digital social media played a strong role in this rise, increasing the concealment of the reality of war-culture.[3] Dower summarizes additional causes of detachment, distraction and war-culture's diminishing visibility: first, paranoia rose out of anti-communist fear, morphing into post-9/11 pathological fear. But second, fear itself was weaponized. "Machiavellian fear-mongering" grew as the clarion call of the national security state. Lastly, heightened awareness of the nation's vulnerability to attack led to desperation. The only way to preserve U.S. "credibility" in the world was through development of "massive cutting-edge military might."[4]

A structural (and in Chapter 3, cultural) investigation illuminates the meaning and phenomenon of moral injury. Why? This kind of questioning helps to show what lies behind the direct violence in moral injury's presenting face. It is easier to understand the environment that makes its generativity possible, even inevitable. When individual experiences of moral injury are set against wider systemic and cultural streams of violence, a deeper frame for understanding takes shape, regarding both of what moral injury *is,* and what is needed to effectively *address* it. Finally, and most important, this book is written for those servicemembers and veterans of war who personally struggle with moral injury. For the resources that have been provided to them, and the frameworks that have been suggested, need to include how moral injury is rooted in a vast structural and cultural landscape. In fact, more narrow conceptual frames, that only address the direct violence of moral injury, may even heighten its devastation in individual lives. The analysis that follows explains why this is the case.

To show how moral injury takes root, I explore various structures of war-culture that conceal injustice and violence in the United States and wider world. This spotlight helps deepen understanding of moral injury's least visible beginnings. Three of the most important structural indicators of war-culture in the United States include: 1) the political economy of war; 2) the "empire" of U.S. international military bases; and 3) the dynamics of the "interpenetration" of war in unending civilian sites of life.

Structurally assessing U.S. war-culture

1. The political economy of war

The structural violence of war works hand in hand with practices of concealment in American culture at large.[5] This is connected to one of the most perplexing characteristics of U.S. war-culture – citizens' lack of awareness of it. Indeed, the facts of U.S. war-culture are *absent* from the minds of many, even most people in the U.S. This seems paradoxical. But scratching the surface shows that the institutional scaffolding of war-culture, simultaneously contributes to the way it appears in U.S. culture: it is largely invisible in the minds of most people, or to the extent that people think about it at all, they understand war and militarism in the U.S. to be utterly natural, a given in their lives that they have never really questioned. Three defining and intertwining facets of war-culture, highlighted here, pull away the mask. Readers will remember the definition: *U.S. war-culture is the enduring and increasing interpenetration of the ethos, institutions, and practices of war with increasing sites and social structures and culture of human life.*

First, in the post-9/11 period, one of the areas of least polarization in the houses of Congress regarded decision-making about the federal military budget. It could bewilder and flummox citizens to know that year after year, the U.S. Congress passively approves the by-far largest budget for war-culture in the world. According to the "National Priorities Project" website, the 2019 "militarized budget" was 64.5 percent of the *total* discretionary budget of the U.S., or $730 billion. This amount exceeded the next highest ten countries' military budgets *combined.*[6] And even this gargantuan number includes categories of spending not included in the official military budget, such as:

- the costs of intelligence agencies
- "overseas contingency operations" in the Greater Middle East,
- "black budgets" of the CIA and NSA,
- Veterans Affairs mandatory spending for veterans' benefits,
- interest on the military debt (an especially large cost).[7]

While The National Priorities Project estimates that the U.S. spends *more* than *the next 10 largest* military budgets *combined* in the world, other scholars' estimates of U.S. military spending are even higher. Historian John Dower summarizes the 2017 reported defense budget of the U.S. at $600 billion. But once additional costs are factored, the number for war-related expenditures rose to *$1 trillion.* Such a figure truly is difficult to absorb; but when broken down, this means that people in the U.S. spent about "$2.74 billion a day, over $114 million an hour," on matters related to militarization and war.[8] The figure is even more disturbing when compared with military budgets of the next highest spending nations in the world (See Figures 1, 2, 3).

How did the U.S. get here? By the time of President Eisenhower, in the post-World War II era, the growing interdependence between government, the Pentagon and war-related corporations and industry presented a concern for democracy, and well-being of citizens and the world.

The intermixing structures of what President Eisenhower first called "The Military-Industrial Complex" (MIC) date back to the late 19th century. Its beginnings may be traced to the shipbuilding and steel industries' close work with government leaders in the building of a modern navy. Congress authorized procurement and industrial mobilization planning, and eventually, the

Discretionary Spending 2015: $1.11 Trillion

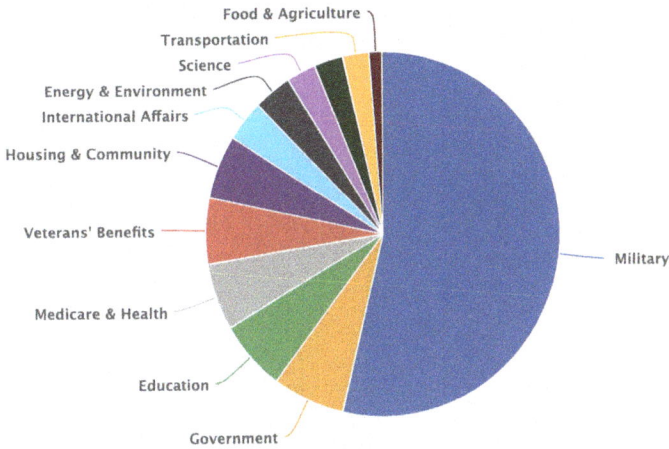

Figure 1   2015 Discretionary Budget of the United States. "Federal Spending: Where Does the Money Go?" *Source: OMB, National Priorities Project.* https://www.nationalpriorities.org/budget-basics/federal-budget-101/spending/ (accessed January 10, 2021).

US vs. World Military Spending, 2019
Global Total: $1.917 Trillion

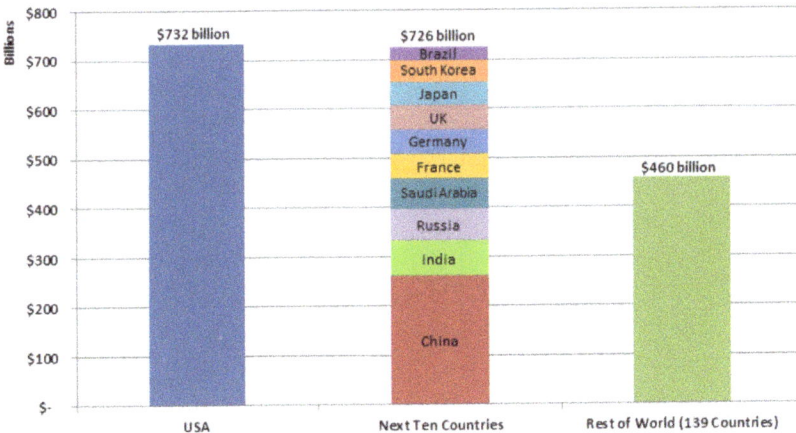

Figure 2   The U.S. Military Budget Compared with Next Highest World Military Budgets. "The U.S. Military Budget 2020," *Source: SIPRI Military Expenditures, National Priorities Project,* https://www.nationalpriorities.org/analysis/2020/militarized-budget-2020/ (accessed January 10, 2021).

THE MAIN EXPORTERS AND IMPORTERS OF MAJOR ARMS, 2015–19			
Exporter	Global share (%)	Importer	Global share (%)
1 USA	36	1 Saudi Arabia	12
2 Russia	21	2 India	9.2
3 France	7.9	3 Egypt	5.8
4 Germany	5.8	4 Australia	4.9
5 China	5.5	5 China	4.3
6 UK	3.7	6 Algeria	4.2
7 Spain	3.1	7 South Korea	3.4
8 Israel	3.0	8 UAE	3.4
9 Italy	2.1	9 Iraq	3.4
10 South Korea	2.1	10 Qatar	3.4
UAE = United Arab Emirates.			

Figure 3 "The Main Exporters and Importers of Major Arms, 2015–2019," *Stockholm International Peace Research Institute Yearbook 2020: Armaments, Disarmament and International Security: Summary* (Oxford: Oxford University Press, 2020), 13. https://www.sipri. org/yearbook/2020 (accessed January 10, 2021).

government created agencies such as The War Industries Board (1918) and, later, the War Production Board (1941).[9]

WWII saw the tightening infrastructure of war between key institutions: "the military establishment, federal agencies, universities and the private sector."[10] This also was the heightening of "industrial war," including such developments as the atomic bomb, radar and radio communications, the military policy of "aircraft over battleships," and concomitant strategic mass bombing of civilian city centers. This military strategy took on enormous importance for both the U.S. and Great Britain in the WWII era. And, overall, convergence meant the tighter interpenetration between industry, politics and military institutions, as "technology, technocracy and amorality advanced hand in hand."[11]

Paul Koestinen, historian of the political economy of war, summarizes that by the time of the early post-WWII era, the interests of the "warfare cohort" joined seamlessly with efforts of Cold War policymakers. "Civilian and military systems were combining in a way that affected and reshaped fundamental aspects of American life," he writes.[12] These were the years when the permanent war economy came into being, the "Gunbelt" formed along the west and east coasts, and in the south and southwest parts of the country, corporations sprang up in aerospace, military and space electronics, aircraft, and other high technology weapons production.[13] These also are the centers for many domestic military bases. An "unprecedented population migration, … generally financed by the Department of Defense" and including scientists, engineers, technicians and skilled labor, created new population centers, requiring enormous building of infrastructure.

Koistinen explains the consequences, "Billions of dollars have been spent to transform the Gunbelt to accommodate the migrating millions." Meanwhile, the same population increasingly could be counted on as a "built-in lobby" for larger and larger "defense" budgets. A kind of "state capitalism" developed. War-related corporations, due to their special relationship with the structures of government, were not subject to the same market pressures experienced in civilian economic enterprises, and "… became characterized by inefficiency, waste and corruption."[14]

Despite the concern of analysts such as Koistinen, in 2018 a long-demanded financial audit of the Department of Defense (DoD) resulted only in demonstrating the continuing difficulty of getting to the bottom of the massive expenditures of the MIC. In no small measure this struggle is due to the growth of the complex, including its incursion into more and more sites of daily life. Today, instead of the term "military-industrial complex," it has been suggested (ironically!) that the structural reality of war-culture is better described as the U.S. "military-industrial-technological-entertainment-academic-scientific-media-intelligence-homeland-security-surveillance-national-security-corporate complex."[15] The more the "complex" has grown, and the greater its diversity and reach of its tentacles, the more difficult it becomes to *see and assess it*, much less protest or resist. This is concealment.

And what is the result of this relative invisibility? The *structures* of "the complex" operate in such a way simultaneously to expand its reach, legitimize it, and encourage its relative absence from citizens' active attention. With regard to the costs of the complex, the story of what took place during the first-ever attempt at a "complete audit" is revealing. Reporting on the 2018 DoD audit, even the complex's own journalistic institutions, such as *Defense News,* admitted to "major flaws" in the way the DoD goes about its record keeping and accounting. Not surprisingly, other investigative reporting was even harsher in its judgment. *The Nation,* for instance, characterized the results of the audit as "The Pentagon's Massive Accounting Fraud."[16] Digging into the weeds, Michigan State University Professor of Economics, Mark Skidmore, after months of research and analysis of DoD financial statement reviews, discovered that between 1998 and 2012, "a mind-boggling $21 trillion of Pentagon financial transactions … could not be traced, documented, or explained."[17]

Meanwhile, Asif Khan of the Government Accountability Office (GAO), the Congress's investigative unit on the federal bureaucracy, seemed to expect the failure of the independent audit. What was missing, in his estimation, was "a good-faith effort from DoD officials; … to date that has not been forthcoming." Despite over 1,000 findings from auditors about necessary remediations, Khan summarized, "So far, hardly anything has been fixed."[18]

Today, the facts of DoD lack of financial accountability are so extensive that some senators have proposed that all defense budgets be frozen until the DoD passes an audit.[19] But Koistinen shows how the huge *scale* of military spending contributes to the difficulty people have understanding or analyzing it. When this is added to questionable accounting practices, intentional concealment of information, and deferral of costs, it's little wonder that citizens' engagement with these issues seems so out of reach.[20]

Nevertheless, questions could be raised about the lack of serious debate about this issue among political leaders in the U.S. And the absence of much-needed public discussion is even more confusing, given the sharp needs of many people in the U.S. How can such expense be justified, given the increasing wealth and income gap, failing national infrastructure, and growing social needs of so many? Why the lack of critical dialogue? At least part of the answer has to do with DoD structures of financing. The costs of the DoD are deeply intertwined with vast civilian structures and systems, such as those described below, that normalize, legitimize, and provide cover over the reality of this war/weapons/militarization financial debacle.

For instance, in the post-WWII era, military money impacted research in universities and think tanks, especially many located along the Gunbelt. By 1980 fully one-third of university and college research budgets were funded by defense dollars. Top tier universities especially were affected, leading to a "brain drain" as many of the best and brightest scientists, and even humanities and social science scholars were courted by generous salaries, and educational and research grants supplied by DoD budgets.[21] This corresponds with "declining discoveries in the civilian sector" and patents for new innovations falling 30 percent between 1966 and 1973. Currently, about one third of all the nation's engineers and scientists, many the best in their fields, are employed by defense contractors.[22]

All in all, Koistinen summarizes, the bipartisan defense establishment, including the defense industry, the Pentagon, the White House, Congress and think tanks, responsible for the expenditure of multiple trillions of dollars over the past six-to-seven decades, "... forcefully resists change."[23] And this same interpenetration of institutions insistently is defended by many millions of U.S. Americans, whose employment is directly or indirectly connected to this "complex." Their dependence on the current state of affairs pushes away acknowledgement of the problem, much less meaningful change. In the end, U.S. citizens' reality is concealed in ways that are willfully encouraged, as well as through systems well beyond individual control. Yet, "according to numerous critics," Koistinen writes, "DoD budgets have distorted public priorities and spending, denying adequate attention to infrastructure, education, Medicare and other public services."[24] These "dysfunctions" of the U.S. American political economy increased in the first decades of the twenty-first century, and the government and public alike seem less capable than ever of addressing and dealing with them.

2. An intricate web of military bases, lily pads and "black sites"

If a closer look at the inner workings of the federal military budget helps explain the structural reality of U.S. war-culture, a second indicator, the intricate map of U.S. military bases scattered across the world, further reveals the enormity of U.S. war-culture. This "empire of bases" (the description first coined by political scientist Chalmers Johnson) includes well over one thousand five hundred domestic and international land-based military bases owned and operated by the U.S. Here I focus on the map of international bases built and maintained by the United States military branches. But not all of these bases "officially" are counted by the DoD. U.S. international military bases also include "lily pads" – these are flexible installations that may be more easily installed or pulled up; "black sites," whose number "exist somewhere between light and shadow;" and "an armada of floating bases," operated by the U.S. Navy.[25]

Examination of the scope of the U.S. empire of bases demonstrates glaring asymmetry in comparison to other nations of the world. Similar to the federal military budget, the numbers and sheer reach of U.S. military bases around the world (not counting domestic bases) are astonishing when compared with how other nations go about the business of security. According to the "Overseas Base Realignment and Closure Coalition," the over 800 international military base sites of the United States (not counting the floating ones, and also omitting an unknown number of black sites), account for 90 to 95% of *all* foreign military bases in the world.[26] In contrast, Russia, the U.K. and France, the countries with the highest number after the U.S., each weigh in at 10–20 foreign bases apiece, while China only has developed one such base. A final statistic really tells the story, for not only is the number of U.S. international military bases skewed in comparison with other nations, over-all the United States has a military base presence in "approximately 84% of the nations on this planet"[27] (see Figure 4).

The frustration encountered by scholars investigating the DoD budget mirrors the experience of analysts who struggle to get to the bottom of the U.S. empire of bases. Repeated rebuffs and disinformation from U.S. mil-itary leaders are common. For instance, sociologist Nick Turse tried to get information about al-Tanf, the U.S. base in Syria where the Syrian govern-ment trains its fighters; this is "an outpost ... with hundreds of U.S. Marines and Special Operations troops."[28] U.S. officials claimed that this particular base "was the key not only to defeating ISIS, but also ... to countering the 'malign activities ... of Iran and their various proxies.'" But the base is never mentioned in the official count of the DoD, in the "Base Structure Report."[29] Moreover, lest we imagine that this was simply some sort of peculiar over-sight or mistake, Turse discovered that negligence was an intentional strat-egy employed regularly by the DoD. As he writes, not only is al-Tanf not included in this report, the DoD also never make mention of bases

> In Syria. Or Iraq. Or Afghanistan. Or Niger. Or Tunisia. Or Cameroon. Or Somalia. Or any number of locales where such military outposts are known to exist, and even, unlike in Syria, to be expanding.[30]

Inquiries to the Pentagon regarding clarification of these matters didn't much help. The Pentagon spokesperson responded to his questions in a way that Turse described as "firmly in line with the Pentagon's well-worn policy of keeping American taxpayers in the dark ..." Spokesperson Lieutenant Colonel Michelle Baldanza's only response was to inform Turse, "... the press officer who is responsible for the Base Structure Report ... has nothing to add and no one available to discuss further at this time."[31]

Pentagon lack of cooperation notwithstanding, scholars such as David Vine have managed to amass a lot of information about the U.S. empire of bases. The Overseas Base Alignment and Closure Coalition website displays a map from Vine's investigation of the numbers and locations of U.S. inter-national bases (that are known) on every significant land mass on the plan-et. The map, upon examination, makes the Roman Empire look like child's play. The highest concentrations of U.S. international bases reflect the after-math of WWII in Europe and Asia, such as the 121 U.S. bases still in Japan. But the spread and number of bases around the world also are a consequence of the U.S. military doctrine of "full spectrum dominance," defined in *Joint*

U.S. Military Bases Abroad, 2020

In 2020, the United States controlled around 800 bases outside the 50 U.S. states and Washington, DC. Map reflects bases' relative number and positioning given best available data. For ease of comparison we use contemporary borders and a Mercator projection.

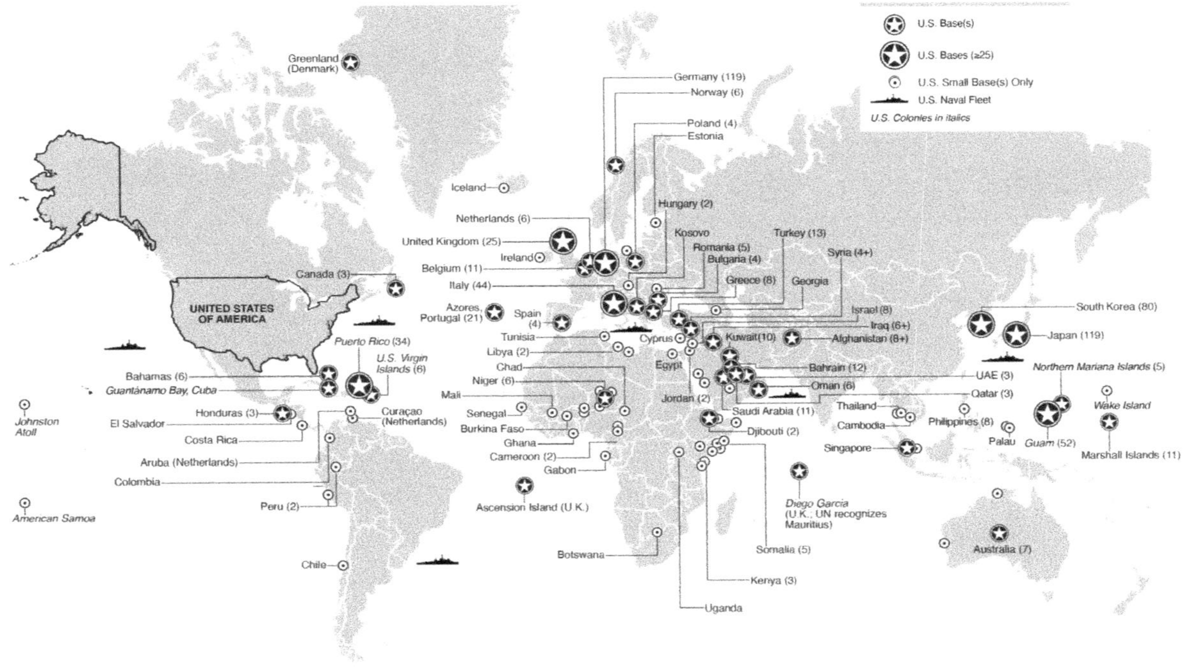

Map by Kelly Martin / kmartindesign.com for David Vine, *The United States of War: A Global History of America's Endless Conflicts, from Columbus to the Islamic State* (University of California Press, 2020).

Figure 4 "U.S. Military Bases Abroad, 2020." *The United States of War: A Global History of America's Endless Conflicts, from Columbus to the Islamic State* (University of California Press, 2020).

Vision 2020 as the freedom and capacity to conduct operations of force that are "prompt, sustained and synchronized" in "… all domains – space, sea, land, air and information."[32]

Why so many and so vast? The rationale for this situation was suggested in 2004 by Chalmers Johnson, and it still stands; the purpose of the bases is five-fold: maintaining "military preponderance" over the rest of the world; facilitating the operation of surveillance and intelligence of citizens and allies as well as adversaries; controlling resources such as petroleum; providing sources of employment and income for members of the MIC; and supplying a comfortable life and entertainment for military abroad.[33]

Meanwhile, between 2011 and 2014 the DoD noted in a press release that special operation forces had been active in "more than 150 countries" – this out of a total of just 193 "recognized nations" in the entire world, as counted by the United Nations in 2011.[34] Additionally, between the end of WWII and 2002, historian Andrew Bacevich suggested that "the U.S. engaged in 263 military operations, large and small."[35] Among these military actions,

> Between 1980 and the terrorist attacks of September 11, 2001, US forces 'invaded or occupied or bombed' a dozen countries in the Islamic world (Iran, Libya, Lebanon, Iraq, Kuwait, Somalia, Bosnia, Saudi Arabia, Afghanistan, Sudan, Kosovo and Yemen).[36]

As the Overseas Base Alignment website further explains, "At least 23 times US bases have been used to launch wars of choice or military interventions in 14 countries in the greater Middle East alone since 1980."[37]

U.S. citizens repeatedly have heard political and military leaders claim that only through such unassailable military might has the U.S. managed to avoid another event like 9/11. But this justification should be questioned. The Overseas Base Alignment not only assesses the scope and number of military U.S. interventions, but includes further analysis. These scholars emphasize that the empire of bases is itself a "target for militants" in places such as Saudi Arabia, Afghanistan and Iraq. Also, the presence of bases in sovereign nations has spurred and energized recruitment of extremists. Finally, foreign bases generate hatred among many people around the world for other reasons, including the environmental degradation they have caused, their links with organized prostitution and sex trafficking, their displacement of indigenous populations, and other harms to local people caused by accidents or crimes (such as rape) incurred by U.S. servicemembers.[38]

John Dower explains that outsized and irrational U.S. militarization is due to a strange combination of factors. On the one hand, we can identify hubris regarding U.S. American military might: "Full spectrum dominance" is linked with notions of U.S. exceptionalism and manifest destiny. This identity emphasizes pride and expectation of hegemonic and unquestioned U.S. military might, not only in the world, but increasingly to dominate the entire cosmos, if the latest extensions of the U.S. military into cyber and outer space are any indication. Especially in the post-9/11 period, inviolability and strength became "what it means to be an American." But on the other hand, U.S. American leaders, especially military leaders, exhibit a kind of anxiety, even "paranoia" and "pathological fear" regarding possible threats to the United States; Dower fears this tendency may be "part of the American DNA."[39] And perhaps these two factors are related: nobody likes being "under someone else's thumb" – but in essence, with regard to military might, this is the role of everyone but the U.S. in the world. We should expect hostile reverberations in response to "full-spectrum dominance."

In addition to fear and anxiety, a third factor regards the lack of questioning, much less protest, in the U.S., regarding the reality of a militarized United States. The U.S. military is thoroughly permeated by corporate interests in security/weapons/war-related manufacture and development. The "defense" world pulls in the commitment and cooperation of millions of citizens, who also participated in the acceleration of militarization of the United States since WWII, a role that has been increasing since the events of 9/11.[40] Dower concludes,

> Fixation on Middle East oil, apocalyptic visions of chaos, … expansion of overseas military bases, acceleration of military interventionism, the wishful thinking involved in assuming that monopolization of sophisticated military might ensures full-spectrum dominance or a quick fait accompli – all [have drawn] the United States ever deeper into a turbulent region that, on its own, [has] long been plagued with strife.[41]

Arguments about the necessity of the U.S. empire of bases, upon closer examination, reveal twisted rationales that perpetuate their maintenance and growth, while concealing the very real negative consequences they have created in the U.S. and world. In conclusion, political scientist Chalmers Johnson, summarizes this context with a telling warning about "blowback" to outsized U.S. militarization in the world:

> The only truly common elements in the totality of America's foreign bases are imperialism and militarism – an impulse on the part of our elites to dominate others peoples largely because we have the power to

do so, followed by the strategic reasoning that, in order to defend these newly acquired outposts and control the regions they are in, we must expand the areas under our control with still more bases.[42]

3. The "interpenetration" of war-culture in unending facets of daily life

This chapter has examined the unparalleled military spending, and the empire of international bases, as two undeniable indicators of U.S. war-culture. But what truly ties together all the various facets of war-culture is the dynamic of "interpenetration." Unending practices of militarism and militarization seep into countless sites of everyday life, shaping people's inattention, lack of awareness, and cognitive distortion with respect to this reality. Or perhaps the process of militarism is more like the aggressive kudzu vine that rapidly spreads over and overwhelms native trees and bushes. If one was to stop and think, it might seem unfathomable that people in the United States, living in the most extensive war-culture the world has ever known, have so little consciousness of it.

The environment of war and militarism provide a deep, but mostly unexamined yet fundamental nucleus of the national imaginary, and sense of what it means to be a citizen. The most prized national symbols define and understand patriotism through the lens of militarism and war, such as the national anthem, and national festivals, like the Fourth of July and Memorial Day. Militarism and war in the United States shape citizens' sense of identity – but they don't often stop to think much about this; in addition, war influences everyday life in all kinds of ways.

Facets of "interpenetration" in war-culture impact the economy, education, patterns of labor, manufacture and consumption, entertainment and popular culture, especially youth culture, sports, religious understandings and practice, the landscape and rituals of the nation's public sites, the list goes on and on. Perhaps most pernicious are the effects of war-culture on citizens' cognition in the United States. In ways visible and invisible, on top of the surface and below, war-culture shapes people's very imagination, both individual and collective, making it difficult to conceive any *alternative* to the current state of affairs.

While researching and writing about war-culture over quite a few years, I have come to develop a perverse hobby – I collect examples of the kinds of interpenetration here mentioned. For instance, whenever I attend a local movie theater to see a film, I count the number of trailers for "war-movies" that inevitably will be part of the pre-screening advertisements. From my count, I can expect that at least half of the trailers will advertise upcoming war films, and often the number rises to over 75%. I wonder, is it simply innocent entertainment that I'm being exposed to in the theater? How should I analyze what is happening in this very common collective American experience?

One of many war-films of recent times was part of a franchise, *Independence Day: Resurgence.* Released in 2016 by a conglomeration of film production corporations, headed up by Twentieth Century Fox, it was marketed and screened across the U.S. and world, in addition to being sold for digital home viewing. The film is listed on IMDb (the Independent Movie Database) as falling into the "action, adventure, sci-fi" category, and rated "PG-13." By early 2019, its gross income was almost $400 million (it cost $165 million to produce). Briefly, the plot of the film involves military forces of the earth banding together to fight against a violent invasion of aliens from outer space.[43]

The trailer is easily accessible through an imdb.com link that takes one to a second link in YouTube.com. As I open the trailer in YouTube, a fictional female president of the United States appears, speaking in front of a vast audience that has gathered in a photogenic nationalistic public square, reminiscent of a Leni Riefenstahl film setting. The president forcefully addresses her people with a powerful admonition about "strength through unity; that strength has brought us the power to survive!" Soon after the trailer shifts to a different scene, as a male leader of the U.S. army appears on the screen, standing in front of silent but ominous troops, and speaking directly to the camera:

> When the world was brought to its knees, the Army was there to fight back. They promised us this would never happen again. They have been the driving forces in the United Nations around the world to form the most powerful weapon against another attack: the Earth Space Defense.

But at this point, watching the trailer, a small communication box appears in the upper left-hand corner of the screen, with the message: "Defend Tomorrow. Enlist Today. Join the ESD."

I click on the link in the left-hand corner to join up and it takes me to a U.S. Army recruitment website.

As part of an ongoing campaign to target "young geeks and gamers," the United States Army partnered with the blockbuster film. Spending millions of dollars, they created supposedly "fantasy" websites and commercials that went viral, ostensibly urging people to join the Earth Space Defense, a fictional, multinational military to battle "aliens." The *ArmyTimes* explains the rationale for these efforts: "The Army's latest recruiting effort dips into a parallel universe, attempting to engage young sci-fi fans who may not be aware of the service's high-tech career paths."[44]

One commercial that was produced to market the film portrays a middle-aged man, casually dressed and puttering with tools in his garage, as he is interviewed about his daughter, a servicemember in the U.S. Army/ "Earth Space Defense." He wears a baseball cap with the Army logo: "GoArmy," and tells the interviewer that he "fought in the war back in '96, and I know what those things [the space aliens] are capable of." As he speaks the camera slowly pans across his garage wall, decorated with photos of the daughter, a "support our troops" sign, a collection of military medals, and a newspaper clipping from the first war (and first film in the franchise, *Independence Day*), with the headline, "VICTORY: ALIENS DEFEATED." "I know this planet is safer because she's defending it," he emphasizes, as the trailer shifts to its final screen. Against a backdrop of black space filled with stars, we see various catchphrases: "#Independence Day," "Paid for by the U.S. Army," the official U.S. Army logo with a single star, and in the center of the screen, in the largest type, the message: "BE SOMEONE'S HERO."[45] (See Figures 5–7.)

In this example of interpenetration that embeds war in popular youth culture (young men in particular are the intended audience), the film's fantasy world of high tech war and militarization of outer space blends seamlessly with real-world institutions of war in the U.S. The Army spent $2.4 million

US Army Earth Space Defense Recruitment

Figures 5–7 (*above and opposite*) Ryan Hunt. "US Army Earth Space Defense Recruitment," *Youtube.com*. May 15, 2016, https://www.youtube.com/watch?v=Uzkp1m1wmMk (accessed January 13, 2019).

US Army Earth Space Defense Recruitment

US Army Earth Space Defense Recruitment

toward production of these media. James Ortiz, director of marketing for the Army Marketing and Research Group, unapologetically explained the purpose: to respond to public perceptions about the army as "low tech and low skill," in order to show potential recruits the Army in a better light. This collaboration produced video games/sites, studio-produced television commercials, and traditional advertising to double traffic to *GoArmy.com*. Those fans who want to unlock Independence Day movie extras in the website must allow US Army recruiters access to their Facebook pages. The goal was to bring 3 million people to the website.

Collecting and exploring diverse examples of war-culture's interpenetrations is a crazy-making hobby indeed! This isolated example involves not only gaming and film corporations who now leverage with the U.S. military to boost recruitment and enhance the Army brand, but also their various marketing divisions, film studios, television corporations, movie theater corporations, and more. And of course, interpenetration of this sort encourages the legitimation, the normalization of war. Militarization and war fade into invisibility, becoming just another part of the landscape we expect and are accustomed to experiencing, even applauding and enjoying as entertainment in our everyday lives. Meanwhile, not only is the militarization of space normalized, but the funding for unending technology of war also is legitimated, while any potentially negative consequences of war are ignored, hidden from view.

Teaching a college course focusing on ethics and war-culture, when we studied the vast terrain of the interpenetration of war-culture with diverse, supposedly "civilian" sites of popular culture, such as the example above, a student-veteran of the Iraq War responded in a way I have not been able to forget. "And we were told that there wasn't enough money to buy us body-armor," he told the class.

War-culture also infiltrates the world of sports – remember the "Penn State Blue Band Military Appreciation" halftime show, for example, with the complex band formations on the field mimicking various types of war-machines and symbols. As if this educational setting were some sort of commercial, the halftime commentator boomed that all military forces are "a global force for good," ensuring American citizens' "unparalleled freedom."[46] In fact the sports halftime show *is* connected to a commercial! Even this supposedly "innocent" depiction of the U.S. branches of the military has a perfidious cast; "a global force for good" precisely was a branding motto developed by the U.S. Navy for a series of sophisticated commercials that also were viewed commonly across the United States in movie theaters.[47] One commercial featured a vast array of football field-sized aircraft carriers, sophisticated war-aircraft, and military servicemembers using highly advanced digital tools of surveillance communications to track down and bomb "the enemy" (viewers never see who this is, what countries are involved, or in fact any human face of the destruction). As the bomb hits its target and the explosion rises into the air, words in bold red font come onto the screen, "TARGET ELIMINATED," followed by a scene of U.S. servicemembers cheering. Eerily, the commercial resembles any number of video wargames featuring high-tech weapons and surveillance that youth expect and enjoy. The commercial ends with the branding slogan: "U.S. Navy: A Global Force for Good."[48] (See Figures 8, 9.)

AMERICA'S NAVY- A GLOBAL FORCE FOR GOOD

Figure 8　Thedudekuz. "America's Navy: A Global Force for Good," *Youtube.com*. April 29, 2010, https://www.youtube.com/watch?v=bao2aPV9uUw (accessed November 28, 2020).

Penn State Blue Band Military Appreciation Halftime Show

Figure 9　Gerry Balz. "Penn State Blue Band Military Halftime Show," *Youtube.com*. October 3, 2015, https://www.youtube.com/watch?v=kwa94MI5Vc8 (accessed November 28, 2020).

War-culture is embedded in the lives of U.S. citizens 24/7, and this very ubiquity contributes to its normalization. It is colored and shaped by clever intentional marketing and communication strategies that benefit its purveyors. From products people purchase and rely on every day that are produced by corporations also involved in the manufacture of the implements of war; to educational institutions, that since 9/11 and the passage of "No Child Left Behind," have been required to allow military recruiters on their campuses to receive federal funding; to the institutions of the media and entertainment – people in the U.S. live in a social and material world deeply shaped by the violence and values of militarism and war.[49] After the events of 9/11, interpenetration especially expanded between the military and civilian contractors and corporations, as well as in the growth overall of the security–surveillance complex.

In addition to entertainment, interpenetrations of war-culture have mushroomed in other ways. By 2014, the number of military and civilian federal agencies dedicated to surveillance and national security had grown to at least 17, making the United States' security complex " ... more gargantuan, cumbersome, compartmentalized, faction-ridden, redundant, wasteful, corrupt and non-transparent than anything the nation had seen before."[50] But funds used to support this work generally are not included in the overall DoD budget. William Arkin and Dana Priest, authors of the Pulitzer-prize winning investigation, "Top-Secret America," discovered that a minimum of 20% of the government organizations with the mission to subvert terrorism were either newly created or redesigned *after* 9/11, while those that pre-existed the terror attacks "grew to historic proportions."[51] The sheer size and unwieldy nature of all these different organizations led to confusion, a struggle to oversee what is taking place, and vast opportunities for over-reach and error. For instance, Arkin and Priest found that each day, the National Security Agency alone was intercepting "1.7 billion emails, phone calls and other types of communications." Millions of dollars of federal funds were spent on the construction of new "SCIF" buildings (sensitive compartmented information facilities) in Springfield, just south of Washington DC. But this growth impacted the culture of the security–surveillance complex, as one three-star general told the investigators, "You can't find a four-star general without a security detail ... 'If he has one, then I have to have one.' It's become a status symbol."[52] By 2017 The Department of Homeland Security began to collect and store all the social media data that immigrants bring with them into the United States, including naturalized citizens and green card holders. Less and less of human life was free from military surveillance and intrusion: "It makes more sense to think of modern borders as overlapping and concentric circles that change size, shape and texture depending on who – or what – is trying to pass through."⁵³

Arkin and Priest found that the immense weight and volume of the information being collected by so many different agencies resulted in "serious overlap" that "... appears to be gumming up the national security machinery."⁵⁴ In one of many such instances, in 2009 a servicemember from the U.S. Army opened fire at a domestic military base, Fort Hood in Texas, killing and wounding many, despite strong evidence that might have been noticed and acted upon by intelligence agencies before the lethal attack. But the shooting came as a complete surprise. Among other details that emerged, the alleged assailant, Major Nidal Malik Hasan, earlier at Walter Reed Army Medical Center, spoke about "adverse events" that might occur if Muslims were not allowed to leave the Army, and exchanged emails with a cleric being followed by U.S. intelligence.⁵⁵

Nevertheless, the increasing size and interpenetration of "the Complex" in civil society continues, despite serious indications that things aren't working, despite the dangers war-culture poses for a wide range of democratic values and social needs within the United States, and despite its impact on many countries outside of the U.S. It now is estimated that approximately "... 854,000 military officials, civil servants, and private contractors [hold] security clearances."⁵⁶ According to one study, in 2005 alone, $390 billion in government funding went to "the private sector" for work related to the DoD, State Department and Department of Homeland Security.⁵⁷ By 2010, during the Iraq War, the ratio of individual private contractors to U.S. servicemembers was 1:1.⁵⁸

William Hartung characterizes the post-9/11 environment as a "security spending binge," that enriched contractor-corporations involved in rebuilding and support, private security, and weapons development and manufacture.⁵⁹ He comments, "... weapons purchases that have been enabled by the political environment fostered by the Global War on Terror *have had little to do with actual defense requirements*"⁶⁰ (italics mine). There was increased "influence peddling," as retired military commanders cycled out of government and into the corporations of media, weapons and security manufacturing, and other lucrative corporations. Hartung describes the various methods through which such peddling occurred:

Campaign contributions to key legislators, use of the revolving door to influence decisions over major weapons purchases, hiring of high profile lobbyists and public relations aides, and leveraging of plant locations to garner support on pork barrel grounds are all tools of the trade for military contractors. In most instances these practices are perfectly legal ...[61]

Both the size and diversity of the interpenetrations of U.S. war-culture increased exponentially in the post- 9/11 era. But in contrast to what political, military and media figures proclaim, according to Dower, the actual threat and direct violence of international terrorism in the post-9/11 period does not measure up to other eras in the 20th century.

Though political leaders insisted that the only effective response to the attacks of 9/11 was to launch "A Global War on Terror," others argue that such a response made little sense. The "patchwork of non-state adversaries" who lacked "massive firepower" and who did not "follow traditional rules of engagement," really did not add up to a world more threatened than ever, or to a situation that best would be mitigated through all-out war.[62] But assessing "actual defense requirements," seemed to become less and less the purpose in a nation hyped up on war. Citizens were hammered with the message that only through war could any security for the nation be purchased. But some scholars argued that this is backwards reasoning, both in terms of assessing the actual threat of terrorism, and also in terms of analyzing the costs of the militarized violence waged in response.

The "Costs of War" research project based at Brown University tallied the number of deaths from the most recent wars of the U.S. According to these scholars' findings, in the post-9/11 period the direct violence of war and terror resulted in approximately 480,000 deaths. About half of these deaths were civilian deaths. But measuring deaths directly caused by armed violence fails to get at the seriousness of the destruction that has taken place. How then should we measure the costs of violence, if not solely through counting deaths directly related to the actions of war? In the post-9/11 period, while the enormous explosion of war-culture was taking place, what *increased* was the number of *indirect* deaths, and the destruction of social, economic and political stability *as a result* of war's violence and destruction. But the normalization of war-culture in the minds and imaginations of citizens subdues critical questions about what this culture actually produces in our lives, and around the world.

The "Costs of War" project does not try to pin down a specific number of deaths related to war's *indirect* violence. These indirect or secondary deaths happened because of the destruction of infrastructure caused by war, the growth of political instability, and damage to health, employment, education and welfare institutions in those places where these wars have been fought.

Research strongly suggests that the number of people who died indirectly is many times greater than those from the direct violence of war and terrorism.

The devastation wrought in the post-9/11 world may be best understood through the astronomical growth in the number of refugees now in the world: "21 million Afghan, Iraqi, Pakistani, and Syrian people are living as war refugees and internally displaced persons, in grossly inadequate conditions."[63] This begs the question: have these wars really resulted in a safer and more flourishing world? People in the U.S. seem unable to ask. By 2019 the U.S. was fighting in 80 different countries, and the financial cost of the wars of the post-9/11 period in 2019 was estimated at $5.9 trillion.[64]

Structural violence: creating fertile ground for moral injury

Moral injury is a phenomenon as old as war itself, as Jonathan Shay suggested with the title of his groundbreaking book, *Achilles in Vietnam.*[65] But this important insight may perpetuate unhelpful assumptions that foster an attitude of fatalism. Fatalistic perspectives interpret moral injury as an unfortunate but necessary reality that has dogged human communities since the invention of war; it is inevitable and perpetual, an inescapable part of human nature and cultures. The best we can do is to try to ameliorate moral injury in individual cases, through individual therapeutic methods, pharmaceutical treatments, and communal efforts; or military leaders can try to improve their structures of command to lessen these outcomes. In contrast, in this last section I argue against fatalism in order to better reveal the inner workings of structural violence and systemic injustice that lie at the heart of moral injury's direct violence in the lives of servicemembers and veterans. Clarity about moral injury's upstream sources is needed to fully understand this phenomenon, and develop a more holistic response to it.

Fatalistic attitudes about moral injury derail a big-enough analysis. While most moral injury research necessarily centers on the human individual, especially the human psyche, too much research never gets past this level. A more complex understanding of violence is needed. To return to the image from an earlier chapter, focusing only on direct violence in individual experiences of moral injury is like exploring the tip of the iceberg appearing above the waters, only to miss the more monumental jagged edges beneath. Fatalistic attitudes thus lead to short-sighted research and understanding of moral injury. These attitudes also stunt the imagination regarding how to respond not only individually, but also collectively. They fail to uncover how and why the structures (and culture) of U.S. ways of war are so damaging.

But there is another way forward. It is possible to get closer to the root of the problem, by exploring the less visible dynamics of violence that lie beneath the surface (both structural and cultural), and the ways these forces of violence ready the ground for moral injury's direct violence. The final section of this chapter explicitly explores this link between structural violence, and the direct violence of moral injury. The next chapter takes up the issue of the involvement of cultural violence in the triad of violence.

Moving past focus on the individual

Veterans Affairs Chaplain Chris Antal, a veteran of the Afghanistan war and chaplain who has developed a unique program for veterans with moral injury, has come to see this deeper connection between the individual and the structural. He writes, "Veterans have the capacity to lead the U.S. public in the adaptive work of deep remembering and inspire a moral revolution against U.S. militarism." What does this mean? Antal continues, "The prophetic message [of veterans] is a counter-narrative of resistance, as it resists both the increased propensity to use force and the normalization of war." Because of everything they have experienced, "veterans are uniquely equipped to guide the U.S. public away from misremembering and selective remembering, and toward deep remembering."[66] The question is, is the U.S. public prepared for what such deep remembering may reveal?

Some moral injury researchers recognize the need for analysis that moves past sole focus on the individual. For instance, scholars report on the collectively brutalizing consequences of participation in the violence of the wars of the 21st century. According to statistics compiled by the Mental Health Advisory Team Study (MHAT), servicemembers reported deeply troubling changes in their characters, ethical perspectives and actions. Post-deployment, fewer than 50% of servicemembers felt it was necessary to treat non-combatants with dignity and respect. Up to 44% of U.S. Marines believed torture was acceptable if it might save the life of a brother in arms. Thirty percent reported having insulted and sworn at Iraqis, and 25% reported being in ethical situations where they didn't know how to respond.[67] These statistics about troubling collective trends among servicemembers emphasize the need for more pointed questions about the waging of these wars, their systemic and structural environments, and their consequences in the lives of those fighting.

The lethality and ambiguity of modern warfare

In addition, some military leaders have suggested that the changes in modern ways of war are at least part of the reason for the increase in the incidence of moral injury. Among those changes, Brad Allenby mentions confusion and difficulty due to the multiples roles servicemembers are required to carry out simultaneously. Not only "fighting and killing," but policing and nation building requirements "… are jammed together so that the same person must shift rapidly between them." Though Allenby doesn't question the ethics of U.S. hegemonic power, he does allow that an "increasingly multicultural and polarized world" makes the use of hegemonic power more complex. Lastly, "moral influence and soft power," in other words, the rise of increased international law, centers of diplomacy and human rights challenge and shine a spotlight on unjust and inhumane military actions. Allenby also mentions the influence of leaks (he mentions Edward Snowden in this regard). These cannot be ignored, and may themselves become "weaponized" (his word). Allenby concludes with a blanket endorsement of the need for a culture of war that encompasses more and more of human life and experience. What is needed, Allenby suggests, is, "a deliberate, strategically integrated process of long-term, intentional, coordinated conflict *across all aspects of a culture*"[68] (italics mine). But the very spread of war that is recommended here, stretching across ever more spheres of existence, only further increases moral ambiguity for servicemembers on the ground. As one researcher imagines the internal conflict servicemembers face:

> Can I kill that girl with the AK-47 assault rifle? Am I a coward for kill-ing by remote control? Why am I fighting on behalf of local "allies" who seem just as bad as the enemy?[69]

Was war *ever* a "seesaw-like arrangement" between "two foes facing one another," and each understanding what drove the other, as researcher Deane-Peter Baker suggests was the case in earlier eras?[70] There is little doubt that today the field of battle is wider, more highly complex and, as a result, deeply ambiguous. Baker illustrates: In the Afghanistan War, military leaders from Australia understood the need to win the support of local people; but local people in Afghanistan perceived what took place in entirely different terms from the professional militaries who infiltrated their villages – they were less interested in conflicts between the Taliban and the Afghanistan government, for instance, than with concerns closer to home, the safety of property and people. Baker comments, "We may well have 'won' the battle in our own definition of the event, but [others] … will have their own political interpretation of the event, be it apathy, anger, satisfaction, or disappointment."[71]

How does this implicate moral injury? Because today's servicemember carries a whole world of war-culture with him/her into the fields of war;

because the fields of war have become much more diverse, and incorporate vast spheres of everyday human life; because war today is more highly urbanized; and also because modern weaponry has so greatly increased in power and lethality – all these changes expand the intensity and power of the stakes that are involved in war, even as the battle environment has become more ambiguous. But to what extent do recruits understand this complex terrain, such as teenagers whose first exposure to recruitment comes through venues such as "The Earth Space Defense"? Nevertheless, narratives of veterans show pained awareness of these insights.

Dehumanization, the "triplet evils," and moral injury

Ethicists Shannon French and Anthony I. Jack agonize about troops who may "animalistically dehumanize the enemy." They understand that military training that "overrides the recruit's moral integrity, so that he or she will have no scruples about killing on command," is ethically unsound. Methods of training and philosophy that eviscerate recruits' moral codes are bound to lead to moral injury and psychological disorders. The "enemy-as-subhuman" method of propaganda may be effective for developing motivation to kill, but it leads to dehumanization, murder and atrocity. For these ethicists, deceptive and misleading language, such as using "neutralizing" instead of "killing" to talk about the work of soldiers, is counter-intuitive. Instead, they suggest reframing the act of killing by "justifying it in a broader moral framework that accounts for the harm servicemembers prevent to their fellow troops, and appeals to more abstract notions of honor, service, duty and just cause."[72]

But will this framework prove adequate for the experience of people such as Stefan J. Malecek, Vietnam veteran? Malecek traces his own moral injury to multiple experiences and sources in his background. His father, a WWII vet, was violent, perhaps also a survivor with moral injury, who inculcated the behaviors of shame and self-repudiation in his son. Later, Malecek's own experiences in Vietnam led him to try anything (eventually he would become addicted to marijuana, amphetamines and opium) to "staunch feelings of tremendous negativity about the military culture that daily betrayed my core values and that lied about essential aspects of the war and why we were there..."[73] But the strong links between the moral injury of war, and the deeper structural political and economic issues supporting war, and military culture and institutions also perpetuating it, go unaddressed in the work of many moral injury researchers and ethicists. Nevertheless, William Nash, one of the foremost experts on moral injury has put it plainly: "The most crucial way [to minimize moral injury] would be improving our society by reducing *the preconditions* for Moral Injury, and by ensuring that unnecessary wars that inflame this grave condition no longer flourish"[74] (italics mine).

At least since the dropping of the atomic bombs in Japan, it has become harder to avoid questions regarding whether war can ever be justified. In 1960 Martin Luther King, Jr. shared his convictions about "how my mind has changed." Like many Americans, King earlier believed that war was a "necessary evil," that should and could be called upon as a "negative good," in order to prevent greater evil, such as the rise of totalitarian systems. Why did he change his view?

> More and more I have come to the conclusion that the potential destructiveness of modern weapons of war totally rules out the possibility of war ever serving again as a negative good ... The choice today is not between violence and nonviolence. It is either nonviolence or nonexistence.[75]

Embracing a "realist pacifism," King did not see his position as "sinless," but as the only rational response to a nation and world gone mad on weapons and power. He could not stay silent while humankind "... faces the threat of being plunged into the abyss of nuclear annihilation."[76]

The destructive nature of war continued to haunt Dr. King in his civil rights leadership, until, in the last year of his life, he publicly came out against the Vietnam War. By this time King was concerned not only about the immorality and senselessness of the Vietnam War; he was worried about the destructiveness of U.S. war-culture overall, and its impact on the moral health of the nation. In his unforgettable speech, "Beyond Vietnam," he proclaimed, "If America's soul becomes totally poisoned, part of the autopsy must read Vietnam. It [the nation] can never be saved so long as it destroys the deepest hopes of men the world over." King addressed "the triplet evils – racism, excessive materialism, and militarism" as central for a moral analysis of sickness of spirit in the nation. He saw how all three elements were (and, I would add, still are) deeply intertwined, mutually exacerbate one another, and rob the nation of its health. "Violence and militarism" drown out democracy and freedom. Vietnam was but "a symptom of a far deeper malady within the American spirit," and getting on "the right side of the world revolution" would mean a "radical revolution of values."

King's thorough-going ethical analysis of U.S. war-culture is taken up in Chapter 5. His prophetic and difficult truth-telling about the intersecting

forms of violence, including the structural violence of militarism, helps clarify a deeper understanding of reality. At the same time, his message not only
then, but today also is very difficult for many to hear. It is difficult to hear for
some because they dedicated their lives to military service, and bled, were
injured, and experienced immeasurable losses along the way. For others, especially civilians, King's analysis sharply contradicts dominant acculturation of citizenship and nationalism based in the ideal of U.S. military might.
Yet getting to the bottom of moral injury requires our reaching deeply to
determine, to the best of our ability, how all the various structures and systems (and culture of violence) of war-culture, give rise to the phenomenon
of moral injury, an inevitable scourge borne by the few.

King's awareness and call for for greater structural justice remains a work
in progress, and could affect how moral injury is interpreted and addressed.
For instance, Pete Kilner, retired lieutenant colonel of the U.S. Army, suggests that moral injury may be less likely if soldiers are encouraged to consider the morality of what they will be asked to do *in advance* of entering
the field of battle. Treating all people, including enemy combatants, with
respect, integrating moral reasoning into tactical training, and working with
soldiers post-battle to help them process and make sense of what happened,
all are helpful and practical suggestions, and LTC Kilner claims that such
practices will help to mitigate the incidence of moral injury.[77]

But what then should we make of the case of Charles Pacello, a former
Air Force Officer who was assigned to the Los Angeles Air Force Base,
where he served as Chief of the Nuclear Detonation Detection System Mission Processing? Officer Pacello sounds like the model citizen ethicists and
military leaders alike hope will enter the armed forces. He was raised with
strong family values and a sense of "honor and integrity" that shaped his decision to serve, "… to preserve, honor, protect and defend all life."[78]

Pacello was commissioned to work at the LA Air Force Base, where he
was given the responsibility for maintaining the readiness of "ground survivable mobile units" to be used in any nuclear conflict. He writes, "Under
my leadership, these [ground units] became operational for the first time."
He responsibly followed through with his duties of ground testing and writing Officer Performance Reports on his work. But one day, not unlike any
other really, his world turned upside down. While sitting in one of the mobile units, overseeing a regular day of testing, suddenly the reality of what he
was doing cut through him, slicing open "a deep moral, psychological, and
spiritual wound": "I realized that I was participating in plans to destroy and
annihilate humankind from the face of the earth." He writes, "In that pivotal
moment, I lost my innocence."[79] Officer Pacello "did everything right," but

his humanity would be overwhelmed by the structures of modern weapons in U.S. war-culture. Pacello's moral injury may not be understood apart from the systemic development of the nuclear weapons/stockpiling apparatus of the United States and the rest of the world.

Or what should we make of the case of Christopher Aaron, drone operator for the Counterterrorism Airborne Analysis Center in Langley, Virginia? Especially after the attacks of 9/11 he wished to emulate his grandfather who had served in WWII, and dedicate his life to a heroic cause. After seeing an email from the DoD about a task force to determine how drones could help to defeat Al Qaeda, he answered the call to become a drone warrior, and worked for the U.S. military and also for military contractors. He was very good at his job and everything seemed fine, until it wasn't. Something was very wrong:

> The distress began with headaches, night chills, joint pain. Soon, more debilitating symptoms emerged – waves of nausea, eruptions of skin welts, chronic digestive problems ... suddenly he felt frail. Working for the [military] contractor was out of the question. "I could not sign the paperwork," he said. Everytime he sat down to try, "my hands stopped working – I was feverish, sick, nauseous."

What happened? Aaron was only at the beginning of facing his own experience: "In the years that followed, as his mood darkened, he withdrew, sinking into a prolonged period of shame and grief. He avoided seeing friends and had no interest in intimate relationships. He struggled with '"quasi-suicidal' thoughts," and dreamed about being forced to sit in a chair and rewatch the violent deaths of people killed by drones he operated. "'It was as though my brain was telling me: Here are the details that you missed out on ... Now watch them when you're dreaming.'"[80]

We might visit many such cases, that directly illustrate how moral injury rises out of individuals' confusion, distress and even despair as they are overwhelmed by their lived involvement in very specific structures and systems of war and militarization, such as nuclear weapons development, policy, stockpiling and maintenance; or the structures and policies of drone warfare that grew so drastically in the post-9/11 timeframe. But to visit one last case here, what about the experience of Eric Fair, whose story was referenced in the introduction to this book?

I open his memoir, *Consequence,* to the second chapter: It's 1995, and Fair has been successfully recruited into the U.S. Army, and tested into a program to become an Arabic language specialist. Entering Basic Training in Leonard Wood, Missouri, he writes about a military cadence used by the Sergeant First Class to bolster recruits' tiring legs and spirits during a long formation run:

> I went to church
> Where all the people pray
> I took out my Claymore
> And I blew them all away
> Singing left right, left right, left right kill
> Left right, left right, you know I will.[81]

Such a cadence has a horrifying resonance, given the rise of mass shootings and violence in the U.S. in recent years in churches, synagogues and mosques. But there's nothing unusual or especially new about these deeply disturbing ways of acculturating people to the military, not to mention the ways in which messages like the one above run utterly counter to the values of honor, service, and respect, that all military branches espouse and celebrate. It gets worse. Fair's memoir is a chilling cautionary tale about one soldier's descent into the hell of what political and military leaders post-9/11 will call "enhanced interrogation." In his case, the structures of government/military policy and law, as well as the systems of corporate contracting for war, will have an inescapable and deeply damaging personal impact. He writes,

> I've abused prisoners in Fallujah and in Abu Ghraib. I have pulled chairs out from underneath young boys. I shoved an old man into a wall. I was silent about the use of the Palestinian chair. I failed to protect the men in my care. I tortured them. And now I believe they like me.[82]

Like so many people in this era, Fair cycled between service in the formal branches of the U.S. military (in his case, the U.S. Army), military contracting and, eventually, work for the National Security Agency. But he is haunted by a recurring nightmare:

> … someone I know begins to shrink. At first I can hold them in my hand or put them on a table, but as they grow smaller I begin to lose track of them. They slip through my fingers and disappear onto the floor. I know they're still there but I cannot find them. I hear their screams in my panic as I scramble to avoid stepping on them.[83]

Another repetitive dream regards a pool of blood on the floor that "nips" at Fair's feet as he struggles to avoid its lifelike movement towards him.[84] There are so many pages of this narrative that are difficult to open, much less read. Fair was required to submit his memoir to the DoD for classification review and, in the process, many passages were blackened and deemed unsuitable to be made publicly available. Nevertheless, he decided to keep the unreadable passages in the book. On one such page there are three big black rectangles where the story was censored. Little text remains, but a single line beneath one of the black rectangles reads, "There is to be no redemption for me in Iraq."[85]

The structural scaffolding of war

If what happened to Eric Fair is a kind of moral injury, was it some sort of unfortunate accident? A tragic but inevitable outcome of necessary wars? Is this just the story of a "bad apple," or the "too sensitive soul"? Fair's participation in torture (and its impact on him) is impossible to fathom, without serious consideration of the structural scaffolding put in place for the Global War on Terror. In 2001, just six days after the 9/11 attacks, President George W. Bush signed a far-reaching "Memorandum of Notification" (MON). This covert order authorized an array of new powers for the CIA "to undertake operations designed to capture and detain persons who pose a continuing, serious threat of violence or death to U.S. persons and interests or who are planning terrorist activities."[86]

According to the Intelligence Committee of the U.S. Senate, the significance of this MON cannot be understated: it "provided unprecedented authorities, granting the CIA significant discretion in determining whom to detain, the factual basis for the detention, and the length of detention."[87] By November of 2001, a mere few months after the MON, Guantánamo Bay was identified for the incarceration of detainees, additional covert "black sites" were in the process of being developed, and within one more month, further "blanket approval" was granted to CIA officers "… to determine who poses the requisite continuing threat of violence of death to US persons and interests or who are planning terrorist activities, and how and where to detain them."[88]

But these plans and their systems of implementation already had been imagined and written up as a memo years earlier by the CIA, at the end of the Clinton era. And within just five months of the fall of the Twin Towers, additional new presidential memos from the Bush administration rewrote legal interpretation of such longstanding moral roadmaps as the Geneva Conventions and the Convention on Torture.[89]

The "Senate Torture Report" of 2014, compiled after exhaustive investigation, outlines a series of decisions and action plans in the highest echelons of government, through which many forms of torture previously used in the Vietnam era were rehabilitated for service post-9/11. It also outlines newer methods that came into use, such as "rectal hydration, forced grooming, the use of insects in confined spaces, the combination of stress positions [think of Fair's description of the 'Palestinian chair' as one example] combined with diapering detainees, and more."[90]

If we are to believe Fair, these heinous practices, systematically developed and even given legal justification in the United States, were like the proverbial pool of blood in his nightmares, nipping at his feet and threatening to pull him in. This was indeed the structural foundation, the quicksand beneath Fair's descent into moral injury. A final point: Fair is excruciatingly unambiguous about his own choices to walk this path; the last thing he would say about himself is that he is "innocent." However, hearers of his story also need to be clear on the following point: though he willingly stepped onto this path, he did not create it. I wonder, how could he have any idea what he was getting himself into? How could one possibly give consent to such things in advance?

Many citizens of the United States demonstrate little appreciation for this ambiguity, or for deeper thought regarding connections between the structural, systemic environment of war-culture, and the phenomenon of moral injury among so many on its front lines. U.S. Americans have yet to build any significant movement of protest about these longest wars in U.S. history. Not only nuclear weapons and drone warfare, many Americans also endorse so-called "enhanced interrogation," and some approve of torture outright, including President Donald Trump. While campaigning, during a television interview Trump blithely stated his approval, "torture works!"[91] But not only he, President Obama signed an executive order in 2011 for a review process "… to hold detainees indefinitely and without end." The incidence of drone attacks mushroomed in Obama's administration, including operations he approved that led to the deaths of U.S. citizens. Though President Obama declared in May 2013 that "the Global War on Terror is over," the federal military budget was not significantly decreased, drone warfare grew alarmingly, and hopes to close Guantánamo Bay seemed impossible to carry out.[92]

The ethics of determining responsibility: Systemic violence and individual choices

According to military ethicist Matthew Beard, moral injury "… involves the difficulties an individual faces when forced to integrate the wrongdoing of a moral authority into their broader conception of the world as a morally reliable place."[93] Beard distinguishes between PTSD and moral injury. PTSD is "a traumatic event that triggers judgments about one's continuing safety," he writes. It leads to a sense of "perpetual or potential victimhood;" these individuals feel continually vulnerable and fearful. Most important, Beard suggests, PTSD reactions originate outside of a person's reasoning capacities. In contrast, Beard continues, moral injury *does* involve human reasoning. Experience leads to a rational conclusion for the morally injured – the world is essentially "untrustworthy", no longer "a reliable place;" war *changes* the world, such that "the world is no longer adequately explained by pre-existing moral beliefs."[94]

Beard sorts through the issues of responsibility and culpability that are involved in moral injury. Certain experiences, while morally "unpalatable," may be nevertheless justified. But human beings will still suffer. There is a "moral remainder," that has to do with those instances in which human beings experience a sense of remorse or regret for "irresolvable dilemmas" for which they are not truly culpable. Response to moral injury is most effective when it helps "… meaningfully integrate their non-culpable responsibility into a personal narrative in a way that avoids unrelieved guilt and persistent shame. They must accept responsibility for what they have done *without* allowing the action to define their identity."[95]

But Beard would have us believe that such a "moral remainder" is different from actions that truly involve culpability. For him, the case of Eric Fair helps to illustrate the difference: "His [Fair's] moral injury is … a manifestation of unresolved guilt … It is not maladaptive to feel guilty when one has done the wrong thing." Beard agrees with Fair's own conclusions about his behavior: he tortured people – he *should* feel guilty. Beard summarizes, "Combatants who have genuinely done wrong, either legally or morally, do not need to have their perception of the events corrected by therapy."[96] Fair's anguish about his behavior is morally justified, and he should make some sort of recompense, according to this line of thinking.

Nevertheless, is Fair's case any different from that of Corporal Sanchez, who killed a 14-year-old boy in an ambiguous series of events at a U.S. military checkpoint in Iraq? Official military judgment determined that "he did nothing wrong," though Sanchez found this inadequate. "How can I say I am a good soldier and a good man when I killed an innocent boy?"[97]

In both cases, don't we have to ask about the shaping influence of structural violence on Fair and Sanchez? Both men abided with structures and systems that intentionally were developed by governmental, legal, military and military contracting institutions. Each man made choices within a certain environment that he had little responsibility for creating. But serious consideration of this structural violence does not strongly figure in Beard's analysis; and far too little thinking about moral injury considers this oversight. Why? To bring the deeper structural realities into analysis of moral injury would necessitate questions that many do not wish to ask. For instance, though Eric Fair "confessed" to his participation in torture not only in his memoir, but in many newspaper op eds, no one from the military or government ever officially prosecuted him. How could they? To prosecute Fair would lead inevitably to having to prosecute all those systems put into place, the "preconditions" (following Nash) for his moral injury. It would call into question a host of immoral structures and their authorities.

By and large, reluctance to question the deep frame of structural violence predominates, because such interrogation could lead in a direction that might challenge the entire enterprise of U.S. war-culture. If anything, Beard is worried that to pull on such a thread may "… make it extremely difficult for soldiers to avoid thinking that their very involvement in war is a moral transgression."[98] Unfortunately, he doesn't take up this question further. He might ask whether indeed, human beings *can* be accommodated morally, ethically, and spiritually to the demands and realities of modern ways of war and its structures and culture. Pulling the thread far enough, this question inevitably rises to the surface. Instead, Beard concludes, the experience of warriors at war, in the end, may yield insights about life that will never be available to civilians. True. But won't at least some of these insights pull the curtain back on the realities of war-culture itself? Beard is right: to pull back this curtain is to lay eyes on an uncomfortable reality, and many might not like what they find.

Structural violence and "the fog of war"

Along with fatalism about moral injury, there exists a similar and related apathy about the reality of war itself. According to this perspective, "the fog of war" makes ethical analysis excruciatingly difficult, and thus war is summarized and distanced as an inevitable horror that always will be part of human experience. But these descriptions and attitudes actually play into an apology *for* war, because their distancing effect diminishes the motivation people might muster to mount a larger investigation as to the deeper grounds of violence in the sediment of war-culture. One begins to think, as bad as war is, there is little that can be done about it, people have survived it from time immemorial, and we will too. At the opposite end of the spectrum are those thinkers who posit that war is an individual and collective good (remember Ian Morris as an example). Sure, there's plenty bad about war, but it leads to stronger human character and communities in the long run. Both attitudes are found throughout the historical record, as Robert Meagher writes, "Freud was far from the first 'thinker' ... to float the theory that war can be waged without moral violation and the destruction of character."[99]

But despite much apathy and fatalism, some *are* paying closer attention to the painful structural dynamics of moral injury. Some researchers describe moral injury as "an occupational hazard organically related to military service."[100] But even this description may be understood in different ways. On the one hand, perceiving a strong causal relationship between moral injury and war may summon motivation to do something about structural war-culture. On the other hand, others might return to the same old apathy about war (and moral injury), approaching moral injury as just another facet of human existence to be borne by some, and ignored by the many. However, apathetic and fatalistic characterizations of both war and moral injury derail the deeper investigation attempted here. A compassionate endeavor to understand moral injury involves exploring structural violence at the subterranean levels of this assault.

Jonathan Shay agrees with those who assert an inevitable link between war's structures, experience, and moral injury. While some ethicists assign the phenomenon of moral injury, fatalistically, to an experience of "bad luck," Shay is more sanguine regarding the cause-and-effect relationship between war and this wound: "I fully concur with the importance and gravity of these horrific incidents that war will *always*, in ever-changing forms, produce ... It will always arise here and there in war even in the best circumstances ..."[101] Shay's insight helps to counter opposing deeply ingrained assumptions, such as the widespread belief that as long war is waged *the right way*, it largely can be withstood, and even build the character of individuals and the nation.

Shay further emphasizes that moral injury involves "culture, social system, mind and brain/body."[102] But this could be taken further. What would Shay say, or for that matter, what would many of the military leaders who are concerned about moral injury say, about the strong social statements from religious bodies that unequivocally address the unrelenting and unjust systems of violence in U.S. ways of war? The Unitarian Universalist Association social statement, "Creating Peace," includes a decidedly structural approach. War inherently involves injustice, according to this analysis; war grows out of "… economic exploitation, political marginalization, the violation of human rights, and a lack of accountability to law." *War's violence is like a poisonous plant that grows out of deep structural and cultural injustice.* The statement also includes this plank that highlights very specific violent structures of war as wielded by the United States:

> We repudiate aggressive and preventive wars, the disproportionate use of force, covert wars, and targeting that includes a high risk to civilians. We support international efforts to curtail the vast world trade in armaments and call for nuclear disarmament and abolition of other weapons of mass destruction. We repudiate unilateral interventions and extended military occupations/imperialism.[103]

A countercultural deconstruction of war-culture, spotlighting the structural factors that give rise to war's direct violence, clarifies the connections between U.S. structures of war, and their consequences in the lives of the morally injured. In the final section of this chapter, these connections are further explored through the concept of "the grey zone." Sorting through structural violence and individual moral injury is difficult and sensitive, and my hope is that this conceptual tool will be of help.

Conclusion: Moral injury in "the grey zone"

Moral injury researchers Duane Larson and Jeff Zust outline the systems of moral support in military branches that help servicemembers faithfully and ethically live out their commitments, including four pillars of moral responsibility: a) mission orders and military principles – in essence their "moral compass;" b) commanders' intents that define how to achieve mission objectives ethically; c) "situational awareness" of context and local customs on the ground; and d) "professional competence."[104] At the same time, these researchers underscore, "War creates conditions that morally injure soldiers by betraying the ultimate values that define their existence."[105]

The dissonance between "ultimate values" defining basic human existence, and the lost world in the fog of war, begs further attention. I draw on the metaphor of "the grey zone" to better understand this dissonance, and its ethical dilemmas and conundrums that are faced by servicemembers. In particular I emphasize the deeper structural foundations that make such dissonance unavoidable. For "the grey zone" is the site of "choiceless choices" in the midst of environments where the world has been turned upside down. Here one's existence is characterized by "double binds" and the necessity to choose between "one form of abnormal choice or another."[106] This description of an "abnormal world" is important, for experiencing the world as "turned upside down," implies a context in which the world one knew is no more; it has become a place that no longer can be trusted, where all the values one formerly trusted in, and the authorities one trusted to be able to sink roots into life, have been eviscerated – the "abnormal world" precisely *is* the world of moral injury.

The metaphor of "the grey zone" was developed by Primo Levi, a survivor of the Holocaust. His contribution to philosophy and ethics remains inestimable, for with respect to this framework alone, the "grey zone" helps us "… not only for judging, but [also] for understanding the true nature of humans and their limits …"[107] Initially Levi created the metaphor of "the grey zone" to describe the indescribable – those inconceivable ethical dilemmas faced by Jews in the morass of the Holocaust. "The grey zone" since has been utilized in many other contexts, and in different disciplines. Philosopher Adam Brown explains how use of "the grey zone" cuts through complex ethical cases such as those explored in this chapter. Brown writes,

> The "grey zone" is important as it destabilises clear-cut distinctions, such as that between "good" and "evil," and warns against hasty moral judgement – or, in some cases, calls for it to be withheld entirely.[108]

Philosopher Dominick LaCapra emphasizes further why "the grey zone" is unique: it is

> "… a condition of extreme equivocation that is created largely through the practices of perpetrators and imposed on victims, typically in the form of a double bind or impossible situations."[109]

Levi's exploration of "the grey zone" took shape in his recounting of the histories of victim/perpetrators, the *Sonderkommandos* of death camps such as Auschwitz. The majority of these were Jews who were forced, upon pain of execution by their Nazi masters, to participate in the industrial machinery of death. Assigned to work in the gas chambers and crematoriums, they received supplies of food, clothing and other goods that were stripped from new arrivals to the camps; but these coerced individuals, whose lives were spared for a time so that they could perform the most awful work of death, also faced constant threat of extinction. Regarding such labor, Brown quotes Levi: "'here one hesitates to speak of privilege.'"[110] In Levi's mind this human reality only could be described as a "grey zone" in which every customary form of ethical deliberation seemed impossible, and inadequate.

Levi struggled to tell these stories, reflected on what became of these human beings, and pondered what to think of them. He discovered a variety of human reactions in this unimaginable environment. Some of the workers of death committed suicide, others tried to escape through alcohol, and others became completely distanced and depraved, as though completely lost to themselves. Meanwhile, still others took great pains to keep what records they could, burying diary pages, resisting through preserving memory.

Philosophers disagree about many things with regard to ethics in the grey zone, but at least two areas of insight from their analyses are helpful here. First, Brown emphasizes that the existence of the grey zone does not excuse one from being judged, or others from the necessity of weighing in with judgment. "The grey zone" is a profoundly *human* existential situation and condition in which both innocence and guilt are excruciatingly mixed up, but throwing up one's hands in apathy or dismissal is not an option. Brown writes, "Levi's 'grey zone' warns against judgement but at the same time requires it."[111] Levi writes, "to confuse [murderers] with their victims is a moral disease or an aesthetic affectation or a sinister sign of complicity."[112] Human beings need justice as much as water or air.

Sonderkommandos by and large, "… continued to facilitate the killing process until they themselves were exterminated." Levi describes how a new squad of "crematorian ravens" was "initiated" by being forced to burn the corpses of its predecessors.[113] Thus we are led to the second insight to be underscored, regarding the deeper structures that created this "extreme destitution," as Levi described it. The behaviors and "choiceless choices" of the *Sonderkommandos* are impossible to understand or analyze, much less make any judgement about, without focused attention on the unthinkable structural violence of the camps and the structural apparatus of the totalitarian Nazi regime altogether. Levi writes,

Certainly, the greatest responsibility lies with the system, the very structure of the totalitarian state; the concurrent guilt on the part of individual big and small collaborators (never likeable, never transparent!) is always difficult to evaluate. It is a judgment that we would like to entrust only to those who found themselves in similar circumstances and had the opportunity to test for themselves what it means to act in a state of coercion.[114]

We are tempted to turn away from this unthinkable setting. But as one philosopher writes, the only way to "exorcise" the individual and collective evils in these humanly created structural realities is through "steady looking," in other words, by refusing to distract or distance ourselves.[115]

Steady looking inevitably points beyond the terrible and haunting stories about the individuals in Levi's narration, to the deeper structural foundation of this violence. And this precisely is why the framework of "the grey zone" matters for any understanding and analysis of moral injury. My point has nothing to do with any simplistic comparison between the *Sonderkommandos* and military servicemembers or veterans in the United States. It has to do with what happens to people in a world that is no longer the world, no longer a place one knows or can trust. The existential experiences in the world turned upside down by war and war-culture, also are "grey zones" that are painfully difficult to understand, much less ethically resolve. And honestly exploring "the grey zones" of individual experiences faced by servicemembers who struggle with moral injury must eventually lead us to "the roots of conflict," the structural violence that undergirds individual experience.

But an important distinction must be made. For in the case of the *Sonderkommandos*, what matters is the nature of this particular structural violence. The history of Nazi Germany and the reality of the death camps is a story of the building of a human infrastructure of violence and inhumanity whose horror never has been replicated in human experience; the image of such terrifying degradation has been seared into the collective human consciousness and stands apart from all other historical examples of structural violence, as awful and terrifying as they frequently are. Even the far too frequent incidences of "Holocaust denial" serve to underscore overall growth in human collective consciousness – we *know* we must never forget, or allow such structures to take root ever again.

In Levi's mind, the structural creation of the squads of *Sonderkommandos* was the height of National Socialism's "demonic crime."[116] For the squads not only made it possible for members of the SS to find relief from this unspeakable labor, in addition, "This institution represented an attempt to shift onto others – specifically the victims – the burden of guilt, so that they were deprived even of the solace of innocence."[117] Yet even here, Levi still found judgment inevitable. He ranks the different levels of collaboration of these laborers with the Nazis, as well as the different extremes of violence that victim/collaborators rained down on others beneath themselves in the hierarchy of the camps. "Until the end of 1943 it was not unusual for a prisoner to be beaten to death by a *Kapo* (leader of the work squad) without the latter having to fear any sanctions."[118] One thing truly is clear: no one escaped the forces of such deep brutalization.

There can be no comparison of the structural violence of U.S. war-culture with the other-worldly setting Levi describes. Nevertheless, Levi's metaphor helps to sort through the confusion and complexity of "the grey zone" in U.S. war-culture; and his writing clarifies an important difference between these settings. For not only is the structural violence of U.S. war-culture *not* burned into the collective consciousness, by and large, people of the U.S. are relatively blind to it altogether. It is largely and unthinkingly celebrated and revered. The collective imagination remains deeply constricted with regard to any question of changing it. Remember that this tends to be the character of embedded structural violence; it is concealed and normalized in human consciousness, even as its practices of exploitative violence, marginalization and oppression remain hidden within the structure and justified. One has to work much harder to *see* it, and to make a moral accounting of it.

Levi's work opens an important area of inquiry with regard to moral injury. He shows how moral assessment must account for the structures of injustice and violence. Yet as so many of the narratives of the morally injured demonstrate, this wider field of accountability, especially structural accountability, is missing. For those with moral injury, it might be asked, what is the impact of separating individual choices and behavior, from the responsibility that rests with the structures of violence that shaped and eventually required such action? Does this disconnection exacerbate moral injury? How can any healing take place without this accounting?

Pondering "the grey zone" also raises questions about locating "innocence" in the stories of moral injury from this chapter. Can "innocence" be ascribed, or at least a very different kind of "guilt" once there is increased awareness about what it means to be subject to the systems of war-culture? These are deeply dominating structures, from which escape is difficult, if an option at all. In this chapter's examples, the experiences of military servicemembers with moral injury could be characterized with similar language of "choiceless choices," where one only had the option to choose between equally abnormal possibilities. Robert Meagher tells the story of a servicemember who was required in her military training, before being deployed, to practice a training exercise, a reflexive conditioning simulation, over and over again. The simulation forced her to "virtually" run over a child with the huge military convoy truck she steered. She needed to be prepared reflexively to kill a child in order to protect the convoy. Thankfully, once she was actually in Iraq and doing such driving in real time, this terrible possibility never arose. But after the war, she found herself unable to return to the work she had done before becoming part of the military; she had been a preschool teacher.[119]

Some philosophers claim that "only a free choice is morally binding." If this is the case, and taking into greater consideration the reality of the dominating violent structures of war-culture, is any judgment on an individual (whether self-judgement on the part of servicemembers, or collective external judgement) unwise and unfair? Given this socially constructed world, it is hard to imagine that anyone ever is completely "free" from being deeply influenced and shaped by our social and structural realities.

However, Levi teaches that at the same time "the grey zone" warns against judgment, it nevertheless requires it. Human beings always are mixed up in both shaping and being shaped by the world they have helped to construct. Once vision is clearer with respect to the structural violence that surrounds us, it can seem overwhelming; for structural violence both shapes and limits human decision-making, it penetrates human *imagination* in inescapable fashion in war-cultures such as the contemporary United States.

Indeed, the systematic and structural violence of U.S. war-culture can overcome human beings, distort their humanity, and confront them with "choiceless choices." Remember the perverse interpenetrations of militarism with the entertainment industry, and its shaping and dehumanizing tentacles in the lives of young potential recruits in the U.S. Remember people like Stefan Malecek, Christopher Aaron, Eric Fair, Anthony Pacello, Corporal Sanchez. Both analysis and address of moral injury are inadequate without insight about "the grey zone" in which countless servicemembers have struggled to live morally in vast structures of unremediating violence, and to make decisions that would not haunt them for the rest of their lives. And without acknowledgement of massive structural violence in the sediment of moral injury, military servicemembers and veterans are abandoned to to facing its overwhelming violence in isolation, mostly on their own. They are cut off from deeper contextualized insight that shows how *all* of those whose lives are connected to U.S. war-culture, in other words, all citizens of the United States, are implicated and involved, both victims *and* perpetrators.[120]

At the same time, as Levi wrote, life does continue "in the most extreme degradation." Life, ethics and judgment still continue both within and under the structural conditions of war-culture. This *is* ambiguous. For, on the one hand, judgment and repair for the moral injury of U.S. military servicemembers is meaningless *without* inclusion of the powerful factor of structural violence in which they are inevitably caught up. This judgment is needed, not only for servicemembers, but also for society as a whole. Eric Fair knew this, and he also knew that such judgment was never going to be forthcoming from a trustworthy source within the institutions he belonged to, so he assumed the role himself by writing his memoir. The point is, to what extent will collective judgments incorporate an adequate accounting of our own reality in the U.S.? And not only structural, but cultural sedimentary violence also must be taken into account (see Chapter 3). *Taking responsibility for moral injury is impossible without also taking responsibility for the world of war-culture human beings have created.* This accountability will not permit a view of war-culture as inevitable, unchangeable, or beyond repair. It will not provide comfort for a fatalistic perspective about war as an unavoidable consequence of human conflict/nature. No, the vision needed for transformation must include both the individual servicemember or veteran who is suffering, and collective responsibility for the whole road of war-culture that makes moral injury its natural destination.

Moreover, bringing the framework of "the grey zone" into moral deliberation has implications for recommendations about fomenting greater "resilience" to forestall moral injury.[121] Resilience training without social analysis slides into moral accommodation to the structural violence of war as a given, as something *we must learn to withstand.* Without social analysis, training in resilience may shape individuals who are primed for the increasing abnormality and violence of the world turned upside down, world no longer a world, in today's modern ways of war. Military leaders such as Lieutenant Colonel Douglas A. Pryer, find this chilling; as he writes,

> The real reason why U.S. military leaders do not talk about moral injury when they talk about war lies in military culture. The prevalent belief in American Exceptionalism nurtures the idea that American soldiers are exceptional, not because of what they do but because of who they are. Accepting that American soldiers may sometimes do things that seriously trouble them runs directly against that belief. It is thus no wonder that instead of better educating servicemembers so that they will make choices in combat that they can live with, the institutional response to the issue of psychological injury has been to try to create resilient, relentlessly positive automatons.[122]

The next chapter takes up investigation of the cultures of violence that acculturate citizens and soldiers alike to militarism and war. Pryer clearly hopes for deeper thinking, but how far should this critical investigation go? I suggest that the way forward is to ask: How can individuals be strengthened to more clearly *see* the structures of violence that create this upside down world, that undergird the extreme circumstances in which escape seems hardly an option? Moreover, how can individuals whose moral injury has arisen out of "abnormal choices" in such a world be supported in their lives going forward? Finally, what should citizens do about the reality of war-culture, once they understand how its structural violence contributes to moral injury? What is the responsibility of "the rest of us"? One thing is clear: not only is it demonstrably unjust, it is also unrealistic to encourage any treatment/response, much less judgment of the individual (or encouragement of his/her self-judgment), without a strong and clear accounting of the entire structural environment of violence, that led to this situation. Levi is best left with the final word: "It is a judgment that we would like to entrust only to those who found themselves in similar circumstances and had the opportunity to test for themselves what it means to act in a state of coercion."[123]

3 Moral Injury and Cultural Violence

Introduction

In 2018 the American Psychological Association (APA) released "Guidelines for Psychological Practice with Boys and Men."[1] In comparison with previous APA Guidelines (addressing race, sexual orientation, disability and/or age identities), the new release sparked heated debate in the wider public because, for the first time, the APA was addressing "traditional masculinity" and suggesting that all is not well with the cultural norms, practices and values that tend to go along with "what it means to be a man" in the United States. What comprises "traditional masculinity"?

> Masculinity ideology is a set of descriptive, prescriptive, and proscriptive cognitions about boys and men … A particular constellation of standards … have held sway over large segments of the population, including: anti-femininity, achievement, eschewal of the appearance of weakness, and adventure, risk, and violence. These have been collectively referred to as traditional masculinity ideology.[2]

The publication stressed the pain and struggle boys and men too often experience (the study did not address the consequences of the struggle and pain for women or the LGBTQ community, who also are impacted by dominant modes of masculinity). Overall, the study emphasized, what is needed is deeper self-understanding on the part of men, as well as those who provide them psychological services. Research shows that men of differing backgrounds, race and class suffer from the following:

- limited psychological development,
- gender role strain and conflict,
- negative mental and physical health consequences,
- increased learning disabilities and behavior problems among boys,
- high male prison populations, and high incidence of violent crimes committed by men, even while men also most frequently are the victims of violent crimes.

Meanwhile, dominant cultural mores exacerbate these problems. Gender/ race/ethnicity stereotyping and bias, the acculturation of traditional masculinity through various social processes, and the stigma men regularly face if they seek behavioral health treatment, make the problem worse.[3] The guidelines propose, "Understanding the socially constructed nature of masculinity, and how it affects boys and men, as well as psychologists, … is an important cultural competency."[4] Among the ten guidelines emphasized for psychologists, the authors encouraged care providers to "… understand and strive to change institutional, cultural, and systemic problems that affect boys and men through advocacy, prevention and education."[5]

Pushback to the published guidelines came quickly: "the American Psychological Association wrongly declares war on 'traditional masculinity,'" wrote one columnist for the *National Review.*[6] In this view, neither "traditional masculinity," nor its supposed "toxicity" is the real issue. No, what is at stake is the "essential nature" of men. Becoming a man is a process that requires other, older men as mentors for the shaping of "inherent characteristics" in males (including aggression, adventure, physical strength, etc.) toward "virtuous ends." Developing discipline and stoicism are primary to this process, including the need to "endure pain" and "suppress natural emotions."

The debate about the APA Guidelines reveals disagreement about important questions: Do modes of masculinity lead to men's and others' suffering? Moreover, sharp differences also are illuminated about beliefs regarding gender and human nature. The assumption of the *National Review* senior writer, that maleness (however it is understood) is "essential nature," is challenged by research about the socially constructed development of masculinities (this chapter in particular will examine several examples). At the end of the op-ed, the writer suggests popular actor Dwayne Johnson's philosophy for "life improvement," as an example for young men to emulate: "'blood, sweat and respect.' You sweat and bleed and in return you earn respect. It's a more vivid version of 'no pain, no gain.'"

When my younger brother was a second-year high school student, he was on the school's swim team. One day, during a particularly difficult workout, he developed a raging pain in his head. He made his way to the edge of the pool and told the coach he couldn't go any further. "Swim it off," he was told. Precious minutes passed while my brother tried to comply, but when he finally was helped out of the pool, he was losing the ability to control half of his body. It turned out that he was in the midst of a life-threatening stroke caused by muscle tissue that was sloughed off during the intense workout, and attacked by his immune system, turning into a blood clot that then lodged in his carotid artery. This painful memory was reawakened for me years later, when my own children were on the town swim team. One day, as the children were swimming laps in their workout, a boy stopped and tried to speak with his mother about pain he was experiencing. "Pain is just weakness leaving the body," she told him. It was astonishing to witness this slogan from the Marine Corps migrating to the childhood site of the swim team, now recommended by a mother to her young son.

The examples above illustrate the conflicts and complexity at the heart of this chapter, to explore the sediment of cultural violence as the nutrient soil and deep source in military moral injury. Bringing the relationship between gender and war-culture out of the shadows is essential for better understanding of the phenomenon of moral injury, and imagination about how it could be better prevented and addressed.

First I return to Galtung's theory of violence to provide an overview of the dynamics of cultural violence, and the ways it interacts with both direct and structural forms of violence. This will provide the underpinning for the next step, to examine three types of cultural violence that impact moral injury: ideologies of military masculinity, the role of religion, and understandings of nationalism.

Take a step back to think more deeply about what is involved in cultural violence as a whole. Two images/diagrams from Galtung's theory of violence help to visualize the relationships and dynamics between different types of violence, and their distinct valences. Galtung suggests that we imagine violence as an iceberg, or as layers of sediment going deep into the earth. At the top of the diagram, direct violence is the event of violence that is most visible to us. It's the tip of the iceberg that appears above the water, or the topsoil of the sedimentary layers. With regard to moral injury, direct violence is *most visible* in the range of behaviors creating harm in the lives of the morally injured, and their loved ones. Direct violence includes self-harm, relational struggle, danger-seeking, addiction and other dysfunctional behaviors; it is related to a loss of identity and, too often, suicide. The majority of moral injury research focuses on how to prevent or ameliorate direct violence. But remember, this is just the tip of the iceberg. Taking Galtung's theory seriously means digging deeper to excavate and analyze the violence beneath. To *understand* what is going on, one must dive into the water, and shovel beneath the surface of the topsoil. Intentional and committed labor is required, for beneath the event of direct violence, the dynamics of structural violence are harder to see; they have been legitimated and normalized in society. Here, below the water's surface, and exploring structural constructions that give rise to direct violence, one finds the interplay of repression, exploitation and marginalization. Chapter 2 examined structural violence in U.S. war-culture to shed light on the interplay of structural violence in moral injury.

This provides important ground for the current chapter, sinking deeper, to investigate the role of *cultural violence.* This is not to leave behind insight regarding structural violence. For structural sediment breeds, as well as feeds off, deeper cultural mulch in the process of destruction. In addition, becoming more conscious of the connections between different layers of violence impacts judgment about what moral injury *is*, and how to *address* moral injury. A much wider field of assessment and action opens, and new questions arise. Rather than conceive of moral injury as an inescapable consequence of war, as an unlucky event, or as an individual disorder or pathology, a different reality comes into view. It becomes clearer that moral injury develops because of the world dominated by the structures of war and war-culture, a world that human beings have created. Understanding and recognition sharpen at this point; for without the will to examine ourselves, and hold ourselves as U.S. citizens accountable as a people, a society, a nation, not only for the structures of war, but also for the culture that shapes our very *imagination* regarding human conflict, military moral injury heedlessly will continue.

Taking this further, the images of iceberg and layers of sediment increase insight regarding the *causal* relationships in violence. These images connote how reverberations of violence generally seep upwards in structures and actions, and sink down in streams of collective consciousness. Cultural violence gives rise to and justifies structural violence, and eventually bursts into the event of direct violence. But the deep sedimentary layer of cultural violence is the *least* obvious, and the most *concealed* vector of violence, though this same vector profoundly shapes the forces of violence that lie closer to and above the surface of the ground.

Finally, by way of introducing this chapter, the reader is invited to imagine one other visual image in addition to the iceberg/sedimentary diagrams. Galtung suggests the *triangle of violence*, as a second heuristic. Here, direct, structural and cultural violence occupy the three points of the triangle. This image helps Galtung to express and investigate a multitude of interactive dynamics between all three facets of violence simultaneously. Yes, direct violence is sourced and maintained by the other two types, but in addition, each vector of violence continually interacts with the other two types in a mutually reinforcing dynamic. Violence percolates in more than one way. While cultural violence remains the deepest strata of violence, and tends to move upwards in the sedimentary layers, simultaneously, additional collisions between all three aspects of violence also reverberate in real time with very real consequences.

Galtung writes,

> By "cultural violence" we mean those aspects of culture, the symbolic sphere of our existence – exemplified by religion and ideology, language and art, empirical science and formal science (logic, mathematics) – that can be used to justify or legitimize direct or structural violence. ... The study of cultural violence highlights the way in which the act of direct violence and the fact of structural violence are legitimized and thus rendered acceptable in society.[7]

Cultural violence "lives" in specific sites of human existence and history. Exploring cultural violence is to enter the realm of the cosmological, and to shed light on generally hidden assumptions in human consciousness and subconscious. It is to examine how "pre-reflection," shapes human beings' sense of value and identity. In other words, the realm of cultural violence is like water that we fish swim in unconsciously and seemingly naturally. And as Galtung suggests, cosmological frameworks are present in many diverse spaces and sites. Not only religion, as one would probably assume, but also mathematics and science acculturate human beings in subterranean and subconscious assumptions about the very nature of reality. Remember, for instance, the claims about "essential masculinity." Intentional investigation of the sources of cultural violence is important, because this investigation helps *unmask* the dynamics that justify structural and direct violence. Cultural violence may be diagnosed wherever particular attitudes, values and identities that define what is "normal and natural" are tied to violence, "assault to basic life needs that *could be avoided.*" Humans absorb these intuitively, through vast and subconscious continuous processes of acculturation even before we are born, and throughout our lives.

Galtung maps cosmological frameworks of cultural violence across social geography and chronology.[8] "Chosenness," for instance, is the framework that one belongs to a people that that have been set aside by destiny or God to be in a special position *vis-à-vis* others. Or the "Center-Periphery" framework creates an "us and them" divide that frequently leads to dehumanization. Along with these examples, additional patterns of thinking (such as those found in much just war theory) that create division between the means of achieving one's goal, and the very goal one is seeking, are another hallmark of cultural violence. Galtung also stresses how frameworks of thinking that separate "unity-of-life" are related to cultural violence. Failing to see the profound connection of all life, and hierarchizing different forms of life, prepare the ground to justify destruction of some for the sake of others. Lastly, Galtung emphasizes that "linear" patterns of understanding existence, and "either/or," and "black/white" patterns of thinking, further exacerbate cultural violence.

One further important distinction regards the difference between "violence" and "conflict." If violence is an assault to basic life needs that could be avoided, in contrast, conflict is a fact of human existence. Galtung writes, "Deep inside every conflict lies a contradiction, something standing in the way of something else." Conflicts "generate energy." There is a question posed by any conflict: will its energy be addressed constructively, or destructively, descending into violence? May this conflict become "life-creative," or "life-destructive?" The very concept of "peace" is non-linear; peace involves a cyclical way of thinking and acting. Gandhi's statement about peace "as the way, not the goal," is important in Galtung's thinking. Peace is taking place wherever violence is in the process of being reduced, and conflict being approached (not avoided!) nonviolently.[9]

Tracing the "life-cycles" of various conflicts and analyzing them lead to better understanding of the nature of conflict and how to transform it. Patterns of thinking matter, such as whether the life-cycles of conflict are imagined in linear or more cyclical terms. According to Galtung, linear cultural frameworks tend to increase violence. In this way of thinking, conflict is imagined as having a beginning, and a specific ending involving *crisis* or *apocalypse* or *catharsis*.[10] In contrast, "… *conflict transformation is a never-ending process.*" Human beings never will arrive at a "contradiction-free" society, but we can positively impact the course of conflict through avoiding polarization, complexifying understanding, growing in conscientization (multi-pronged awareness), mobilizing and struggling for increased nonviolent change, and reducing violence whenever and wherever we can.[11]

In his discussion of conflict and cultural violence, Galtung especially highlights the two central axioms from Gandhi's understanding of peace alluded to above: unity-of-life, and unity-of-means-and-ends. When and where these two axioms are preserved in conflicts, the pathway of less violence and greater positive transformation is strengthened. At the same time, the lack or absence of these axioms in any context helps to diagnose cultural violence at the base of both structural and direct events of violence. But this work of "pathology," as Galtung describes it, where violence is diagnosed in a way that is similar to investigating and diagnosing disease through a study of the whole human body, is challenging for the following reason: cultural violence not only renders direct and structural violence *acceptable*, but cultural violence also is *invisible* without intentional labor to pull it out of the shadows. Thus, the remainder of this chapter is devoted to just such interrogation of *three primary forms of cultural violence* deeply imbricated in the toxic soil, the dead water, the poisonous landscape sourcing the growth of military moral injury: ideologies of military masculinity, the role of religion, and cognitive metaphors of nationalism.

Colliding masculinities in U.S. war-culture

Sovereign masculinity

Bonnie Mann asks a wonderful question in her analysis of "sovereign masculinity" as a cultural force that shapes gender, valorizes violence, and infuses national and military identities: "How does the 'making sense' of gender relate to the 'making sense' of war?"[12] Disentangling the links between gender constructions and early justifications of The Global War on Terror, Mann shows how violence has endured, though President Obama officially declared it over, and despite massive destruction and costs.[13] She exposes subterranean threads and processes beneath the surface, uncovering cultural formations of masculinity that operationalize war-culture in the United States, and shape human self-and-other understanding. In this section, following Mann's focus, I explore the consequences of these gender constructions. Bringing this cultural violence into clearer view both complexifies understanding of moral injury, and clarifies vision regarding various forms of response.

According to Mann, a significant shift in national ways of understanding and defining "manhood" took place in the United States at the end of the 19th and into the 20th century. "Maleness" historically was associated with the powers of "reason," and transcended "femaleness." In turn, "femaleness" has tended to be assigned culturally with the body, vulnerability and the emotional and mortal life of human beings. But a new collective worry arose in the U.S. around the time of the presidency of Theodore Roosevelt. Men (in this view) had become too soft, distanced from their own physicality, weak and lacking in primal bodily strength associated with the wild animal world. This also was the era of Reconstruction and the corresponding backlash of Jim Crow in the United States. White Americans were "obsessed with the connection between manhood and racial dominance," Mann explains. Certain strands of evolutionary thinking gave rise to anxiety among white men regarding those who had been consigned to the role of "savage" (African and indigenous people in the U.S.) by dominant racial ideology. Were these groups gaining an upper hand in terms of brute power and strength? Perhaps the "white man of reason" was becoming emasculated and even impotent.[14] President Theodore Roosevelt warned, "over-sentimentality, over-softness, in fact washiness and mushiness are the great dangers of this age and of this people. Unless we keep the barbarian virtues, gaining the civilized ones will be of little avail."[15]

At this moment in the United States, the cultural wells shaping white masculinity shifted. Masculinity became a *hybrid*; "the white man of reason" now took it upon himself to "'introject' a certain imagined primitive manhood of the African American and American Indian." Mann writes, "White men in America 'borrowed' or 'took back' the primitivity they had previously deposited in the figures of Black and American Indian subjects."[16] This was the era that produced *Tarzan of the Apes,* whose protagonist became the epitome of white manhood. This masculinity combined notions of white Anglo-Saxon culture, emphasizing intelligence and rationality, with characteristics of brute strength and skill, supposedly necessary to live among "primitive apes." This "man" became adept at killing (not only animals but also Black men), and his "hybridity made him both invincible and fascinating."[17]

But this blockbuster was accompanied by another that also galvanizeed the nation. Even as this new hybrid of masculinity was shaping culture, the film, *Birth of the Nation*, reinforced the continuing dominant cultural U.S. portrayal of African American men as rapacious, out of control, hyper-sexualized, dangerously perilous for white women, irrational and full of bestial strength – in essence, as a challenge to white manhood that only could/would be met with unrelenting violence (thus the need for the hybrid ideology of masculinity, combining both "rational whiteness" and bestial strength). As we explore the cultural material embedded in colliding ideologies of masculinity, contradictions are to be expected as they mix and spin different characteristics.

Mann explains that the changing nature of white masculinity was always "aspirational;" in other words, white masculinity never was fully achieved or settled, but always in play, and needing to be proven again and again (the same could be said about the forms of masculinity assigned to Black and indigenous men; this assignation too would be re-enacted, as a justification for violence).[18] And all this became central in the development of "sovereign masculinity."

The Oscar-winning film, *The Hurt Locker,* is singled out by Mann to illustrate the dominant characteristics of sovereign masculinity in the post-9/11 era.[19] This is a departure from other war films that emphasize masculinity as pure hyper-physicality and power. In the multifaceted portrayal of sovereign military masculinity in *The Hurt Locker*, the film's protagonist, Sergeant "William James," shares his name with the famous philosopher, alluding to a very different message right from the start. James is intelligent, and highly trained and successful as a bomb detonator in the Iraq urban field of war. Mann describes him as "a combination of soldierly calm, ruthlessness, and technical skill."[20] But he also is "an adrenaline junkie, as much as he is emotionally incompetent." At the same time, his masculinity is "… infused with heightened primitivism, an instinct-driven animality that is ferociously focused on triumph and survival."[21] "Putting on the [bomb detonation] suit" requires a contradictory combination of technical acuity, raw animal power, relentless purpose and cynical bravado. Mann notes that actual veterans of the military were not enamored of this soldierly figure who they saw as all too likely to get himself and others killed. Veterans especially were suspicious of the knee-jerk excitement of the American public to the film, who "… called it awesome," and remarked on the "'large balls' [it took] to go over there." Reviewers declared that the bomb detonator was "an iconic figure," "the 21st Century GI Joe."[22]

It does, however, seem odd that Americans so little focused on other contradictions in the film, such as when James comes home after deployment. For this soldier's transformation into the iconic warrior/man, making it possible for him to "succeed" in the Iraq theater of war, doesn't work at home. There he seems helpless, confused, numb, isolated and just angry. He goes into a supermarket to make a simple purchase and is overwhelmed by aisle upon aisle of so many consumer goods; he looks on at a distance as his wife cares for their young child, emotionless. He may have exhibited superlative technical skill on the battlefield, but seems utterly at sea with respect to critical thought or emotional maturity state-side; he is unable or unwilling to engage any process of self-reflection, to think about what happened to and in himself, and what he might do about it. He will return willingly to the armed services, and redeploy to the fields of war; what else can he really do?

Mann would say that James' reaction to coming home should have been expected. The cultural process of masculine formation that shapes men like James inevitably leads to such ends. At the heart of sovereign masculinity is a process she names as "the shame-to-power conversion."[23] The prospect of experiencing shame, or being shamed, for boys and men in particular, relates to holding off and forestalling inevitable experiences at the heart of what it means to be a human being: awareness of one's deep vulnerability, one's bare need of others, experiencing limits and ambiguity. Though as Judith

Butler has written, "one's life is always in some sense in the hands of another," the "shame to power" conversion is the attempt to rise above this, and achieve inviolability and control. In sovereign masculinity formation this cultural violence especially is worked out through shame related to gender and sex, such as through the fear of rape, of penetration.[24]

The ritual of the "field-fuck" enacts the process of shaming. Related to "resilient cultural practices" of hazing involving primarily young men (such as sports, fraternities, gangs, etc.), in military contexts these practices take on a unique intensity (these practices also impact and involve women).[25] A victim, perhaps someone who has not "played by the rules," who offended the group in some way, or who failed to live up to the masculine standards that are expected and demanded, is held down while others mimic penetration from behind. Bystanders egg on and applaud the process. Victims are expected to endure the ritual and laugh it off afterwards. Mann notes that this is a common practice in the Marine Corps, has been recounted by various memoirists, and also has deep roots in much broader culture.[26] The practice also has been identified as an entry ritual in the United States Armed Forces.[27] Culturally speaking, to be a "female" means to live in an "I suffer" body; in contrast, the goal in becoming a man, is to achieve an "I can" body liberated from any such infringement or risk of assault. The point is to rise above the shaming faux-penetration, and grow into the kind of person to whom nothing of this sort ever will happen again.

Mann especially turns to linguistic evidence to make her point about gender shaming that is ubiquitous in all the branches of the military. New recruits face continual misogynist and LGBTQ verbal assaults, "pussy, girl, bitch, dyke, faggot, and fairy." To be aligned with woman or the LGBTQ individual is to be shamed and not a man. Women and LBGTQ people in the military are in multiple binds with respect to the "trash talk" they not only must endure, but according to some female soldiers, participate in if they are to win acceptance. Either they are a "soldier" or they are relegated to "slut" or "bitch." One memoirist and former soldier recounts how, attending a concert with fellow servicemembers, she wore mascara. This was a mistake; now her military colleagues only could see her as sexual bait, and weigh whether she might be available sexually. "I was tits, a piece of ass, a bitch or a slut of whatever; but never really a person. Bros before hos."[28]

Military gender-based violence is ubiquitous and "an inherent part of the military institution," according to scholars of military culture. Today, in Western liberal militaries, between 85 to 95% of servicemembers are men, and while the violence within the military is directed at both *women and men*, it is perpetrated "almost exclusively" by men. Scholar Ben Wadham writes, "Militaries foster military masculinity and their violence but they also fail to be accountable for it."[29] Even shocking revelations in recent years regarding gender-based violence within the military, and the "constitutive violence" of military cultures, have not been sufficient to change military command's tendency toward "forms of denial based on inward looking solidarity."[30]

How does one hold shame at bay, or overcome it altogether? Mann writes, "Gender lends itself to justificatory operations."[31] Sovereign masculinity must be performed over and over again, as shame is converted to power not just once, but repeatedly. Why? A "self-justifying fantasy" constitutes the heart of this masculinity formation. In other words, the human realities of mortal limitation, intersubjectivity, and plain uncertainty and vulnerability that characterize all of human life, are "put out of play."[32]

Sovereign masculinity is a chimera, a delusion, a nightmare – and its illusory nature necessitates that it be continually re-enacted. It is a very enticing dream for human beings whose culture esteems authority, control and freedom from fear or lack of power. This explains why a figure like James is so popular in the American imagination, or Chris Kyle, the Navy SEAL upon whose life the hugely popular film, *American Sniper*, was based. In both cases, their life and work in the world of war is clearcut, unapologetic, and devastatingly violent; they achieve their goals, and they survive in the most radical of environments. Their lives and actions are marked by a power that seems superhuman, based on highly developed technical skill, combined with unpredictable displays of overwhelming violence. According to the Internet Movie Database (IMDb), Kyle's technical expertise joins with the same kind of superhuman power and bravado as James': his "pinpoint accuracy [as a sniper] saves countless lives ... and turns him into a legend." But he has the same inability for critical thought or self-examination of his internal emotional world: "Back home to his wife and kids after four tours of duty, ... Chris finds that it is the war he can't leave behind."[33]

And individual boys and men are not the only targets/objects of such formation – Mann argues that the very *nation* requires it. "It [the nation] needs to have its citizens read the headlines, 'Shock and Awe,' and feel their most visceral identity commitments expressed in the hyperbolic display of agency, the spectacle of invulnerability, that the headline announces."[34] Sovereign masculinity meets the national imaginary. Is it any wonder that "Full Spectrum Dominance" became the justification and doctrinal base for the massive structural overkill of U.S. war-culture in the post-9/11 era?

Sovereign masculinity plays out not only in the lives of individual soldiers and boys/men, but simultaneously this cultural violence interacts in a justificatory operation to promote and mask the outlandish forms of structural violence in U.S. war-culture examined in the last chapter.

Honest examination of the cases of William James, Chris Kyle, and others, reveals that sovereign masculinity, combined with their experiences in the world of war, deforms the capacity for meaningful lives. The world "turned upside down," (the way I have described the world of war), has taken hold of their very beings at such a deep level, they now find it impossible to thrive anywhere else. Kevin Powers, the novelist/poet/veteran of the Iraq War, captures the deep pain of this reality with his poem, "Separation." A twenty-four-year-old "boy" who has returned from deployment in the Iraq war weeps with rage and despair as he sits in a bar back in his hometown, and contrasts his inner world with that of other boys, "Young Republicans in pink-popped shirts" who sit at the opposite end of the bar. "I want to rub their clean bodies in blood," he imagines. He's been home for three years, but still finds it impossible to be without his rifle, and remembers another day at another bar, his first day home, when he got drunk and wept and begged for people at the bar to return his rifle to him.

> "How will I return
> fire?" I cried. I truly cried.
> But no one could give it back
> because it was gone and I felt
> so old: twenty-four and crying
> for my rifle and the boys
> at the end of the bar
> were laughing.[35]

Sovereign masculinity robs boys and men of the capacity to live as full and complex human beings. The delusion of control and threat of shame, the use of rage-filled violent means, experience of extinguishing the life of others, and the rejection of vulnerability, permeability, emotional ambiguity and open-ended critical thought, are diminishing to full personhood. And as Mann warns, such is not only the case of cultural violence with respect to individuals in the United States, these frameworks and practices also seep into vast collective imaginaries, both religious and national. Dominating masculinity integrally is related to the use of "legitimate" violence required of servicemembers. It is a "… rich cultural seam permeating all aspects and relations within militaries with military masculinities."[36]

2. Making men (and women?) expendable

Many of the characteristics of sovereign masculinity parallel those from another important study, *Unmaking War, Remaking Men.*[37] Feminist sociologist Kathleen Barry investigates "expendability" in the process of *core masculinity*. Her work further expands understanding of cultural violence at the base of moral injury. For if girls and women are taught from a very early age to know themselves as sexual objects, boys' and men's gendered acculturation in society is shaped by way of being taught that their life is expendable. She writes,

> ... *expendable lives* refers to the class of human beings who are identified by their male gender, are socialized and then trained to know themselves – years before a gun is pointed at them or their truck triggers a roadside bomb – as those who can be sacrificed in war[38] (italics mine).

Barry calls this *core masculinity* because cultural violence precedes all other ways of being formed as a man, and also because this cultural pedagogy transverses culture, ethnicities, race, and class – and I would also emphasize, chronology and religion. It is found in ancient as well as contemporary formats, and both "high" and "popular" forms of culture. *Dulce et decorum est, pro patria mori,* wrote the Roman poet, Horace: *it is sweet and proper to die for one's fatherland.*[39] Compare this ancient message to the popular bumper sticker, "Freedom isn't free!" The idea of expendability as a necessity for the survival of the nation-state, and the way religion is commoditized for this same process, will be examined further on in this chapter.

To drive through the state where I live, Pennsylvania, especially through its many small towns in the rust belt, is to experience this public pedagogy first-hand. Expanses of road through farmland and wooded areas regularly give way to two-lane roads marked by signs to slow down as you enter small historic towns (many of these date back to the 18th century). Lined with homes and small-town squares, one also sees signs of former industries from the eras of mining and steel. Almost inevitably, the streetlights or utility poles will be decorated with mounted placards featuring photos of young men from the wars of the 20th and 21st centuries, in their military uniforms, and with their names, military ranks, and dates of birth and death. These lampposts, statues and other commemorations of wars are ubiquitous in Pennsylvania small town parks and squares. As a researcher of war-culture, such landmarks stand out to me, and I wonder, what it is like to come into contact with them as a regular part of one's daily life?[40] In 2017 the website *CareerCast* rated "enlisted military personnel" as the most stressful job in the United States. Its median salary was just under $28,000. Among the 11 factors that were rated as most stressful in this employment, were the following: "physical demands, environmental conditions, hazards encountered, competition, risk of death or grievous injury, immediate risk of another's life."[41] But do the young men who see the "Hometown Heroes" banners every day have any awareness of this? Indeed, this is a rite of passage to manhood, however distorted.

Barry also has wondered what it is like for boys to grow up with this acculturation. She writes,

> I want to know what happens to you as you learn to conform to the death wish of masculinity. As you watch the photos and IDs of men killed in combat rolling down your television screens on the evening news, how do you internalize the awareness that you could die in a few years in combat somewhere?[42]

Like Bonnie Mann, Barry identifies *shame* as a key component in the shaping of *core masculinity*. To experience fear is shameful and must be rejected; thus, fear is addressed by "papering it over" with violence, and managed through distancing. Simultaneously, the knowledge of one's own expendability goes hand in hand with contempt for women; the worst shame is to be identified as female. Yet women themselves frequently are the strongest reinforcers of these very dynamics. Most important, Barry emphasizes the following: "… neither male expendability for war nor female vulnerability to male violence arises independently of each other."

Does this explain, in the extreme context of male military expendability, why women who are servicemembers find themselves at such high risk of violence from men in their supposed "fraternity"? In 2017 the "Service Women's Action Network," (SWAN) reported that sexual violence, *not* deployment, is the greatest factor undermining mental well-being for women in the U.S. military branches. SWAN's research director explained that 61% of service women have been diagnosed with depression, and 41% with PTSD; but "…what is most distressing is that 49% attribute their poor mental wellness not to combat deployments but to the bias, harassment and sometimes assault that they received at the hands of fellow servicemembers."[43]

Barry emphasizes that this is *learned*, not "essential;" *core masculinity* must be reinforced and performed, over and over. It is powerful not because it is universal or rooted in biology, but because "states and movements require men's lives for combat." Barry writes, "The devaluation of their lives is shown to them as heroic, manly sacrifice." She writes,

> *Core masculinity* seals anger and aggression away in the unconscious where it becomes the source of the rage that the military will tap to prepare you for combat. It is the same expendability that feeds into the expectation that you exist to protect others, women and children especially, which often turns to violence against women. Here is the unconscious source of men's emotional disconnect and suppression of their own feelings.[44]

Basic Training exhibits the development of *core masculinity* in concentrated form. And remember, this is but one of many institutions to examine with respect to Galtung's triangle of violence, to see at close range how cultural violence reverberates mutually with structural violence, and erupts in events of direct violence. In addition to the internal structures of Basic Training, many institutions exhibit vulnerability to this reverberation, such as Junior ROTC, public education mandating information sharing about high school students with military recruiters, popular militaristic entertainment aimed especially at young men, and recruiting practices such as we already have examined. We also might examine the interplay of formation between what takes place in the institutions above, and the role of families, especially those steeped in strong military values and cultures.

Basic Training involves the stripping away of previous civilian identities, combined with exposure to extreme physical and mental stress. Sleep deprivation and hyper-physical exertion are combined with the bombardment of humiliation, as Barry describes, "your identity is reduced and degraded." Identity is reshaped in the service of becoming one with your unit, and shaming mechanisms play a central role:

> That is how you become a unit, one in your degradation. You fear being belittled, ridiculed, humiliated if you do not hold up your part ... In effect, your empathy and connection to shared human consciousness are being reconfigured to serve military needs – to make remorseless killers.[45]

Some readers might think Barry has gone too far with her conclusions at the end of the quote above, but this sociologist claims that in Basic Training the use of degradation and shame is purposeful. These practices are designed to build resilience, but more important, they overcome recruits' basic human resistance to killing.[46] As the process builds relationships between the recruits, emphasizing the fact of their deep need to rely on one another, simultaneously it creates suspicion of those outside the group: "friendships form in context of fear and intimidation; you feel different from all others 'on the outside.'"[47]

Researcher Patricia H. Hynes echoes this analysis of so-called "friendship," but goes further to explain how violence and misogyny are central:

> ... hostility toward women pervades military training – often out of deep antipathy for the presence of women in traditionally male space, sometimes stemming from competition, always linking manliness with sexual dominance ... it functions like a glue to solidify male bonding over women's status as sex objects.[48]

Hynes describes the environment of the military for women in this era as one of *sexual terrorism*. Some researchers claim that war also contributes to male sexual violence in civil society: during the WWII era, the rates of rape in the United States increased by 27%, but other forms of violence, such as murder and manslaughter, declined.[49] Acculturation to sovereign or core masculinity achieves two important goals: first, it forms powerful bonds between servicemembers that will be of utmost importance in the actual waging of the violence of war; and second, through this process, violence itself is lubricated and normalized.

Barry also analyzes the powerful reflexive conditioning exercises now commonly used in Basic Training; this development followed upon the discovery that only 25% of soldiers actually fired their guns while in battle during the WWII era.[50] Reflexive conditioning is intended "... to bypass their thinking and their own moral code. It is the same method that Pavlov used to train that dog," Barry writes.[51] But one wonders what else is bypassed when these cognitive and moral shifts are drilled into people. Think about the young recruit who was compelled through an advanced simulation to practice, over and over again, purposely running over a child with her military vehicle, in order to protect the convoy.

Galtung emphasizes that one of the deep cultural wells of violence is the "self/other gradient." To the degree that human beings ossify differences between ourselves and whomever we identify as "other," we become increasingly disposed toward violence. Yet practices of domination and dehumanization of the other (whether based on gender, sexual orientation, race or ethnicity, or other characteristics) are necessary to overriding basic human tendencies not to kill our own species. In the post-9/11 period this dynamic of cultural violence ignited and spread not only outside the nation, but within it as well. However, such values embedded in Basic Training are needed for the work that will have to be done. Soldiers need to act quickly and without hesitation, and more complex and empathetic assessments and questions about "the enemy" and themselves are discouraged. There isn't time or mental space for this kind of ambiguity. Nevertheless, these cultural formations raise questions about their long-term impact on human persons.

Contradictions in gender and masculinity acculturation in the military reveal fields of incongruity, especially with regard to orientating human beings to the task of taking life. For this formation involves *both* crass military cadences *and* the glorification of killing as "the necessary sacrifice" one must make in order to protect the unit and country. Barry quotes from an Iraq Veteran Against the War,

> I callously screamed out brutal chants about slaughtering kids in schoolyards and laughing about the way napalm would stick to their skin. We must've screamed 'Kill!' hundreds and hundreds of times to get into our heads that this was our purpose as soldiers.[52]

More confusing still, the combination of crass cadences and sacralized interpretations of killing are mystified through further layers of culturally produced violence that links everyday civilian life with the fields of war. From 2008 to 2010, in a popular Philadelphia mall, next to an indoor skate park, the Army operated "The Army Experience Center." At one point I went to visit this place and had a lengthy conversation with its commanding officer about its purpose and his own work of recruiting. Dressed in khakis and polo shirts so as to appear more civilian, military recruiters encouraged young people who visited the center to "play" in sophisticated military simulations and their faux (through frighteningly specific and accurate) weapons and vehicles. Photos of the spectacle showed boys in tee shirts and shorts in military Humvees with their arms wrapped around weapons on military simulation stages, huge smiles on their faces. The lifelike simulations took advantage of the popularity of wargaming among youth with this stimulating virtual environment. Boys could walk over with their skateboards and in just a few minutes be fully immersed in a virtual firefight taking place in the dense urban environment of an Iraqi village. From the simulation they then were guided to kiosks for further internet surfing, this time through slick digital advertising focused on matching them with Army career opportunities. The Center also had small conference rooms where those who expressed interest could be further encouraged into enlistment.[53]

These recruiting practices were developed during some of the toughest recruitment years of the wars in the early post-9/11 period, when it was estimated that soldiers like the military officer I spoke with had to reach out and interact with about 150 people to successfully recruit one new soldier. But in addition, this cultural violence, masking and mystifying the violence of militarization and war, and mobilized with young people to solidify a certain brand image, also reverberated with other sedimentary institutional layers of structural violence in the U.S. economy: The Army contracted with Ignited Corporation, a marketing company, and the makers of *Halo*, a popular video game at the time, to create the center, at a cost of $12 million, paid for through tax dollars. Cultural violence seeps upward, like water rising through the different layers of sediment, through structure, bursting into direct violence. Additionally, and simultaneously, all three prongs of the violence triangle bounce off and mutually increase each vector's influence. Embedded in structure and culture, violence takes root in the deep recesses of human life, preparing the ground from which moral injury will grow.

3. Military base masculinities

Lastly, I turn to a third researcher, David Vine to investigate cultural violence in "militarized masculinity." Vine shines light on the structural sexual violence that is ubiquitous on U.S. military bases.[54] "Camptown-style prostitution," "sexually objectifying entertainment" (think Playboy bunnies and Dallas Cowboy Cheerleaders) and "pervasive pornography" characterize the culture of these places, and double-messaging from commanders is the rule of the game. Official communication stresses "responsible drinking" and staying away from "juicy girls" while, simultaneously, sexual violence on the bases is excused through a "boys will be boys" attitude. Vine describes the cultural and structural violence that shapes these military bases as "highly *unnatural* ... [it is] created by human decisions made over time (mostly by male military government officials) ... in which women's visible presence is overwhelmingly reduced to one role: sex": He writes,

> Institutionalized military prostitution draws on existing gender norms – cultural ideas about what it means to be a man and a woman – but it also intensifies these norms. It trains men to believe that using the

sexual services of women is part of what it means to be a soldier and part of what it means to be a man.[55]

Vine focuses on the internal operations of this cultural violence. Training in how to kill goes hand in hand with the acculturation of dehumanization that makes this possible. As we saw in Chapter 2, military ethicists Shannon French and Anthony Jack agreed that it is very difficult to actualize training to take the life of others without *some* form of dehumanization, though they hope the internalization of dehumanization will be temporary.[56] But internalizing dehumanization additionally leads to the cementing of misogyny, as Vine writes, "One of the central forms of dehumanization promoted by military training and the culture of daily life in the military has been the supposed inferiority of women."[57] In addition, cultural violence associated with gender differentiation joins with reinforcement of other negative stereotypes related to race and ethnicity, especially on many international U.S. bases.

In 2015 there were approximately 52,000 U.S. military living and working at the bases located on the island of Okinawa, Japan. Just eight days before President Obama flew to Hiroshima, a historic first-ever visit of an U.S. president to a site of atomic bombing, a 20-year old woman from the Urama Prefecture of Okinawa was raped and murdered. Soon after, a contractor working for the U.S. military was arrested and charged with the crime. Sixty-five thousand Okinawan Japanese came together in a demonstration protesting the U.S. military bases and the sexual violence of U.S. servicemembers and contractors. They stood together in silent solidarity, choosing not to shout, "worrying that if we raised our voices, those voices might erase the sadness of other people." Suzuko Takazato, head of the Rape Emergency Intervention Counseling Center Okinawa, described the scene:

> We held in front of us images of butterflies said to represent the souls of those who have died in Okinawa, and held up signs in English and Japanese reading "Withdraw all U.S. Forces from Okinawa."[58]

In her work of advocacy with the victims of sexual violence, Takazato came to the realization of a strong connection between this sexual violence and "the true nature of the armed forces." She summed it up, "If you don't have the perception of discriminating against others and making them comply with your will by force, then you can't make it as a soldier." Meanwhile, the Okinawa Prefectural Government reported that between the years of 1972 and 2015, 5,896 crimes took place perpetrated by U.S. military personnel, including 129 alleged rapes.

However, even in the #MeToo era, this cultural and structural violence continues. Without more women in key leadership positions, without "fully investigating and clearly identifying the command failings which may have contributed to the under-detection of these sexual assault crimes;" and without "requirements that commanders uphold those rules or face dismissal," significant change is unlikely. In addition, resources for victim/survivors, including heathcare, legal resources, and confidentiality, need further development.[59]

The *Truthout* reporting series on military sexual violence squarely raised the unanswered questions:

What is it about military culture that results in such extreme sexual crime? Why is sexual assault so traumatizing for women soldiers? What are the responses of the Department of Defense and the Veterans Administration to the epidemic of sexual crime in their midst, with its multiple health consequences? And what are the radical changes necessary to reform a recalcitrant military?

During the post-9/11 wars, *one of every three* women servicemembers was the target of sexual assault by other members of the military, the series reports. Women face "a pervasive, normative culture of deep-rooted misogyny – with women treated as sexual prey rather than as adult soldiers – in military training and service." During the years of U.S. occupation of Iraq, at "Camp Victory," some women soldiers died as a result of dehydration in their barracks. Despite 120 degree weather, "they stopped drinking water because they feared being raped by other GIs while using the unlit latrines at night."[60]

The sacred canopy over U.S. war-culture: links between military masculinities, and religious and nationalist forms of cultural violence

Thus far, this chapter illuminates a deep and painful contradiction, in that military cultures proclaim to be based on longstanding values that guide everyday interactions and practices, such as the core Army values, "loyalty, duty, respect, selfless service, honor, integrity, and personal courage." But these values collide with actual practices of military structures, acculturation, and required standards and formation of military masculinity. Examining cultural violence increases awareness of a world of contradictions in social systems, cultural norms and everyday values and practices that people tend to take for granted.[61]

But there are additional contradictions to investigate as well. In addition to colliding military masculinities, a second area regards religion, and the sacred canopy over U.S. war-culture. Barry's unpacking of "expendability" provides a place to begin. The cultural norm of expendability is inculcated before all others, she claims, as "pre-reflection" conveyed to boys and men, preceding all other elements of acculturated masculinities. Expendability is based on the understanding that one lives in order to sacrifice one's life for others, especially in the context of war, though we find it also in other vocations, such as policing and firefighting. It seems odd and contradictory that messages of expendability would go hand in hand with the "shame to power conversion" at the heart of sovereign masculinity, but deeper analysis shows how these different thrusts of cultural violence interact and reinforce one another. Barry's analysis of expendability in *core masculinity* gains further traction when examined through the lens of religion, especially Christianity as it is popularly understood in the U.S.

I began researching "U.S. sacrificial war-culture" soon after the events of 9/11. My background as a feminist theological ethicist sensitized me to notice distinct changes taking place in the culture of the United States, and eventually I wrote a book to unravel what seemed a mystery at the heart of its cultural contradictions, *U.S. War-culture, Sacrifice and Salvation.* I took up questions regarding the strength and seeming inviolability of the frame of "expendability" in *core masculinity* and, indeed, in U.S. and other sovereign forms of nationalism, especially investigating the religious roots of this cultural violence.[62] How is it that people are encouraged to see their lives as expendable? How and why have we developed the idea that we demonstrate what we most value by dying for it? Why is our understanding of what it means to be a citizen so consolidated as willingness to die for the nation-state? And how have such concepts "bled" into the sanctification and mystification of U.S. militarism and ways of war?

The months and years following 9/11 were a fraught and emotional time in the country, full of grief, confusion and fear, and the nation rallied, for a brief time, around the idea of unity through shared suffering; but very quickly, hearts and minds turned to the framework of war, and the "necessity" of violent response. Chants of "USA! USA!" became common at sporting events. National leaders issued threats of violence toward the perpetrators. And behind the scenes, the government drew on projects that had been developed many years before in the security and surveillance apparatuses of the nation, involving disturbing plans that soon would be implemented for practices such as "extraordinary rendition" of suspects, "enhanced interrogation," and "black sites."[63]

Simultaneously, in this early post-9/11 period of the U.S., language of "the necessary sacrifice of war" surged everywhere in politics, popular and military cultures, glorifying the practices of war as the ultimate form of citizenship, the most prized way of belonging to the nation. The same language effortlessly drew from Christian images and frameworks of salvation. This (civil) religious nationalism relied on a "sacred canopy" to justify ideology of "the necessity of war-as-sacrifice." Throughout the nation this cognitive pattern about the meaning of nationalism became commonplace – expressed both fairly crudely through popular social media messages, and also in the language of high culture traceable as far back as the Roman Empire, such as we already have seen in the poetry of Horace: *Dulce et decorum est pro patria mori* – it is sweet and honorable to die for one's fatherland.[64]

Of course, none of this was new either to the U.S. or other nations; no, this vector of nationalism has a long and deep history; but it sprang into bold life as citizens and leaders struggled to respond to the tumultuous events of 9/11. Social media versions of this message/framework of war easily intermixed with (civil) religious references to Christian understandings: "Remember that only two forces ever agreed to die for you, Jesus Christ and the American soldier. One died for your sins, the other for your freedom. Pass it on!" Today the message is printed on coffee mugs and tee-shirts, and marketed and sold.[65] But it also is heralded in politics and military culture; preached expansively in Christian churches, especially at times such as Veterans' Day; made a required ritual observance in countless educational settings; and featured in widely read Christian periodicals. The below selection from one church-related periodical, *The Gospel Herald,* clearly demonstrates this logic:

> For believers, Veteran's Day should serve as a reminder of the ultimate sacrifice that was paid on our behalf – that Jesus Christ, the Son of God, willingly bore our sins on the cross at Calvary so that we might be reconciled to Him, offering free forgiveness and new life to all of those who call on His name.
>
> John 3:16–17 says: "For God so loved the world, that He gave His only Son, that whoever believes in Him should not perish but have eternal life. For God did not send His Son into the world to condemn the world, but in order that the world might be saved through Him."
>
> This Veteran's Day take a moment to thank the veteran – and continue to pray for those in active duty and the families of those who

have sacrificed so much for our freedom. More importantly, remind the younger generation of their duty towards their country, and inspire them to uphold the tradition of liberty and justice for all.[66]

A distinct pattern of sacrificial logic joins a certain kind of thinking about Christian *soteriology* (the study of salvation) with a mystification of the costs and consequences of war.[67] Language about "the ultimate sacrifice" is drawn upon *equally* to speak of the death and injury of military servicemembers, *and* to describe the saving work of Christ on the cross. In both cases, the framework of "the ultimate sacrifice" provides justification while also hiding the costs of violence. Christianity becomes a handmaiden to war, and is utilized to sacralize war.

Not only in popular, religious and military cultures, diverse public sites in U.S. politics also are rife with the same version of sacralized nationalist logic, and it silences dissent, blesses war-making, and shuts down critical thought. And, as the final part of this chapter will explore, examination of this cultural violence *also* confronts citizens with sharp questions about the direct violence seen in the phenomenon of military moral injury. Cultural violence at the seabed of both military masculinities *and* U.S. nationalism, shapes the deep sedimentary layer of violence in U.S. nationalism. And true to the nature of cultural violence, though standards of masculinity and nationalism are indelibly tied to popular forms of Christianity in the United States, this remains mostly invisible in citizens' critical awareness. The interplay of this cultural violence is widely legitimated; throughout the post 9/11 period I have traced the use of this language and framework in every presidential administration, both Democratic and Republican.[68]

Contemporary martyrdom narratives drawing on these cultural tropes in the post-9/11 era of war-culture of the United States were colonized and capitalized upon in political campaigns, by government leaders, military spokespeople, through citizens' and veterans' organizations, and in vast reams of popular culture. This cultural production promoted disciplined framing that influenced *both* popular perspectives *and* high-level decision-making about militarism and war. Sacrificial linguistic patterns transcendentalized the violence of war, while simultaneously *dis*couraging consciousness and clear-eyed ethical deliberation about the true costs of war. In other words, this is language that makes war a sacred enterprise. By "transcendentalize," I mean that the very concept of "war" in common thinking is affected.[69] War is a human institution and construction; but this cultural violence changes the hold "war" has on the collective subconscious, such that "war" moves into a position of "ultimacy." Understanding what it means to be a citizen similarly changes, such that one's tie to the nation also is framed as ultimate. And if sacred, it cannot be questioned or challenged; critical analysis is viewed as a threat.

One of many examples of this cultural violence, the sacred canopy of "the necessity of war-as-sacrifice," involved the ill-fated campaign of Hillary Clinton to become the first-ever female president of the United States.[70] In what follows, I trace the relational pinging back and forth of all three elements of the triangle of violence, and the interactions of this violence with the mystifying and contradicting mores of masculinity, religious values and norms. Lastly, I highlight the impact of all these elements of cultural violence, on dominant forms of U.S. nationalism.

At a critical moment on the final night of the Democratic National Convention in July, 2016, a carefully planned spectacle was televised to the nation, beginning with a sophisticated short film featuring Hillary Clinton speaking to the convention (and everyone watching the convention at home).[71] "If you want to see the best of America," she proclaimed in the film, "you need look no further than Army Captain Humayun Khan." Against a backdrop of American flags and somber music, the camera zeroed in on Clinton's face as she detailed Kahn's immigration with his family to the U.S. as a small child, his stellar educational credentials, and his enlistment in the U.S. Army. Then she launched into the narrative of his martyrdom.

Approaching a "suspicious vehicle" that drew near to the gates of the U.S. army base in Iraq where he was stationed, he was killed when the vehicle exploded. Clinton's speech emphasized characteristics of altruistic self-sacrifice in the actions leading to his death. He told the members of his unit to step back as he approached the vehicle. "Captain Khan was killed, but his unit was saved by his courageous act." At this point in the short film, the shot toggled between Clinton, speaking on the stage, and flashes of audience members, who openly wept as they listened. She continued, listing the medals Khan was awarded posthumously. Meanwhile, the video shifted to a backdrop of a flag-draped coffin carried by horse and carriage in a U.S. military cemetery, while Clinton stressed Khan's youth; he was only 27 when he died.

As patriotic background music built to a climax in the film, Clinton continued her speech by quoting Humayun Khan's father, who in an interview proclaimed that his son's "last ten steps" toward the suspicious vehicle were motivated by "all the values of this country" that he had absorbed in his life here. The film now centered on the figure of Khizr Khan, the father, holding a triangle-shaped folded American flag, standing prayerfully before a shrine to his son in his home, with photos of the handsome young man in his military uniform, military certificates and medals of commendation. "Those ten steps told us that we did not make a mistake in moving to this country," he said as the film concluded. As the convention stage's big screen turned black, both parents of the young man who was killed emerged onto the stage and walked to the convention podium, to a long and emotional standing ovation by the crowd.

Finally, the applause dying down, Mr. Khan began a short speech to the convention crowd, stressing a dual identity: he is *both* an American Muslim who immigrated to the U.S., *and* the father of a son sacrificed for the nation. "We are blessed to raise our three sons in a nation where they were free to be themselves and follow their dreams. Our son, Humayun, had dreams too, of being a military lawyer, but he put those dreams aside the day he sacrificed his life to save the lives of his fellow soldiers ..." Now Mr. Khan contrasted Hillary Clinton's character with Donald Trump's, clearly the main point of his speech. Emphasizing the theme of sacrifice again in a direct accusation to Donald Trump, he asked, "Have you ever been to Arlington cemetery? Go look at the graves of brave patriots who died defending the United States of America. You will see all faiths, genders and ethnicities. You have sacrificed nothing, and no one."

The video and live speech were among the moments that elicited the strongest emotional response of the entire convention, if we are to judge from the faces, voices and applause from the audience. But this sacrificial momentum did not end at the convention. Later, when Mr. Trump, the Republican presidential candidate, was interviewed by *ABC News* and asked about Mr. Khan's speech, he focused on Mrs. Khan's silent presence beside her husband. Speaking in a way that was offensive to many citizens, Trump wondered aloud about whether Mrs. Khan had been prohibited from saying anything because of her religious and gender identities: "She probably, maybe she wasn't allowed to have anything to say, you tell me."[72] A furious response ensued. In particular, "Gold Star Families" of the U.S. took up the banner by writing a public letter to Mr. Trump. Understanding the role of the Gold Star Families in the United States sheds light not only this specific moment, but a much longer enduring relationship between sacrificial discourse such as in this example, the role of martyrdom, and the connection to U.S. war-culture both present and past.

In 1936, the U.S. Congress passed a resolution to create a yearly "Gold Star Mother's Day," launching the beginning of this organization. To honor and remember "the sacrifice" borne by mothers whose sons died in "The Great World Wars," the last Sunday of September every year was set aside for a national remembrance.[73] Americans were encouraged to display the flag in civil and religious settings, and organize meetings to engage in "public expression of the love, sorrow and reverence of the people of the United States for the American Gold Star Mothers." Today programs such as the "Luminary Initiative" continue the tradition by encouraging thousands of luminaries to be lighted on the last Sunday of September. On the Marine Corp webpage detailing this commemorative activity, John 15:13 holds center stage and provides the sacrificial logic: "Greater love has no one than this; to lay down one's life for one's friends."[74] Meanwhile, efforts are in place to create Gold Star Family memorials in every state. One such recently constructed memorial in Valley Forge, Pennsylvania, spells out the central message: "Gold Star Families: A Tribute to Those Who Sacrificed a Loved One for Our Freedom." On the rear side of the memorial, four scenes are depicted: "Homeland, Family, Patriot, Sacrifice" (see Figures 10, 11).[75]

Clearly, by raising questions about Mrs. Khan's silence at the Democratic Convention, Mr. Trump was treading upon a national sense of identity that is sacred to many Americans. As the Gold Star Families' public letter excoriated Trump:

> Your recent comments regarding the Khan family were repugnant, and personally offensive to us. When you question a mother's pain, by implying that her religion, not her grief, kept her from addressing an arena of people, you are attacking us. When you say that your job building buildings is akin to our sacrifice, you are attacking our sacrifice. You are not just attacking us, you are cheapening the sacrifice made by those we lost.[76]

Gold Star Families' grief must be honored and respected; simultaneously these events beg a deeper analysis. Though (civil) religious sacrificial understandings, like that of the Gold Star Families, mostly are driven by popular Christian understandings, the Khan's Muslim identity now was embraced and consolidated within the Gold Star Families through a parallel and unquestioned sacrificial logic. In earlier eras of U.S. history, participation in "the sacrifices of war" also opened the door to national inclusion for other minority groups held in suspicion or considered "inferior" in dominant nationalist ideologies. The popular film *Glory*, about the Civil War all-Black volunteer military company, narrated just this framework, an ideology of cultural violence that celebrated, while also mandating African Americans' sacrificial death for the nation as the cost for the claim to full citizenship. In addition, similar logic was applied in the World War II era to

Figure 10 "Memorial Monuments." *Hershel Woody Williams Medal of Honor Foundation.*
http://hwwmohf.org/monument-projects.html (accessed January 8, 2021).

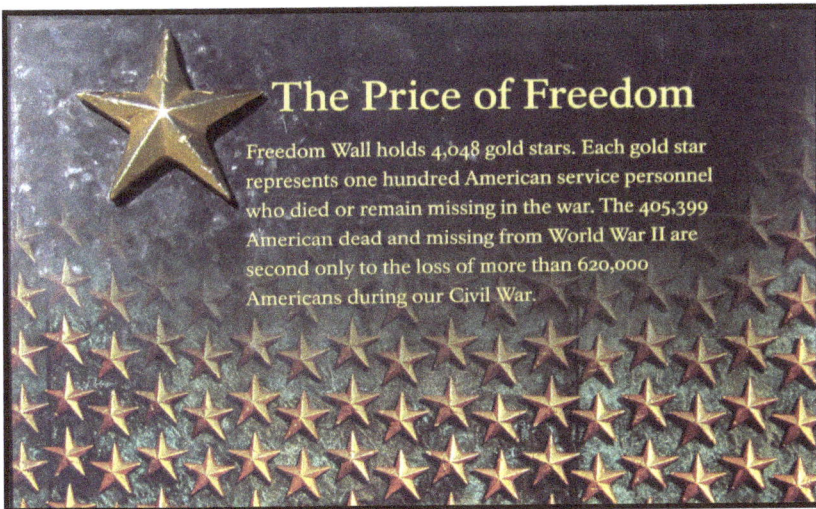

Figure 11 "The Price of Freedom," "*World War II Memorial*," *Wikipedia.* By Billy Hathorn – own
work, CC BY-SA 3. https://en.wikipedia.org/wiki/World_War_II_Memorial (accessed January 10,
2021).

Japanese American troops who fought and died for the same reason, even while their family members were interred in concentration camps by national authorities.[77]

According to this way of thinking, one proves or earns one's right to citizenship through willingness to sacrifice life for the nation; but of course, not *all* citizens face such an equally stringent requirement, only those whose right to citizenship is held up for question because of negative stereotypes applied to their minority status. Sacrificial requirements tend not to be equally distributed across society; this precisely is why they should be questioned and critically examined. But sacrificial justification generally is not part of collective conscious thought; like other forms of cultural violence, sacrificial logic discourages critical thinking and reinforces both structural and direct forms of violence.

The ubiquity and longevity of this framing, "the necessity of war-as-sacrifice" should not surprise us, for sociologists such as Catherine Albanese long have noted how the rhetoric of sacrifice *surges* in times of actual or potential war.[78] Emotion-based and familiar, the rhetoric catches people at a deeply subconscious level, and dictates an expected pathway of response. This dynamic was on full display, witnessing the faces of those at the convention. And surely, the tragic loss of the Khan family must be grieved honestly. What is the right way to approach and understand such grief? It would be remiss not to recognize that in the case of this convention, Humayun Khan's terrible death was commoditized for a very specific purpose, to solidify Clinton's candidacy and unify her base. But this insight did not dawn on those listening. Remember, cultural violence runs very deeply in the collective human psyche, and shapes and forms "pre-reflection." The convention spectacle demonstrated the deep tie to an embedded framework of a sacrificial identity (linked both to religion *and* nationalism); emotion naturally was roused, and critical thought diminished.

But if one was to stop and think critically, uncomfortable questions would come to the surface. There might be consideration of the deep contradiction of a presidential candidate who capitalized on the suffering and death of an American family's loss in the very "preventive war" that she voted to enact as a senator. Citizens also might remember the false premises sold to the American people (one memorable example is Secretary of State Colin Powell's defense of the war to the UN) through which national acquiescence, in addition to congressional obedience, was purchased. This might raise further questions about the meaning and purpose of this fine man's death: was it truly "necessary?" Compassion and grief with the Kahns could grow into increased anger regarding dawning awareness of the many unjust and illogical structures of U.S. war-culture that grew so quickly and at such expense during the post-9/11 years. The sedimentary layers of structural violence provided grease for the direct violence of war to appear as inevitable and seemingly "necessary," while in actuality, the steep costs of its direct violence were borne by very few. Cultural violence, the sacred canopy of sacrificial ideology, provided plausible concealment, springing to the surface in widespread justificatory operations. The response of convention participants easily was channeled, linked to a wider national response to 9/11, and the concomitant U.S. reaction of war.

In addition, continuing to think about the nature of the war that took this young man's life, and investigating the interplay of different forms of violence, it should be noted that *both axioms* of conflict transformation noted earlier were absent. Not only unity-of-life, but also unity-of-means-and-ends were nowhere present. Judith Butler's important question, "what is grievable?" might help to assess this loss, and examine cultural modes of addressing grief. For sacrificial narratives like the Democratic Convention pushed certain storylines to the front, while thrusting others completely out of view.[79] The martyrdom of Captain Khan was glorified, but the massive destruction of Iraq, the enormous weight of its people's grief, and loss of infrastructure necessary for their well-being, remained completely out of sight. No unity-of-means-and-ends. There were no tears at the convention for this massive violent assault to life; only some lives were "grievable." No "unity-of-life" here. In the end, a "pathological investigation," along the lines of Galtung's method, clarifies how U.S. citizens continue to be deeply influenced by cultural violence. Citizens' imagination in the post-9/11 era emphasized a linear pathway of thinking, conceiving conflict with a beginning and apocalyptic end, a way of thinking that could only imagine addressing conflict by way of conflagration.

But is it possible to imagine an alternative? What if the deep cultural wells influencing collective thought instead were guided by imaginatively working through the question of the "least violent" ways of dealing with the very real dangers and conflicts citizens face? This would mean refusal of the conflict as "us against them," and doing the opposite, digging into its complexities and illuminating its many vectors. What if the deep cultural wells were such that the requirement to *remember,* and take into account *all affected life*, was paramount?

Such would not be the case. Instead, that very familiar frame encountered so often in both religious and (civil) religious contexts, leapt (and still leaps) to the surface "Honor their sacrifice," so goes the saying. To overlay the destruction of war with a sacrificial canopy is to render war sacred, and to remove it from critical assessment. In this case, the sacred canopy over the ideology of "the necessity of war-as-sacrifice" very successfully buttressed Clinton's credibility as a presidential candidate. She emerged from the convention and that evening triumphant. Even questions that were raised about her as a female candidate (was she capable of performing as a commander in chief?) were suppressed by the clever framing in this performance. For like every other male president before her, she demonstrated loyalty (even more important for her as a woman?) to the required sacrificial nationalist justification for war and war-culture in the United States.

Cultural violence and the Christian Bible

Religious texts provide potent fuel for the sacred energy associated with war. Remember how the centralizing of sacrificial logic in the Marine Corp "Luminary Initiative," harnessed John 15:13: "Greater love has no one than this; to lay down one's life for one's friends." Or we might recall John 3:16–17, the verse drawn upon by *The Gospel Herald* to draw a continuous line between the work of Christ and a particular interpretation of the violence (interpreted as sacrifice) of soldiers (both through killing *and* being killed) in war: "For God so loved the world, that He gave His only Son, that whoever believes in Him should not perish but have eternal life. For God did not send His Son into the world to condemn the world, but in order that the world might be saved through Him."

As the post-9/11 period dawned in the United States, I began to listen more carefully to these religious allusions. Steeped in the literature of Christian *soteriology*, in particular I was influenced by the scholarship of many women writers who raised important criticisms about sacrificial logic in Christian thought and practice, and its impact on women's lives. For instance, Christian theologian Delores Williams came to the realization that the Christian portrayal of Jesus as "the surrogate/substitute who sacrifices himself for human sin," consolidates destructive cultural constraints in the lives of Black women in the United States. For Black women, hearing sermons about mirroring their own lives on this "substitute" only led to reification of their socially required subjugation and sacrifice. Williams traced links between sacrificial theology and three dominant social roles imposed on Black women: "mammy," sacrificing care for her own children in order to provide domestic labor for white families; "sexual surrogate," who was disallowed ownership of her own body, and preyed upon sexually by white men; and "field slave/sharecropper" whose physical labor was demanded as a surrogate for male labor, and expected to match that of any man's. This theologian came to the conclusion that to attach *any* spiritual value to Jesus' death on the cross as a sacrifice/surrogate to be emulated, only encouraged ingrained destructive religio-cultural assumptions that were deeply oppressive and unjust. The meaning of the life of Jesus of Nazareth, she emphasized, was not to *die*, but to promote a vision of a different way of living that did not require *any* sacrificial grist. To ponder Jesus' execution by the Roman empire, was to look upon *sin* in its most degraded form.[80] It was to visualize more clearly the consequences of war-culture: *this is what happens when societies insist on maintaining themselves through the sacrificial practices of violence and war.*

Others also have addressed these concerns, such as biblical scholar Joana Dewey.[81] She investigated the inequity in sacrificial logic that is placed on the backs of the least powerful, and justified and sacralized through use of the Bible. For instance, "taking up one's cross" has become a cognitive metaphor in many cultures. It is shorthand for understanding suffering as a redemptive experience. But Dewey turned to Mark 8:34 to investigate this cultural interpretation of the biblical passage: "Then he called the crowd to him along with his disciples and said: 'Whoever wants to be my disciple must deny themselves and take up their cross and follow me.'" New Testament verses like this have been appropriated culturally to sacralize military service, injury and especially, death, as sacrificial. Taking on the suffering and risk that accompanies war is valorized as the way to redemption; and the biblical passage adds the aura of the sacred. We might remember the common Facebook message: "Remember only two forces ever agreed to die for you: Jesus Christ and the American soldier!" (see Figure 12).

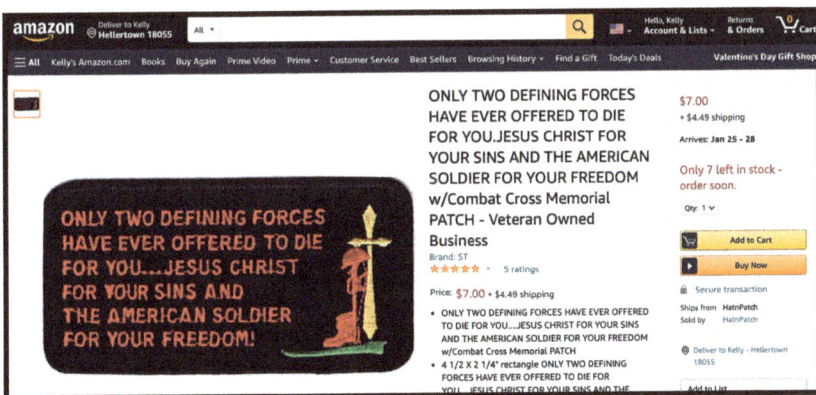

Figure 12 "Only Two Defining Forces." *Amazon.com.* https://www.amazon.com/DEFINING-OFFERED-AMERICAN-SOLDIER-Memorial/dp/B00RWUOV0Q (accessed January 10, 2021).

In contrast, Dewey showed that this interpretation is not consistent with biblical scholarship that explores the significance of "taking up one's cross" in its first century context. "Glorification of victimage" was exactly the opposite of what the gospel writer hoped to emphasize. "Taking up one's cross" signified remaining faithful and committed to the work of discipleship. And how should "discipleship" be understood? According to Dewey, Jesus of Nazareth's vision of discipleship included insistence on *naming* of the violence (not sacralizing it!); and a *nonviolent* means of living and understanding of ultimate reality. But this vision was in conflict with prevailing powers of his society. Jesus' teaching and actions drew inevitable violent response his way, and he was killed.

There is need for increased intellectual labor to highlight the dissonance between historical critical exegesis of sacred texts, and *both* longstanding *and* contemporary popular biblical interpretive framing in the discourse of war. Biblical "reception history" investigates this interplay between biblical interpretation and the role of culture. With regard to our own era, scholar James Crossley wonders, "What should we do about the use of the Bible in contemporary American politics, a significant area of contemporary reception-historical research?" He describes biblical scholars who explore various uses of the Bible in advertising, fashion and popular culture, and interpretive intersection with race, nationalism, and global capitalism; added to his list, I emphasize the need for deconstruction of Bible reception as it intersects with the three points of the triangle of violence in U.S. war-culture. This labor should address today's dominant biblical interpretation with respect to U.S. war-culture, a framing that only may be described as an abuse of text, consolidating a distinct message: "the sacred canopy over the necessity of war-as-sacrifice."[82]

Finally, in addition to the thinkers above, biblical scholar Elisabeth Schüssler-Fiorenza also helps unravel these complexities.[83] Her investigation focused on the cultural landscape of Rome/Palestine, and its 1st century values, socio-religious and political structures and practices. She explored dissonance in conflicting messages from Christian texts of this period, regarding the nature of the vision of Jesus of Nazareth. Along the way she uncovered traces of a distinct vision in early texts that she described as "the discipleship of equals." But this vision conflicted with other threads from early texts that emphasized the values of "kyriarchy," a view of reality based, not on equality, but on hierarchized roles, acquiescence to coercive power, and control through violence. In other words, the dominant culture of the first century was not all that different from our own in the 21st century. There, too, "necessity of sacrifice" prevailed as a cognitive framework, and especially was assigned to those most vulnerable, or to marginalized or other sectors of the population that were perceived as a threat to the existing powers. As Schüssler-Fiorenza uncovered these signposts in early Christian texts, she concluded that it is up to each generation, through the moral energy mustered anew in every age, to determine which interpretive road will be followed.

All these scholars provide a context for this chapter's focus on *contemporary* interpretive Biblical frames, and the commoditization of them to buttress popular understandings of war. With regard to common popular use of the Bible, the dominant tendency today mostly leans toward *reproduction* of oppressive and unjust kyriarchal first-century realities. Use of the Bible provides sacred justification and simultaneous concealment of the ways of war, violence, and war-culture in the United States.

I highlight one additional scholar's work lighting a different pathway that resists this tendency. Liz Theoharis, one of the founders of "The Poor People's Campaign," (this title intentionally is linked with the Poor People's Campaign begun by Martin Luther King, Jr., in the last year of his life), shines light on abusive and intellectually deceitful New Testament interpretations of poverty.[84] She digs into longstanding biblical reception in the United States of Matthew 26.1: "The poor you will always have with you." The passage frequently is interpreted to suggest that poverty is inevitable, and if we are to do anything, it should be within the bounds of individual charity. But Theoharis' biblical exegesis demonstrates that in its original context, the gospel language was intended to highlight destructive structural economics of Roman imperialism, and to promote a vision of equitable security and flourishing for all people. Theoharis' reading reveals that the dominant popular biblical reception of "the poor you will always have with you" in the United States not only is unjust, but even contradicts the biblical message intended in the first century. Justification of poverty cannot be rationalized through rigorous biblical exegesis, and such communication only encourages cultural violence, and a worldview that lubricates both the structural and direct violence of poverty.

Theoharis' work helps illuminate how to assess interpretations of sacred text with regard to war-culture. Similar to her work on poverty. Theoharis' method helps to diagnose and address the cultural violence in New Testament (NT) interpretations that sacralize war, especially the costs of war, as "the ultimate sacrifice" of supposedly "necessary violence" that may not be avoided. In addition, a second insight emerges from Theoharis' work, regarding the importance of deep listening to individuals and communities most directly affected by injustice. The best way to counteract the concealment of structural and cultural violence, mobilized through abusive biblical interpretations, is to prioritize silenced voices. In the case of NT passages about poverty, this involves prioritizing the voices of homeless families, college students, the unemployed, and others whose very lives challenge dominant assumptions and popular biblical interpretations of NT texts. The same could take place with respect to prioritization of voices with first-hand experience of the struggle with moral injury. Prioritization of their voices could increase imagination to develop alternatives to dominant interpretive frames that operationalize sacrificial violence. These voices amplify awareness of "the radical features of the biblical message" too often missing. This process could start with the following question: how did "a nonviolent messiah" become the archetype for the nation's understanding of soldiers waging war?

Three final points bring this section to a conclusion. First, spectacles like the Clinton performance at the Democratic Convention are far from new in the American political-cultural landscape. Barack Obama's presidency, the administration of George W. Bush, and the Trump era all reveal very similar sacrificial tactics. Requisite New Testament verses regularly are inserted into political speech, and interpreted with a familiar sacrificial logic to sway voters and mystify the contradictory realities of war and militarism. These interpretive frames not only elevate U.S. military injury and death to the level of the sacred; they simultaneously conceal as much as they reveal. But this biblical reception could be subjected to deeper critical thought and resisted. Prioritization of silenced voices could face civilians (especially those with Christian commitments) with their own responsibility. These civilians might then refuse to cooperate with cultural violence bolstered through biblical reception that uncritically aligns metaphors of Christian salvation with the work of war. Collective vision might widen the redress of moral injury and emphasize that this reality does not "belong" only to the individual servicemember.

Second, while the rhetoric and cognitive frame of "the necessity of war-as-sacrifice" disciplines all citizens, in the case of Basic Training, and military cultures generally speaking, these frames are drilled with particular intensity. And the most common response to anyone who dares to question the frame of sacrifice, is to shame them. All of Donald Trump's obnoxiousness aside, remember how the Gold Star Mothers shamed him (or anyone) regarding any questioning of the sacrificial frame. I have encountered this disciplining first-hand as I speak publicly, and I wonder if servicemembers experience the same, and in even more concentrated form. Does this specter of shame *heighten* the burden of moral injury, as those who struggle with it find it impossible both to honor grief, *and* at the same time question the sacrificial frame, and the violence it conceals? Clinton's performance showed how the frame of sacrifice places limits on "what is grievable;" this lens minimizes the losses and destruction experienced by people outside of the United States. It channels personal grief into one allowable framework. But not only grief, the frame equally limits critical thought: certain questions – "is it a good idea to describe servicemembers' lives and work as 'sacrificial'?" – are impermissible, never allowed to come to the surface.

As of yet, military moral injury research has not explored how the sacrificial framework of war impacts the development of moral injury. However, moral injury research *does* include insight regarding the consequences of witnessing or participating in the destruction of the other; this witnessing/participating plays a very strong role in the development of this injury (see Chapter 1). This leads to the following question: do cultural frames that sacralize violence, and discourage grief for these "others," along with acculturation in masculinity that is linked to processes of dehumanizing others, exacerbate moral injury?

Moreover, the analysis here applies not only to servicemembers. Cultural violence that is associated with dehumanizing cognitive frames, such as, "the necessary sacrifice of the enemy," also places thick scales over the eyes of U.S. citizens. It creates "moral blinders."[85] Grief for "others" never gets onto the table of awareness because these others never come into view as fully human, only as "those who must be sacrificed." Citizens are shaped to gloss over, or remain blithely oblivious to the unthinkable losses in Iraq, Afghanistan and other nations around the world as a result of the post-9/11 wars. But for many servicemembers, their time in Afghanistan, Iraq, and elsewhere has keenly sensitized them to this inherent contradiction. *These people are every bit as human as I.* What does broad collective lack of awareness among civilians mean for those who are morally distressed as a result of their immersion with these others, in war? And how is this problem figured into any treatment or response offered for their moral wounds?

Finally, third, not only does cultural violence derail critical thought about "what is grievable," it also obstructs critical social analysis about war and the impacts of U.S. war-culture domestically and in the world. Citizens fail in our responsibility to see and take charge of our own reality. This leads to additional loss of vision, for people find their imaginations inhibited regarding *alternatives* to address the real conflicts and dangers that face citizens. War is "transcendentalized," covered with a sacred canopy that protects it from question or analysis, and simultaneously constricts social imagination. But to date, very little moral injury research includes the importance of a wider and deeper social and cultural analysis. Does this in the end also work against more fully understanding and addressing these wounds?

There are voices that speak about a different vision; I think of spiritual leaders such as Thich Nhat Hanh, Claude AnShin Thomas, and more recently, Chaplain Chris Antal, who have pointed to the need for those with moral injury to find ways forward that contribute to human flourishing through speaking unpopular truths about the reality of war. These uncomfortable truths largely will conflict with the "culture Bible" in U.S. war-culture.[86] And they will challenge the social and cultural structures of violence in the nation and illumine their destructiveness.

In the end, cultural violence in the use of New Testament texts is part of a long (civil) religious tradition in the U.S. that misappropriates sacred text to provide *shade* over the violence and costs of war. And all this lies at the base of the ideology of "the necessity of war-as-sacrifice." This cultural violence discourages clarity, and its disciplining force dampens questions about the structures and cultures of violence humans have created. It is the proverbial skeleton within and the seabed beneath the devastation of moral injury. However, increased consciousness leads to resistance; a realization grows that all citizens need to engage unafraid analysis of the U.S. (civil) religious traditions, including the biblical interpretations so central to the cultural violence at the base of U.S. war-culture.

Conclusion: A wider and deeper landscape

One recent investigation that explores psychological treatment for people struggling with military moral injury tells the story of "Mr. Jones," and those who tried to help him.[87] Jones (not his real name), a white male, 41 years old, and a veteran of the Army National Guard, was referred to a Veterans Affairs PTSD clinic after showing signs of emotional stress that led to his being discharged from the service. According to the clinicians' report, his life was rough from the start. Born into a family whose mother died from drug-related addiction early on, his father was not able to handle family responsibility following her death. Jones struggled in school, was learning-disabled, and eventually found his way into the Army National Guard, serving for two decades.

Like so many other members of the National Guard, the events of 9/11 eventually led to his deployment. A part of "Operation Iraqi Freedom," he experienced a series of traumatizing events in Iraq, but none affected him more than when he intentionally ran over a child with his military vehicle.

This action was required to uphold the orders of his convoy. Like the preschool teacher, this was the dreaded possibility he perhaps had trained for with simulation exercises (the case study does not make clear whether this was part of his training or not), but in his case, if he had been trained with such simulations, the nightmare was realized.

At the VA clinic, Jones exhibited signs of discomfort when asked to revisit this memory. His sleeping hours were filled with nightmares about it, and during the day he experienced hallucinations and painful thoughts about the boy, an Iraqi child who did not get out of the middle of the road despite Jones' signaling him, before being smashed with the vehicle. Jones' life demonstrated many of the classic symptoms of moral injury: relational dysfunction, overuse of alcohol, inability to sleep, feeling "on-edge" and alienated. Mostly, he felt shame about what he had done; he could not be forgiven and had lost his sense of self-worth as a human being. The clinicians reported that his anger not only was directed at himself, but also at the commanding officer who ordered him to commit this act, and at the U.S. government as a whole for abandoning him by discharging him.[88]

Thinking through Mr. Jones' moral injury means addressing three layers in this story: the events in Jones' life, the process through which serious and dedicated caregivers at the VA did their best to support him, and the meta-analysis from military scholars who examined this case study to illustrate, from their viewpoint, the complexity of addressing moral injury effectively.

Mr. Jones was not the most compliant subject. He missed appointments at the VA clinic, avoiding them because he found it too difficult to face the emotional distress they elicited.[89] His relational skills were deficient; not only his early family life, but also his life in the military mitigated against deep relational commitment. There were regular changes to his unit following traumatic losses during deployment; this required him to work in an environment without time or resources to build trust with others on whom he would have to depend.[90] Additionally, he experienced the command's decision to discharge and send him home after he began to exhibit disturbing symptoms, as yet another abandonment.

But clinicians discussed various options for treatment with him, and he decided to try a cognitive-behavioral approach. This involved focusing on the impact of the trauma he had experienced, in particular on what his experiences meant for the way Jones made meaning in his life and world. In therapy he was asked to revisit his disturbing memories, write about them, and explore "unhelpful beliefs" that "interfered with his capacity for resilience."[91] One session invited him to participate in an "unfinished business chairing exercise," to have an imaginary discussion with the boy he killed, taking first the boy's perspective, and then his own. Clinicians reported that this exercise unleashed grief, and they hoped this would help Jones to begin to repair his relationships and see what had taken place in a more self-accepting light. In the end, however, they admitted that post-treatment Mr. Jones still exhibited "clinical levels of PTSD/MDD" (Post-Traumatic Stress Disorder/Major Depressive Disorder).[92] His "PMIEs" – "potentially morally injurious events" – could not be fully assuaged through these methods.[93]

The main thrust of Mr. Jones' clinical treatment was to build his resilience, "the capacity to adapt to, cope with, and recover from challenging situations."[94] According to the military analysts of his case, three different types of "adaptive flexibility" are addressed in this therapeutic modality: first, cognitive flexibility helps servicemembers to view difficult situations more positively, or make decisions about when to allow and when to suppress one's emotions. Second, psychological flexibility refers to the capacity to face and endure emotionally challenging events. Third, philosophical/religious flexibility refers to the ability to hold together conflicting moral questions and perspectives.[95]

The military analysts of Jones' case further explain: building resilience in military populations will help them to withstand war's "complex challenges;" "resilient individuals who are exposed to PMIE's will still experience transient stress reactions that are mild and moderate in degree but not significantly disruptive to their functioning."[96]

Not surprisingly, the military analysis of Mr. Jones' suffering and treatment did not include investigation of the role of structural and cultural violence as part of understanding what happened. But there are some telling hints even in this story that reveal structural and cultural layers of violence at work. For instance, these researchers emphasize the "moral environment of deployment." This is a unique environment, one that requires certain "social adaptations" that "are not present in nonmilitary traumas."[97] The analysts continue with a description of military culture,

> … military training explicitly focuses on the formation of tight-knit fighting groups by promoting moral beliefs, identities, emotions and obligations that serve to increase cohesion, thereby promoting the overall combat effectiveness and survival of group members.[98]

But the same necessary "cohesiveness" also "promotes mistrust of others," the researchers admit. Basic Training means entry into "a new culture and community with its own unique values, hierarchy and structure."[99]

Here we begin to see hints and lines of continuity with the investigation of military masculinities that we already have examined. For example, the military analysts make reference to the ways military culture stigmatizes those who seek out mental healthcare providers.[100] Meanwhile, leaders who are focused on completing the mission, formed through this same culture, seem dangerously out of touch with the consequences of their decisions. In Mr. Jones' case, when his unit was attached to another that had experienced many deaths, none of the leaders addressed this "increased psychological stress."[101] Even after the death of the Iraqi boy, no "after-action review" took place, through which some sort of support might have been offered. It sounds as though he mostly was left to deal with what had taken place on his own. In the end, once Jones began to exhibit symptoms of distress, he was blamed for having these issues, by being discharged and sent home, where the possibility for "social support" was even more greatly reduced. Thus, the facts of his case appear to be continuous with a culture that expected "inviolability" and shamed any show of weakness or pain. But further examination of the destructiveness of these military structural and cultural realities remains unexplored in this analysis.

In order to better understand the direct violence of Mr. Jones' moral injury, analyzing the interplay of structural and cultural violence at work reveals a wider landscape of harm. "Civilian society" here is described as having "lax standards of personal responsibility and high expectations of tolerance and cultural and moral diversity."[102] Such language encourages an "us vs them" perspective, even a certain suspicion that one should have toward civilian culture. Perhaps not surprisingly, this analysis makes no mention of the standards of masculinity common in military cultures, their use of degradation and shame, the acculturation of dehumanization, their impacts on women and men, or the questionable nature of acculturation to expendability, though these analysts do admit that being greeted as "heroes" when servicemembers return from deployment may lead to feeling "profoundly misunderstood" for those who are struggling with confusion and guilt.[103] The analysts also recognize that acculturation of suspiciousness toward strangers, widespread in military training, also creates problems after returning home: this may "evolve into stronger attitudes of cynicism, contempt and even hatred of both the enemy and their broader culture and ethnic group."[104] These are hints regarding much deeper springs of violence in military cultures, but they are not taken further.

Military culture is highly praised: "military service members typically have opportunities to cultivate close personal relationships, self-confidence, maturity, strength of character, and a sense of purpose in life."[105] But

precisely along these lines, if these analysts encourage holding together conflicting perspectives as a part of "philosophical/religious flexibility," why is
there not more honesty about the more insidious side of military acculturation that surely played a role in Mr. Jones' injury, much less war-culture as
a whole? For this may be the kind of questioning that Mr. Jones needs the
most, to help him understand his situation and contextualize it. But this analysis does not much poke beyond the tip of the iceberg. The focus remains
limited to Mr. Jones' presenting problem and experience of direct violence/
moral injury as a result of his guilt over the death of the Iraq boy. To do
more, to dig deeper, would be raise questions about the entire enterprise of
military culture required for the mobilizing of the war machine.

Mr. Jones was supposed to develop sufficient "adaptive flexibility" to
endure and even succeed in this environment, and to withstand its horrors.
But is this a goal really worth pursuing? Do its benefits outweigh the terrible costs? Even the first element, "cognitive flexibility," is highly questionable. Mr. Jones should be able to maintain a positive perspective even in
the world-turned-upside down of war, in which nothing, including the most
basic values that have been instilled in a person, no longer can be trusted:
we don't kill children. The development of cognitive flexibility would have
him suppress his emotion in the convoy, and follow orders. Yes, this very
well may have resulted in the safety of his fellow servicemembers, but what
did this requirement do to him? And we have no way of knowing the consequences of this tragedy for the boy's family and community.

In the imaginary discussion with the boy during his treatment, the inci-
dent is described as a "tragic encounter."[106] Here again, the structural and
cultural violence that led to this unthinkable situation is concealed through
a fatalistic attitude. Mr. Jones decidedly is *not* invited to probe further into
the war-culture that gave rise to this war, the massive structural violence
built in the United States that led to him being a part of the convoy that day.
He decidedly is *not* invited to consider the cultural mores that lubricate its
violence. For despite all the military training, reflexive conditioning, acculturation of a particular type of masculinity, and many other aspects of cultural violence in the nation and its military that were absorbed by him, in
the end, Mr. Jones could not wipe away the stain of violating a deep moral
code so fundamental to his very being. He knew that *this should not be.* But
one wonders whether the cognitive behavioral therapy assisted him in understanding and honoring the deep significance of his own moral injury, his
own reflective conscience. For according to the description of this therapeutic mode (cognitive-behavioral treatment), the goal is to explore "a survivor's appraisal of the trauma and 'manufactured emotions' such as shame,

guilt, and anger, which are generated when higher-order cognitive process-es go awry."[107] In other words, the goal is to reduce painful moral struggle by reframing it as "manufactured," the mistaken consequence of "cognitive process gone awry."

This perspective reflects an understanding of violence as instrumental; violence is an objective tool that may be picked up and put down. It may be used to create the goal of peace. Those who wield it may be trained to use it with minimal moral discomfort; and those who can't will be classified as having insufficient "adaptive flexibility."

Galtung would say that this is naive and unrealistic. In contrast, using the triangle of violence to think through this narrative, one has to say that moral injury, far from being manufactured, is the natural consequence of the structural and cultural violence we human beings have constructed. Unlike the treatment modality above, using the violence triangle as a heuristic tool reveals a much wider and deeper landscape of violence in the case of Mr. Jones. His pain reveals a profound truth: this suffering does not belong to him alone, and it was not inevitable.

The next chapter will take up this case study further and compare it with a different approach to addressing moral injury, but even here, we see the beginnings of growing self-awareness in Mr. Jones' anger toward his com-manding officer and toward the U.S. government. He knows that something went very wrong and sorting it all out is immensely difficult. His "maladap-tive coping skills" (alcohol, self-harm and the like) are signposts that he has not had the communal support that would *see* this pain and *investigate* its multifaceted and complex causes. But Mr. Jones is like the proverbial canary in the coal mine. One wonders, if citizens and caregivers had the courage to stay with him in his pain, and together with him explore this violence in all its dimensions, would he be in a different place? Would we?

4 Moral Injury and Atrocity

Beginning reflections

Writing this book has given me pause to reflect on Hannah Arendt's characterization of "the banality of evil."[1] Evil has different guises, but it may be most frightening, pernicious and dangerous, when it operates through modes that have been routinised, domesticated, and normalized. Even more alarming, the very construction of evil's normalizing modes may result from the actions of people who wanted to help, and had good intentions; or equally disturbing, this kind of evil, as Arendt so devastatingly analyzed, is the consequence when human beings fail to *think*.

One case in point involves the ways people in the United States have been acculturated to remember the atomic bombings in Hiroshima and Nagasaki. The documentary film, *White Light, Black Rain,* consists of extended interviews with *hibakusha* (atomic bomb survivors) sixty-two years after the bombings. These individuals mostly were children when the bombs were dropped; now filmed in their 70s and 80s, they speak simply and searingly about the experience of atomic mass horror.[2] Sakue Shimohira was 10 years old in 1945; her mother and brother were killed in their home when the blast came. She survived along with her sister into a post-bomb aftermath that only could be described as other-worldly. Without food, without shelter, the city erased and filled with death, without understanding what had happened to them (U.S. censorship prohibited the Japanese media from publishing any information that would provide explanation), she and her sister struggled to keep going. Now these many years later, facing the camera directly in this documentary, and recounting the meaninglessness, abject suffering and grief of those days, anger rises in her voice as she describes the U.S. doctors who came to Hiroshima to study the radiation effects of the bombings on the bodies of the Japanese, including children. The children were bused to examination centers, undressed and summarily examined, but never given any treatment. Her voice goes flat as she further tells how in that terrible time, her sister lost the will to keep struggling. Eventually she threw herself in front of a train. Shimohira concludes the story by sharing that she would have followed in her sister's footsteps unto death but lacked the courage.

The face, voice and words of a person such as Sakue Shimohira come as a shock to the U.S. American viewer; we're not used to seeing this unadulterated view of the atomic bomb and its real impact on people. To the extent that U.S. citizens consider people "under the mushroom cloud," they may be more familiar with the images of "the Hiroshima maidens," from their middle or high school history textbooks, and from U.S. popular media.³ Arranged through the efforts of Rev. Kiyoshi Tanimoto, himself a *hibakusha*, and *Saturday Review* editor Norman Cousins, 25 young women who had been badly injured in the bombing were chosen to come to the United States in the early 1950s for an extensive visit to undergo plastic surgeries for their scarred disfigurement.

Without question, both Tanimoto and Cousins wished to help alleviate suffering. Rev. Tanimoto had encountered numerous young isolated women who visited his parish in Hiroshima; their scars made them pariahs in Japanese society. Similarly, Cousins believed that the power of love one finds in the best of familial relations could be extended to heal the wounds of war.

But their good intentions too easily melded into a narrative that undermined truthful discourse about the consequences of the atomic bombings, in order to make them more palatable to U.S. American minds. The links between the formation of memory in the United States and Arendt's characterization of evil are apparent to scholar Yuki Miyamoto, who explores how the stories of *hibakusha* were used "to justify violence [and] serve the national narratives in their respective countries."⁴

Even the name, "Hiroshima maidens," suggested a fairytale-like quality to this story that would be marketed and sold in a way that directed attention away from the irredeemable power of these new weapons and their impact. Instead, positive light was cast on the superior methods of plastic surgery in the U.S., and the U.S. American spirit of altruism. As opposed to showing citizens the abject dystopia of the nuclear world the United States had introduced to the planet, the narrative of the Hiroshima maidens stressed U.S. American compassion and scientific superiority: "… the horror of the aftermath [of the bombs] was rendered as 'curable' as a broken relationship, through advanced American medical technology as well as American civilian virtues," writes Miyamoto.⁵ Meanwhile, the two Japanese-American women who had been hired to translate for the maidens, and who had spent the years of the war in U.S. internment camps, received no media coverage in the United States.⁶

As Miyamoto explains further, the banality of evil in this historical example is more than the sublimating of the horror of the atomic bombing. It is more than the omission of all the bomb's real consequences, "the flash, roar, blast, radiation, discrimination, disfigurement, keloids, ..." No, the banality reaches its height in the way these horrors were transfigured through media discourse that utilized cultural imperialism to mask mass destruction. The truth of over 225,000 slaughtered immediately and in the early aftermath of the bombs would be muted by focus on just these 25 young women, in a storyline that reinforced themes of 1950s U.S. American unassailable military might linked with paternalism and innocent benevolence (rendering the actual dropping of the bomb into passive voice, as if a supernatural event). This narrative reinforced supposed U.S. cultural and technological superiority, and altruism for the "less fortunate countries" in the world. Miyamoto describes the cultural context,

> The reconstruction of the American ideal in the 1950s revolved around the image of a white, middle-class, Christian, and heterosexual family based on a patriarchal structure. The US media often portrayed Hiroshima maidens' adoption of American housekeeping and lifestyles as the process of recuperation from their physical and psychological wounds, as if becoming like American women in suburban middle-class families were a process of healing and a goal for them to attain.[7]

Arendt's characterization of "the banality of evil" has at times been misunderstood, as if she was somehow minimizing the depth, destructiveness, and sheer horror of evil by calling it "banal." But this is to mistake her meaning. Evil adopts multiple faces, and human beings participate in myriad actions, both large and small, that encourage others and themselves to domesticate it, making it something lesser, or unavoidable and unfortunate, or again, something for which no one has any responsibility, just part of fate. This is revealed in the representation of the atomic bombings in the story of the Hiroshima maidens, the enormous evil of nuclear weapons rendered banal, as if no one bore any responsibility for these events, and as if the nuclear world was just one more development of human civilization. In this way the urgent need for accountability and reckoning with what the entry of nuclear weapons meant for the world, was deflected.

The narrative thrust in media about the Hiroshima maidens in the United States still plays an important role in the domestication of the use of nuclear weapons. For instance, focus on solely 25 young women neatly eviscerated awareness of the enormous scale of the bombs' destruction. Today the moral blinders of people in the United States motivate emotional distance and unawareness regarding the destructiveness of their country's war-machine, both nuclear and conventional. It is not unusual to hear U.S. Americans blithely compare U.S. losses of 9/11 with the losses of Japan at the end of World War II, as if these were somehow on the same plane of experience. Shortly after the fall of the Trade Towers in New York, I traveled there and viewed the terrible destruction, and the many signs of grief and fear in the city. I also have had the opportunity to travel to Hiroshima and Nagasaki a number of times to spend extended time at their Peace Museums and Peace Parks, as well as the cities at large. These are experiences I wish that every citizen of the United States might have. On first impression, what is striking when visiting the sites in Japan is the overwhelming nature of the numbers of people who were/are affected, and the reach of the destruction. According to the Atomic Heritage Foundation, as many as 166,000 people died from the bombing in Hiroshima before 1945 had ended. In Nagasaki, the numbers reached 80,000.[8] In comparison, there were 2,997 immediate deaths as a result of the terror attacks on September 11, 2001.[9] Bones still are discovered and recovered in the city of Hiroshima, in unexpected places, and names of *hibakusha*, atomic bomb survivors who have died, are still added yearly to the cenotaph in Hiroshima Peace Park, and to the list of names in Nagasaki's National Peace Memorial Hall.

Walking through the city of Hiroshima, frequently I have come across historical markers on the streets, far from the hypocenter, indicating where bodies were discovered, sometimes decades later, during building renovation projects, or other excavations. Visiting the Peace Park in Hiroshima, at the place of the monument dedicated to Korean victims and survivors, the ground height is marked to show the level where people walked before the atomic bombing, and after. The only way to deal with destruction on such a massive scale was just to cover it up and start afresh with new surface about 2–3 feet higher than the old. When I walk through the city of Hiroshima, I am aware that I am stepping on top of the bones of those killed in the bombing. And this is on top of other mass destruction that took place during the last part of WWII, when 67 cities in Japan were incinerated through firebombing, over 100,000 people were killed in one night alone in Tokyo, and 15 million Japanese were left homeless.[10] But allowing the sheer scale of this destruction to sink in is not generally the U.S. American way. If anything, as Robert Lifton described so well, Americans mostly are "numbed" to these realities.[11] And not only the United States, Japan's people have their own struggles to honestly face the truths about their violent aggression, colonialism, racism and virulent nationalism from this era.

This chapter raises questions about "evil" and its connection to moral injury.[12] Why take such a seemingly drastic turn here? The previous chapters of this book emphasize the multiple ways people in the United States, including researchers, cease their thinking and analysis of moral injury after a certain point. While there is much serious and meaningful effort to understand the nature of this trauma, and develop means to ameliorate it, I find too little in moral injury literature suggesting that humans bear responsibility for preventing it in the first place. Some question how military servicemembers can be trained, habituated, shaped in such a way as to withstand it. Military moral injury rising out of the ashes of war seems frequently to be accepted as "a given," an unfortunate reality. Attitudes about moral injury largely are fatalistic if also infused with a desire to help (not unlike attitudes towards the Hiroshima maidens). Not enough research on moral injury moves past analysis of direct violence to explore how structural and cultural processes and systems of violence *also* are deeply imbricated – structural and cultural processes that we human beings have constructed and have the power to rethink and transform.

The beginning seed for this book was planted in my mind about ten years ago, when I attended a gathering of scholars and ethicists who had come together to address urgent issues about conscientious objection to war.[13] The term, "moral injury" was introduced and explored to help interpret the context of veterans' experience of war. Later in the conference, in a small group discussion with ethics researchers, the eminent psychologist Jonathan Shay reflected on the meaning of moral injury. Listening to him, for me, flipped on the proverbial light bulb in my mind. My research on U.S. war-culture had given me new insights about the history, systems, and destructive consequences that war-culture has brought to the U.S. and wider world. But I had never thought about this particular consequence of war – moral injury – in precisely this way. I returned to my hotel room after the day's conference events and found myself writing down impressions on a yellow legal pad. There was a nagging thought in the midst of all this that I needed to pin down and try to articulate. That night it came to me. If people of the United States *began* our thinking and moral deliberation about our ways of war in the United States with this reality, the moral injuries of our servicemembers and veterans, *we would find it impossible to justify what we are doing in the war-culture we have created and continue at all costs to maintain.*

Evil as "atrocity"

The theoretical guidepost I use to explore moral injury as "evil" comes from philosopher Claudia Card, whose book, *The Atrocity Paradigm: A Theory of Evil,* aims at increasing understanding regarding what human beings should do about evils, and how we should respond to them. (p.viii)[14] Card outlines what makes "evil" different from other kinds of harm, and refuses any simplistic assessment of evildoers as "wicked." Her theory provides an important theoretical backdrop that assists moral deliberation about a wide variety of horrific human behaviors, systems and cultural frameworks. With regard to moral injury in particular, Card's theory sets into sharper relief the curious drop off of thinking with respect to moral injury explored in earlier chapters of this book. Her philosophical theory about evil and atrocity makes it more difficult to rest easily with moral injury as a "given" that must be endured, a cost that must be borne, a human reality that some always will bear, a phenomenon that we will always have with us.

In contrast to any fatalistic or unquestioning attitude, Card writes, "We need a theoretical account of what makes wrongdoing serious enough to count as evil or in what ways it is serious. 'Evil' is a heavy judgment." (p.7) Using Card's paradigm of evil as "atrocity," as a theoretical framework, the following questions arise: Does moral injury count as an "atrocity"? If so, why would calling moral injury "an atrocity" provide stronger ethical grist for moral deliberation to comprehend it, and strategize how to deal with it? Will this theory help to better incorporate the roots of structural and cultural violence into an overarching ethical analysis of moral injury? I argue that Card's theoretical distinctions provide a pathway to sift through the many ambiguities and complexities involved in ethical deliberation about moral injury as an "evil," such that in the end, *thought* deepens about the phenomenon of moral injury, leaving us in a better place, as Card hopes, to better know what to do about this evil, and how to transform it.

First, what exactly is "evil"? How is it different from other forms of "harm" or "wrongdoing"? Card's thesis drives straight to the point: "… evils are foreseeable intolerable harms produced by culpable wrongdoing." (p.3) Each of the words here has been meticulously chosen for surgical exactness. First, Card places emphasis on the *intolerable harm* of evil, as opposed to other kinds of harm, and in contrast to primarily focusing on the motivating factors that engender evil.

So first we need to sort through "intolerable harm" and its relationship to "evil." Not all harm reaches the immensity of *evil*. In Card's view, we call harm or wrongdoing "intolerable" – "evil" – when it extinguishes access to "the basics that are necessary to make a life possible and tolerable or decent." (p.16) These "basics" necessary for life include:

- Having one's bare physical needs met: food that is free from contamination; clean water and air; sleep.

- Having one's psychological needs met: Card understands that human physical needs intertwine with psychological and spiritual needs, including the free space to develop positive ties with other humans, opportunities to make choices, and to develop and experience self-worth.
- If the above needs are rooted in freedom *for* life that is "tolerable," the necessary basics for life also imply freedom *from* contexts that create intolerable harm, such as "debilitating fear, ... severe and unremitting pain or humiliation, debilitating and disfiguring diseases, starvation, extreme impotence, and severe enforced isolation." (p.16) Prolonged insecurity, and evisceration of human dignity and self-respect also are basic harms that destroy life. (p.62)

Card's description of "evil" shows remarkable continuity with Johan Galung's central definition of violence: both scholars begin their thinking with an account of basic, necessary life goods and opportunities for a "tolerable life." And both analyze how human forces (whether "evil" or "violent") cut life short or destroy its potential altogether.

Card's understanding of evil as "intolerable harm" segues into Galtung's definition of violence. According to Galtung, violence involves "avoidable insults to basic human needs, and more generally to life, lowering the level of needs satisfaction." Like Card's use of the qualifier, "foreseeable," Galtung focuses on violence that is "avoidable;" humans *could make other choices* to *act* in ways that would prevent such assaults to basic life needs. And Galtung's description of the basic needs that are strangled by violence keenly resembles Card's list, including: "survival, well-being, identity/ meaning, freedom."[15] Though Card and Galtung appear to be unaware of one the other's work, it is striking indeed to see such similarities between "evil" and "violence."

But along with extinguishing the basics necessary for a tolerable life, evil is characterized by additional distinguishing features. Card identifies "evil" as taking place because those who harm are "culpable;" in other words, in addition to "intolerable harm," a second outstanding characteristic of evil as atrocity is that it is *foreseeable. People knew that intolerable harm would take place. Knowing that intolerable harm would happen makes human beings culpable for it.* For Card, evil as atrocity always involves culpability. Galtung, it appears, would agree; violence involves *"avoidable* insults." Evil and violence are different from those circumstances in life in which people are faced only with unjust options, and no matter what they do, someone will be hurt. Card writes, "To be culpable, we ought to have acted differently ...

Nonculpable agents are not evildoers, even when they are used as instruments by others who are culpable." (p.18)

Previous chapters explored how moral injury comes about, not only as a result of direct violence, but also through being rooted and nourished in streams of structural and cultural violence. All this leads to the thesis of this chapter: *Military moral injury* is *an atrocity, a foreseeable intolerable harm produced by culpable wrongdoing.* In what follows, first I explore how previous chapters' analysis of structural and cultural violence in the phenomenon of military moral injury, illuminate moral deliberation. Any passive acceptance or justification of moral injury becomes impossible, in the light of the violence triangle. Moral deliberation must not end with attempts to ameliorate *after the fact* the devastating consequences of moral injury in the lives of servicemembers, veterans and their families; ethical response also must take into account the structural and cultural violence that prepares the ground for this injury.

Moreover, ethical address to prevent moral injury *before the fact*, through attempting to shape a human being who will be impervious to such assault, also will be challenged. *To say that military moral injury is an atrocity is to shine a spotlight on the relations of culpability in the roots of structural and cultural violence.* Card's proposed theory of atrocity assists a more thoroughgoing social analysis of the phenomenon of moral injury. It underscores the importance of examining the seeds of denial and mystification in systems and culture that are responsible for moral injury's eruption into the human world. In addition, her theoretical framework also highlights how and why human beings could act differently, could make other choices. This framework of atrocity counters tendencies to assess war as the regrettable, but only way of dealing with otherwise intolerable harm. Moral injury is a *foreseeable intolerable* harm caused by *culpable* wrongdoing.

Second, the analysis of this chapter is grounded in one additional case study of military moral injury. I explore how Andy's intolerable suffering shifted through his participation in a new Moral Injury Group practice led by chaplain Chris Antal, and clinical psychologist Peter Yeomans in a Philadelphia Veterans Affairs hospital. Their work incorporates a beginning framework of social analysis to better empower Andy, other members of the group, their care providers, and the larger community. I suggest that this Group framework could be strengthened through more rigorous theoretical grounding, and draw upon both Card's theory and Galtung's framework of the triangle of violence to analyze "what happened with Andy," and make suggestions that build upon their social analysis. Finally, I reflect on how and why Andy's experience, and the macro phenomenon of military moral injury as a whole, should be understood as "atrocity," and reflect on the serious implications of making this claim.

Andy's story

A relatively new moral injury practice is taking place at the Corporal Michael Crescenz Veterans Affairs Medical Center in Philadelphia (Crescenz VAMC), in a Moral Injury Group led by a VA chaplain and a VA psychologist. I draw on their work, especially their published study regarding one morally injured veteran, "Andy," who is benefitting from participation with them, other veterans, and listening and supportive members of the wider community.[16] This section builds on the insights from Andy himself, and chaplain Chris Antal and psychologist Peter Yeomans regarding Andy's case, the Group they have developed, and insight emerging through their work regarding the need and role for a social analysis of military moral injury, for people like Andy, their families and care providers, everyday citizens, and people across the world whose lives are affected by U.S. wars.

Antal and Yeomans are unequivocal about the role of community engagement in what they call "adaptive change," in any adequate response to the suffering of people like Andy. In addition to drawing on their important work, the analysis undertaken here includes additional theoretical and moral grist. For juxtaposing Andy's case with Galtung's theoretical framework lays bare the urgency of a deeper collective social analysis of this individual case, and moral injury as a broader phenomenon. Not only do I focus on Andy's (and others' who are morally injured) pathway toward continued healing and self-understanding; in addition, this deliberation enlivens *thought* at large, challenging society to greater conscientization about war-culture and its consequences. Response to moral injury must include honest confrontation with the reality of war-culture; this is at the root of the harm Andy has experienced, and also shapes and impacts all U.S. citizens, and so many others across the world.

A new slew of questions comes to the surface: In what ways is Andy's moral injury "intolerable harm"? And if Andy's moral injury is/was a foreseeable intolerable harm caused by culpable wrongdoing, who then is culpable? How could it have been foreseen? And what kind of reckoning, and recompense is due? What changes to the current world are called for?

Antal and Yeomans claim that analysis and response to military moral injury "lie at the intersection of psychology, spirituality and ethics." (p.6) This parallels the method of this book, to advocate multiple modes of investigation and analysis for increased understanding and development of an ethical framework broad and deep enough to adequately respond to moral injury. But these researchers also stress that U.S. citizens mostly avoid facing what moral injury reveals about our society: "work avoidance mechanisms" are deftly employed in society to disguise, misinterpret and plain detach from the consequences and costs of U.S. ways of war. Three dominating strategies provide ways for citizens and leaders to "disengage" from the devastating consequences of military moral injury in servicemembers and veterans: people *demonize* veterans for the harm they participated in; or conversely, they *valorize* veterans, hiding and blinding themselves to the deep hurt veterans carry; and lastly, they *pathologize* veterans by labeling them with psychological diagnoses so as not to have to bear the deeper truth revealed by the reality of their moral injury. (p.8)

With regard to the third factor of disengagement, *pathologizing*, Antal and Yeomans could not be any clearer: moral injury is anything *but* a pathology; the experiences of guilt and shame at the heart of moral injury are "… normal responses by a moral agent with an active conscience." (p.5) This judgment opens a critically important avenue in moral injury research. For as we will see in the case study of Andy, a thoroughgoing ethical evaluation, and mitigating of moral injury's suffering experience, involve tracing the trauma all the way down to its roots in structural and cultural violence. The bottom-most sources of the problem come into view, as opposed to a focus on moral injury's direct violence, and attempts to "fix" people with moral injury (the pathologizing route). The method argued for here spotlights moral injury's causal conditions; these form the ground of this injury, and are best uncovered through a method of excavation. Only a genealogical investigation of the route of violence will uncover the deepest sources of the wound, and clarify effectively how to understand and determine possibilities for authentic healing. And as we will see, emergent healing involves not only Andy, but a much wider community.

Remember the approach and case study from the last chapter involving Mr. Jones. In that example, well-trained and compassionate mental health practitioners sincerely tried to help Mr. Jones reframe his guilt and shame regarding his killing of the Iraqi boy. They invited him to imagine sitting with the boy, to listen to what he might say, and share his own shame and grief; but simultaneously, it was communicated to Mr. Jones that his pain was the result of a "misguided" interpretation of his own experience. He was asked to explore "unhelpful beliefs" that "interfered with his capacity for resilience." The goal of therapeutic treatment was to assist him to develop "cognitive flexibility." This meant that he should be able to withstand the deep moral divide that tore him apart when he was commanded to crush the Iraqi boy with his convoy vehicle and override one of the deepest moral mandates known to human beings: *we don't kill children.* Nowhere does the case study suggest that perhaps Mr. Jones' deep and long-lasting shame and guilt might be a trustworthy ethical signpost demanding broader self-reflection and collective attention. According to this therapeutic mode (cognitive-behavioral therapy), the goal was to explore "a survivor's appraisal of the trauma and 'manufactured emotions' such as shame, guilt, and anger, which are generated when higher-order cognitive processes go awry."[17] In other words, practitioners encouraged Mr. Jones to interpret the deep emotional and cognitive pain and dissonance within himself as "manufactured" – the mistaken consequence of "cognitive process gone awry." In the end, Jones' shame and guilt were addressed as emotional experiences requiring modification, *not as truth-telling that demanded an open hearing.*

Antal and Yeomans' approach is fundamentally different. They write, "… the distress associated with killing in warfare is more than just neurosis in need of diagnosis and treatment." (p.7) The larger purpose behind their approach, involving spiritual, religious, social and non-pathologizing modalities, is to "shift the framework from one that is exclusively medical and clinical." (p.8) This opens a wider landscape and deeper understanding of what is at stake. "Moral pain from combat is normative, not disordered." (p.12) Even the common terms used by practitioners, such as "diagnosis" and "treatment" of moral injury, connote an interpretation that moral injury somehow is pathological, the result of a person's weakness or malformation, or the result of inadequate training and preparation. (p.13) As these researchers underscore, common clinical practices that label the morally injured with various psychological diagnoses not only are unhelpful, but may exacerbate moral injury's pain in the lives of veterans (one wonders if this has something to do with Mr. Jones' continued suffering and dysfunction following his time of treatment).

One example involves the stigmatizing pathologizing involved in the system of VA disability pay. Financial recompense to those who suffer a range of psychological problems is determined through "rating" the veteran according to the severity of his/her "disability." (p.15) Moral Injury has not yet been recognized by the DSM; people like Andy or Mr. Jones, who suffer life-threatening dysfunctions, commonly may be given pathological diagnoses; and categorized along a spectrum that measures the psychological severity of "disability," to determine financial support.

Antal and Yeomans' model rests on a different starting point with regard to the phenomenon of moral injury; the purpose of their Group is to empower those struggling with moral injury, through honoring, highlighting and modeling moral engagement with the dissonance and pain the morally injured express, all the way down, *as an important source of truth-telling to a much wider collective.* In contrast to seeing themselves as "damaged goods," or patients with psychological pathologies, or individuals whose cognition is in need of reinterpretation, participants gradually embrace the role of "prophet," invited and empowered to share a "burdensome knowledge" with the citizens who sent them to war. (p.16)

"Andy" participated in the fourth iteration of their 12-week program at the Crescenz VAMC in Philadelphia. With a long family history of military service and following his own 11-year career in the U.S. military, after his discharge Andy was deeply troubled. Psychologists and psychiatrists treated him with a range of psychotherapeutic and pharmacological approaches over a period of *eight years*. But nothing helped, as he summed it up, "I'm still messed up. There is no therapy that can cure me." (pp.22–23) Given a 100% "service-connected disability rating for PTSD," and ranked as a high risk for suicide, he was referred to Antal and Yeoman's new Moral Injury Group.

In addition to reading about Andy in Antal and Yeoman's research, I also heard him testify publicly at the Crescenz VAMC and at a Philadelphia Episcopal church about his experiences. The first time I heard him speak, Andy was very clear that participation in the Moral Injury Group was a last-ditch effort; this would be his final attempt to do something other than end his life.[18] As he put it, "This group was a desperate last chance." (p.25) It is hard to imagine the strength it must have taken for Andy to withstand eight years of ineffective intervention in the midst of such pain. Nevertheless, entering the Moral Injury Group, he exhibited "perfect attendance" over 12 weeks of 90 minute meetings. (p.16)

The Moral Injury Group sessions address a variety of topics, but what stands out is the way facilitators empower participants to develop their own skills and strength to face themselves and others, working together, and practicing increased capacity for testimony, that is, speaking honestly about their reality. Multiple perspectives are encouraged through advocating the values of pluralism and diverse spiritualities. In addition to defining and studying research on moral injury, participants also are encouraged to reflect on the difference between "moral disengagement" and "telling it like it is ... paying attention to harmful consequences ... [moving from] dehumanization to humanizing the other." (p.19) Perhaps, most important, members of the group are encouraged to reflect on and discuss just how citizens in the U.S.

are "morally disengaged" from the realities of warfare, and how Veterans testimony can help *them.* (p.20)

From the beginning of the Group, participants know that in week ten they will participate in a "community healing ceremony," a ritual in the Crescenz VAMC chapel that will provide them with a pulpit to testify about what they have experienced to a gathered community that has expressed eagerness and willingness to listen. "The Community Ceremony is a safe space for remembrance, mourning and reconnection." (p.20) As they prepare for their public testimony as "prophet," group members are invited to focus on two questions: "What do you need to unburden? … What does the community need to hear?" (p.20) Antal and Yeomans are especially emphatic about the significance of this public exchange: "Veterans experience an identity shift from *patient* to *prophet* as they begin to recognize their testimony contains wisdom [that is] of value to society." (p.20) The ceremony includes ritual practices aimed at veterans, their families, and members of the wider community, symbolizing society as a whole. Lament, confession, sharing of pain, and a commitment to reconnect and act all are addressed through various rituals involving movement, candles, water, touch, seeing and listening.

Andy not only has testified publicly about his life, but also gave permission for Antal and Yeomans to write about his life story. One profound shaping experience from his childhood occurred when Andy witnessed younger children in his family being abused by an older relative who was a "devout Catholic." (p.22) His inability to intervene in the abuse left him with a strong desire "to be a protector of the innocent." (p.22) Andy identifies a second telling event from much later in his life. Like Mr. Jones, during his deployment to Iraq, Andy made a decision that resulted in others' death, in Andy's case, thirty-six people, including nine children.

While working in Iraq as an intelligence operative, during one mission Andy identified a "target," and what he concluded was the target location. He joined the ground unit one night to kill or capture that person thus identified. But as the unit approached the home/"target," shots were fired at them from inside the home, so they called for an airstrike. A U.S. gunship appeared and fired missiles into the home. Afterward, Andy entered what was left of the house to "clear the building," only to find inside a heap of bodies, thirty-six men, women and children, "slumped together in a pile." (p.23) More than eight years later, at the Episcopal Church in Philadelphia, during his testimony, I would hear Andy say that the sight of those bodies in the Iraqi home was "etched into the back of my eyelids forever," his hands fluttering before his contorted face as he spoke from the front of the church.[19] Whatever acculturation he had received in his training and earlier life to help him compartmentalize difficult experiences, it all bled out of him when he saw that pile of bodies that night. "I could not stomach handling these bodies long enough to discover my intended target." (p.20) A "half-singed Minnie Mouse doll" mirrored "… the lifelessness of a six-year-old girl holding it." (p.23) Describing it later as a moment when "… a part of himself – his soul – left his body," Andy could not get past "… the shame of my unholy perpetration." "I relive this alone, the steel cylinder heavy with .38, knowing that to drive one into my own face will free me from this prison, these sights and smells." (p.23)

During the fourth week of his participation in the Moral Injury group, Andy testified aloud about the experience above. Chaplain Antal, in a clergy education seminar about moral injury I attended, further revealed that before agreeing to participate in the Moral Injury Group, during the more than eight years Andy suffered with this terrible knowledge and experience, he had never told anyone about it.[20] But now, his disclosure in the Group of something so painful and shameful "… inspired other MIG Veterans to follow with disclosures of their own." (p.24) Andy also decided that he would testify publicly at the Community Ceremony in week ten. By the time I heard him in Philadelphia, some time later, Andy was testifying in more settings, "empowered by guilt, not imprisoned by it," as he said. (p.25)

Andy described the experience of the Moral Injury Group: "this is a place to listen to the screaming soul, to acknowledge your true self, let down your armor, and react in a positive way, be a prophet." (p.25) One of the most important impacts of the experience for him involved the emphasis on community involvement: he began to experience "reconnection and gaining a sense of belonging to community" because in some way the ceremony began the process of "let[ting] the community accept their brunt to share." (p.25)

Andy's "prophetic" work continues since his time in the Moral Injury Group, through testifying in different settings, and also in a symbolic spiritual practice through which he is intentionally rebuilding the ties of humanization. He refers to the nine children in the airstrike who were killed as a result of the intelligence he provided as "my kids," and is carving memorial soapstones for each of them, with "culturally appropriate" names identifying each child. He takes the stones with him when he testifies, and people get in long lines to come forward, view and touch them. (p.26) Clinically speaking, two months after completing the group, Andy's psychological tests revealed "… reductions in depression, religious struggles and negative effects of morally injurious experiences, as well as elevations in self-compassion and social functioning." (p.26). Chapter 5 further takes up Andy's story and prophetic healing work.

Taking the analysis further: What happened with Andy?

I draw on Andy's story, and the practice of the Crescenz VAMC Moral In-jury Group, because the foundation of this unique program promotes an emerging social analysis of structural and cultural violence in U.S. war-cul-ture. The very framework buttressing the program speaks powerfully about important differences between this approach and others. How does this take place? First, the VA program empowers the morally injured with respect to their concept of *identity*. The process of the group is designed to support a transformation of self-understanding, from disordered *patient*, to *prophet,* a person whose suffering is heard, and taken seriously as important truth for a larger community. But equally important, second, the program clearly identifies how wider society is "morally disengaged" from the realities and consequences of war and war-culture. It has to be risky to do this sort of work, because it begins to tread on territory that is very carefully protected, not only by the institutions of war and militarization in the United States; but by everyone (that is, all citizens) whose lives are shaped by the influences of war-culture.

I wonder about the ways that moral injury care providers who are em-ployed by the U.S. Department of Veterans Affairs, and Department of De-fense Health Affairs may find themselves in a difficult bind.[21] They are "on the front lines" in their immense dedication to encourage healing for the morally injured. But how does the deep military culture of these environ-ments affect the work they do? To what extent does the atmosphere in these institutional structures complicate seeing the need for, and implementation of, a thoroughgoing analysis of the roles of structural and cultural violence associated with the war-culture of the United States? The same bind exists across U.S. war-culture in a myriad of institutions, educational, corporate, religious, government, etc., in particular for those whose livelihoods are mixed up with Pentagon/DoD-related funding streams.

A long but little-known history explores eruptions of conflict between U.S. military institutions, and servicemembers of all military branches who protested from within. In different eras, perhaps culminating in the era of the Vietnam War, "laborers" in various military branches rose up and protest-ed the violent work they were commanded to do. They identified structural and cultural violence in intersecting forms of oppression that especially tar-get minorities and women within the military, and institutional and cultur-al mores that require and justify violence. One example from the Vietnam War era regards the creation of twenty or more "GI Coffeehouses" that were set up across the nation in Army towns, near domestic military bases. As researcher David L. Parsons writes, "the coffeehouses served as resource centers and organizational bases for the growing movement of active-duty soldiers organizing against the war." With "comfortable, hip environments that featured live music, poetry readings, rock posters and other accoutrements of 1960's youth counterculture," they also created space to address "the army's serious racial issues" and "narrowly proscribed gender roles" assigned and enforced by military culture.[22] But they would be met with "… repression, harassment and intimidation" by military institutional power.[23] Nevertheless, despite the strong shaping influence of militarism in the United States, especially celebrated in U.S. civil religion and in the rituals, doctrine and acculturation within all military branches, significant numbers of U.S. servicemembers have been anything but passive or unthinking celebrants of U.S. ways of war. At the same time, protests from within generally have been met with forceful opposition from military and other systems of power. Thus, today's context is complicated for providers who care for the morally injured: to what extent, as part of the care and healing for the morally injured, can providers analyze (and criticize) the structural and cultural violence of war-culture itself?

Given the fraught nature of this context, witnessing what takes place in the Moral Injury Program developed by Antal and Yeomans, especially the "Community Ceremony" in week 10 at the Crescenz VAMZ chapel, is to see an act of amazing courage. The ritual begins with music that the veterans in the group have chosen, played by a small group of musicians, including keyboard, electric guitar, drums, and vocalist. Twice I have heard the musicians begin the ceremony by playing John Lennon's familiar "Imagine," and the air grew thick with emotion, especially when these lyrics filled the space:

> Imagine there's no countries
> It isn't hard to do
> Nothing to kill or die for
> And no religion too
> Imagine all the people living life in peace, you
> You may say I'm a dreamer
> But I'm not the only one
> I hope some day you'll join us
> And the world will be as one.[24]

Along with lament, confession and pain, the veterans' testimonies also included sharp questions and criticisms about the nature of U.S. wars of the 21st century, and questions about why U.S. society seems to care so little.

They also testified about "the cost" of U.S. wars in the lives of those who fight them, and the costs for people in places across the world, who struggle to persist amidst the fields, urban contexts, villages and highways of battle.

Researchers Antal and Yeomans hope to do additional qualitative research to better learn what members of the wider community take away from participation in these ceremonies. They want to know more about people's reaction to the ceremony's emphasis on "taking some responsibility for sending these Veterans off to warfare." (p.27) At the same time, they cite evidence about the mountain of resistance in U.S. war-culture. Acceptance of responsibility is "something heavily resisted in cultures and countries like the U.S. that value individualism, individual responsibility, and achievement." (p.27) These caregivers find themselves squarely in the midst of complexity of the double bind described here, as people who are employed by The U.S. Department for Veterans Affairs, and whose work with the morally injured also inevitably is leading them into a deeper critique of U.S. war-culture itself. As they work to further develop "adaptive space" for veterans, their friends and family, and the community at large to face the costs of war, this work also must involve a constant monitoring of the cultural temperature, so as not to elicit reactive sabotage.

This important research and practice taking place at Crescenz VAMZ and beyond is deeply moving. At the same time, strengthening the robust theoretical framework in their program, to trace the genealogy of violence in moral injury, would further sharpen Antal and Yeoman's research and practice; and further underscore the need for all citizens to stop avoiding, and face the war-culture that gives rise to this reality. At the same time, I also understand that the social analysis I continue here is one that many citizens will find offensive, and will be resisted institutionally as well, because it challenges a deeply entrenched status quo, the dynamics of violence at the pillars of war-culture.

In order to work through such a social analysis, I return to Andy as a case study, to ask "what really happened here?" I explore how Andy's story *not only* shows the devastating nature of *direct violence* in his individual life, *but also* the role of *structural and cultural violence* intertwined with his own experience, and military moral injury more widely. Tracing the threads of violence in Andy's story is an important first step of this social analysis, and lays the groundwork for the final part of this chapter, a return to Card's theoretical framework of evil as atrocity. At that point I address the implications of the claim that moral injury is an atrocity, and reflect on the reverberations of moral injury tied to foreseeability and culpability of U.S. society as a whole.

Andy's moral injury and the triangle of violence

1. Direct violence

In order to mobilize the social analysis regarding "what happened with Andy?" I return to the theoretical framework of the violence triangle, to place the story of one individual into a more comprehensive context. Using this theory mitigates the overarching problem in moral injury research and clinical practice, regarding the tendency to focus on what happened with the individual as if it occurred in a vacuum, like a lightning strike or tsunami. Moral injury is not this kind of violence – it is not an act of God, a matter of fate, or an unlucky consequence of life. Its violence has deep roots that penetrate very specific human institutions, social constructions, values and understandings. This is territory we need to explore.

So first, what happened to Andy with respect to point of direct violence in the violence triangle? The initial indication of direct violence in Andy's story involves his witness of the abuse of younger siblings. From there his narrative jumps to what happened on that terrible night when his unit called in the airstrike on the "target" he identified. While no doubt Andy might describe and discuss other events of direct violence over the course of his life, in terms of the way he tells his story, these two events stand out for their enduring importance in his own psyche.

The missiles that were fired that night in Iraq, in addition to killing thirty-six people, also were soul-destroying for Andy. Clearly, the destructive consequences of moral injury, leading to Andy's resolution to take his own life, emerged from this direct violence. And in addition to self-harm, destructive impacts in his relationships also resulted; for instance, Andy relates that during many years following his discharge from the military, he found himself unable to interact with his niece and nephew, because the vision of healthy children only underscored his guilt regarding those he "murdered" (his own language). (p.23) Researcher and veteran of the Iraq War Michael Yandell emphasizes that moral injury doesn't just develop in a moment, even when veterans link it to specific events of direct violence, like Andy does with the night of the airstrike. No, moral injury builds over time, as the reverberations of violence grow, and their destructive impact spreads throughout the lives of individuals and communities.[25]

Along these lines and continuing to explore the direct violence involved in Andy's case, we have to consider not only Andy, but also the impact of the airstrike's direct violence on its "targets." Thirty-six people were killed. We may imagine, but it is impossible to measure the expanding destruction of the airstrike's direct violence on the other members of Andy's unit, as well as the family, friends, and wider communities of those children, women and men who died so violently and suddenly.

These are the immediate aspects of direct violence that are most visible in Andy's story. If we remain and dwell with Andy in this reality for a time, it is easier to understand why so much moral injury research and clinical practice stop at this point: already it seems overwhelming to deal with this pain and loss, and imagine pathways of response. But the theory of the violence triangle compels the further push forward of this social analysis, because there are yet two other elements of the triangle to be assessed. Remember that direct violence never "stands alone," but always is sourced by, and impacts other forms of violence, both structural and cultural.

2. Structural violence

So the focus here shifts from direct violence, to thinking about the ways direct violence is embedded and interacts with systems of structural violence. This hearkens back to the three outstanding indicators of structural violence in U.S. war-culture identified in Chapter 2: the political economy of war, the U.S. "empire of bases," and the dynamics of "interpenetration." In war-culture, violence winds its way through vast systems and structures of war, long before it erupts into direct violence, such as the airstrike.

This social analysis places Andy's story against this backdrop, in order to take into account the different vectors of structural violence, and their formational role in the wave of events leading to the Iraq War, though Andy enlisted and deployed a few years before the launch of this war. The declaration of "A Global War on Terror," as identified earlier in this book, arose largely as a result of structures of war that had been developed long before. Insistent increase of militarization, and the march toward war were presented as the only avenues through which there could be adequate interpretation and response to the events of 9/11. This is the thought-restricting nature of war-culture; its structures of violence constrain human imagination, and shut down creative thinking regarding alternatives to violence to address the very real dangers faced by human beings.

Moreover, paucity of thought also results because of the structural violence throughout the political economy of war in the United States, involving well over half of the federal discretionary budget (and additional national resources). The vast sums of money and human resources structurally devoted to war and war-culture not only have shaped the national economy, but also U.S. citizens' ways of thinking and imagining. The war-economy is deeply normalized in the minds of U.S. citizens; additionally, for many, legitimation further is cemented because their jobs and way of life are ever more deeply tied to this economy. Not only the U.S. economy, but also the political system is engineered so as to ensure its stability and growth. The result is people who remain mostly unaware and unconcerned, and who by and large willingly justify and support this reality.

In addition, war, its institutions and practitioners, have been elevated and sacralized in national identity. This dynamic further disables critical thinking; thought is "put off the table" through the process of sacralization. Sociologist Hans Mol investigated how the development of sacralization prohibits criticism or protest. As he writes, "sacralization produces immunity against persuasion." Making something sacred inevitably introduces characteristics of "untouchability and awe."[26] Questioning or protesting this bulwark is akin to challenging the divine! All this helps to explain why, as the VA Moral Injury Group emphasizes, the nation remains "morally disengaged."

The development of the "Military-Industrial Complex" may be traced in U.S. history at least to the end of World War II. By Andy's time it had morphed into a vast complex colonizing wide-reaching sectors of civilian society, a "military-industrial-technological-entertainment-academic-scientific-media-intelligence-homeland-security-surveillance-national-security-corporate complex" (religion also should be added to this long list).[27] All this is important to remember with respect to Andy's deep sense of shame and guilt, his "unholy perpetration," as he calls it. How was he shaped by these intertwining and penetrating systems of war-culture in the United States? The Moral Injury Group at the Crescenz VAMZ wished for the wider community to "bear its brunt of responsibility," but what does this mean, without an analysis that explores and strives to understand just how war and militarization shape all citizens, and give rise to the inevitable social conditions that are the foundation for the direct violence in Andy's case?

Given this normalization, given this lack of consciousness, it is *less* difficult to understand the speed through which government leaders successfully convinced much of the U.S. American public that the only possible reaction to the events of 9/11 was a "global war," concomitant with the enormous military buildup that took place post-9/11. Where did Andy's own life fit into this history? Remember theorist Paul Koistinen, and his dire diagnosis of the political economy of war in the U.S. This is a system that is deeply damaging to the nation. Nevertheless, as the same political economy grew and claimed a greater hold on the life of the United States, it was becoming only more difficult to build political will for meaningful change. In light of this environment, we may ask to what degree, if any, were political and military leaders able or willing to weigh the impact of this development on the lives of so many young men and women, the children of the nation, like Andy, who were sent to war?

Surely the overarching U.S. military doctrine of "Full Spectrum Dominance" in every conceivable environment – land, air, water, space, the cyber-world – as the dedicated position and plan of the U.S. military, deeply characterized the context shaping Andy's own decision-making, as well as the structures of the military he would enter. Yet Andy was just 17 years old when he volunteered to enlist, in 1999.[28] One wonders, what educational resources, religious or familial support existed in his life to help him seriously, and with the deepest consideration, evaluate this decision and its possible impact on his own life, and others' lives?

Additional vectors of structural violence also are at stake in the case study involving Andy. For instance, what of the impact of the "empire of bases" both rising out of and anchoring the same political economy of war? How do we measure the impact of this structural reality of war-culture in what happened? Andy's work as an "intelligence operative" took place in this system of bases, and the aircraft that fired the missiles that day was sourced by the same system. Yet Andy's agony over his decision regarding the airstrike, prior to his participation in the Moral Injury Group, does not include awareness of any responsibility of these vast systems and structures in these events. (The next chapter explores how since his participation in the Moral Injury Group, and sharing moral responsibility with the larger community, Andy is finding some relief from the moral pain and despair.)

Lastly, what about the impact of "interpenetration" of the ethos, institutions and practices of war with unending sites of supposedly "civilian culture"? How was Andy's own thinking shaped by this same interpenetration to view going to war, and being part of the machinery of war, as his own vocational pathway? As a youth growing up in the United States, how was Andy impacted by the interpenetration of war-culture with popular youth culture? Remember the Navy brand, "a Global Force for Good;" at the time Andy enlisted, the Navy tagline was "Let the Adventure Begin."[29] Was he exposed to video wargames produced by the military branches in partnership with video-gaming corporations?[30] How were the traditions of his own military family shaped by deep connection with the values and practices of military cultures, and religio-cultural rituals and theology such as this book has examined?

At the clergy training seminar on moral injury that I attended, led by Chaplain Antal, I raised some of these questions. Antal responded, "Andy says that his disability pay is 'blood money.'"[31] Here is Andy's own dawning awareness that in some way, he was "bought out" by systems and structures much larger, and with more immense power, than his early awareness could be expected to perceive.

In the end, it would have been impossible for Andy to be in Iraq, have access to such immense power through these weapons of war, or be involved in his unit's calling in the airstrike that night, without a vast structure of violence not only supporting, but encouraging such action as the right and only way to deal with threats. Yet in much moral injury research, when moral injury is assessed and analyzed, this landscape is omitted entirely – none of these structures or systems ever comes into play in the analysis regarding *why* this moral injury took place, and *what* should be done about it. In fact, in too much moral injury research, the agony of people like Andy, that shines a piercing light on the destructive consequences of the war-reality humans have created, is bypassed. We see this in the valorizing, demonizing and pathologizing modes through which moral injury so often is miscategorized. Many citizens and medical practitioners collude in protecting war-culture from deeper examination, by insisting on naming moral injury as an unfortunate and inevitable byproduct of war; or by insisting that with proper training and support, such moral agony may be prevented, resisted, or withstood; and by failing to connect this pain to the wide and deep structures of violence that lie deeper at its base. Andy knows better.

I deeply appreciate the beginnings of the social analysis being brought to bear for Andy and others in the CrescenzVAMZ Moral Injury Group. I also believe that Andy's and our own understanding will grow, through tools and support to analyze *what* happened with him within the systems and structures of U.S. war-culture, and *why*. Saying, "the wider community needs to bear its part of the burden," is an important first step but, simultaneously, it is urgent that this step be taken further, to explore just what that burden is, how it has developed, and what its impact is on people like Andy, not to mention its consequences for other affected human beings, such as the 36 people who died by way of U.S. firepower that day in Iraq. Finally all U.S. citizens are implicated and bear responsibility for what took place.

3. Cultural violence

This social analysis, in addition to acknowledging direct violence, and bringing the *structures* of violence more clearly into view, finally addresses the role of *cultural* violence in Andy's life. Here the vectors of cultural violence identified in Chapter 3 are explored: colliding masculinities, the role of religion, and dynamics of nationalism. A number of important hints from

Andy's story come to the forefront, especially the few bare details he shares about his early life. Our social/cultural analysis begins with those details. Andy was from a family with a long and deep history of military service. He witnessed the abuse of his younger siblings by a relative who was a "devout Catholic." He developed a desire to "protect the innocent."

How was Andy shaped by dominant modes of masculinity within military cultures and families examined in this book? Was he raised, as Kathleen Barry analyzes, to understand his life as "expendable"? I would encourage Andy to examine his understanding of how he was shaped as a "man." It would seem that in his family, as with many others, the abuse of his siblings was protected through silencing mechanisms, because Andy felt "helpless to stop it." (p.22) Yet Andy also felt responsible, as though he should have been able to do something. As he grows into a man, his desire "to protect" becomes a strong force in his decision-making. Ability to protect and control became a central value for him, and as we saw, this premium on control and protection is deeply linked to dominant tropes of masculinity – men are those who protect others, they stop bad and wrong situations from continuing through coercive (and often violent) acts of power.

There is no reference anywhere in Andy's story regarding any trusted confidants he turned to when he witnessed the abuse. They might have told him that there was little he could do to protect his siblings, other than tell an adult, and ask for help. Andy was a child, and to expect himself to be able to stop such a terrible situation, was not realistic or just. Even more confusing and painful, the abuser was a "devout Catholic." (p.22) Perhaps one of the most destructive aspects of abuse is the way that perpetrators manipulate positions of moral authority and trust to groom, disable and silence their more vulnerable victims. What impact did all this have on Andy as a child, and as an adolescent young man, as he moved toward resolution to enlist? According to the case study, Andy seems to have been mostly on his own to deal with this situation; he felt alone, he was unable to ask for help. He became "vacant of faith," experiencing the loss of religious resources and community. (p.22)

Does Bonnie Mann's "shame to power" analysis of contemporary military masculinity play a role in Andy's story? I sense shame in Andy with regard to his perceived failure to protect his siblings. He responds with growing determination to protect the nation by enlisting. What is the connection between Andy's deep desire to protect his siblings, and his own shame and vulnerability in that situation as a child? How did this history affect his growing desire to become the sort of man who could "protect the innocent"? Dominant masculinity formation in military cultures refuses the realities of human vulnerability, limitation, even pain. Because shame is related to vulnerability, any perceived weakness must be rejected and overcome over and over, through performances of violence. Did identity dynamics such as these play out in Andy's life?

I also wonder about the distinct possibility of moral injury (and other forms of injury) among Andy's other family members; he reveals that both his father and grandfather experienced war, specifically his father in combat as a Green Beret in Vietnam. (p.22) We might ask to what extent moral injury is passed down from parent to child in military families across the nation, and about the confusing and little-understood dynamics within military families with respect to this generational legacy of violence.

We can only imagine what *would* come to light if Andy was encouraged to explore narratives and practices of military masculinities, such as those examined here, that were passed down through the generations in his family. At the same clergy moral injury seminary that I attended, it seemed as if every clergyperson in attendance had stories along these lines regarding their fathers and grandfathers who had been to war. One woman sitting at my table expressed her frustration and grief, because it seemed to her that she only was permitted to learn the full truth about what her loved ones (who were veterans) had experienced in war *after* their deaths, by reading their private papers; so strong was the unspoken family rule that such things could not be discussed in the light of day. Did Andy experience something similar in his military family?

More than anything, I would want to ask Andy about the ways he was schooled in philosophies and practices of dehumanization. Can he trace the threads of his life to see how and when such schooling began, and what were its strongest shaping moments? How was his education in dehumanization reinforced through absorption of narratives about what it means to "be a man"? How did all this become an unconscious way of being through his military acculturation, especially by the time of that moment in Iraq, when his unit called in the airstrike? What about the confusing nature of the military culture he was a part of, the juxtaposition of the code of military values on the one hand, and widespread dehumanization of women, people of color, other ethnicities, and LBGTQ individuals, on the other hand? Chaplain Antal relates that Andy was in the Air Force, attached to a Special Forces ranger regiment, mostly Army.[32] A robust social analysis of "what happened to Andy" must take up these issues as well, yet this is difficult and painful work.

U.S. Marine veteran Christine Pedersen's story reads like a cautionary tale with respect to the many internal contradictions between the ideals and realities of military life. Like Andy, born into a proud military family, she and her brother were raised according to a strong ethic based in Marine Corps values, as she says, "We grew up believing that standing at attention, yelling cadence on runs to our activities after school and listening to lectures about honor, courage and commitment were norms in every household." Yet even as a child, she experienced dissonance between her father's deep internalization of Marine Corps values and culture, and the facts of his own relationship with this institution. His greatest disappointment was being medically discharged after a "botched foot surgery," performed by U.S. military doctors in Okinawa, Japan. Yet he refused to apply for VA disability benefits, ever downplaying his injury. All he wished for was to be accepted for re-enlistment into the Marine Corps Reserves. Though this never came to pass, his proudest moment was when Christine herself was accepted into the Corps. However, this same decision grew into something that Christine admits "... forced us to confront sides of the military neither of us wanted to see. My enlistment became a bond and a wedge between us, and eventually forced us on a journey toward truth." In the end, "The truth was that sexual harassment was a continual element of my enlistment ... I felt exhausted by my career and angry that my father still felt so loyal to an institution that had repeatedly dehumanized me."[33]

Andy's story does not indicate any pause in his thinking before the airstrike; we do not know how or if he thought deeply about the possible and terrible all-too-human consequences of his unit's act. It sounds like a reflexive action on his part, no doubt following upon the acculturation of all his training, all his formation. But hearing, smelling, then seeing and touching the pile of bodies was for Andy a rude and horrifying experience of coming to consciousness about the false premises he had internalized.

More than anything else, on the night of the airstrike, Andy was struck to the core with regard to the destructive results of dehumanization. This should give us pause to consider just how, and through what processes, his own schooling in dehumanization took place. Moreover, as time passed, after that day in Iraq, he found himself less and less able to live with the results of this formation. There was no justifying it; no rationalizing of it, no medicating of it, no sidestepping of it by way of psychological diagnosis or treatment. His soul left his body.

As we turn to the role of religion to explore its contribution to cultural violence, Andy's story spotlights the disingenuous nature of dominant civil religion. *Both* the violence servicemembers absorb *and* the violence they mete out consistently are described as "the necessary sacrifice" they make on behalf of the nation. But Andy's pain cuts through any (civil) religious masking of the consequences of his dehumanization by way of religious frameworks. His story undermines any justification based in (civil) religious characterization of military service, injury and death. This thinking falls apart; the distortion is clarified. A "necessary sacrifice"? Cognitive dissonance abounds. To use Andy's own words, this was an "unholy perpetration" and "unforgivable sin;" such is his description of the visceral experience of the airstrike and its aftermath. Andy's description makes me want to hear more about his own experience of the cultural violence at the seabed of U.S. culture that connects religious ideas, metaphors and practices, with militarization and war. Over time, his own "screaming soul" could not allow him to rest or accept any such justifying, mystifying measures.

A deeper social/religious analysis would invite Andy to trace those threads of his life where religion played a role in the cultural violence at the deepest level of his own moral dissonance and pain. One wonders, for example, as a child, and later, a young man in the early post-9/11 era, how many (civil) religious experiences, involving religious cultural violence such as that explored in this book, Andy witnessed. When he met with recruiters at the tender age of 16 or 17, to what extent was his "desire to protect" manipulated through such narratives of expendability regarding "the necessity of sacrifice" to protect the nation? Were these narratives also a part of his own Catholic military family tradition and ethos? Did he attend (civil) religious military rituals that taught the conflation of Christianity with U.S. ways of war? Did his church chimes ring out battle hymns of the nation on Memorial Day?

Any sense of spiritual life, much less Catholic religious practice, remained dormant and dead for Andy through most of his life. Following the abuse of his siblings, through enlistment and eleven years of military service, and over more than eight years of psychiatric and psychological interventions post-military service, it was not until he began to embrace and practice his role as "prophet," who would testify to the truth about his experience of war, that a new idea of spirituality began to germinate. (pp.22–25) Spirituality could be more than "an ominous dark force." Andy described his work in the Moral Injury Group as "soul work, a battle for your true self, … true spiritual rehabilitation." (p.25) This was indelibly linked with reconnecting with a wider community that could "accept their brunt to share." (p.25)

As Andy continues to explore and develop this new sense of spirituality, I believe his "soul work" can be strengthened through the social analysis outlined here, to more explicitly examine his life, and name the role religion played in the cultural violence shaping his own formation, decisions and experience leading to those actions in that Iraqi town that night. To what extent did (civil) religious narratives regarding "the necessary sacrifices of war," and "the soldier who agrees to die for you, like Jesus Christ," provide cover over the work of war that would be required? Moral injury research has documented that witnessing and participating in the suffering, harm or death of others is a key causal condition of this wound, yet very little research examines the cultural violence of rhetorical sacrificial frameworks that not only justify the destruction of some for the benefit of others, but mandate it. Who in Andy's life was present to review all this with him, and help him think more deeply about what he might be trained and ordered to learn and do? It is indeed difficult to think about the strength and fortitude it must take for someone like Andy, to demonstrate perseverance in digging through all the different layers of toxic cultural sludge, to adequately and fully tell his truth.

But in addition, he and others with similar experiences also will be morally strengthened when the wider community "accepts its brunt to share" by joining with Andy in a deeper self-examination of society and the church's (ab)use of religion in U.S. civil religion. This involves communal dedication to digging out and shining light on the myriad forms of cultural violence in civil religion. It *also* involves people of faith who will be dedicated to excavation and examination of the myriad forms of cultural violence specifically in their religious doctrines, proclamation and practices. Only then will society at large better understand what really makes up moral injury. For moral injury not only involves *direct* violence, and not only the vast *structures* of violence in U.S. war-culture. At moral injury's deepest and most unconscious level, troubling and destructive strands of *cultural* violence link individuals such as Andy to a much wider network of denial, mystification, sacralization of violence, and untruth. "The necessity of the sacrifices of war," superimposed over the narrative of Jesus of Nazareth, aids, abets and masks war-culture, is exploited to justify war and militarism, thrusts the actual devastation of war's violence into the distance, and through all this, develops into the poisonous mulch at moral injury's least visible root.

In particular, "bearing the brunt" rests with religious communities and their leaders, whose responsibility is to create those necessary spaces and opportunities to do the work of theological reflection, as they wrestle with and study their own traditions, assumptions and practices. "Accepting their brunt to share" will mean insisting on leadership to *think*, study, confess, name and work to change the ways their religious discourse and practices contribute to increased violence through collective blindness, lack of adequate *thought*, and deflection of responsibility. The church's "brunt to share" will mean prophetically calling the nation to account for its colonization and commoditization of the church's own tradition, through which the nation rationalizes and mystifies its own violent imperialistic practices.

This leads us to the final element of cultural violence to be addressed here. By now it should be visible to the reader how various elements of cultural violence intermix with and influence each other. Colliding narratives of masculinity interpenetrate with religious language and metaphor regarding the "necessary sacrifices of war." When one stops to think about it, the contradictions between "expendability" and being shaped for "inviolability" are stark, but such is the case in U.S. war-culture. Cultural violence grows in ratio to the lack of availability of critical thought; the tropes and practices that undergird and mask cultural violence may be filled with internal contradictions, but people have "pre-reflectively" accepted them as normal, routine, even divine! Thus the ground of culture only rarely is called into question.

But contradictions notwithstanding, colliding masculinities and (civil) religious formulations come together to shape and impact the deepest subconscious strata of identity in U.S. nationalism. For sovereign masculinity not only is the training ground for boys and men, but for the nation itself, as Bonnie Mann argues. "Inviolability" has become the most cherished element of nationalism, performed through "Shock and Awe," and developing into the justification for the doctrine of "Full Spectrum Dominance." Nationalist spectacles of supposed invulnerability are regularly performed, with promises (but these promises are lies) about the unencumbered agency of the nation. Outlandish and exorbitant excesses of structural violence in U.S. war-culture are justified and celebrated by way of this cultural violence even as they simultaneously distract attention from those who are at the receiving end of their most devastating consequences. How was Andy impacted by the displays of dominant forms of U.S. nationalism, centered on pride and expectation of hegemonic and unquestioned U.S. military might? How did such exposure shape his own decision-making, including his decision regarding the airstrike?

Remember that John Dower characterized contemporary forms of U.S. nationalism as "wishful thinking… assuming that monopolization of sophisticated military might ensures full-spectrum dominance or a quick fait accompli…"[34] But if Andy's story tells us anything, it reveals that schooling in this kind of nationalism, intermixing with his military acculturation, also is training in dehumanization. In the end, everything Andy had absorbed was revealed as delusion when he encountered the pile of bodies in the bombed-out structure. As he later said, "My targets were proud Iraqis in an occupied state, bakers and merchants, cousins and priests, mothers and fathers, big brothers and baby sisters." (p.23)

Returning one last time to the story of Mr. Jones, we may remember how his care providers attempted to help him deal with his pain through addressing his "unhelpful beliefs" and "misinterpretations" in his higher order cognitive processes. In other words, "correct" interpretation of what happened with the death of the Iraqi boy would mean to place it in the context of just war ideology, to understand this as an unfortunate necessity required by the dictates of the mission in a just war. It does not appear as though any space ever emerged in his clinical treatment to raise questions about whether such a framework could in fact be truly just, or whether it was just to require human beings such as himself, in a supposedly "just war," to develop the capacity to override their deepest moral sensibilities, such as *not killing children*, in order to abide by the mission tasks and goals. But sorting through this cultural violence is confusing and difficult. As researcher Marysia Zalewski writes, such violence "... persistently masquerades as something 'other' through its sanctioning by the state. Buried in this authoritative frame is a quagmire of hidden violence – state violence itself, gender/sex violence, the violence of colonialism and racial brutality."[35] The emphasis here is on that particular type of state violence that "masquerades" as just war thinking. Nevertheless, *all* these strata of cultural violence lie deeply buried in military cultures, law, and systems of organization and practice, in addition to pervasively influencing dominant strands of U.S. national identity. Yet, as Robert Meagher argued in *Killing from the Inside Out*, the phenomenon of moral injury has an imploding impact on just war thinking and ideology (Meagher's important insight will be further explored at the end of this chapter).[36] Cultural violence takes place through a process of misnaming, as Galtung describes, "changing the light from red to green – killing for some other reason as wrong, but killing in the name of the nation is patriotic."[37]

We can characterize the different types of cultural violence at the seabed of Andy's moral injury as "derealizing narratives," borrowing from Judith Butler.[38] In essence, each of the three aspects of cultural violence identified here were just different types of training in derealizing dehumanization. Where they bear any truth, such narratives only tell part of the truth; they hide more than they reveal. Think back to the Clinton Democratic Convention, and the sacrificial spectacle that encouraged an outpouring of grief for Captain Humayun Khan. Derealized narratives determine "what is grievable." Yes, there were honest and deeply felt tears on the faces of many at the Democratic Convention for the loss of this beautiful young man, but where was there any display of grief for "the proud Iraqis in an occupied state"? And we remember how the same derealization simultaneously and cleverly subjugated Clinton's own role in approving the war that stole Captain Khan from the family that so clearly adores him. Cultural frames that disallow or discourage grief for these "others," combined with acculturation in masculinity that is linked to processes of dehumanizing others, exacerbate moral injury. Like citizens at large, Andy's acculturation in U.S. nationalism led to a tendency to gloss over, or worse, remain blithely oblivious to the unthinkable losses in Iraq, Afghanistan, and other nations as a result of U.S. wars – until that day, when the sight, sounds, smells and touch of those losses tore away the mask of delusion.

Andy's schooling in all these philosophies and practices of dehumanization placed blinders on his capacity to *see and grieve.* We can sum it up by saying that before the airstrike, he was a person who did not have the imagination to adequately perceive the consequences of his own violent action. Can any of us say that we would be any different? And, in the end, we also have to wonder about the way this cultural violence additionally prevented him from developing into the full potential he had as a human being – yes, a vulnerable human in need of others, and equally able to give and contribute to others. Card would describe such acculturation as a form of oppression, a "reducing, molding and immobilizing" process in Andy's life. (p.99)

But the unforgiving and unrelenting truth of what he witnessed in the aftermath of the airstrike, the pile of bodies of children, women and men, swept away the delusion of Andy's former way of living. The sight, touch, and smell of this reality, and his own intact moral conscience, came together like an icy bath washing over him. He woke up, and simultaneously began to break down, unable to continue in all the ways he had been educated, formed and valued. Andy would have to find a new and different way forward. It would become increasingly difficult to continue an unquestioning way of life in all the various institutions, systems, structures and culture that had so deeply shaped him before.

Conclusion: Moral injury and the atrocity paradigm

Moral injury is an atrocity, a foreseeable intolerable harm, produced by culpable wrongdoing. In this final section, I return to Claudia Card's theory of atrocity to bring to a conclusion the social analysis of moral injury, and "what happened with Andy." Card developed this theory in order to respond to "the ethically most significant, most serious publicly known evils of my lifetime." (p.5) I would place the evil of war and war-culture somewhere near the top of that list. One of these publicly known evils Card analyzes regards the urgent issue of sexual violence as a weapon of war. But I find only two tantalizing hints in her book regarding the potential for the atrocity theory to apply to war and war-culture overall. She writes, for example, "perhaps the best argument against modern warfare is that it cannot be conducted without atrocities," but she does not take the application any further. (p.12) Later in the book I find another reference: "War is, after all, the deliberate infliction of intolerable harm." (p.122) But though Card's vision led her in a different direction from mine, nevertheless, in what follows, I draw deeply on her important work, and take her thinking further in support of the argument here. For Card's theory provides a generative backdrop to re-examine the analysis of moral injury as a whole; the atrocity paradigm is a model that insists we take a large step back and widen our sight. Vision has to encompass *both* Andy's individual story and suffering, *and* a global ethical vision regarding moral deliberation, judgment and rectifying action.

What is most "salient" about atrocities, Card insists, is their "harm." Remember the different vectors of harm outlined by Card that render life "intolerable." But those who perpetrate atrocity tend not to see their actions as problematic; they regularly do not understand that they are, in fact, committing atrocities. (p.9) And victims also commonly do not understand or label the violence enacted against them as atrocities. Why? This curious state of affairs with regard to atrocities as a whole, also may be extended to the phenomenon of moral injury. Despite everything that is known about it, and despite the depth of its harm in so many people's lives, collective thinking has yet to name moral injury as an atrocity. This remains the case equally for those powers responsible for war-culture, and the laborers of war-culture on the front lines.

Card's primary method of critical analysis is philosophical; she does not delve into the sociological except occasionally. But Galtung's socio-cultural framework of the traingle of volence may be used to further explore her emphasis on the mystifying dynamics of misrecognition and concealment. Misrecognition at the base of atrocity is related to the basic nature of structural and cultural violence; concealment takes place regularly by naming this violence as something other, something different from violence. In addition, both structural and cultural forms of violence are sacralized and simultaneously domesticated; and they take shape in human beings pre-reflectively, through vast processes of acculturation. Thus they go unseen and unnamed, increasing their concealment from greater vision. More than anything else, Galtung stresses: *structural and especially cultural forms of violence are masked, hidden beneath the surface of things, legitimated and normalized.* This is why diverse forms of atrocity pass as something else, as something other than intolerable. At the same time, ways of war are presented as facts of life that are impossible to change. But we know that *these are human constructions.* This is violence that humans have built, and they bear responsibility for it.

Because of the very normalization of this violence, to use the word, "atrocity" in connection with moral injury has a way of stopping us in our tracks. Calling moral injury an atrocity feels serious indeed; it is to place moral injury in a more urgent frame of reference than has been permitted up to the present time. It is to say something new and different about the nature of the harm that moral injury entails. In short, moral injury is "intolerable;" *it should not be.* Immediately, thought springs to other types of atrocities in human history: torture, genocide, femicide, ecocide, slavery, the list goes on and on. Atrocities call human beings into action; they are not something human beings should just live with, just get by with. No, atrocities demand collective human responsibility. This is why Card's language is so striking; it sets the tone and moral imperative attendant to the phenomenon of moral injury into starker relief.

In addition, Card's theory helps to connect "atrocity" to the concept of "culpability." As she describes, once human beings begin to absorb that an atrocity is taking place, there emerges a reaction of shock because the realization coming to the surface is that human beings *engineered this or failed to act to prevent it. What have we done? Who have we become?* How could human beings do such things, or omit taking necessary action to prevent them? And how might people have intervened, so that it could have been otherwise? (p.5) Culpability is double-edged; it can involve *intention* on the part of perpetrators to inflict harm; but *failure* also is part of culpability, failure to pay attention, and take seriously developing contexts of harm, so that they can be stopped. In this way, Card finds culpability not only with "inhumane purposes" (she describes bullfighting as one example), but also in those instances "… when [intolerable harm] is reasonably foreseeable by those with power to change it." (p.20). Capital punishment, in her view, is an example of such harm. There are people with power who see (if they are willing) the harm this practice inflicts; they have the capacity to work to stop it. To call something an atrocity not only signals that intolerable harm is taking place, but also that human beings *know about it, and could do something about it.*

The social structure of power with regard to moral injury reveals a compelling portrait of culpability. *Who is responsible for the death and destruction of war?* For there is little doubt that people in power – in military, political, health and other sectors – are aware of what is happening. Not only has sincere alarm been expressed, but dedicated work is taking place to create avenues to ameliorate moral injury after it has occurred, or prevent it through various sorts of advance training. Nevertheless, Card's exploration of culpability opens the door to a landscape that demands deeper reflection regarding the ways that people in power, whether researchers, practitioners, religious professionals, military or political leaders, lack both vision and will with regard to doing something meaningful to stop moral injury at its root. Instead, with a few possible exceptions, current trends follow along with dominant forms of treatment of all wounds of war; this one too is to be managed; help will be given. Nevertheless, seen through the lens of Card's understanding of atrocity, it becomes more difficult to rest comfortably with such an assessment. For atrocities are not to be lived with; we should not accept them; things could be different. They are "evil." To say something is "evil" is to see "monstrous deeds" at work. Atrocities demand all the will and energy that social justice movements can muster, they deserve our "priority of attention" to deliver us from evil, by addressing and transforming the evil at their root. (p.23)

But again, priority of attention is deflected or avoided. Card explores why this is the case. First, she wonders why "recognition takes so long;" she asks, why are human beings so frequently unable or unwilling to recognize something as "an atrocity"? (p.23) She mentions the systemic rape of Korean comfort women during World War II as one example, and ponders how and why it took so many decades for the world to name these practices as an atrocity, as torture. But such trends continue. In 2019 the United States backed away from an international resolution it had spearheaded in the United Nations a decade earlier, that recognized and named conflict-related rape as an atrocity. Earlier the U.S. pushed for a full array of health resources to be available for women who are raped in war. The United Nations resolution proclaimed that being forced to carry a pregnancy due to war-related rape, to term, is a form of torture. But ten years later, the Trump administration refused to support the international resolution, unless every reference to "sexual reproductive health" was removed from the resolution; they were unwilling to sign off on anything that might enable women to pursue abortions, even following such sexual violence.[39] Willful blindness to atrocity continues. But Card's theory pushes exploration regarding what makes it possible for individuals and societies "not to see" atrocities while they are taking place, and after. *Analysis* of the dynamics of concealment is required; one must press further.

Second, and equally troubling, Card emphasizes that victims may become complicit with perpetrators in the very violence, the "evils" they have experienced. (p.11) People's "characters become corrupted." (p.11) In too many instances, "the dominated take on the perspective of the dominator." (p.40) In cases such as this, she writes, "... slaves have succumbed to a belief about the world that cannot see the world in any other terms other than the master's." (p.40) They have internalized "slave values," that exalt qualities such as "tameness." Virtues that are required in these oppressive circumstances cleverly are renamed, so as to disguise them and make them more palatable. Thus, "servility" is called "respect;" service is called "love;" obedience is called "loyalty;" and attachment to one's oppressors is "faithfulness." Those who internalize "slave values," Card writes, are "... like good dogs – good for their owners. A good dog does not necessarily have or lead a good life; a good dog is well trained; likewise a good slave, good children, and a good woman." (p.40) I hesitate, but will dare to add the following inevitable question: should we add being "a good soldier" to this typology? How about "a good citizen;" or "good patriot"?

All this is more complicated still when we consider the wide spectrum of veterans' attitudes and beliefs about the military branches and their own military identities. For many veterans, deep loyalty, identification with and affection for the U.S. military remains paramount throughout their lives. Remember, for instance, Christine Pedersen's father, a deeply loyal and enthusiastic veteran of the Marine Corps, who simultaneously had experienced serious personal harm as a result of his life within that institution. Not only a "botched surgery," (Christine's own words), but in addition Mr. Pedersen's internalization of Corps' values, resulted in a way of thinking that made applying for VA disability compensation appear to him as something negative, even shameful. Meanwhile, truthfully acknowledging his beloved daughter's sexual harassment was near impossible. He believed that accepting military financial disability would forever prevent his successful re-entry into the reserves – was this true? Living up to the identity he had adopted meant portraying strength and self-sufficiency at all costs, and refusal of assistance, refusal of vulnerability. Even his own daughter's experience of lasting harm at the hands of the same institution was difficult to integrate into his own identity, and set of values about the Marine Corps. The conflict created a "wedge" between them.

But unlike Mr. Pedersen, in her analysis of atrocity Card emphasizes that in many instances, people in oppressive contexts find the means not to succumb. Some hold onto or develop a larger perception and imagination that hint at a vision of a different world. One of the strongest forms of enslaved people's survival and subterfuge involves laughing at the authorities or masters even while maintaining a pretense of obedient compliance. Card writes, "seeing the oppressor as evil is a creative act on the part of the oppressed." (p.44)

I see defiance, imagination and the rejection of "slave values" especially in Andy's spiritual practice of carving the soapstones. He refuses to forget the children who were killed as a result of the airstrike. This practice directly conflicts with all the attitudes, philosophies and reflexive practices of dehumanization that he was encouraged to internalize and make central to his own identity.

Remember that some military ethicists, such as Shannon French, are aware of the dangers to servicemembers from training in dehumanization. These military scholars weigh the burden of dehumanization within the framework of a cost/benefit analysis. Yes, servicemembers can or will be harmed through being required to develop and enact such training; but the nation needs this. There is no other way but to require some people to do the nation's destructive work, its killing. However, nowhere in their analysis do they stop to ask whether this vision of the world should be criticized. Instead, they attempt to minimize the costs of dehumanization by applying themselves to the creation of new mechanisms that they hope will reduce the damage, and promote the quickest recovery, the best practices of "rehumanization" following immersion into war, and development of moral injury.

But all we need to do is think about Andy to understand that such an approach is both cynical and unrealistic. Being shaped in the ways of dehumanization is not a suit of clothing that one can put on and take off. The sharp wires of dehumanization are not easily controllable; they go past the surface of the skin; they penetrate deeply into the depths of one's body, into one's very soul. All the individual experiences of moral injury in this book demonstrate this insight. However, dominant atttudes about violence widely held in the United States shape its war-culture, and promote unrealistic and instrumental views of violence as a "tool." These assumnptions infuse both militairism (the culture of war) and militarization (development of all the structures and systems of war). This lack or refusal of sight leads to and supports the "enslaved mentality" of dehumanization that war-culture requires.

Further, uncritical assumptions regarding the instrumentality of violence also shape the decision-making of those in power who respond to the consequences of dehumanization after the fact. They *believe* in violence; it will bring certain, quick and determinative results, and any negative consequences can be managed or ameliorated; *there is no other choice*. This by and large shapes the way that moral injury is addressed in the United States. But Andy knows that such lack of *thought* is yet another example of the banality of evil. It is directly the opposite of the profound understanding Gandhi arrived at over the course of his life, and his continual experiments with peacebuilding, and analysis of the truth about violence: violence is *brutalizing* to the human spirit, both for those who implement it, and those on the receiving end. Violence degrades the dignity of human beings and human community.

Human inter-relationality includes a necessary bearing of one another's needs, being exposed in our own and others' vulnerability, and experiencing moral pain. Nevertheless, Card insists, the atrocity paradigm reveals with crystal clarity: "… there are some things that no one should have a 'share' of, such as torture and rape, toxic air, water and soil." Why do we not think more deeply about the burden of moral injury we are asking some of our brothers and sisters to carry? Card writes, "Social justice requires not only fairness in distributing both benefits of social cooperation and burdens necessary to produce or maintain them, but also *prevention of gratuitous, cruel and inhumane burdens.*" (p.97) (italics mine).

Given all this, it is hard to imagine anything more powerfully defiant than for Andy to bring his carvings to the Crescenz VAMC in Philadelphia. He sets himself and his life directly at odds with the status quo of the culture of violence, by imagining possible names those children might have been given by their families, and carefully positioning the stones for others to view and touch as so many sacred objects. But social analysis does not stop there; we additionally are challenged to reflect further on the meaning of this symbolic action, for if we agree with Andy that the killing of these children *should not have been,* what does that mean for any way forward? How do we begin to address all the forces of direct, structural and cultural violence that led to such a state of affairs? Andy's action insists that we not rest comfortably with the status quo of detachment, deception, misrecognition and concealment. This reality is intolerable, we cannot permit ourselves to live this way. *And if we do live this way, who are we?* Card writes, "tolerating evils should not be tolerated!" (p.113) Mourning and lamenting lead us out of complacency. But sorrow is meaningless without the process religion names as *metanoia*, literally, turning around and moving to a changed relational status, a different course of action, a transformed way of seeing and being in the world.

Military moral injury is an atrocity, a *foreseeable* intolerable harm, produced by *culpable* wrongdoing. How is moral injury *foreseeable*? Moral injury researchers and clinicians, military and political leaders, and especially the family and friends of those who struggle with moral injury show keen awareness of its soul-and-life destroying impact. But deeper vision to perceive, name and root out the structures and culture of violence and evil that set moral injury alight, eludes most. Yet Card emphasizes the following about "diabolical evil":

Diabolical evil, in my view, consists of placing others under the extreme stress, even severe duress, of having to choose between grave risks of horrible physical suffering or death (not necessarily their own) and equally grave risks of severe moral compromise, the loss of moral integrity, even moral death. This is stress geared to break the wills of decent people, to destroy what is best in us on any plausible conception of human excellence. For that reason, it deserves to be regarded as diabolical. The devil wants company and is a willing corrupter, plotting others' downfall. This is how evil extends its power ... But diabolical evil in human beings is very real. (p.212)

Card may as well have been speaking about the internal dynamics of moral injury in the quote above. The question is, if we *know* that these consequences will result from the structures and cultures of war we human beings have created, for the very people we *say* are most dear, beloved and respected by the nation, our servicemembers and veterans, why do we place them in the way of such intolerable harm?

I can hear all the just war theorists and thinkers clamoring to respond with an unlimited array of just war philosophical planks, justifications, and apologies. In the end all their arguments will emphasize the plaintive explanation: *there is no other way to respond to injustice. The nation must be protected. Only through such systems can the innocent be saved.*

This too is a cost/benefit analysis, similar to French's thinking. But a social analysis of the direct, structural and cultural sources of violence in U.S. war-culture, in the end, demonstrates the utter untenability of this justification. U.S. structures of war are anything *but* decisively the outcome of a true measurement of the dangers the U.S. faces, *or* the result of an honest evaluation of the best methods of security that might be devised. The final assessments of Andrew Bacevich and Robert Meagher are stark reminders of this. For Bacevich, after a long survey of successive and continuous chapters in the U.S. wars "for the Greater Middle East," neither the costs nor any suggested benefits find enduring justification. Yet U.S. Americans cannot be roused from what he describes as a deep "slumber" about the senselessness of their wars. More than anything else, war has become the ultimate tautology; going to war is what we do. Meanwhile, Robert Meagher's assessment is equally bleak. Taking moral injury seriously, he suggests, implodes the logic of just war theory and thinking altogether. As he writes, "... war has its own rules, and they have little to do with serving justice or preserving humanity."[40] He continues,

... it is our veterans who have lived and endured the inescapable contradiction between the touted necessity of violence and its inherent immorality. The nation that sent them to war sees them as heroes, deserving our lasting gratitude and esteem; but all too often they return from war unable to accept that gratitude and respect, finding themselves inwardly darkened and eaten away with guilt and shame. This reality is something we all need to understand, and this understanding will never come unless we listen to our veterans and learn from them, rather than from our political representatives and leaders, about the "rules of war"—referred to as the "rules of the road" by our president [Obama] in his Nobel Peace Prize acceptance speech—and whether they matter for much in the end.[41]

In the end, there is little cover left, no breathing room for us to say, "we just didn't know." The intolerable harm of moral injury is *forseeable.* And that makes all U.S. citizens *culpable.* They share "the gray zone" with servicemembers and veterans of the military. The vehicle of war-culture has taken citizens and leaders in with their own knowledge, to that territory of being deeply imbricated in their own and others' moral corruption; leaders and citizens alike have "put them [the morally injured] into situations where in order to survive they must, by their own choices, risk their own moral deterioration or moral death," as Card said. (pp.211–212) Or as Meagher quotes writer/veteran Tyler Boudreau, "… one's humanity can be quite difficult to recover once it's been evicted."[42]

We are so accustomed to thinking about war as something we win or lose, as a (semi)sacred act that creates and sustains the nation, or as a "necessary evil" or "sacrifice" that may not be avoided. But these too are thought patterns that arise out of the culture of violence; they are linear ways of thinking that conceal far too much along the way and promote violence as the only antidote to conflict. We may bemoan the ways this culture and these systems have become so deeply a part of human world-building. We may grieve their impact on us all. But we remain responsible for them, culpable. And if culpable, then it is impossible to rest with the world as it is. In the end, the military moral injury of our sisters and brothers turns the internalization of war and war-culture on its head. All those people whose case studies are considered in this book, and so many more who are suffering, or who have ended their own lives because their suffering became unbearable, are like the proverbial canary in the coal mine. We see them gasping for air, choking on the toxic way of life we have built. The coal mine is imploding all around us. We can't stay there any longer. Like Andy, we have to find a different way forward. The final chapter explores just what this may mean.

5   Towards Building a Different World:
A National Swerve

Can we be honest about the world as it is? Is it possible to envision and then build a different world? What would it mean to love one's country, one's planet and all its inhabitants?

Introduction

"I can't breathe." In June, 2020, after the killing of George Floyd, as hot summer protests exploded across the United States and world, the *New York Times* found 70 cases from the last ten years about incidents involving individuals apprehended by law enforcement departments in the United States, who spoke these exact words. They were not listened to, their very access to oxygen was cut off, and they died. *The Times* reported, "The dead ranged in age from 19 to 65. The majority of them had been stopped or held over non-violent infractions, 911 calls about suspicious behavior, or concerns about their mental health. More than half were Black."[1]

People can't breathe. We might pause and consider the weight of these words, and the way they cut across so many crises facing human beings. Along with race-based police brutality, additional suffocating effects of violence reach far and wide. Reflection also could include how and why this suffering is so unequally distributed across the nation and world. Sam Grant, Executive Director of 350MN.org, explains how the desperation of "I can't breathe" links racial social violence with racial environmental violence. "All voices – white, black and brown; indigenous and immigrant; rural and urban – need to be heard if we are to secure a safe and livable climate."[2] Poor communities, and Black and brown communities especially have been disproportionately affected by social and environmental injustice.

The summer and fall 2020 historic fires across the West and Southwest of the United States made it harder to breathe. Even as Donald Trump's administration prepared officially to end U.S. involvement in the Paris Agreement beginning November 4, 2020, *Scientific American* underscored that climate change is a major force in the fiery devastation on the ground, and resulting toxic air across much of the western part of the United States. Climatologist Daniel Swain of UCLA emphasized, "Climate change also affects how much moisture is in the air. It's actually drying out the air during these extreme heat events, which zaps plants of additional moisture."[3] But the burdens posed by this global shift are not suffered equally. Violence is intersectional: environmental *and* police injustice fall by implicit design and disproportionately on communities that have been marginalized in the United States because of race, ethnicity, or class. The Environmental Protection Agency, reporting on environmental disproportions, finds that "people in poverty are more exposed to more fine particulate matter than people living above poverty," and "non-Whites tend to be burdened disproportionately to Whites."[4]

Moreover, by the end of 2020 the Center for Disease Control projected over 390,000 deaths in the U.S. from Covid 19 – more people struggling to breathe. The number of deaths in the world climbed near 1,700,000, according to the World Health Organization.[5] The facts and visuals of having breath cut off, life cut off – choked, denied, unseen, constrained, poisoned – all this became more and more impossible to ignore or deny in the lives of too many human beings, not to mention non-human life as well. As 2020 drew to a close, stark contrasts grew even sharper; Donald Trump crowed about his supposed "immunity" from Covid, telling people "don't be afraid," while so much of the country, and especially poor and minoritized Black and brown communities, continued to face daunting losses and risks, one more indicator of structural racial health injustice.

Against this backdrop, the toxins of U.S. war-culture continued to intermix, enhancing all these dynamics of death-dealing constraint, denial, poisoning and cutting off of breath. "The Costs of War" researchers at Brown University summarized the budgetary costs arising from the U.S. post-9/11 wars. Between 2001 and 2020 the bill of war-related appropriations and obligations amounted to $6.4 trillion. Meanwhile, since 2001, the sheer geographic range of the wars expanded from Afghanistan and Iraq, to "wars and smaller operations elsewhere, *in more than 80 countries*"[6] (italics mine).

Honesty about our reality

The purpose of this book is to shine light on the crushing weight and consequences of war-culture, especially for military servicemembers, their friends, families and communities, to better illuminate the dynamics of violence that seed and maintain the suffering of moral injury. A direct line of continuity and culpability runs between the scaffolding that supports the structural and cultural violence of war-culture, and the devastation of military moral injury. But if people are to try to imagine a different way of living, or build a different world – if people want to understand how such intractable, large-scale and longstanding intersectional crises may be addressed – first we must dare to be honest about the world as it is.

Last year my husband and I sold the house we had lived in for over fifteen years, and downsized to a smaller house closer to my work. We're now in a small town within the Lehigh Valley, the third largest metropolitan area of Pennsylvania, with about 842,000 people. Our moving date coincided with the shutting down of the college where I teach, as we all pivoted to online teaching and learning in the face of the looming pandemic. The entire nation was facing so many uncertainties on the horizon, health-related fears, economic and employment catastrophes, an increasingly volatile political climate, and following May 25, 2020, the day that George Floyd was killed by Minneapolis police, a renewed and surging insistence on national reckoning with racial injustice.

In contrast to many other citizens, my life as a college professor and a white woman in the United States is privileged, including during this time, by layers of security to which others have little or no access. My job remained intact, and I had the means to implement necessary social distancing, since I live in my own home, and was able to switch over to remote work – unlike many other women, especially Black and brown women whose jobs disappeared in greater numbers during the pandemic. I did not have to worry about getting evicted, unlike so many other fellow citizens. The public health crisis exacerbated many existing inequalities in the United States, and the gaps have only continued to grow wider.

There was a massive and jagged sense of discontinuity during this time. For me, it was the jarring experience, on the one hand, of managing in this new environment, and on the other, witnessing and participating in the sharp and unrelenting unfolding of events related to protest, environmental catastrophe, fear of infection, rapid and disconcerting change all around, and the sense of the very ground opening up as so many fell through the cracks of the world we have made.

Shortly before Memorial Day, 2020, Borough city workers appeared at the corner where our house is located, with a cherry-picker truck. My husband and I watched from a window as the lift raised a worker higher than our second floor, and we assumed that electrical work on the utility pole had been planned. We were wrong.

I had seen this in many smaller towns, in areas of Pennsylvania situated more centrally in what is called "the rust belt." But somehow, I never imagined that this particular practice of war-culture would encamp literally twenty feet from my front door in the Lehigh Valley. However, when the city workers left, we saw that they installed a banner directly in front of our house on the utility pole, with the words "Hometown Hero" flying at the top. Against a backdrop of stars and stripes, a black and white photographic facsimile of a young man in military uniform was prominently featured. Below the photo we read his name, rank and the military conflict in which he fought. When I went out later to look at the rest of the street, I saw that similar banners, each one bearing a different photograph and information, had been installed all along our street, two to three banners per block. The banners memorialized and heroicized servicemembers from eras going back to World War II, and as recent as the First Gulf War[7] (see Figure 13).

Shortly thereafter, St. Theresa's Catholic church and parochial school, situated on the corner, perked up despite also being locked down. Parishioners appeared and installed about fifteen shoulder-high white crosses on the front lawn, with lights to illuminate them at night. Curious, I made a point of walking by to see what was going on. On each cross the name of a U.S. military conflict was painted in black letters, and the total number of U.S. military deaths (I actually looked up a number of the conflicts and discovered that the many of the numbers of U.S. military deaths posted on the crosses were incorrect). During Memorial Day and Fourth of July, the church chimes of St. Theresa rang out battle songs and war-related hymns for about a week.

As a researcher of U.S. war-culture, and as someone who has lived in this part of Pennsylvania now for a good part of my life, I have come to expect these practices. But I also find myself becoming angry, and feeling oppressed. No one from the Borough consulted with my husband or me before hanging that banner directly in front of our house; such is the widespread assumption that we all share in and agree with the national imaginary it represents, a national identity with war sacralized at its center. I think it's safe to imagine that St. Theresa's across the street is not engaging in study or conversation regarding the actual social teaching of the Catholic Church regarding morality and war, which they would find in conflict with the glorification of war on their front lawn and in the lyrics of the chimes ringing out.[8]

In both the banners and the church crosses, supposedly the emphasis is on remembering and memorializing U.S. military deaths. But to do so in a vacuum is unthinkingly to sacralize war. The public pedagogy in these examples really is stunning when one stops to think about it more deeply. For

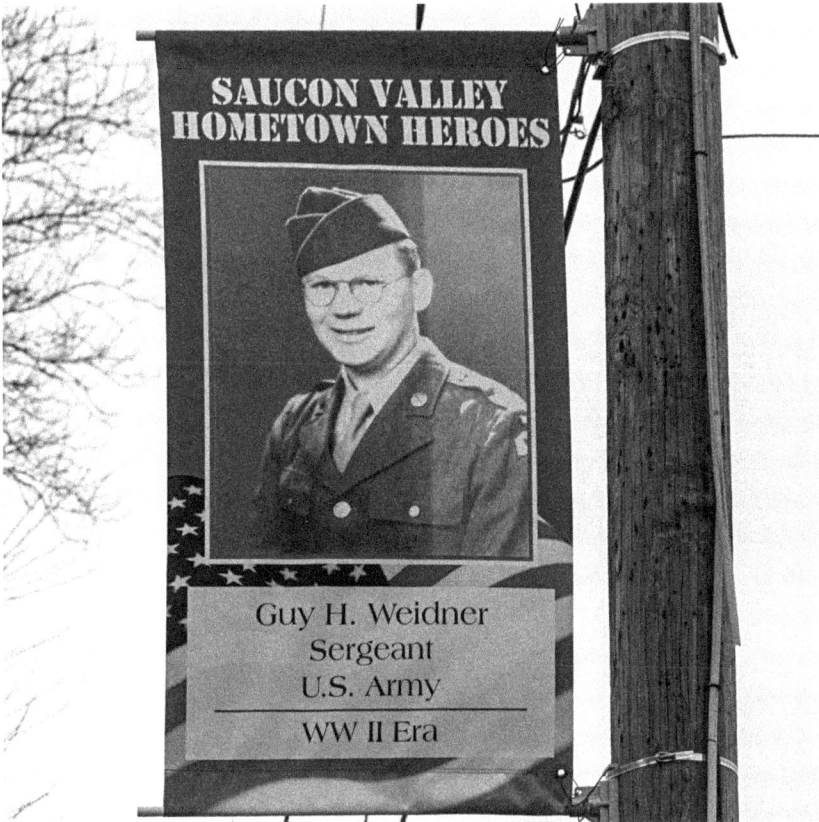

Figure 13 "Hometown Heroes." Photograph by Thomas Denton-Borhaug (January 10, 2021). Used with permission.

instance, we might stop and ponder how the banners and crosses underscore and encourage obliviousness to the consequences of U.S. involvement with conflicts/wars in over 80 countries abroad since 2001. We could reflect on this pedagogy's avoidance ever to mention the current status of U.S. militarization, the concentration of U.S. military bases around the world, the extent of military spending at home, and the role of U.S. politics, money and war-related industries ever escalating the global arms bazaar abroad. Meanwhile, in this pedagogy any "enemy" is completely faceless. There is no grief, no remembering of these "others" – it is as if they don't exist at all. The assumed narrative is that the U.S. is always right in these conflicts, and that the laborers of war on the front lines are "heroes." There is little to no mention regarding how, if ever, the wars of the 21st century might end.

These practices of war-culture are ubiquitous across the United States, in many communities large and small. On Veterans Day, people at my college innocently plant yellow and/or American flags commemorating veterans on the same corner where the college has its "Peace Pole," seemingly unaware of any contradictions! There is little inclusion or mention (or thought!) regarding the wider and deeper context of our war-culture, and its consequences both for people in the United States, and many others around the world. Nevertheless, as this book has emphasized, commemorative practices such as these, though well-intentioned, run counter to the painful and conflicted truth-telling of many laborers of war. The barrier already created between the practitioners of war and the rest of us is only reinforced; and these rituals deepen the silence and the isolation.

Meanwhile, in the summer of 2020, the surge of protest and cries for racial justice indicated growing collective awareness across the United States about the depth of systemic domestic police violence, as a symptom of pervasive and longstanding structural and cultural racial violence in the nation overall. Though it was widely misinterpreted and misunderstood, the cry to "defund the police" became impossible to ignore. What was behind this cry? Activist and theorist Angela Davis explained: with surging awareness of the "massive problem of racist state violence," what should the country do? While many misinterpreted "defund the police" as a disrespectful slam on police officers, Davis' understanding was more nuanced. She saw that only addressing "individual police officers to bear the burden of that history" through prosecuting them, would encourage little progress in the overarching goal of eradicating structural police racism and violence. Instead, the cry to "defund the police" was a reference point to *revision* security and safety overall. As she said in multiple interviews, it makes little sense, when someone is having a mental health crisis, to send someone to address the situation with a gun.[9] We would do better to connect the call to "defund the police" with what Davis terms, "abolition feminism," an intersectional analysis that points to a different mindset and aim altogether,

> ... recognizing that threats to safety, threats to security, come not primarily from what is defined as crime, but rather from the failure of institutions in our country to address issues of health, issues of violence, education, etc. So, abolition is really about rethinking the kind of future we want, the social future, the economic future, the political future. It's about revolution.[10]

Davis' inspirational analysis points toward a horizon of rebuilding the world, and redressing structural injustices to create a world where people are pulling together. But there is deeper digging yet to be done, to continue the effort at honesty about our reality, and to imagine a different world.

Continuing this excavation uncovers further links between different vectors of violence. Criticisms about police violence from the summer and fall of 2020 connected the dots between domestic policing and the militarization of war-culture. Some researchers and journalists explored the 1033 program in the Department of Defense, arising out of the 1997 National Defense Authorization Act, that streamlined a pipeline for discarded military products, creating a pathway from the fields of war to local policing authorities in the United States. It was reported that "over $7.5 billion of property has been transferred ... [with over] 8,000 law enforcement agencies enrolled" in the program. In addition to "ordinary" items such as "office equipment, clothing, tools, radios," the pipeline also moved "rifles, armored vehicles," "night-vision goggles and pipe bomb materials" and who really knows what all else.[11] One report indicated,

> A year after Ferguson, then president Barack Obama signed an executive order that prohibited state and local law enforcement from receiving certain types of property, like grenade launchers and weaponized aircraft, under the 1033 program, but these restrictions were short-lived: Trump lifted them in 2017.[12]

Meanwhile, Anna Gunderson, a political scientist at Louisiana State University who studied the program, emphasized the difficulty in pinning down the actual numbers and activities of the program, because "the agencies themselves are inconsistent in keeping track." Ryan Welch, political scientist from the University of Tampa, reported, "Our research suggests that officers with military hardware and mindsets will resort to violence more quickly and often."[13]

But though the alarm was sounded about this increased use of militarized equipment in domestic police departments; and though activists and theorists also underscored how the same militarization ignites and escalates potential violence in any crisis, the connections go deeper still. Davis and the abolitionist feminists call out structural streams of violence that must be faced. And even deeper still, violence endures in the heart of U.S. national identity, stubbornly anchored in the bottom-most streams of culture in the United States.

Violence in the heart of national identity

To put it bluntly, people in the United States need to think about our relationship with cultural violence, in other words, the way that violence shapes our very identities. In the U.S., violence is the tool we reach for; it is the banner we wrap ourselves in; violence is the practice we unthinkingly worship – we bestow vast sums of our monies on it, we can never have enough of it "in the bank," as it were, whether through military armaments, or ever-expanding policing budgets, or the 2nd Amendment. Our national rituals, ways of commemoration, holidays and sites of identity are shot through with references to the violence of war as the bedrock of who we are as a country, a nation. During the turbulent and uncertain time of public health, political, economic and race crises in 2020, gun sales to individuals skyrocketed in the United States. In Pennsylvania, background checks related to gun sales surged by 45% in one year.[14]

Necessary violence is the story we tell ourselves to ward off fear of an uncertain future and uncontrollable events as well as imagined foes: violence will save us; we are in control; we will overcome whatever danger comes our way with our own unvanquishable violence. To say that this is the only language our enemies can understand only underscores that this is our own mother tongue. Yet amazingly, and oh so contradictorily, people simultaneously pretend that we can shield ourselves from the inevitable backlash that violence always unleashes, insisting that we can remain unscathed by the violence we insist on wielding, and imagining that we can build a peaceful world and relations through violence, though one has to wonder, what does the peace we supposedly seek look like in such a violence-saturated context? Meanwhile, the dominant narrative masks the deep inequalities that violence always encourages. Maybe if we just pretend hard enough, squint seriously enough, we can see around it, so it is imagined. What a cognitive distortion, what a conflict.

During the Trump era, it was fascinating, in a horrifying kind of way, to observe U.S. citizens demonstrating their stringent defense of false realities. During an international pandemic in which the U.S., 4% of the global population, experienced over 20% of the world's deaths from Covid, nevertheless, so many people believed that despite stark facts, they could ditch masks, attend large gatherings, and encourage regular school and the opening of all businesses without restraint. Of course, facts themselves were posed as an identity issue open to challenge, such as when the nominated Justice to the Supreme Court, Amy Coney Barrett, answered senators' questions regarding whether she accepted the science of climate change.

Judge Barrett's responses demonstrated "preference falsification" in action, the tendency to misrepresent what one really thinks or values in the face of prevailing social pressures.[15] Asked whether corona virus causes infection, or whether smoking causes cancer, she had a ready response based on scientific data. But when asked about "whether climate change is happening, and it's threatening the air we breathe and the water we drink," Barrett refused to answer. Trying to avoid the question, she said that she could not opine on "a matter of public policy, especially one that is politically controversial … I would not say I have firm views on it."[16] Scientists and activists were outraged. Greta Thunberg's sarcastic tweet said it all: "To be fair, I don't have any 'views on climate change' either. Just like I don't have any 'views' on gravity, the fact that the earth is round, photosynthesis nor evolution."[17]

But again, as this book has shown, if the refusal of climate change science still characterizes a significant swath of U.S. culture, an even more widespread refusal to acknowledge the reality of war-culture is alive and well. Why? No doubt there are many factors to explain this troubling reality but, at a profound level, acknowledgement of U.S. war-culture is out of reach because *honesty about this reality threatens national identity*. Facing sacrificial war-culture painfully clashes with the practices and narratives of identity we have created and regularly perform. It's deeply in conflict with the stories we tell about our lives, the U.S. nation, and the rituals through which people make meaning about citizenship and national belonging. Like other truths that citizens find inconvenient, honesty regarding the consequences of sacrificial war-culture inevitably leads to identity conflict. Thus, just as many citizens blithely *refuse* to acknowledge the science of climate change, or Covid science, the conflicts posed by a national imaginary based in sacrificial war-culture are managed in similar fashion, through denial, falsification, and also through glorification – by way of undergirding war-culture with sacrificial rhetoric and logic.

A struggle to have the honest conversation we need

In the fall of 2020 I was contacted by the producers of "The Gist with Mike Pesca." Produced by *Slate*, the daily show addresses news and culture.[18] Celebrating the five-year anniversary that made it one of the longest-running daily news podcasts, Pesca described the purpose of the program, "It's not a resuscitation of what happened. It's my take on the news. It's not Rush Limbaugh or The Young Turks. It's not ideologically driven."[19]

In their email to me, "The Gist" producers invited me to be interviewed by Pesca about my first book, *U.S. War-culture, Sacrifice and Salvation.* I was intrigued. Responding to Producer Lori Galarreta, I asked how they had come across my work, and whether "there was any particular theme" that interested them. I also sent them two of my recent shorter publications, so that they would have the opportunity to better understand my analysis of sacrificial U.S. war-culture. As producer Daniel Schroeder responded, "Our host Mike came across your writing while doing other research for our show and thought you'd be a great guest to speak with on the topic of sacrifice, your work in that area, what that means now, and the parallels of sacrifice in war and in this pandemic."[20] Producer Galaretta explained further, "Mike's closing monologue in today's episode focuses on the sacrifices of military members and the significance of Trump's dismissal and derision of such sacrifices. Mike even quotes you at one point. So Mike is particularly interested in going a bit deeper on the ideas he touches on in this monologue."

I listened to the podcast the producers sent, in which Gist had explored an explosive news story reporting on Trump's description of military servicemembers as "suckers and losers."[21] After listening to the podcast, I got back in touch with the producers. Were they sure that they wanted me on the show? In the podcast, Gist had characterized Trump's comments as "bad war strategy," in addition to being offensive and ugly. As Pesca argued, "veneration for the sacrifice of servicemen and women is the fuel for the perpetuation of the all-volunteer army," and to be able to support the mightiest military force in the world without having to rely on conscription is "one of the greatest and most ignored accomplishments of the last 47 years." When Trump "denigrated the ultimate sacrifice," he "hurt the military overall, and all of us by extension," in essence, weakening the military. As Pesca concluded, "Sacrificial discourse authorizes war, by building value into the deaths brought about by war ... Trump robs these deaths of that value."[22]

I emailed the producers about my doubt,

Perhaps you'll want to look at some of my work to consider if Mike will want me on. I'm very critical of the way sacrificial frameworks have been used by both Republican and Democratic leaders (including Trump!) to mystify and justify what I call "U.S. war-culture" – take a look at the two shorter articles and why don't you get back to me. In the clip that Daniel [one of the producers] sent to me, I hear Mike falling into the same kind of cognitive trap that so many others do, making war sacred through reliance on this notion. I ask, once war becomes a sacred enterprise, how can it ever be rationally analyzed, much less criticized or protested? … I'm really not sure that you all understand the argument that I'm making here.[23]

Following my email, the producers responded, "We spoke with Mike this morning and he's looking forward to the conversation, including discussing your thoughts on Trump's recent and past comments about sacrifice and the military."[24] The day and time for the virtual interview were confirmed, and it took place on September 10, 2020. As the producers requested, I made my own voice memo with my iPhone, so that I might afterwards send it to them to be mixed in with their own recording. Thus, I have a recorded copy of the interview, and it has been fascinating for me to go back and listen to the conversation.

From my perspective, it was an engaging and forthright exchange. We agreed on the importance of deeply valuing military servicemembers. I explained my analysis of the sacralizing, masking and concealing nature of sacrificial war-culture. We spoke about grief and whether it is possible to ask if war is ever futile. Near the end of the interview, Pesca asked the following question,

> Somewhere out there is a person who doesn't like the way Trump said it, but is very anti-war, and recognizes what you say is true. Our whole culture conspires to tell people that sacrifice is essential. What would you say to this person: I wouldn't call these people suckers, but they didn't give their lives for a greater cause? I'm cognizant of the war machine finding a grain of truth in what Trump says …[25]

Pesca's question gave me the opportunity to discuss grief and grievability. I responded,

> We know that a very tiny percentage of citizens are dealing with these so-called sacrifices, in terms of being in the military, being sent to the fields of war, and experiencing the kind of suffering that they inevitably do. And we thank them, they return to the United States, and then people tend to thank them for their service, often using sacrificial language. But do they really think about the fact that this sacrifice has been distributed so unequally in the United States? Most people, I think, are all too willing to go about their everyday lives, and allow a small number of citizens to bear this burden. That bothers me. But it also bothers

me that this language of sacrifice occludes our vision with regard to awareness, about the lives, the losses in the countries where we have been fighting, in the longest wars of US history. And there really doesn't seem to be any end to them yet. And we seem to be powerless, unable to rouse ourselves to the kind of protest needed to stop them. I wonder about the way that this sacralization of war disables us from the kind of active citizenship we need to engage. Once war becomes sacralized, and I would argue that is what the rhetoric and the logic of sacrifice does, how can we ever protest it? ... You become a heretic in the sacralized world of war, if you say no. And that is as much a disservice to our military servicemembers as it is to the rest of us, and maybe more to them.[26]

There were 14 emails exchanged between the producers and me in the days leading up to the interview. When I asked at the conclusion of the interview if this had been what they hoped for, and whether it was helpful, the producers said, "There's a lot of material here for us to use."[27] They also told me that they would be in touch regarding the date of the upcoming podcast. And that was the last I heard from them. About two weeks later, I decided to get in touch again, emailing,

> Dear Daniel and Lori – I'm curious to know if any of the interview will be published in the podcast? If a decision was made not to utilize the interview, it would be helpful for me to know why.
> Thanks,
> Kelly Denton-Borhaug[28]

To date, I have yet to hear again from them, and nothing from the interview was aired, so far as I know. I can only surmise that in the end, the content of the conversation was not in keeping with what Pesca wished to communicate to his listeners. As I have experienced in many settings over the years, this isn't an easy conversation to have. To get to the bottom of why such is the case, we have to dig deeper into those issues of national identity and its relationship to violence.

Nationalism and identity, violence and equality

Judith Butler's *The Force of Nonviolence,* sets the relationship between national identity and violence into sharp relief.[29] A key plank from her argument opens this exploration: "Most forms of violence are committed to inequality."[30] Relegating certain others to "enemy status" masks the relations of inequality that are central to the dynamics of violence. Exploring how violence works inexorably leads to the structural and cultural frameworks that justify and implement inequality.[31] What does Butler mean?

Inequality is present wherever a particular type of thinking elevates certain lives above others. In short, to practice or condone violence, one must believe that lives on the receiving end of violence somehow are less valuable, and less deserving of protection and preservation. The standard by which Butler identifies inequality at work is the category of "grievability;" readers will be familiar with this idea from earlier chapters of this book.

She asks, "How do we account for the differential ways in which lives and deaths matter or fail to matter?[32] Excavating the ground of "war logics," in other words, the frameworks of language and patterns of thinking in any war-culture, one discovers working assumptions of inequality: "In order to live, the other must die … [or] If you want to live, you must be able to kill."[33] Remember this exchange logic and the cultural catchphrases or memes in the United States that embody precisely this assumption: in the central exhibit of the World War II commemorative plaza on the national mall in Washington, D.C., beneath rows of stars symbolizing the deaths of U.S. military servicemembers, the words are emblazoned, "Here we pay the price of freedom." There must and will be death, a "payment," a blood sacrifice that includes both the deaths of the enemy, and the deaths of warriors. The same thought more casually is expressed on bumperstickers and tee-shirts, "Freedom isn't free!" These sacrificial cognitive patterns have been acculturated in all citizens. But Butler shines light on the inequality hiding in plain sight: not all lives are equally valuable; some lives will not be grieved, mourned or valued enough to have their life safeguarded.

This standard of valuing holds true not only for those labeled as "the enemy," but also the servicemembers who wage this violence. Where are the places in U.S. culture where citizens are encouraged to reflect on the question, *what is the impact of this violence on those who perpetrate it and/ or experience it as a form of betrayal?*

Those who are trained to do such labor, supposedly on behalf of the security needs of all citizens, are relegated to atrocity; they both inflict *and* experience intolerable harm. Lingering on the question posed above, the clouds of confusion begin to clear, and honesty takes greater shape. But achieving this consciousness is not easy, or simple.

Over and over in the last two decades, presenting this material, I observe painful emotions regularly arising among listeners. We don't wish to think of ourselves in this way, as abetting atrocity; we say that equality is at the heart of what it means to be a U.S. citizen. Is this why, in order to try to counter the notion that these lives were not equally valued, people in the U.S. go to such lengths in their methods of commemorating military servicemembers? Remember the banners 20 feet from my house. Moreover, lest we imagine that this exploration is inconsequential, Butler insists that "naming practices," in other words, the very language/rhetoric that is commonly accepted and used, already inculcates certain ways of thinking and valuing.[34] This means that language such as that used in "war-logics" has a way of muting, justifying, and making more acceptable the forms of state violence to which people give their assent. It now appears less "direct, less spectacular, less orchestrated," and more necessary and inevitable.[35] In other words, it muddles requisite clarity about reality that we need.

U.S. citizens are pre-reflectively educated in broad formats of war-culture's public pedagogy, such as the WWII memorial, and thus shaped not to see, or to assume that these frameworks of inequality are normal and necessary. Certain lives will not be preserved, certain losses must be accepted. And sacrificial logic and metaphors lubricate these cognitive patterns; they not only justify inequality, but necessitate it, even sacralize it! Along the same lines, just war theory always involves a similar exchange and cost/benefit analysis. Butler writes, "to be subject to a calculation is already to have entered the gray zone of the ungrievable."[36]

Most importantly, what about the inculcation of this kind of thinking in the lives of the military servicemembers whose struggles are recounted in this book? How were these assumptions about identity, inequality and sacrifice embodied or addressed in the treatment that Mr. Jones underwent? It's easy to see the role of prevailing cultural memes and assumptions in Andy's story. The abject shock he experienced once he entered the bombed structure, finding the pile of bodies, points to a particular logic that was at work in his thinking previously, to "mute, justify, and make more acceptable" the devaluing and destruction of certain lives. But again, the inequality of violence did not end there: his own life also was deemed "a necessary sacrifice" – not subject to the same conditions of protection and preservation as other lives. In addition, and taking a collective view, the working mantra of the Trump presidential administration, "America First," demonstrated a nationalizing of such assumptions regarding the prioritization of sovereign individuality of the nation, and subsequent justification of the inequality of all other nations. "America First" means that everything and everyone else is less, secondary. As with other forms of war-logics, this suggested banner of identity was justified and implemented through fear, in this case the specter of supposed "American carnage."[37]

Such is the state of affairs in U.S. war-culture. What of its consequences? Butler reflects on how the violence in collective reality "takes its toll on the body." It is "an attack on the structure of being" itself.[38] Because so little thought is paid to the embodied and spiritual consequences of violence at the heart of war-culture, Butler's insight is worth further reflection.

In other words, deeper digging is required, beyond individual identity, and beyond national identity, to an even more profound set of questions. One might ask, what does it mean to be human, to have a human life? Remember how the logics of war stress "individual freedom." People in U.S. war-culture, especially men, and all military servicemembers, are educated and shaped to long and strive for "impermeability" as individuals, and warriors. At the same time, and contradictorily, they also are shaped for "expendability." The earlier chapters of this book explore how this formation not only impacts individuals, but also military cultures, and masculinist national identity. But though widespread in the nation, and despite the hold this identity formation has on people individually and collectively, honesty about reality reveals this as a cognitive and moral distortion: assumptions of impermeability *and* expendability amount to a false reality, a thought pattern little more than a chimera. *Human beings are not impermeable.* In contrast to supposed impermeable individuality, Butler insists, *"life requires infrastructure as an immanent feature of life itself."*[39] *"'I' requires 'you' to survive and flourish, and we both require a sustaining world."*[40] The only survivable, flourishing, good life is one that is "lived with others." To truly value equality, *we must reject expendability*: every life is deserving of preservation and protection in a web of mutuality.

The emphasis on impermeability, individuality and expendability all contradict the very heart of human existence. Speaking truthfully about the human condition requires us to name our "vulnerability, exposure, even dependency," along with the abiding and irreplaceable value of all human life. Humans have "the right to persist," *and* human flourishing always and everywhere is inextricably bound up with other lives, as well as the well-being of non-human life.[41]

We have to be honest – the central ways that U.S. citizens are pre-reflectively acculturated to imagine and centralize their ideals of belonging to the nation, inevitably lead to the justification and the need to defend inequalities that always are enforced with violence. But if we were instead to highlight "grievability," in Butler's mind, a diametrically opposed value would come before our vision: "this loss is unacceptable." In essence, grievability "is a defining feature of equality."[42] We only grieve if lives are of value, if losing them would matter so much to us that we insist on something different. And we need this "utopic horizon," for without insisting on the morality of "equal grievability" of all life, not only do we fail to recognize all lives as valuable, in the end, we arrive at a point where some lives "will not be registered at all." Not only war, but racism and other forms of structural and cultural violence also exhibit the same patterns. Butler quotes Ruth Wilson Gilmore's definition of racism:

> Racism, specifically is the state-sanctioned or extralegal production and exploitation of group-differentiated vulnerability to premature death.[43]

How can such death-dealing methods of identity formation and the determining of life's value be countered? We must be honest about our reality, and the world we have built. Butler calls for the work of "tracking and exposing the oscillation of frameworks" of violence, that are as deceptive as they are one-sided. Acknowledgement of the misrecognition, the justifications, all the masking and sacralizing, is the work that is demanded. [44]

This book's purpose is to track and expose the deeper wells of structural and cultural violence that give rise to moral injury. But this last chapter raises two additional questions. First, *how can we dismantle the destructive scaffolding that supports so much structural and cultural violence?* Second, in addition to exposing the destructiveness in frameworks of violence, there is equal need for energy and insight to inspire a different consciousness, and to envision scaffolding for a different world. *What are the signposts that help us to imagine a different world, and for what larger rationale, toward what deeper hope, may such work be directed?*

Cultural swerves and stranded ethics

The intersection of multiple crises facing the United States and wider world face human beings with danger and opportunity. In 2014, Robert Jay Lifton highlighted the notion of "swerves;" these are moments in history when cultural forces unexpectedly and powerfully shift. The solid ground beneath suddenly morphs into something more fluid and uncertain. I will never forget being in San Francisco when the 1989 earthquake took place. That was a visceral and physical experience of hard ground suddenly out of joint. In some parts of the city, especially those that were built on landfill (and ironically, much of the landfill was put into place following the 1906 earthquake!), scientists spoke of "liquification" of the ground, where some of the worst damage from the earthquake occurred.

Believe me, the sense of ground falling away is not a comfortable sensation. Similarly, "cultural swerves" are ambiguous hinges in history, capable of destruction as well as change. These tectonic shifts jolt societies when cultural, social, historical ground seems to liquify, becoming newly unstable. The former ways of thinking and believing now are experienced as jarring, they just don't fit any longer, and one is overcome with a sense that things have to change.

On "Bloody Sunday," in Selma, Alabama in 1964, as they attempted to cross the Edmund Pettus Bridge, civil rights marchers led by John Lewis and Hosea Williams were trampled by Alabama State Troopers, and a "posse" on horseback organized by Sheriff Jim Clarke. The state and local forces ran directly through the nonviolent and unarmed protesters, beating them with police night sticks and suffocating them with tear gas, raining down a blizzard of violence on people whose conscience insisted on this symbolic bridge crossing as a declaration of change. They *would* register to vote in Alabama.

Only a few days before, people in Selma, as well as across the nation, watched as the nightly TV news showcased film of Amelia Boynton at the hands of police violence. Sheriff Jim Clark grabbed this middle-aged professional Black teacher by the neck in front of the city courthouse, and dragged her half a block down the street to a paddy wagon. The ground was shifting in ways that segregationists and white supremacists could not control. In the days that followed, other Black professionals stepped into the fray, creating additional teachers' protests, beauticians' protests, undertakers' protests. A wave of insistence on equality grew, and the forces of resistance to change ineffectively and violently tried to prevent it. Finally, following the bloodshed and violence at Edmund Pettus Bridge, Dr. Martin Luther King Jr. put out a call to the nation, asking people to come to Selma to continue the insistence. It is fascinating to listen to voices who responded from all over the country, as they were interviewed by journalists. Dropping whatever they were doing, they changed their plans, and got on planes and trains, cars and buses to head to Selma. "I just decided, I had to come. I've got to see what it's all about." "These ideals that have been expressed here by the people have been mine for a long time."[45]

King and other leaders described such moments as "creative tension;" and this tension goes along with cultural swerves. The creation of new collective consciousness and awareness, though preceded by long and hard work on the part of social justice actors, still surges with the sense of surprise; like Boynton, Lewis, Williams and King, we have to be ready to recognize this new opening when it comes.[46] The swerve of awareness about racial justice in

Selma surged and then culminated in the Voting Rights Act of 1965, though access to fair and free voting remains a work in progress in the U.S.

Lifton describes additional social/cultural swerves that altered collective consciousness in the United States. These include the nuclear threat, and the climate threat. Swerves accompany "breakdowns in the social arrangements that ordinarily anchor human lives."[47] In these cases, "experience, economics and ethics" coalesced in new ways, such that earlier "fragmentary awareness" leaped to a different level, "a formed awareness." Selma ignited change; white people were challenged to understand themselves and their society differently; Black people's collective insistence on full personhood and human rights grew to new heights. In this emerging consciousness, a new and profound realization overtook an earlier blindness. The previous ethical assumptions that benefitted some while dealing death to others, could be defended no longer; that moral formation not only was now outdated, but more widely recognized as "evil," similar to the way that segregation and white supremacy have culturally been identified as "evil," in the United States, even if eradication of these threats remains to be fully accomplished, an unhealed national wound, and urgent ongoing social responsibility.

The "nuclear swerve" began to form in the 1980s, when the imaginary of a "nuclear freeze" collectively took hold across the world, and millions of people were moved to rise up and demand a freeze on the testing, production and potential use of nuclear weapons on the part of the United States and Soviet Union. Clearly, long before this, there existed some awareness about the danger of nuclear weapons and the horrific suffering they posed for people and the planet; but as Lifton writes, now, with this swerve, suddenly "emotions related to individual conscience were pooled into a shared narrative by enormous numbers of people."[48] The development of the language of "nuclear freeze" became a mobilizing rhetorical banner capable of uniting people across many forms of difference.

Lifton identifies the climate crisis as an additional swerve. Since his first writing about the "climate swerve" in 2014, additional signs have coalesced, suggesting that the swerve is taking ever greater shape, "a transnational demand for cutting back on carbon emissions in steps that are systematically outlined." Could the banner of "climate freeze" come to unite and mobilize people across the world as powerfully as the language of "nuclear freeze" took hold in the 1980s? Nuclear freeze mobilization never stopped, but in fact continued to gain ground, through regional nuclear freezes in the world, and also, more recently through ratification in 2020 by fifty sovereign nations of the United Nations' "Treaty on the Prohibition of Nuclear Weapons."[49]

Two threads from Lifton's thinking about cultural swerves inform this chapter. First, Lifton emphasizes the links between a changing narrative, a shifting imaginary, and concomitant changing set of ethics. "People came to feel that it was deeply wrong, perhaps evil, to engage in nuclear war, and are coming to an awareness that it is deeply wrong, perhaps evil, to destroy our habitat and create a legacy of suffering for our children and grandchildren," he writes.[50] New language, and a new narrative, came into being simultaneously with a reconsidered collective self-understanding. All this informed the deeper change taking place, and helped to spread and anchor the swerve taking shape. The rhetoric of "nuclear freeze" became an imaginary that people could unite behind, a straightforward, evocative, immediately understandable, and powerful framework, demanding change. Imaginaries are capable of evolution; they can change and grow.

Second, Lifton describes the "passionate ethics" that arise along with new awareness, consciousness and identity. Passionate ethics inspired Selma and washed across the country. This was a result of the hard work of so many, and also a result of a changing national consciousness, leading to national legislation and frameworks for equal access to the right to vote. In the case of the climate swerve, ethicists and activists now speak of "stranded assets" to describe the urgent change in moral thought and behavior in accord with climate crisis awareness. "Leave it in the ground," has become the rallying cry of protesters with respect to the remaining oil reserves across the world.[51] This is a sharp turn away from the principles that guided fossil fuel corporations, and their "focus on the maximum use of their product in order to serve the interests of shareholders."[52] Like "stranded assets" that should be left in the ground, Lifton suggests that "stranded ethics," are those moral frameworks that also remain better buried and left behind. Fossil fuel corporation ethics, shaped by values and actions that we are better off saying goodbye to, are "stranded ethics" that have led to destruction; they are "evil" and should be rejected for something new.

Lifton makes reference to an additional stranded ethic, the "amorphic ethic of 'national security.'"[53] This ethic masks and justifies not only unremitting and destructive militarization; it also papers over the consequences of militarization and war, the destruction of people, infrastructure and the natural world. Yet this ethic has not yet been stranded. Along with other factors, religion plays a strong role in undergirding and sacralizing it. Lifton emphasizes, "Over the course of my work I have come to the realization that it is very difficult to endanger or kill large numbers of people except with a claim to virtue."[54] This book illustrates that Lifton's insight is all too true.

In the cases of both the nuclear swerve and the climate swerve, people evolved from a more elemental form of "tangential awareness," including doubt about the status quo, and fragmentary thoughts and ideas, to "the more active knowledge associated with formed awareness."[55] A decisive change, and development of "ethical passion," took place both cognitively and morally; now they identify and articulate as "wrong" the behaviors based on former assumptions and values that excused or justified both nuclear weapons and climate change. And they seek new frameworks of justice, and wider landscapes of flourishing.

Reimagining our belonging: Returning to Andy's story

The moral injury of veterans and servicemembers is an atrocity, an intolerable and foreseeable harm produced by culpable wrongdoing. Is it possible, that like "nuclear freeze," or "climate crisis" or "climate freeze," the simple rhetorical banner, *"moral injury is an atrocity,"* could encourage a cultural swerve? Could it prompt growth in collective consciousness regarding the devastating consequences of the militarized and violent world we humans, especially those of us who are U.S. citizens, have built?

When I first heard Jonathan Shay talk about moral injury in that conference years ago, I knew instinctively that this phenomenon called out for deeper reflection. The lightbulb turned on in my mind: if we would challenge ourselves to truly understand moral injury in the lives of too many servicemembers and veterans, we would by necessity find it impossible to rest comfortably with the contradictions, justifications and sacralizations of war-culture that so characterize the United States.

This book follows that initial thread of insight to its inevitable conclusions. Moving past the direct violence of moral injury, and setting into sharp relief the structural and cultural violence that undergirds it, we are confronted with unavoidable clarity: the foreseeability of moral injury is undeniable; moral injury is not like a lightning strike, or tsunami. Its violence and harm grow out of the structural and cultural violence of the social world humans have built. Thus we share collective moral responsibility. We cannot – should not – rest at ease with this destruction, this pain, this death. We can no longer deny the line of continuity between the suffering and degradation being experienced by veterans and servicemembers, and the structural and cultural violence in the war-culture that we have built together and continue to sustain.

There is no room left for excuse, justification, concealment. Moral injury is that flashpoint that pulls our vision (however reluctantly!) to the truth about war and war-culture in the human world we have created. Hearing the voices of those who live with moral injury, seeing their faces, and taking in their stories, is akin to the nation viewing the manhandling of Amelia Boynton on the national evening newscast. If Claudia Card expressed how impossible it is to inaugurate war without atrocity, defining moral injury as atrocity clarifies this vision further. Think, for example, about how and why Andy has carried its pain and destruction. The formation he underwent in "unequal grievability," involved all the training and consequences of his work as a servicemember. But this identity, this consciousness was burned to the ground, along with all the other destruction that occurred the night his unit called in the airstrike on a "target" and location Andy had identified. And not only Andy, once the bath of ice-water awareness rushes over us, as it did for him, all those who belong to the United States also must face our own culpability. As Chaplain Antal and the veterans say in their ceremony, this means "accepting our brunt of the burden," even as Andy also has made exactly this process his life's ongoing work.

But what does this mean, and how shall we carry that weight? If the *scales have fallen* from our eyes regarding the atrocity of moral injury; after *the swerve in consciousness springs up in us* related the structural and cultural violence that gives rise to moral injury; when we *understand* that this phenomenon is a foreseeable and intolerable harm – then we cannot but *recognize that all of us*, everyday citizens as well as leaders in our common life, share *culpability*. Here a new "passionate ethics" begins to grow.

Nevertheless, I pause at this juncture, because the awareness outlined above appears to be very far away for the majority of citizens in the United States. The cognitive and moral processes through which citizens automatically frame war as "the necessary sacrifice" and, further, foreground this with sacrificial templates from their religious traditions, have for so long successfully justified and legitimated a muddy rut of unequal grievability; and this runs very deeply in the U.S. American psyche. However, at the same time, signs of a swerve of consciousness are visible. The enormous increase of research about moral injury in recent years, the emergence of more voices demanding to be heard among those who live with moral injury, and the new language, understanding and efforts to address it, all signify that change is afoot. The question is, will we allow ourselves to be impacted?

Moral injury education and training

During the last few years, Chaplain Antal of the Veterans Health Administration included me in various public trainings growing out of the Moral Injury

Group he and psychologist Peter Yeomans have developed. These workshops educate clergy and chaplains about moral injury, and promote the development of skills to support healing among veterans, their families and the wider community. Due to the recognition that many veterans who are suffering will never break their silence to seek help from medical professionals, especially within the Veterans Health Administration, leaders of the VHA determined to increase education and training for clergy and chaplains as a specific goal.[56] The VA concluded that local religious institutions and their clergy could provide an invaluable role, if they can develop willingness to openly listen, and build and sustain relationships of trust, as well as learn how to refer to the VA and community mental health professionals when appropriate. I have a unique role in these educational settings, to help participants think about the background and context of sacrificial war-culture, the triangle of violence, and the ways in which direct, structural and cultural violence inevitably give rise to the moral injury of too many servicemembers and veterans. It should also be said that my role is clearly outside of the authorized VA structure.

I first heard Andy speak publicly in one such VA-sponsored ceremony at the Philadelphia Crescenz VAMC, then again later, when he agreed to give his public testimony about the truth of war to a gathered group that met in an Episcopal church in Philadelphia (recounted earlier in this book). Since then, I have worked with Chris in clergy trainings about moral injury, to present on my research, and raise the questions about the triangle of violence in sacrificial war-culture that this book has explored. In October of 2020, one such collaboration took place virtually with about 40 clergy and chaplains from Pennsylvania. Chaplain Antal, with Andy's permission, gave an update on Andy's most recent activities since he "graduated" from the Philadelphia Moral Injury Program. As I listened, I realized that Andy is pointing the way forward for all of us, civilians, servicemembers and veterans alike; he is creating the model for how to meaningfully address the direct, structural and cultural violence of moral injury, and reframe our way of life.

These days Andy is a part of a "Moral Injury Leadership Group" that continues to meet and has developed a specific set of goals. All the members of the group completed the 12-week Moral Injury Program at Philadelphia, and Andy describes them as "a cadre of combat veterans who wish to serve as emissaries to spiritual communities affected by our actions as soldiers." Their mission is threefold:

1   Promote awareness of Moral Injury in spiritual community;
2   Make amends through acts of piety/volunteership;
3   Engage the public with intent to develop leadership that eschews the MIC [Military-Industrial Complex][57]

There's more. Chaplain Antal also shared a published article that Andy wrote for a local Philadelphia newspaper, the *Friends, Peace and Sanctuary Journal*. The journal is "rooted in the idea of cultural exchange … to reinvigorate a presence in the City of Philadelphia."[58] The newspaper is written in Arabic, with some articles translated into English. Titled "Bees and Love," Andy's article tells how the same "cohort of veterans … intent on repairing their war-torn souls agreed to meet up with the family of this newspaper's founder." Meeting at the home of four brothers associated with the paper, all Iraq refugees from the Diyala Governate, Andy's initial "trepidation and nerves" were transformed through generous hospitality and honest conversation. Sharing "many plates of expertly-BBQed meats," and kettles of "cardamom-infused black tea (EXTRA sugar)," Andy writes, "Before I knew it, I had four new brothers."[59]

It's important to acknowledge that Andy still struggles, though now he connects his own wrestling with the pain of people he once considered to be his enemy, as he writes,

> Life can be overwhelming; People can be difficult. This is double so for the surviving witnesses of war – those of us forced to flee, and those of us who did the forcing. Refugees and Veterans are bonded by war in this way: both groups must learn to function in hindsight of their actions or reactions, in a world with totally different rules than they are accustomed. And here we all are.

Along the way, Andy and one of the Iraqi brothers discovered a shared interest in bee-keeping. Mohaned was "trained in the art" as a boy in Iraq, and Andy is a small-scale farmer. Now the entire "motley crew" began a venture to raise bees, and "laboring and training together," for over a year, they have sustained two hives whose honey they donate to those in need in Philadelphia. A photo accompanying the article shows the four brothers and Andy beaming at the camera, with a quote from Maya Angelou that Andy describes as "honey in my ear: 'We are more Alike, my friends, than we are Unalike.'" In the article's last words Andy addresses the reader, "Life can be Sweet; People can be Angelic. How will you choose to spend your day today?"

Rehumanization and honesty toward reality

Andy's story not only points toward greater hope, and a swerve for healing and well-being among those who struggle with moral injury; his life also reveals a passionate ethic involving a set of pathways of rehumanization that might inform all citizens, and their very conception of the nation itself.

Naming the structures of dehumanization

First, Andy's insistence on naming the structures of dehumanization is central. He refuses to pretend that everything is fine; he does not paper over or excuse what happened. There is ongoing honesty about reality here, but not only regarding his own individual pain, limits and wounds. Andy has refocused his struggle as a kind of window through which to see, take in and be present to the pain of refugees from Iraq. Earlier in his life he was shaped to perceive these people as his enemies, he knew them as something other than fully human; but now they are co-conspirators, friends, "beloved brothers." Lest we imagine that this has been a simple or easy process, we might return to other parts of Andy's story from previous chapters. Remember his agony in publicly telling his story, even to the gathered community that had expressed willingness, even eagerness, to listen. Remember the soap stones he hand-carved over months and years, each stone with the imagined name of one of the children who died in the bombed building that day.

At yet another training, at Kirkridge Retreat Center in Pennsylvania in 2019 where, once again, I had been invited by Chaplain Antal and Rev. Scott Hutchinson to participate, Andy also came to share his story. He brought the stones he had carved for the children, and laid them carefully on a huge boulder on a beautiful lawn at the retreat center. He knelt by the stones as people approached to view, touch and be near them. There is no forgetting of this destruction. But Andy shows that this is not the end of his story. There also exists the possibility of kinship that is joyful.

The work of rehumanization goes hand in hand with continuing to tell the truth about war and its grounding in dehumanization. In the ritual that takes place in the tenth week of the Philadelphia Moral Injury Group, Andy and other veterans take on the role of "prophet" to testify, speaking the painful truth about their experiences of war, experiences that run completely counter to the ways war and militarism are commemorated and sacralized in the United States. One particular part of this ceremony stayed with me for a long time, as civilians gathered at the front of the gathering space with the veterans, and we were asked to look into each other's faces. It was uncomfortable, to be honest, to engage in this act that felt so intimate, and unsafeguarded. We civilians had only just listened to their testimonies, and now the veterans met our eyes with their honest gaze. Together in silence we jointly held the challenging and painful truths just spoken. I was reminded of Vietnamese

Buddhist peace activist, Thich Nhat Hanh, who has told veterans of war to think of themselves as "the light at the tip of the candle, illuminating the way for the whole nation." Leading retreats for war veterans since 1987, Hanh has a very specific message for them:

> We who have experienced war directly have a responsibility to share our insight and experience concerning the truth of war. We are the light at the tip of the candle. It is very hot, but it has the power of shining and illuminating. We can gather into groups to support each other. Practicing mindfulness, we will know how to look deeply into the nature of the war and, with our insight, awaken our own people. We know what war is. We also know that the war is not only in us; it is in everyone – veterans and non-veterans. We must share our insight, not out of anger, but out of love. Our people need us to do it. I am trying my best, and I hope my friends will do the same.[60]

Such honesty and openness are unnerving. No wonder many would rather "thank veterans for their sacrifice and service," and move on as quickly as possible. But what is that, really, but another form of dehumanization of veterans and servicemembers, not to mention a complete obliteration of war's victims?

If we hope to come to terms with its dehumanization, the truth about war has to be spoken. But the work Andy has dedicated himself to does not stop with this truthful narrative. Along with telling the truth about what war really is, and what it means to experience it directly, Andy and the others in the Moral Injury Leadership Group have taken another all-important step: they have committed themselves to the analysis of war-culture's structural and cultural scaffolding of violence. In other words, they are taking on that social analysis that can help all of us better understand the layers of violence in our world-building that have made war and militarism so central. In the third plank of their mission statement, Andy and the others declare their intention to "develop leadership that eschews" the Military-Industrial Complex.

This too is honesty toward reality. As this book has argued, we cannot dispense with the truthful telling and hearing of servicemembers' and veterans' experiences; *and we must set those same narratives over against the deeper and wider analysis of the structural and cultural violence of war-culture.* Why? For veterans and servicemembers, this analysis has to do with better understanding what has taken place in their own lives, and why. Far too often, forms of redress and support for the morally injured stop at the level of direct violence. But joining with those we say we most

esteem – our military servicemembers – and taking on their social analysis of violence and war-culture, would have a far-reaching impact. The individual sense of shame and self-loathing that so many describe, begs for
this larger frame of understanding. We saw that Andy blamed himself, as
if he and only he was responsible for what took place that night of the airstrike. In moral injury literature there is too little reflection directly linking
the sense of betrayal felt by many to a wider social analysis of war-culture,
and exploration of communal cultural culpability. Meanwhile, Andy's story
demonstrates that very little, if any, of the treatment he experienced over
eight years, before entering the Moral Injury Group at Philadelphia, encouraged him to analyze how his own struggles could only be adequately
understood through a wider lens, and deeper investigation addressing the
ocean of war-culture in which the entire nation swims. His truth, and ours,
is entirely more ambiguous.

U.S. war-culture shapes all citizens to normalize practices of dehumanization; but those on the front lines of combat are at particular risk, as if the
dehumanizing formation and expectations of them was on steroids. At the
most recent training I helped to lead, in response to my presentation, one of
the veterans in attendance reflected that the social analysis of war-culture,
sacrifice and the triangle of violence wouldn't have much helped her as a
17-year-old getting ready to enlist. "My brain wasn't fully formed; I don't
think I could have taken this in; I was going to enlist, and nothing would or
could stop me."[61] Her words underscore the absence of well-informed and
thoughtful mentors, wise guides to help young people imagine their futures,
and think seriously about the consequences of their decisions. Such thoughtful and measured mentorship is lacking in much of the United States. When
the philosopher of war, Camilo Mac Bica, came to lecture in my college
courses, he summed up the mindset of many teenage enthusiasts of war with
a story about a young man who likewise was incapable of hearing Bica's
warnings about the truth of war. He was more excited about Bica's military
tattoos: "Chicks dig those!" the young man said.

If civilians are to "take on our brunt of the burden," we will remedy the
widespread vacuum of thoughtful education regarding war-culture and its
consequences. So much of war-culture, as demonstrated, has been designed
to do the very opposite, not only present war as attractive and exciting, but
even as a sacred enterprise. We shall have to search for ways to break the
cognitive connections that assign value to military veterans and servicemembers, through the sacralization of war itself.

Superseding his own 17-year old self at his time of enlistment, Andy's
thinking evolved, informed by his hard experience, and eventually arriving

at a completely different place. And if civilians are to join with Andy and others like him, they too will strive for a deeper understanding, including an honest and thoroughgoing criticism of the war-culture human beings have built, and its pervasive streams of structural and cultural violence. However far off this lies for the majority of U.S. citizens, nevertheless, a deeper awareness of the dynamics and causes of moral injury could inspire a cultural swerve with regard to what Lifton called "the amorphic ethic of 'national security.'"[62] The revelation: "*moral injury is an atrocity*" strips away the distortion through which moral injury is justified and normalized as an outcome of war that must be accepted and tolerated, a "necessary sacrifice" that must be paid in blood, the necessary cost for the purchase of "security." *We do not have to accept this.*

Can we begin to raise those deeper questions and rethink our ways of dealing with conflict and security, as well as what it means to belong to the nation? The glue that for so long has solidified war as "the necessary sacrifice," and even an unchangeable fact of human nature, can begin to crumble, to give way to a more humane imaginary, one worthy of our celebration of equality.

False stereotypes about violence and nonviolence

During Mike Pesca's interview with me for *The Gist* podcast, he began early on by acknowledging that we probably have conflicting views regarding whether war ever can be justified. But certainly I would agree with him, wouldn't I, that World War II was "a good war"? I responded by noting that these kinds of questions seem inevitably to arise in defense of war-culture. Over time I have come to understand that the lurch to defend war in the face of criticism, is linked to a sense that one's identity is under threat. It is just plain hard for people to imagine their lives without war and militarism; in the United States war-culture has become such a given, and has so permeated our lives, that people are blind to it. They misrecognize this deep infiltration, this undying and unholy connection of our national identity with the violence of war. Absent war-culture, how might the people of the United States describe their nationalism, their understanding of national security; how might they confront the depth of our social and economic and cultural infrastructure in the nation now built upon war and militarization? What alternatives can we envision? Facing up to war-culture's iron grip on human life is indeed difficult, and requires both courage and then imagination to reconceive who we are.

But isn't this naïve?

Erika Chenowith, political scientist at Harvard Kennedy School and the Radcliffe Institute for Advanced Study, is familiar with this conundrum. She tells the story of how she once approved without question the idea that "power flows from the barrel of a gun." But invited to a workshop on non-violent resistance to address conflict, she agreed to go, though she thought such a position was "naïve." Using protest, boycotts, and other strategies of nonviolent response to conflict could never be ultimately successful, she thought. When conference scholars presented material about positive cases in the world where nonviolence worked, she responded, "Those were probably exceptions. Maybe this works for environmental reform, but it will never work if you're trying to overthrow a violent, ruthless dictator." Maria Stephan, another academic at the conference, challenged her, "Are you willing to test this empirically?" Chenoweth was curious.

So over the next few years she collected data on all major violent and nonviolent campaigns in the world for the overthrow of an unjust government or territorial liberation since 1900. There were hundreds of cases. She was "blown away" by what she discovered. From 1900 to 2006, she learned, nonviolent campaigns were two times more likely to succeed than violent ones. Moreover, the collected data showed that the trend of greater success in nonviolent campaigns increased overall over time, becoming more common. Perhaps most surprising, she found, nonviolent campaigns had greater success even in brutal authoritarian conditions. Digging deeper to ask, "why were the nonviolent campaigns more successful?" Chenoweth discovered the reason: "people power." Analysis of the hundreds of cases showed that if just 3.5% of the total population was engaged in the campaign, success was very likely. And campaigns that drew in more than 3.5% participation of the populace *all* were nonviolent. In addition, she found that nonviolent campaigns were more inclusive, and representative of diversity of all kinds. Why? "Safety in numbers" tended to draw even "risk-averse" people into the campaign. The visibility of civil resistance actions helps to attract involvement; even more initially ambivalent people will join in; so that these campaigns spread across all kinds of populations and institutions. In addition, through increased tactics of "dispersion," people learned practically over time how to avert violent repression of civil resistance. Civil resisters use "strikes, banging on pots and pans, staying at home, turning off the electricity at a coordinated time of day," etc., to avoid violent repression. Chenoweth observes, "The movement stays disruptive, and it's also very hard to repress with violence."[63]

These research discoveries forced Chenoweth to reexamine her former assumptions about violence, the nation, and how human beings collectively deal with conflict and power. She asked herself,

> Why was it so easy and comfortable to think that violence "works"? Why did I find it acceptable to think that violence happens almost automatically, because of circumstances or by necessity, that it is the only way out of some situations? In a society that celebrates our focus on battlefield heroes on national holidays, it was natural to grow up believing that "violence and courage," were one and the same, and that true victories cannot come without bloodshed on both sides. But for people serious about seeking change, there are "realistic alternatives."[64]

The role of religion in the scaffolding of violence

Chenoweth shows impressive candor regarding prior assumptions that shaped her thinking; these presumptions unwittingly justify violence, and represent a failure of imagination. She also demonstrates courage through willingness to speak publicly about how her mind has changed. How many people have bothered to explore so deeply the formative roots of their national identity? Her example underscores the urgency of critical thought about U.S. national addiction to ways of violence. All this requires further excavation, if we are to strive for the honesty we need. It is particularly imperative to explore the role religion plays in these dynamics.

Earlier chapters of this book explored the tight link between popular Christian elevation of the sacrifice of Jesus of Nazareth, and the work performed by U.S. laborers of war. In both cases, "the necessity of sacrifice" is assumed, and the death and injury of these heroes is "the ultimate sacrifice" they make for believers for the sanctity/security of the nation. We can further explore "the U.S. war-culture Bible," to spotlight how sacred texts traditionally are mined and misinterpreted in the U.S., both in churches and in national settings, so as to present a divinized and uninterrupted portrayal of war and militarism as a sacred enterprise.[65]

In many cases, reliance on Christian language, cherry-picked sacred texts and doctrines prevent deeper critical thinking or protest of U.S. ways of war. This too is cultural violence; and we should ask, what impact does this (civil) religion have on the development of vulnerability to moral injury among our laborers of war? In the October 2020 clergy training mentioned earlier, when I raised these questions, clergy attendees responded with a range of reactions. There was confusion, because they had never been invited to think about such matters before. I sensed a heaviness in the gathering, because facing and working toward greater awareness about our national identity, and the ways it is mixed up with religious commitments, understandings, and practices, is difficult work. One attendee, a white male who had worked as a military chaplain for over 30 years, grew angry, and took me to task. As he vented, it was especially poignant when he lamented, "For over 30 years, when I worked in the military, I wasn't allowed to have my own opinion." Now I was asking him to think critically in ways that were so unfamiliar, and threatening to the identity he had carried unthinkingly for many decades.[66]

Maria Pilar Aquino wastes no time in getting to the heart of the matter: if we are to strive for honesty, and understand our reality, we will have to dig into the very *patterns of thought* that give rise to the ways we define identity, and understand our institutions and societies. She writes, "conflict and peacebuilding studies today appear to be severely hindered due to kyriarchal forms of thought."[67] The term, "kyriarchy" first was coined by biblical scholar Elisabeth Schüssler-Fiorenza. It refers to "relational patterns marked by domination and subordination." In other words, kyriarchy is an umbrella term to describe what this chapter has explored, those identities and behaviors marked by lopsided grievability, and the inequality of violence.

Pilar Aquino understands the destructive links that merge state and religion; kyriarchy is like an invasive kudzu plant that embeds in societies and "intertwines with religious discourses, texts and traditions." "Kyriarchal religions … cultivate violence," – even as they simultaneously use the language of peace! And these formations and practices collude with and legitimate inequality; they enforce both domination and subordination.

Pilar Aquino summarizes what is at stake. Kyriarchal religion masks "the ideological instrumentalization of religion." For religion is a vulnerable human enterprise. In cultures such as the United States that glorify and sanctify war and militarism, religion easily joins the state apparatus, there to become mobilized to conceal the state's "violent proclivities." For those who would resist this instrumentalization, the first task is to "expose the ideological instrumentalization of religion," says Pilar Aquino. However, there also is a "constructive role" religion can play. How? Through supporting "processes of constructive change," people and institutions of religion can align their words about peace, with the things that actually make for peace. Embracing "conflict transformation," people of religion may "enhance conditions and foster the growth of societies that affirm human dignity, through meeting basic human needs, and protecting human rights within sustainable communities."[68]

But such work truly is challenging in the context of the United States, once we recognize the depth, breadth and insistence upon war-culture that touches upon every aspect of everyday life. This book already examined religion's tendency to intermix with kyriarchal gender identity formation to lubricate the inequality and destructiveness of war-culture's violence. And, in addition to gender inequality, insistence on a deeper national reckoning with racial inequality in the United States in 2020 made it impossible to ignore the deep white supremacist cultural violence of the nation. This too is kyriarchy in action, and the white supremacist bedrock is equally as oppressive and inhumane as gender inequality, if not more so. Following the failure of professional pollsters in November 2020 to accurately gauge the immense voter support for the person and policies of then-President Trump, the poet Caroline Randall Williams wrote these words:

> The polls failed last time, and they failed this time, in part because they can't tell you what so many Black Americans know and live every day: that so much of white America is deeply racist, in ways that are impossible to quantify but that are nevertheless felt, and that bear out in the vote. Every time this fact is underestimated, democracy pays for it. Black lives pay for it. White lives pay for it. There are 235,000 Americans dead in the ground who could back me up if only they had their breath.[69]

To what degree was voter support for a second Trump presidential term influenced by subterranean (and overt!) cultural streams of white supremacy in the U.S., including those that are mixed up with religion? Robert P. Jones tells how the religious denomination into which he was born and raised, the Baptist Church, "was founded on the proposition that chattel slavery could flourish alongside the gospel of Jesus Christ." This was justified as "divinely mandated," he writes.[70] Compelled to investigate the U.S. Christian embrace of white supremacy, he explains, "I have always been fascinated by the ways in which beliefs, institutional belonging, and culture impact opinions and behaviors in public space."[71]

Kyriarchal streams of violence are intersectional. The inequality of violence in both white supremacy and war-culture not only work in similar ways, but also mutually inform and influence one another. Like war-culture, there is "willful amnesia," says Jones, involved in the stubborn resilience of white supremacy in Christianity. Christian institutions and people can and do reject or sidestep acknowledgement of these continuing trends.[72] More-over, the "instrumentalization of religion" jumps easily between white su-premacy and war-culture. Jones writes, "the Jesus conjured by most white congregations was not merely indifferent to the status quo of racial inequali-ty; he demanded its defense and preservation as part of the natural, divinely ordained order of things."[73] Similarly, the same Jesus' "ultimate sacrifice" became the cultural template for military death and injury in the U.S. Some-how, the gospel accounts about Jesus of Nazareth's clear disavowal of mil-itarized violence became a non sequitur in the universe of U.S. war-culture. Meanwhile, Jones argues, Christian misinterpretation of biblical texts, also worked hand in glove with other academic disciplines, such that "virtually every tool for the production of human knowledge about the world has been co-opted to justify white supremacy."[74]

Despite widespread lack of acknowledgment of this theological abuse, certain voices identified the severity of the problem with crystal clarity. Theologian James Cone cut to the bone with his exposure of the violence in white Christian theology, underscoring seven related failures behind the current status of "crisis" in Christian theology in the United States.

- Failure to see or speak about "the moral evil of anti-black racism in America;"
- Failure to be in solidarity with the victims of violence, be it economic, social, political, or class-related;
- Failure to develop theological language that can challenge the oppressive structures of society;
- Failure to critically analyze patriotism that serves a "racist government" and "systems of inequality and injustice;"
- Failure to theologically explore what it means to be human from the perspectives of "the light of the Gospel for the poor and the weak in society;"
- Failure to address the crippling problems that plague our historical moment in time: "human poverty and greed, physical deprivation and destitution, economic dispossession and income inequality, oppression and injustice, child and sex slavery, suffering and hunger, white supremacy and racial discrimination, imperialism and capitalism;"
- Failure to "champion better race relations, economic uplift programs for the poor and the lower-class, to support protest activism for racial and social justice politics, and to sustain Gospel-centered peace and reconciliation conversations."[75]

The lack of adequate language to analyze the kyriarchal intertwining of religion, racism, imperialism, patriotism, and inequity, all of which intermix in the stew of war-culture, leads to moral blinders; inadequate language and analysis alike render this violence invisible. Rev. Beth Reed, an Episcopal priest who works closely with *The Poor People's Campaign*, observes that the signs in front of so many church buildings that offer words of welcome, and information about church services, should be changed. "White Comfort Available Here," would be a more truthful messaging of the actual work and brand of the dominant U.S. white Christian church, she suggests.[76] Jones also understands that the work of addressing the crisis of white theology, if it happens at all, frequently is undertaken as a form of white altruism, and this only makes the crisis worse. "White Christians must take up this work not just because it is morally right or politically prudent, but also because it is the only path that can salvage the integrity of our faith, psyches, and legacies," he writes.[77] I would take this further, for the work of addressing these intersecting crises that are suffocating all of us, is a matter of life itself.

Rehumanization and swerving the national imaginary

What will clear the pathways for breath? When Buddhist monk/Vietnam veteran Claude AnShin Thomas lectures, he often begins by asking audience members very directly, "what is the most important thing in life to you?"[78] This can be somewhat disconcerting for individuals, and they scramble to come up with some sort of adequate answer. They may respond by offering up their understanding of ultimate reality/God; or family, or something else. AnShin listens patiently. Then he asks his co-lecturer, Buddhist monk Weibke Kenshin Andersen, to assist him. "Please cover my mouth and nose so that I am not able to breathe," he instructs. The audience watches with spellbound interest as Kenshin constricts his breath as long as possible. His face begins to change color, and he shows signs of physical distress before finally moving her hands away and drawing a deep inhale. "Breath is what is most important," he says, "without breath there is nothing."[79] A combat veteran whose experiences and wounds (both physical and psychic) disabled him, AnShin came to the centrality of breath through Buddhist practice over many years. As he says, focus on breath provided a pathway to "live more peacefully with my unpeacefulness." Like Andy, AnShin does not forget his experiences of war-culture, and war. But the way forward is only possible with unflinching honesty about what has taken place, including honesty about the cultural and structural reality we humans have built, that makes such history possible.

Following Andy's example, and "pursuing leadership that eschews the Military-Industrial Complex," what does this look like? If the truth about moral injury swells into a flashpoint, and the reality of this atrocity pierces through denial and blindness, we finally cannot avoid the conclusion that the world out of which moral injury emerges, is not the world we want for ourselves, for one another, or for the planet itself. So what are our next steps? Recognizing our morally injured brothers and sisters as "the canary in the coal mine," inexorably leads to the conclusion that the entire coal mine, the war-culture of the United States, is in need of deep remedy, and profound change. In such a time as we are now living on the planet, the metaphor of "coal mine" itself is highly evocative, for we know that if we and so many other inhabitants of the planet are to survive and flourish, coal mine economies must become a thing of the past, another "stranded asset" we need to leave behind.

Rehumanizing steps

Honesty about reality works hand in hand with the best steps toward rehumanization, and efforts toward peacebuilding. Remember Johan Galtung's emphasis: "conflict transformation" may be misunderstood, because we are acculturated to think in black and white extremes, and also because we may wrongly assume that peace means the absence of conflict. Moreover, because the enormity of the intersecting crises we face is so great, it's easy to become overwhelmed. But when and wherever we are taking steps to *address* conflict nonviolently (as opposed to avoiding conflict), we are in the midst of building greater peace, and lessening the scope of violence.

Martin Luther King Jr. famously said, as he prepared for the "Beyond Vietnam" speech, that he "didn't want to study war no more," but his own example shows that the intentional study of U.S. war-culture informs greater honesty about our reality, and is, in fact, an irreplaceable step toward greater peace, and rehumanization.[80] When I introduce the concept of "U.S. war-culture" to different audiences, I've learned to expect that some listeners will reject this notion entirely, because the truth about war-culture contradicts deeply valued assumptions about U.S. identity. But I also find that there is hunger to better understand this reality. A more thorough understanding of the reality of war-culture can be encouraged through focus on three main indicators of war-culture that have been analyzed with detail by a range of scholars. Readers will remember these indicators from earlier chapters of this book:

1   The sheer amount of money spent to maintain and expand U.S. war-culture;
2   The range and disproportional numbers, in comparison with the rest of the world, of the "U.S. Empire of Military Bases";
3   The depth and breadth of interpenetration of the ethos, practices and institutions of war and militarism, with vast sites of civilian life across the nation and world.

Studying U.S. war-culture *is* peacebuilding labor, especially given the continuing unawareness, blindness, and rejection of this reality in the United States. Experiencing hostility and offense to the very notion of U.S. war-culture is shocking, but such reactions also are revelatory as to the true nature of the national mindset. Continuing with the example of Dr. King, we may remember what happened when he dared to name and speak truth to power in his speech, "Beyond Vietnam." Following this address in 1967, he was vilified and isolated in the last year of his life. Seventy-five percent of white America declared him to be "irrelevant." And almost sixty percent of Black America rejected his insistence on the "triplet evils of racism, materialism, and militarism."[81] Institutions of all sorts, from the NAACP, to the media, other civil rights leaders, and the White House, showed him their backs.[82] Some accused him of arrogance for daring to speak about foreign policy; others accused him of being a communist, for so criticizing the United States. All these charges surely grew from the deeper explicit threat his words provoked, regarding sacralized U.S. ways of self-understanding and identity. How else are we to understand what ignited such a vicious and undeserved attack?

Perhaps Dr. King was aware of the hostile reaction this address would provoke, for in the speech he declares that it is not at all clear that the United States will have the "maturity" to acknowledge, much less accept responsibility for the triplet crises he outlines. He warned, "The world now demands a maturity of America that we may not be able to achieve." What would this maturity involve? King unequivocally called for religious institutions, "churches and synagogues" (and today we would add temples, mosques and other religious traditions and communities) "to match actions with words by seeking out every creative method of protest possible." He counseled young people and all clergy of draft age against enlistment, adding that when drafted, they should be "challenged ... with the alternative of conscientious objection." Why? King now broadened the analysis to a much wider view, "The war in Vietnam is but a symptom of a far deeper malady within the American spirit," he said. An all-encompassing response must address the stranded ethics of "the immense profits of overseas investments." Economic injustice perpetuates the neglect of "fairness and justice of many of our past and present policies," both domestic and international.

Dr. King did not call for withdrawal from the world, nor did he advocate for the ethics of "America First." Instead, American maturity would necessitate acknowledgement of our own violence, so that we might come to say of war, "This way of settling differences is not just." The revolution he called for, and squarely challenged people to face, would involve a decisive shift for religious institutions, and for the country as a whole, from "a thing-oriented society to a person-oriented society." He did not pause to articulate the enormity of the stakes involved in whether U.S. citizens would be able to achieve this maturity, for "a nation that continues year after year to spend more money on military defense than on programs of social uplift is approaching spiritual death."

King unrelentingly outlined "the revolution" essential to heal the structural and cultural violence of both religious institutions and nation. This was what people in the U.S. found most disturbing, and what led to the rejection and venal attacks against him. Alluding to a well-known gospel passage that would be immediately recognized by millions across the nation, King swept away customary interpretations surrounding it. In the well-known parable known as "The Good Samaritan," a man who has been robbed, beaten, and left for dead on the Jericho road, is avoided by various passersby who hold different forms of social and religious privilege. Finally, a social outcast, the Samaritan, stops to help, binding the man's wounds, carrying him to a local inn, and providing for his continuing care. But responding to countless sermons' interpretation of this story to encourage individual acts of charity, King thunders that any individual response only represents "the initial act." This is not what justice demands. Instead, "the whole Jericho road must be transformed," he insisted. The entire "edifice" of the nation (including, we might also say, white churches and white religious institutions, as well as all the myriad institutions of war-culture) are in need of wholistic change. "True compassion is more than flinging a coin to a beggar. It comes to see that an edifice which produces beggars needs restructuring."

King's words are as provocative and far-reaching today as they were in 1967. In light of this astounding critique, and its incisive analysis of war-culture, it is striking to witness how the United States celebrates his birthday each year. There is little acknowledgement, let alone deeper study and analysis, of this, his most significant speech, as part of the national dialogue. At least up to our own time, with few exceptions, we won't find political leaders from either the Democrats or Republicans who draw from this speech as a basis for their candidacy. The United States and most of its religious institutions still show little tolerance for King's clear call for an end to war as integral to the peacebuilding infrastructure that will undo the intersecting triplet evils of poverty, racism and militarism.

Rehumanization with the world

A last emphasis from King's speech helps uncover another pathway of rehumanization. As Andy graduated from The Moral Injury Group in Philadelphia, and began to forge a way forward with other veterans, he sought ways to develop friendship, and meaningful joint projects with refugees from Iraq. Andy's story calls to mind the culmination of King's speech, "the call for a worldwide fellowship that lifts neighborly concern beyond one's tribe, race, class, and nation is in reality a call for an all-embracing and unconditional love for all [hu]mankind."

King stresses that multifaith encounter, openness, good will and working together will be inspired through "Love ... the key that unlocks the door which leads to ultimate reality." This rehumanization practically reaches across the boundaries humans have imposed between themselves and others, boundaries institutionalized by way of both religion and the nation.

Perhaps the most far-reaching element of the speech was King's audacity to counsel the nation to rethink its fear-driven foreign policies, and its failure to promote better understanding of other nations, with peoples' hopes, needs, aspirations and goals. Writing in the midst of the Cold War, and having been accused many times himself of being a "communist," King responds to the climate of fear that gripped the U.S.:

> Let us not join those who shout war and, through their misguided passions, urge the United States to relinquish its participation in the United Nations ... We must *not engage in a negative anticommunism, but rather in a positive thrust for democracy, realizing that our greatest defense against communism is to take offensive action in behalf of justice.* We must with positive action seek to remove those conditions of poverty, insecurity, and injustice, which are the fertile soil in which the seed of communism grows and develops."[83] (italics mine).

Clearly, the nation evidenced little readiness to hear the call to action King laid out. Looking back, one sees how better attention to King's words could have impacted the Cold-war era. Can we hear these words now in our own post-9/11 era, that is so driven by fear of terrorism? Is it possible to imagine a different post-9/11 national response, involving refusal to "engage in a negative anti-terrorism" relying on the vast implements of violence? King's admonition might have changed the history of the last two decades. Instead of the overwhelming response of war and increased militarization to the 9/11 attacks, the U.S. could have chosen a different way forward.

Not avoiding conflict, people might have addressed it nonviolently, through systems of national and international legal justice, combined with insistence on a deeper understanding of the other, and profound support and empathy with terrorists' victims, while rejecting violence and revenge. Is it possible, along the way, that the United States could have centralized what King describes as the necessary "offensive action … to remove those conditions of poverty, insecurity and injustice" that so often are at the root of violence? The last twenty years' retreat into armed violence and fear fed and bolstered these longest wars in the history of the United States, wars that we still seem not to know how to end. Meanwhile, and in contrast, Andy's rehumanization through friendship and peacebuilding with the brothers from Iraq represents a small-scale model of precisely what King hopes the nation will do. Andy writes that when "love and honest conversation flowed as liberally as the tea … before I knew it, I had four new brothers." He describes what happened,

> My new brothers pulled me into their arms, and out of my Cave of Solitude, so to speak. Our friendship blossomed into true brotherhood: before I knew it, I was having masgouf and tea every weekend, and we worked together to build a support network to flesh out and fund our beekeeping adventure. We labored and learned together, and in less than one year from meeting, we are happy to share the success of our two hives with you![84]

Of course, there will be those who label this as just so much naivete, much as the critics of King labeled him as critically and intellectually incapable of adequately addressing the foreign policy of the United States. Up to the current moment, U.S. political leaders who dare to seriously question the enormous financial outlays for war and militarism in the United States similarly are tarred, and the legislative changes they suggest to the federal military budget are easily swept aside.[85] But along with King, Pilar Aquino and so many others, including Andy, we may unapologetically assert that it is time to encourage a swerve in our ways of thinking, and try a different way forward, based on "enhancing conditions and fostering the growth of societies that affirm human dignity, through meeting basic human needs, and protecting human rights within sustainable communities," as Pilar Aquino asserts.[86] Does this mean that all violence, conflict, and injustice magically are solved? No, because this *is* what peacebuilding looks like: we move the needle forward with every act to expand the conditions and growth of human dignity described above, not by avoiding conflict, but by responding to conflict nonviolently. Every act, large and small, matters.

Flourishing in a community of sister-and-brotherhood

Andy's peacebuilding venture is linked to action and advocacy quietly taking place on a much greater scale. Remember Andy's own Catholic upbringing, and the long time in his life that he was "vacant of faith." What might Andy think about courageous steps Pope Francis is taking to move the needle of the Catholic Church, and wider world? It's important to remember, at the same time, the ambiguous and ambivalent nature of religious institutions, and theologies. The perpetration of abuse such as Andy witnessed in his early life by a Catholic relative, and structural institutional protection and dismissal of this violence on the part of the Catholic Church as a whole, must continue to be protested, and may not be forgotten. Nevertheless, the way of peacebuilding advocated here rejects black and white methods of moral response; protest and demand for change with regard institutional abuse is urgent. *And also urgent is* the positive use of institutional resources, to unsparingly spotlight violence in all its forms, and work toward nonviolent transformation.

Pope Francis' encyclical letter, *Fratelli Tutti,* released in October 2020, echoes many of the themes already outlined in this chapter.[87] Francis powerfully describes with deep honesty the death-dealing reality that characterizes not only those in the United States, but indeed all world powers:

> ... the dream of working together for justice and peace seems an outdated utopia. What reigns instead is a cool, comfortable and globalized indifference, born of deep disillusionment concealed behind a deceptive illusion: thinking that we are all-powerful, while failing to realize that we are all in the same boat. (p.26)

The narrative of supposed peace through dominating power and violence is a false story; it breeds distrust and cynicism, and perpetuates cycles of revenge. We fail to recognize our *naïve reliance on violence*, and are thus blind to violence's destructive consequences for both perpetrators and victims. Francis does not hesitate to describe both structural and cultural violence at the heart of war-culture. Our world has become increasingly influenced by "outbreaks of tension and a buildup of arms and ammunition in a global context dominated by uncertainty, disillusionment, fear of the future, and controlled by narrow economic interests." (p.29)

The Pope's encyclical especially has garnered attention for its call to leave behind just war theory and principles as a moral defense of war. This theory and way of thinking is another stranded ethic; today, the ideology of just war is bound to breed cynicism and dishonesty, because just war principles routinely are called upon facilely to mask the truth about war: "war is the negation of all rights and a dramatic assault on the environment. If we want true integral human development for all, we must work tirelessly to avoid war between nations and peoples." (p.225) He further explains,

> War can easily be chosen by invoking all sorts of allegedly humanitarian, defensive or precautionary excuses, and even resorting to the manipulation of information. In recent decades, every single war has been ostensibly "justified." The Catechism of the Catholic Church speaks of the possibility of legitimate defence by means of military force, which involves demonstrating that certain "rigorous conditions of moral legitimacy" have been met. Yet it is easy to fall into an overly broad interpretation of this potential right ... At issue is whether the development of nuclear, chemical and biological weapons, and the enormous and growing possibilities offered by new technologies, have granted war an uncontrollable destructive power over great numbers of innocent civilians. The truth is that "never has humanity had such power over itself, yet nothing ensures that it will be used wisely." (p.258)

The sheer weight and breadth of war-culture makes it impossible to pretend any longer that war may be approached from a neutral or objective perspective; any suggestion of ethical reflection about war that presumes a beginning "blank slate" should be regarded with suspicion. People in the United States especially have been pre-reflectively shaped to perceive militarization and war as "the right answers" to the conflicts we face. Francis' conclusion regarding the practical reliability or moral justification coming from any just war defense is incontrovertible: "*We can no longer think of war as a solution, because its risks will probably always be greater than its supposed benefits. In view of this, it is very difficult nowadays to invoke the rational criteria elaborated in earlier centuries to speak of the possibility of a 'just war.' Never again war!*" (p.258) (italics mine).

The Pope's letter mirrors Andy and his veteran cohort's stress to tell the truth about war. They are united in the mission to underscore war's structural and cultural violence (the MIC) that continues to be masked as it is justified in our world. Like Andy, the Pope's letter makes clear the truth about de-humanization and inequality that inevitably attend and exacerbate war and militarization: "The first victim of every war is 'the human family's innate vocation to fraternity,'" Francis writes. (p.26) We might pause to reflect on what this sentence conveys regarding the Pope's understanding of human beings. Humans have a "vocation" for what the Pope calls "fraternity." Human beings are built for that flourishing that only takes place through mutual relationship, in a community of brother-and-sisterhood. Butler's insistence on life together with others as a condition for life itself, comes to mind here.

Yes, peacebuilding "demands hard work, craftsmanship," but human beings are uniquely and brilliantly capable of this "social peace." (p.217) In a way that cannot but help remind one of the new bonds that Andy and the four brothers from Iraq are forming, Pope Francis calls for a "culture of encounter" among individuals and peoples. (p.217) These are "processes" that help people develop the necessary skills to deeply listen to one another, build the capacities they need to accept difference, and work together. (p.217) The letter also addresses the hard work that is involved in not forgetting atrocities born of war and other destructive injustices, and working toward equitable recompense as much as possible, while also refusing to allow atrocity or violence, fear or revenge to have the final word.

In the end it is Francis' theological view of the human person's intrinsic and inestimable worth that drives and justifies his assertions, as he writes, "Every human being has the right to live with dignity and to develop integrally; this fundamental right cannot be denied by any country" (p.107) And again, "… every human being possesses an inalienable dignity." (p.118) The dignity of human persons is accompanied by the immeasurable worth of the planet itself, that cannot be carved into pieces and relegated on the basis of power, "narrow interests" and violence. No, "the world belongs to everyone." (p.118)

What follows from this passionate ethics, this way of valuing human lives as "equally grievable," is a vision on a macro scale equally as beautiful and inspiring as Andy's:

… if all people are my brothers and sisters, and if the world truly belongs to everyone, then it matters little whether my neighbour was born in my country or elsewhere. My own country also shares responsibility for his or her development, although it can fulfil that responsibility in a variety of ways. It can offer a generous welcome to those in urgent need, or work to improve living conditions in their native lands by refusing to exploit those countries or to drain them of natural

resources, backing corrupt systems that hinder the dignified development of their peoples ... if we accept the great principle that there are
rights born of our inalienable human dignity, we can rise to the challenge of envisaging a new humanity. (p.118)

Reframing national and religious identities: An experiment in imagination

It is uniquely human to long for connection with transcendence; but in practices of U.S. nationalism, this beautiful capacity has been devastatingly
misplaced in sacralized war-culture. In the 1960s sociologist Robert Bellah
wrote about the significance of the spark of transcendence in the U.S. national imaginary. He defined "civil religion" not as worship of the U.S. American nation, but as the experience of assessing this belonging "in the light of
ultimate and universal reality."[88] Having faced the "trials" of the U.S. American Revolution, and the Civil War, the nation now faced the Vietnam War,
a third time of wrenching national trial. Bellah's description of the stakes in
that "third trial" in U.S. nationalism equally pertains today: "We have in a
moment of uncertainty been tempted to rely on our overwhelming physical
power rather than on our intelligence, and we have, in part, succumbed to
this temptation. Bewildered and unnerved when our terrible power fails to
bring immediate success, we are at the edge of a chasm the depth of which
no man [sic] knows."[89]

Does sacrificial war-culture in the longest wars of U.S. history amount to
"a fourth national trial"? Though too easily colonized by "petty interests"
and "ugly passions," Bellah hoped that practices of national belonging in
the United States would break through such chains, as citizens challenged
themselves to ongoing collective self-examination and critical appraisal, to
push the meaning of national identity to "new growth and insight." In particular, he emphasized that the era of Vietnam obliged U.S. citizens to reject "worship of the nation," for a different mindset, one that would judge
and interpret U.S. American experience, "in light of ultimate and universal
reality." To do this would require citizens to move past any easy notion of
U.S "chosenness" to a wider conception of being "part of one civil religion
with the world." This would mean looking beyond national boundaries, and
searching beyond "biblical religion," to explore symbols of transcendence
from many world religions; and understanding one's identity not only as belonging to a particular nation, but to a plural world. In contrast to Bellah's

Figure 14 "God, Guns, Trump Flag," by John Moore. Getty. In David Klepper and Matt O'Brien, "Tech Giants Lock Trump Accounts," *Associated Press, The Morning Call*, January 8, 2021. https://enewspaper.mcall.com/html5/desktop/production/default.aspx?&edid=4b8ec97f-0b86-449c-926e-6e0584f6ae67 (accessed January 12, 2021).

hopes, the January 6, 2021 insurrection at the United States Capitol building featured violent followers of President Donald Trump brandishing huge U.S. American flags, and carrying guns as they stormed the building where the Congress was meeting to certify the electoral votes for President-Elect Joe Biden. But the flags had been changed, now emblazoned with a large cross in the middle of the stars and stripes, flanked with guns and accompanied by the words, "Gods, Guns, Trump" (see Figure 14).[90]

In addition to Bellah, theologian Paul Tillich, writing about ten years earlier, also understood the dangers of (civil) religious nationalism. Tillich described "ultimate concern" as central to the existential human condition; all human beings experience "the state of being ultimately concerned."[91] Humans are compelled and drawn by the ultimate and unconditional; their lives involve risk, doubt and courage as meaning-seekers. Remember also Berger's summary statement about human life and world-building; the task of every generation is to pass on a meaningful world to the next. Tillich took this realization further, for the very notion of "ultimate concern" begs the question about how and where to place ultimate concern, and why human beings locate it in one site as opposed to another. Tillich's German heritage and his experiences of war, both the senseless destruction of World War I, and also the genocidal consequences of World War II, clarified for him the danger of situating ultimate concern in the nation. He saw the consequences that resulted in his own context.

Tillich's insight about the nation and ultimate concern remains a cautionary tale; beware of placing ultimate concern in that which is not ultimate! The nation, wealth, prestige, even family and friends, cannot bear the weight of ultimate concern, for none of these realities finally is ultimate. This precisely is the danger of sacrificial war-culture in U.S. nationalism in the 21st century. An honest and deeply felt human longing for transcendence, and need to find and place one's ultimate concern, wrongly is sacralized and seeded in the finite. But the primary longing, and need to deal with ultimate concern, remains an ongoing project in human experience, both individual and collective, including at the level of nations.

A thought experiment

A thought experiment brings this book to a close, regarding a re-envisioning of a day of national commemoration in the United States, say, Veterans' Day, or Fourth of July. Central to this vision is a shift in consciousness, a growing national swerve regarding the meaning of national belonging, and the passionate ethics accompanying this swerve.

People come together in small and larger gatherings across the nation to participate in rituals, ceremonies and celebrations that reflect elements of Chaplain Antal's work with veterans. These groups intentionally unite veterans, their friends, family, and other community members who have expressed willingness to listen. Specific preference is given to people like Andy, veterans and servicemembers, and refugees from war-torn lands, like Mohaned, who can speak openly and prophetically about the truth of war and war-culture. Space for telling difficult truths, lament, and grief for the losses of daughters and sons of the United States, *equally are accompanied by attentive naming* of the injuries and deaths to people outside of the United States, and damage to infrastructure, non-human life and the environment worldwide. Voices of refugees of war are sought, and heard. *We listen, grieve, and unlearn war.*

Community groups, religious congregations, and educational institutions take advantage of these days to provide educational resources for the study of war-culture: they explore war-culture's never-ending consumption of resources of all kinds; and investigate its breadth and depth, such as through study of the empire of U.S. military bases across the world. They analyze examples of the interpenetration of war-culture in U.S. economics, education, media, government, religion, youth culture, sports, foreign policy, entertainment, and so much more. Churches take up serious study of *Fratelli Tutti*; and beyond this, interfaith encounter between diverse religious institutions takes place, as people share the very best of their traditions' understandings and teachings about conflict, ultimate reality, and ways of flourishing together. Museums mount exhibits such as The Moral Injury Study and Art Installation. *We engage in social analysis and theological/religious reflection; face our reality, and explore equality, democracy, justice, love.*

Instead of the mono-war-culture of borough street banners such as the one in front of my house, that centralize one uncritical identity and consolidation of sacrificial war-culture, civic efforts encourage a multiplicity of voices, and visual and artistic forms of commemoration from as many perspectives as possible. This means that some will continue to hang banners that celebrate war-culture unthinkingly; but other citizens, representing the swerve in imagination that is taking place, create very different works of civic art and remembrance. In the wake of national insistence on racial reckoning in the summer of 2020, beautiful, challenging and soul-filled works of street art sprang up in so many places across the United States. Sometimes these works of art featured the faces of people like George Floyd or Breonna Taylor; while other inspiring art took the shape of messages posted in places to inspire civic protest and dialogue, such as the renaming of "Black Lives Matter Plaza" in front of the White House in huge yellow letters covering the entire street, supported by Washington D.C. Mayor Muriel E. Bowser.[92] Art for Veterans Day or Fourth of July will include new rhetorical banners, such as *End the Atrocity of Moral Injury;* or *Come Let us Build a New World Together* (the rhetorical banner that was created by the Student Nonviolent Coordinating Committee in the 1960s). Not only visual art, but music, drama, and creative expression of all kinds are encouraged to explore the costs of war, militarism, and militarization, and imagine steps toward a different world.

One example comes from Touchstone Theater in Bethlehem Pa, where the musical comedy, *Dictators 4 Dummies*, was produced, using music and dance to dethrone "the fascist playbook" taking root in U.S. culture, and promote laughter at its "slave values." In this "satirical send up of the art of tyranny," two ex-dictators who once were rivals for world domination, after becoming friends while in prison, now have formed a Las Vegas lounge act called *The Generals*. Through song, dance, and thinly veiled violent rejoinders, the former dictators attempt to raise (extort?) money from the audience in their "Tyrants of Tomorrow Telethon," while the audience cackles at their unrestrained antics.[93] *We build capacity to resist domination, and expand vision, critical analysis, imagination, and appreciation.*

In addition to such forms of collective celebration, slowly other ways of marking, honoring and coming together on these days may begin to take shape. People increasingly seek out and celebrate narratives about the nonviolent transformation of conflict, and specific skills to enhance peacebuilding. Instead of ceaseless news articles on these days of national commemoration that focus on battles and their warriors, the stories of communal peacebuilding in U.S. and world history take center stage. Imagine using the 4th of July to dramatize King's "Beyond Vietnam," or celebrate the lives of people like Amelia Boynton, James Lawson, Water Protectors like Eden Jumper or Jean Roach, Jody Williams (Nobel Peace Prize recipient for her leadership to ban landmines), Beatrice Finn (Nobel Prize recipient for her work to ban nuclear armaments), Sam Grant (leader for environment and racial justice), Greta Thunberg, and so many more. Patrisse Khan-Cullors and asha bandele, founders of *Black Lives Matter*, write in the memoir, *When They Call You a Terrorist*,

> We know that if we can get the nation to see, say and understand that *Black Lives Matter*, then every life would stand a chance. Black people are the only humans in this nation ever legally designated, after all, as not human. Which is not to erase any group's harm to ongoing pain in particular the genocide carried out against the First Nations peoples. But it is to say that there is something quite basic that has to be addressed in the culture, in the hearts and minds of people who have benefited from, and were raised up on, the notion that Black people are not fully human.[94]

Imagine lifting up the stories of successful nonviolent revolutionary change in the plethora of historic examples from 1900 to the present, discovered by Erica Chenowith.

Along with planting the yellow flags near the peace pole, people at my college develop initiatives to inspire tree-plantings on such days. The swerve in consciousness that addresses war-culture joins together with the climate swerve and the racial justice swerve, prioritizing ways of reframing national identity through national commemoration focused on saving the planet, prioritizing equity, and honoring all living inhabitants. Think of Andy, the Iraq brothers, and their work on the beehives. What powerful material for a new way of conceptualizing what it means to belong to the nation; we are people who promote the "culture of encounter" to come to know and support refugees; we practice multicultural global engagement and just relationship; and intertwine such work with our care and advocacy for the planet itself. *We decentralize war-culture, study the things that make for peace, and prioritize the whole human community, and the planet.*

In addition to heading out to enjoy and commune with the natural world, students and others on such days also engage in advocacy to impact legislation, local and national, to decentralize war-culture and increase peacebuilding infrastructure of many sorts, including legislation to address environmental labor and racial justice. They might engage in protest: why should so much be laid at the feet of the gods of war, when so many students are drowning in educational debt, and so many citizens lack adequate social safety nets? What does the "climate swerve" require? People learn about and sign up with organizations such as ICAN (The International Campaign to Abolish Nuclear Weapons), to join in proclaiming its central message:

> Nuclear weapons are the most inhumane and indiscriminate weapons ever created. They violate international law, cause severe environmental damage, undermine national and global security, and divert vast public resources away from meeting human needs. They must be eliminated urgently.[95]

In December, 2016, at least 2,000 U.S. veterans responded to the call of Wesley Clarke Jr., son of retired General Wesley Clarke, and traveled to the Standing Rock Indian Reservation in North Dakota to form a "human shield," acting as an "unarmed militia" to support peaceful protestors of the Dakota Access Pipeline project, and nonviolently deter the police action against them. One Navy veteran who participated described the action as "not a mission of war, but a mission of peace."[96]

Speakers are brought in; there is study of the scholarly literature regarding how to promote a positive conversion of the war-culture economy of the nation; there is support for awareness about the remarkable intellectual work taking place, reimagining military bases' conversion to better support peacebuilding efforts, and decentralize war and militarization.

One specific example could involve economists such as Robert Polin and Heidi Garrett-Peltier, who have determined that "investments in clean energy, healthcare and education will produce between 50 and 140% more money than if the same money were spent by the Pentagon."[97] These public intellectuals challenge the old argument that technological advances through war-culture research and development are worth the costs, both financial and human; and they deconstruct the false argument that any change to the military budget will create inestimable economic damage to the nation as a whole. As they write,

> ... the most pressing areas for technological development are not in ever more dazzling weapons systems, but in clean energy, mass transportation, and high end manufacturing. Given these priorities, there is no reason that such industries should continue to be controlled by the Department of Defense.[98]

Meanwhile, scholars who work on the positive conversion of U.S. military bases write that "increased commitment to diplomacy, economic and cultural engagement, and international institutions," not only will promote better security for the United States with regard to its relationship with the wider world; in addition, "moving half the $51.5 billion spent on [U.S. military] bases would mean 450,000 infrastructure jobs, 300,000 elementary school jobs, 3 million Head Start slots, or 2.2 million vets with VA health care."[99] This does not sound like an economic disaster! How might media, foundations, think tanks and other institutions be encouraged to centralize and support similar consciousness-building and learning on days of national commemoration and celebration?

In addition to the structures of war-production, citizens also use these days to study and rethink U.S. military bases and branches of the military themselves; one place to start will be to invite women servicemembers to testify about the realities of sexual terrorism in the military; others gather to study reports addressing the conversion from armed force to practices of just peacekeeping and peacebuilding; this development has been growing over many decades in the world. Still others examine and work to change the dearth of peace education in educational institutions and student textbooks. *We promote decisive structural and cultural change, and challenge reliance on violence as the premier method to achieve a better world.*

Finally, in addition to the intellectual work above, the rhetorical banner, *End the Atrocity of Moral Injury*, directly questions the destructive ideology of "the necessity of the sacrifices of war" that is bolstered through exploitation of Christian understandings of salvation, and that gains traction through streams of sovereign masculinity, and tropes of expendability. Remember how this sacrificial rhetorical formation, and patterns of sacrificial cognition generally, uncritically centralize Jesus of Nazareth's death as the interpretive template for U.S. military losses. This distortion too must be faced, and addressed. Swerving the national consciousness with regard to practices of civil religion means that people of religious commitments will have to get to work. They will strive for greater honesty regarding what is going on in their own communities, activities, sermons, commemorations of national holidays, theologies, and service. Would that every divinity school across the United States prioritized courses for all potential clergy regarding social analysis linked with theological reflection on the intersecting crises of racism, materialism, war-culture, climate and more! Would that every course on Christian soteriology seriously addressed the vulnerability of Christian understandings of salvation in war-cultures, and promoted not only theological analysis, but reconstruction. Imagine religious institutions using these days to encourage their people to salvage their ultimate concern by criticizing the false god of sacrificial war-culture, and engaging in dialogue about the meaning of ultimate concern, and how to live with its ambiguity and risk.

Continuing in this thought experiment, the mere act of religious institutions' hosting and promoting of such rituals/ceremonies like Chaplain Antal's, will be a powerful beginning, because it is impossible to participate in something like this without coming away with so many new questions. Former ways of seeing and belonging are broken open, and new vision and understanding begin to form. After hearing someone like Andy tell his story, it feels utterly blasphemous to suggest that what he experienced was "a necessary sacrifice akin to what Jesus did on the cross." *War-culture is not sacred.* It cannot bear the weight of ultimate concern. Additionally, these rituals could promote an end to the old opposition between "pro-military" and "anti-war" factions, because these gatherings centralize care, concern and the deep valuing of members of the military, precisely through commitment to honesty, and openly hearing about what these people have experienced.

Nevertheless, the work must not stop with the hearing of these testimonies. An additional moral exercise, setting the narratives about moral injury against the backdrop of deeper engagement, study and dialogue about the structural and cultural violence of war-culture, outlined above, also is ongoing work needed in the United States. This is the second indispensable step. For people of religious commitments in particular, the labor of excavating the deep religious undercurrents that mask and sacralize war-culture, is the process of dismantling concealment. Suspicion regarding sacralizaton expands the continuing swerve towards a different world less suffocated by institutionalized structural and cultural violence and injustice. *People of Christian commitments study their traditions, and engage in theological reflection with diverse partners to name and face both structural and cultural (civil) religious violence and injustice.*

6   صيف ٢٠٢٠   parabicnews@gmail.com   صحيفة اصدقاء، سلام، ملاذ آمن   ٦

(Arab Interest in Culture... cont'd from pg. 2)
the originality of this society and not extraneous as some believe. Their scientific destination was to a very wide field, based on their great ability to visualize and their imagination in building and crystallizing ideas into scientific concepts based on which their theories and philosophies were built. Therefore, one of their first interests was to explore the sky and draw maps of the Zodiac that they identified and the paths of the stars that they followed, through which they knew the seasons and times, and wove various stories and myths on this topic. Today it is an important source for the study of astronomy in different cultures and our culture.

In the field of ethics, the pursuit of a sound life and the aspiration towards noble values were among the most important goals that they sought because it achieves happiness and strengthens family and social relations.

In the field of mathematics, physics and nature, they had implications that indicate their expansion and development of interest in this aspect of books in which they recorded their research and scientific discoveries that are still used mainly in various scientific fields.

In the field of geography and maritime navigation, the Arabs were the first to penetrate the seas and wrestled with them and defeated them. The Phoenicians and the Canaanites were the ones who had the lead in this field before other nations. Al-Idrisi was the best proof of that, because he drew a map of the world at a time when the various nations were ignorant of geography. The Greeks

Bees & Love

"We're more alike my friends, than we are..."

Life can be overwhelming; People can be difficult. This is double so for the surviving witnesses of war– those of us forced to flee, and those of us who did the forcing. Refugees and Veterans are bonded by war in this way: both groups must learn to function in hindsight of their actions or reactions, in a world with totally different rules than they are accustomed. And here we all are. Together on these pages, in this moment in time! What do you and your family do to handle to stress of life? I'm usually rotten at this mundane cognitive process (like many of you dear readers, I face the consequence of PTSD on the daily) but I have been taught a sort-of magic trick to help cope: Just Bee. Two "E"s. Let me explain…

As it turns out, one year, ago, a cohort of veterans (myself among them) intent on repairing their war-torn souls agreed to meet up with the

واحة الشعر

قلت وقررت

ولا عاد نور هو النور...	قلت لكن لم أفعل...
ولا عدت انا اطير مع اسراب الطيور	وقررت لكن لم أقرر...
ولا يغريني ضوء القناديل...	كنت خائفة
فأنا الان نجمة في السماء	مبعادرة البصمات تجربي
وانت القمر وفتان بين الاثنين...	الهبيات الى ذلك الوتر
لنا سأقول وأقرر...	الذي عزف أول لحن حب.....
لا ان أقول سأدعها في على الكتمان	ما بيننا.
بين ضلوعي تصارع نبضي ...	وربما ابعدها أكثر وأعلى أسوارها
وتكي حلمي ...	سأركب في أشيال ومعها حبي
تداوي جرحي...	سأركب ذكرياتي ومعها جراح قلبي
فالبعد ارحم ...	يا استنارة الزمن أسدلي اوجاعي
لكن ستندم...	وكل صباح ...
دكتورة ليلى الحسيني	فقبلات الصباح تبخرت مع ندى
شاعرة الحنين سفية	الزهور
السلام والإنسانية	
-ليلى الحسيني	

Figure 15 Wall, Andy. "Bees and Love." *The Journal of Friends, Peace and Sanctuary*. Summer 2020 (parabicnews@gmail.com).

And there is so much more to explore, such as the ways that people of diverse religious communities may support one another, and learn from one another, regarding the myriad ways that violence and kyriarchy become enmeshed in religious thought and practice; and additional discoveries regarding how to come together for the work to disentangle such threads.[100] Finally, how can all of us build upon the joyful sharing of food and drink, earth-promoting labor, and open and honest conversation with others, that Andy has discovered?

We can only imagine what will happen along the way of this thought experiment. Pope Francis hopes that the world will become better able to "envisage a new humanity." Martin Luther King Jr. hoped for a growth in the nation for "a positive thrust for democracy, realizing that our greatest defense … is to take offensive action in behalf of justice." More honest, capacious and generous forms of imagining and situating ultimate concern may be identified, stressing the centrality of valuing life through human interdependence, inclusion of all humans and nonhuman life, and the unity of means and ends. Perhaps all of us, and especially those so disproportionately impacted by the intersecting forms of direct, structural and cultural violence, finally will find it easier to breathe. Andy asks us, "How will you choose to spend your day today?" (see Figure 15).

Notes

Preface

1   Kevin Powers, *The Yellow Birds* (New York: Back Bay Books, 2011), 142–145.

2   Catherine Lutz, "Making War at Home in the United States: Militarization and the Current Crisis," *American Anthropologist* 104 (3) (September 2002), 723. Also see Denton-Borhaug "Chapter One: War-culture and Sacrifice," *U.S. War-culture, Sacrifice and Salvation*, 1st edition (New York: Routledge, 2014), 15.

Introduction

1   Jack Saul, "An Audio Experience: Exploring the Costs of War," International Trauma Studies Program and Windmill Factory, Debut in 2019 at UNFINISHED festival at the National Museum of Art of Romania, https://www.moralinjuriesofwar.org/about (accessed December 13, 2020).

2   Eric Fair, "The U.S. must open the book on the use of torture to move forward," *Washington Post*, April 11, 2014. Fair's story is explored in greater depth, in Chapters 3 and 4.

3   Darius Rejali, *Torture and Democracy* (Princeton: Princeton University Press, 2007).

4   Rejali outlines three ways that torture persists in democracies: the "National Security Model;" the "Civic Discipline Model;" and the "Judicial Model." See *Torture and Democracy.* Also, Kelly Denton-Borhaug, "A Theological Response to Torture and Democracy," *Dialog: A Journal of Theology*, 47 (3) (Fall 2008), 217–227. The definition of torture from the United Nations Convention against Torture reads as follows: "Torture means any act by which severe pain or suffering, whether physical or mental, is intentionally inflicted by or at the instigation of a public official on a person for such purposes as obtaining from him or a third person information or confession, punishing him for an act he has committed, or intimidating him or other persons." See "Convention against Torture and Other Cruel, Inhuman or Degrading Treatment or Punishment," Article 1.1, *United Nations Treaty Collection*, New York, December 10, 1984,

https://treaties.un.org/Pages/ViewDetails.aspx?src=IND&mtdsg_no=IV-9&chapter=4&lang=en (accessed December 13, 2020).

5   Claude AnShin Thomas, *At Hell's Gate: A Soldier's Journey From War to Peace* (Boston, MA: Shambhala, 2004), 20.

6   Thomas, 2004, 36.

7   Kevin Powers, "Author's Note," *The Yellow Birds* (New York: Back Bay Books, 2011), 2.

8   Richard Sisk, "Alarming VA Report Totals Decade of Veteran Suicides," *Military.com*, September 23, 2019, https://www.military.com/daily-news/2019/09/23/alarming-va-report-totals-decade-veteran-suicides.html (accessed 10/8/2019). Also see Amy Novotney, "Stopping Suicide in the Military," *Monitor on Psychology*, 51(1), January 2020, http://www.apa.org/monitor/2020/01/ce-corner-suicide (accessed December 12, 2020).

9   Eric Fair, 2014.

10   Eric Fair, 2014.

11   Jonathan Shay *Achilles in Vietnam: Combat Trauma and the Undoing of Character* (New York: Atheneum, 1994), 20. William P. Nash, "Commentary on the Special Issue on Moral Injury: Unpacking Two Models for Understanding Moral Injury," *Journal of Traumatic Stress*, 32 (3) (June 2019), 465. https://doi.org/10.1002/jts.22409

12   See Chris J. Antal & Kathy Winings, "Moral Injury, Soul Repair, and Creating a Place for Grace," *Religious Education*, 110 (4) (2015), 384. https://doi.org/10.1080/00344087.2015.1063962

13   Brett T. Litz, Nathan, Stein, Eileen Delaney, Leslie Lebowitz, William P. Nash, Caroline Silva, Shira Maguen, "Moral Injury and Moral Repair in War Veterans: A Preliminary Model and Intervention Strategy," *Clinical Psychology Review*, 29 (2009), 695–706. https://doi.org/10.1016/j.cpr.2009.07.003

14   Albert Bandura, *Moral Disengagement: How People Do Harm and Live with Themselves* (New York: Worth Publishers, 2016), 2. I am grateful to Chaplain Chris Antal for steering me in the direction of this helpful resource.

15   Edward Tick, *War and the Soul: Healing Our Nation's Veterans from Post-traumatic Stress Disorder* (Wheaton, Ill: Quest Books, 2005), 104.

16   Jonathan Shay, "The Trials of Homecoming: Odysseus Returns from Iraq/Afghanistan," *Smith College Studies in Social Work*, 79 (2009), 294. https://doi.org/10.1080/00377310903130332

17   William P. Nash, Brett T. Litz, "Moral Injury: A Mechanism for War-related Psychological Trauma in Military Family Members," *Clinical Child Family Psychological Review*, 16 (4) (2013), 386. https://doi.org/10.1007/s10567-013-0146-y

18 William P. Nash, a retired Navy psychiatrist and pioneer in stress control and moral injury, has asserted that a majority of returning veterans "bear some kind of moral injury," according to journalist David Wood, "The Grunts: Damned if They Kill, Damned if They Don't," *Huffington Post*, March 18, 2014. http://pach.org/from-the-media/the-grunts-damned-if-they-kill-damned-if-they-dont (accessed January 6, 2021). Researchers Blair E. Wisco, et al, summarize, "A significant minority of U.S combat veterans report PMIEs related to their military service. PMIEs are associated with risk for mental disorders and suicidality, even after adjustment for sociodemographic variables, trauma and combat exposure histories, and past psychiatric disorders." See Wisco et al, "Moral injury in U.S. combat veterans: Results from the national health and resilience in veterans study," *Depression and Anxiety*, 34 (4) (April 2017), 340–347. https://doi.org/10.1002/da.22614

19 Brandon J. Griffin, Natalie Purcell, Kristine Burkman, Brett T. Litz, Craig J. Bryan, Martha Schmitz, Claudia Villierme, Jessica Walsh, and Shira Maguen, "Moral Injury: An Integrative Review," *Journal of Traumatic Stress*, 32 (3) (June 2019), 350. https://doi.org/10.1002/jts.22362

20 Griffin, et al. (2019), 356.

21 Griffin et al. (2019), 351.

22 Griffin et al. (2019), 355.

23 Griffin et al. (2019), 356.

24 Warren Kinghorn, "Combat Trauma and Moral Fragmentation: A Theological Account of Moral Injury," *Journal of the Society of Christian Ethics*, 32 (2) (2012), 62. https://doi.org/10.1353/sce.2012.0041

25 Rita Nakashima Brock, comments from Opening Plenary, "Moral Injury: Pathways to Recovery," *USC*, May 29, 2019. This point also is powerfully argued in her book co-authored with Gabriella Lettini, *Soul Repair: Recovering from Moral Injury after War* (Boston, MA: Beacon Press, 2013). See The Shay Moral Injury Center, https://www.voa.org/moral-injury-war-inside. Nancy J. Ramsay directs the Soul Repair Center at Brite University, https://www.brite.edu/programs/soul-repair/.

26 Chris J. Antal & Kathy Winings, "Moral Injury, Soul Repair, and Creating a Place for Grace," *Religious Education*, 110 (4) (2015), 392. https://doi.org/10.1080/00344087.2015.1063962

27 Kinghorn, 2012, 68.

28 Robert Meagher, *Killing from the Inside Out: Moral Injury and Just War* (Eugene, OR, Cascade Books, 2014), 5.

29 See Rita Nakashima Brock and Gabriella Lettini, *Soul Repair: Recovering from Moral Injury After War* (Boston, MA: Beacon Press, 2012).

30   The term used for transitioning soldiers is called "out-processing," defined as "all Soldiers being discharged, separated, retired, transferred to another Service or component, or released from active duty." According to this policy, "Soldiers will be given a minimum of 5 working days to out-process unless it is locally determined that Soldiers can out-process quicker." See "Chapter Three: Out-processing," *Personnel Processing (In-Out-, Soldier Readiness, and Deployment Cycle)* Army Regulation 600–8–101, Headquarters Department of the Army Washington, DC, February 19, 2015.

31   Tyler Boudreau, "The Morally Injured," *The Massachusetts Review*, 52 (3) (2011), 746–754.

32   Boudreau, 2011, 753.

33   Ramsay, Nancy J., "Moral Injury as Loss and Grief with Attention to Ritual Resources for Care." *Pastoral Psychology*, 68 (1) (2019), 110. https://doi.org/10.1007/s11089-018-0854-9

34   Arnold R. Isaacs, "Moral Injury and America's endless conflicts," *Salon.com*, December 8, 2018. https://www.salon.com/2019/12/08/moral-injury-and-americas-endless-conflicts_partner/ (accessed December 19, 2020). Email from Chris Antal to Kelly Denton-Borhaug, December 18, 2020.

35   David Wood, "Moral Injury – Healing: Can We Treat Moral Wounds?" *Huffington Post*, March 20, 2014. http://projects.huffingtonpost.com/moral-injury/healing (accessed January 6, 2021).

36   David Wood, "The Grunts: Damned if They Kill, Damned if They Don't" *Huffington Post*, March 18, 2014.

37   Capt. William P. Nash, Teresa L. Marino Carper, Mary Alice Mills, Teresa Au, Abigail Goldsmith, Brett T. Litz, "Psychometric Evaluation of the Moral Injury Events Scale," *Military Medicine*, 178 (6) (June 2013), 647. https://doi.org/10.7205/milmed-d-13-00017

38   See the list of papers posted by the 2014 Ethics Symposium Archives: 2014 Papers and Presentations, *Command and General Staff College Foundation, Inc.*, September 22, 2014, 78. https://www.cgscfoundation.org/events/ethics-symposium/ethics-symposium-archive-2014/ (accessed November 28, 2020).

39   Nash and Litz, 2013, 368.

40   David Wood, 2014. See also Nash and Litz, 2013, 368.

41   McCloskey, Megan. "Combat Stress as 'Moral Injury' Offends Marines," *Stars and Stripes,* April 18, 2011, https://www.stripes.com/blogs/stripes-central/stripes-central-1.8040/combat-stress-as-moral-injury-offends-marines-1.142177 (accessed December 13, 2020).

42   Lieutenant Colonel Douglas A. Pryer, "Moral Injury and the American Service Member: What Leaders Don't Talk about when They Talk about War," in the 2014 Ethics Symposium Archives: 2014 Papers and Presentations, *Command and General Staff College Foundation, Inc.*, September 22, 2014, 78. https://www.cgscfoundation.org/events/

ethics-symposium/ethics-symposium-archive-2014/ (accessed November 28, 2020).

43   Tick, 2005, 155.

44   Pryer, 2014, 81.

45   See Michael Bottoms, "International Partners Attend Spiritual and Moral Resiliency Course," *United States Special Operations Command,* March 23, 2020, https://www.socom.mil/pages/International-partners-attend-Spiritual-and-Moral-Resiliency-course.aspx (accessed December 19, 2020).

46   Wayne B. Jonas, Colonel Francis O'Connor, Patricia Deuster, Colonel Christian Macedonia, eds., "Total Force Fitness for the 21st Century: A New Paradigm," *Military Medicine*, 175 (August Supplement, 2010).

47   Pryer, 2014, 81.

48   Pryer, 2014, 61.

49   Johan Galtung, "Cultural Violence," *Journal of Peace Research*, 27 (3) (August 1990), 291–305.

50   Galtung, 1990, 292.

51   Peter Hermann and John Woodrow Cox, "A Freddy Gray Primer: Who was he, How did he die, Why is there so much anger?" *The Washington Post*, April 28, 2015, https://www.washingtonpost.com/news/local/wp/2015/04/28/a-freddie-gray-primer-who-was-he-how-did-he-why-is-there-so-much-anger/ (accessed December 25, 2020).

52   Galtung, 1990, 293.

53   Galtung, 1990, 294, 296.

54   Sara Childress, "How Baltimore's Police Policy Led to Freddie Gray," *Frontline: PBS* (August 10, 2016) https://www.pbs.org/wgbh/frontline/article/how-baltimores-police-policy-led-to-freddie-gray/ (accessed December 25, 2020).

55   Galtung, 1990, 291, 295.

56   Meagher, 2014.

57   Ian Morris, *War! What Is It Good For? Conflict and the Progress of Civilization From Primates To Robots* (New York: Straus and Giroux, 2014).

58   Paul A. C. Koistinen, *State of War: The Political Economy of American Warfare, 1945–2011* (Lawrence: University of Kansas Press, 2012. Chalmers Johnson, *The Sorrows of Empire: Militarism, Secrecy and the End of the Republic* (Blackstone Audio Inc., 2007). Andrew Bacevich, *The New American Militarism: How Americans are Seduced by War* (London: Oxford University Press, 2013). Linda J. Blimes and Joseph El Stiglitz, *The Three Trillion Dollar War: The True Cost of the Iraq Conflict* (New York: W. W. Norton and Co., 2008). Robert Polin and Heidi Garrett-Peltier, "The U.S. Employment Effects of Military and

Domestic Spending Priorities: 2011 Update," *PERI Political Economy Research Institute* (Amherst: University of Massachusetts, 2012). Polin and Garrett-Peltier, "Benefits of a Slimmer Pentagon." *The Nation,* May, 2012, 15–18, https://www.peri.umass.edu/publication/item/747-benefits-of-a-slimmer-pentagon (accessed December 13, 2020).

59   Jon Sobrino, *Where is God? Earthquake, Terrorism, Barbarity and Hope* (New York: Orbis Books, 2004).

60   Claudia Card, *The Atrocity Paradigm: A Theory of Evil* (New York: Oxford University Press, 2002).

61   Claudia Card, 2002, 7.

Chapter 1

1   Peter Berger, *The Sacred Canopy: Elements of a Sociological Theory of Religion* (New York: Anchor Books, 1967), 27.

2   Berger, *The Sacred Canopy*, Chapter One, "Religion and World-Construction."

3   Berger, 1967, 40.

4   Berger, 1967, 29.

5   Berger, 1967, 43, 45.

6   See Denton-Borhaug, *U.S. War-culture, Sacrifice and Salvation*, 1st Edition (New York: Routledge, 2014).

7   "Penn State Blue Band Military Halftime Show," YouTube.com. October 3, 2015, https://www.youtube.com/watch?v=kwa94MI5Vc8 (accessed December 13, 2020).

8   Stanley Hauerwas, *War and the American Difference: Theological Reflections on Violence and National Identity* (Grand Rapids, Mich.: Baker, 2011), 4. Robert Emmet Meagher, *Killing from the Inside Out: Moral Injury and Just War* (Eugene, Ore.: Cascade Books, 2014), 1.

9   Nick Turse, *The Complex: How the Military Invades Our Everyday Lives* (New York: Metropolitan Books, 2008), 16.

10 See "Military Expenditure," *The Stockholm International Peace Research Institute Yearbook 2020*, Sipri.org, https://www.sipri.org/yearbook/2020 (accessed January 6, 2021). Also see "The Militarized Budget 2020," *National Priorities Project*, https://www.nationalpriorities.org/analysis/2020/militarized-budget-2020/ (accessed January 10, 2021); and "Federal Budget Tipsheet: Pentagon Spending," *National Priorities Project*, https://www.nationalpriorities.org/guides/tipsheet-pentagon-spending/ (accessed January 6, 2021).

11   Ian Morris, *War! What Is It Good For? Conflict and the Progress of Civilization From Primates To Robots* (New York: Farrar, Straus and Giroux, 2014), 7.

12   Morris, 2014, 9.

13   William Penn, "First Letter to the Delaware Indians," *Nonviolence in America: A Documentary History*, eds. Staughton Lynd and Alice Lynd (Maryville, NY: Orbis, 1995), 2.

14   Andrew Newman, "Treaty of Shakamaxon," *Encyclopedia of Greater Philadelphia*. https://philadelphiaencyclopedia.org/archive/treaty-of-shackamaxon-2/ (accessed January 6, 2021).

15   Andrea Mazzarino, Marcia C. Inhorn, and Catherine Lutz, "Introduction: The Health Consequences of War," in *War and Public Health*, eds. Catherine Lutz and Andrea Mazzarino (New York: New York University Press, 2019) 5–6; Bayla Ostrach and Merrill Singer, "Syndemics of War: Malnutrition-Infectious Disease Interactions and Unintended Health Consequences of Intentional Health Policies," *Annals of Anthropological Practice*, 36 (2) (2013): 257. https://doi.org/10.1111/napa.12003

16   Mark Pilisuk with Jeinnifer Achord Rountree, *Who Benefits From Global Violence and War: Uncovering a Destructive System* (Westport, Connecticut: Praeger Security International, 2008), 199, 27.

17   Pilisuk and Rountree, 2008, 28.

18   Pilisuk and Rountree, 2008, 27.

19   Pilisuk and Rountree, 2008, 9.

20   Historian and retired Colonel Andrew Bacevich made this point about the redevelopment of the U.S. nuclear arsenal. Andrew Bacevich, interview by Amy Goodman, *Democracy Now*, March 10, 2016, https://www.democracynow.org/2016/3/10/andrew_bacevich_why_is_no_candidate (accessed December 13, 2020).

21   Edith M. Lederer, "US urges countries to withdraw from US nuke ban treaty," *Associated Press*, October 21, 2020, https://apnews.com/article/nuclear-weapons-disarmament-latin-america-united-nations-gun-politics-4f109626a1cdd6db10560550aa1bb491 (accessed December 23, 2020).

22   Pilisuk and Rountree, 2008, 28.

23   Barack Obama, "Remarks by the President and the First Lady on the End of the War in Iraq," *The White House: President Barack Obama*, Fort Bragg, North Carolina, December 14, 2011, https://obamawhitehouse.archives.gov/the-press-office/2011/12/14/remarks-president-and-first-lady-end-war-iraq (accessed December 13, 2020).

24   Nick Turse, "Will U.S. 'successes' lead to more Iraqi military failure?" *Middle East Eye*, January 22, 2016, https://www.middleeasteye.net/big-story/will-us-successes-lead-more-iraqi-military-failures (accessed December 13, 2020).

25   Thomas H Kean, Chair, "The 9/11 Commission Report," *National Commission on Terrorist Attacks Upon the United States*, August 21, 2004, https://9-11commission.gov/report/ (accessed December 13, 2020).

26   For one fascinating study of this historical development, see Susan Juster, *Sacred Violence in Early America* (Philadelphia, PA: University of Pennsylvania Press, 2016).

27   Alex José Alvarado, email message to Kelly Denton-Borhaug, January 18, 2016. Permission granted to use email in this book, Alvarado email to Denton-Borhaug, December 30, 2020.

28   Ann Jones, *They Were Soldiers: How the Wounded Return from America's Wars—The Untold Story* (Chicago, IL: Haymarket Books, 2013), 167.

29   See Denton-Borhaug, *U.S. War-culture, Sacrifice and Salvation*, Chapter Two: "Building and Maintaining the Drive to War: Victimage Rhetoric, Framing and the Language of Sacrifice;" and Chapter Four: "Rehabilitating Sacrifice?"

30   Berger, 1967, 44.

31   Additional examples of sacrificial rhetoric may be found in additional articles and book chapters listed under Denton-Borhaug in the bibliography of this book.

32   Tucker Gates, writer, "Season Three: Chapter 30," *House of Cards*, Media Rights Capital and Panic Pictures, February 1, 2013. Television.

33   For a historical-critical analysis, see Simon J. Joseph, *The Nonviolent Messiah: Jesus, Q, and the Enochic Tradition* (Minneapolis: Fortress Press, 2014).

34   "Season Three: Chapter 30," *House of Cards*.

35   See David Martin, "Building a Monument to Wounded Warriors." *CBS News: Sunday Morning*, September 28, 2014, https://www.cbsnews.com/news/building-a-monument-to-wounded-warriors/ (accessed December 13, 2020; "Disabled Veterans Memorial Underway Near the National Mall." *Associated Press*, July 23, 2014, https://wjla.com/features/veterans/disabled-veterans-memorial-underway-near-the-national-mall-105344 (accessed December 13, 2020).

36   All quotes come from Martin, "Building a Monument," (2014) and *Associated Press*, "Disabled Veterans Memorial" (2014).

37   For further discussion of this poem, see Denton-Borhaug, "Sacrificial U.S. War-culture: Cognitive Dissonance, and the Absence of Self-Awareness." *Journal of Religion and Violence*, 5 (1) (April 28, 2017), 5–26. https://doi.org/10.5840/jrv201742538

38   Wilfred Owen's poem, "Dulce et Decorum est," was written in 1917–18, *The War Poetry Website*, https://www.warpoetry.uk/ (accessed December 13, 2020). Elizabeth Samet, professor of English Literature at West Point writes, "Suggesting that a death in battle was in vain—'Lives

were wasted' in Fallujah, a former Marine told the Times, 'and now everyone back home sees that'—also starkly exposes what the World War I poet Wilfred Owen described as the 'old Lie' about the unadulterated sweetness of dying for one's country." "Can an American Soldier Ever Die in Vain," *Foreign Policy*, May 9, 2014, https://foreignpolicy. com/2014/05/09/can-an-american-soldier-ever-die-in-vain/ (accessed 11/04/2019).

39   See Judith Butler, *Frames of War: When Is Life Grievable?* (New York: Verso, 2010).

40   See Hans Mohl, *Identity and the Sacred* (Oxford, UK: Basil Blackwell, 1976), 12.

41   See Chapter 5 for more extensive analysis drawing on the work of Judith Butler.

42   Ian Morris, 2014.

43   This material comes from Denton-Borhaug, "'Like Acid Seeping into Your Soul'; Religio-cultural Violence in Moral Injury," in *Exploring Moral Injury in Sacred Texts*, ed. Joseph McDonald (London: Jessica Kingsley Publishers, 2017), 111–134. See Kevin Powers, *The Yellow Birds* (New York: Backbay Books, 2013).

44   Ben Fountain, *Billy Lynn's Halftime Walk* (New York: Ecco, 2012). Also see Johan Galtung, "Cultural Violence," *Journal of Peace Research* 27 (3) (August, 1990), 291–305.

45   Kevin Powers, *Yellow Birds* (New York: Back Bay Books, 2013), 142–145, Author's Note, 2.

46   Ben Fountain, *Billy Lynn's Long Halftime Walk* (New York: HarperCollins, 2012).

47   Fountain, 2012, 59.

48   Fountain, 2012, 306.

49   Fountain, 2012, 37.

50   Fountain, 2012, 38.

51   Fountain, 2012, 59.

52   Fountain, 2012, Front Pages. Karl Marlantes, *What it is Like to Go to War* (New York: Grove Press, 2012).

53   Kristen Bakotic, "The Most Tested Among Us," *The White House: President Barack Obama*. November 11, 2014, https://obamawhitehouse. archives.gov/blog/2014/11/11/most-tested-among-us-vice-president-biden-pays-tribute-our-nations-veterans (accessed December 25, 2020).

54   Galtung, 1990, 296.

55   Martin Luther King, Jr., "Beyond Vietnam: A Call to Conscience" delivered April 4, 1967 at Riverside Church, New York City. Stanford University, The Martin Luther King Jr., Education and Research Institute,

https://kinginstitute.stanford.edu/king-papers/documents/beyond-vietnam (accessed December 13, 2020).

Chapter 2

1   William Arkin, "My Departure Letter from NBC," *William M. Arkin Online*. January 4, 2019, https://williamaarkin.wordpress. com/2019/01/04/my-departure-letter-from-nbc/ (accessed January 7, 2019).

2   Arkin, "Resignation Letter." Also see Paul A. C. Koistinen, *State of War: The Political Economy of American Warfare, 1945–2011* (Lawrence: University of Kansas Press, 2012); Chalmers Johnson, *The Sorrows of Empire: Militarism, Secrecy and the End of the Republic* (New York: Henry Holt and Co., 2005); Andrew Bacevich, *The New American Militarism: How Americans are Seduced by War* (London: Oxford University Press, 2013); Linda J. Blimes and Joseph El Stiglitz, *The Three Trillion Dollar War: The True Cost of the Iraq Conflict* (New York: W. W. Norton and Co., 2008); Robert Polin and Heidi Garrett-Peltier, "The U.S. Employment Effects of Military and Domestic Spending Priorities: 2011 Update," *PERI (Political Economy Research Institute)* (Amherst: University of Massachusetts, 2012). Polin and Garrett-Peltier, "Benefits of a Slimmer Pentagon," *The Nation,* May 2012, 15–18. Jon Sobrino, *Where Is God? Earthquake, Terrorism, Barbarity and Hope* (New York: Orbis, 2004).

3   John Dower, *The Violent American Century: War and Terror Since WWII* (Chicago, IL: Haymarket Books, 2017), 8.

4   Dower, 2017, 8.

5   I draw from the method utilized by theologian Jon Sobrino, in his analysis of the concealment of systemic injustice and institutionalized violence in U.S. militarized culture, and its impact on El Salvador. See *Where Is God? Earthquake, Terrorism, Barbarity and Hope.*

6   "The Militarized Budget 2020," *National Priorities Project*, https://www. nationalpriorities.org/analysis/2020/militarized-budget-2020/ (accessed January 7, 2021). According to the NPP, "In recognition that the U.S. maintains both the world's highest military spending, and one of its highest incarceration rates, the militarized budget includes the traditional military budget, as well as spending on veterans' affairs, homeland security, incarceration, law enforcement, immigration enforcement, and the still-ongoing war on drugs."

7   John Dower, 2017, 12.

8   Dower, 2017, 12.

9   Koistinen, 2012. Denton-Borhaug, "U.S. War-culture and the Political Economy of the United States," *Word and World* 34.4 fall (2014), 376–377.

10   Dower, 2017, 23.

11   Dower, 2017, 22.

12   Koistinen, 2012, 163.

13   Koistinen, 2012, 237.

14   Koistinen, 2012, 105–106.

15   Nick Turse, *The Complex: How the Military Invades our Everyday Lives* (New York: Metropolitan, 2008).

16   Aaron Mehta, "Here's what the Pentagon's first-ever audit found," *Defense News,* November 16, 2018, https://www.defensenews.com/pentagon/2018/11/15/heres-what-the-pentagons-first-ever-audit-found/ (accessed January 9, 2019); Dave Lindorff, "The Pentagon's Massive Accounting Fraud Exposed," *The Nation,* November 27, 2018, https://www.thenation.com/article/pentagon-audit-budget-fraud/ (accessed January 9, 2019).

17   Lindorff, 2018.

18   Lindorff, 2018.

19   Koistinen, 2012, 231, 227.

20   Koistinen, 2012.

21   Koistinen, 2012, 127–130.

22   Koistinen, 2012, 208–209.

23   Koistinen, 2012, 225.

24   Koistinen, 2012, 235.

25   Nick Turse, "One Down, Who Knows How Many to Go?" *Tomgram: TomDispatch.com.* January 8, 2019, https://www.tomdispatch.com/post/176513/tomgram:_nick_turse,_one_down,_who_knows_how_many_to_go/ (accessed November 28, 2020). Dower, 2017, 81.

26   "U.S. Military Bases Overseas: The Facts," *Overseas Base Alignment and Closure Coalition,* https://www.overseasbases.net/ (accessed January 11, 2019).

27   Turse, 2019.

28   Turse, 2019.

29   Turse, 2019.

30   Turse, 2019.

31   Turse, 2019.

32   Dower, 2017, 79.

33   Chalmers Johnson, *The Sorrows of Empire*, 152. Also see Denton-
      Borhaug, *U.S, War-culture, Sacrifice and Salvation*, 1st Edition (New
      York: Routledge, 2014), 23.

34   Dower, 2017, 107.

35   Dower, 2017, 81.

36   Dower, 2017, 81. Dower quotes Andrew Bacevich, "Even If We Defeat
      the Islamic State, We'll Still Lose the Bigger War," *Washington Post,*
      October 3, 2014.

37   "U.S. Military Bases Overseas: The Facts," *Overseas Base Alignment and
      Closure Coalition.*

38   "U.S. Military Bases Overseas: The Facts," *Overseas Base Alignment and
      Closure Coalition.* See also David Vine, *Base Nation: How U.S. Military
      Bases Abroad Harm America and the World* (New York: Metropolitan
      Books, 2015), especially Chapter 3, "The Displaced," Chapter 7, "Toxic
      Environments, and Chapter 9, "Sex for Sale."

39   Dower, 2017, 8.

40   Dower, 2017, 8.

41   Dower, 2017, 84.

42   Johnson, 2005, 152. Also Denton-Borhaug, 2014, 23.

43   *Independence Day, Resurgence,* directed by Roland Emmerich (2016;
      Twentieth Century Fox); See the Independent Movie Database, imdb.
      com. https://www.imdb.com/title/tt1628841/ (accessed January 13, 2019).
      Also see "US Army Earth Space Defense Recruitment," YouTube.com.
      May 15, 2016, https://www.youtube.com/watch?v=Uzkp1m1wmMk
      (accessed. January 13, 2019).

44   Kevin Lilley, "Army's New Recruitment Drive: Sign up, maybe fight
      aliens," *Army Times,* May 18, 2016, https://www.armytimes.com/off-duty/
      movies-video-games/2016/05/18/army-s-new-recruitment-drive-sign-up-
      maybe-fight-aliens/ (accessed January 13, 2019).

45   "US Army Earth Space Defense Recruitment," YouTube.com.

46   "Penn State Blue Band Military Halftime Show," YouTube.com. October
      3, 2015, https://www.youtube.com/watch?v=kwa94MI5Vc8 (accessed
      November 28, 2020).

47   Many of these commercials also may be seen on YouTube. For example,
      see "America's Navy: A Global Force for Good," YouTube.com. April
      29, 2010, https://www.youtube.com/watch?v=bao2aPV9uUw (accessed
      November 28, 2020).

48   "U.S. Navy: A Global Force for Good," YouTube.com.

49   See Denton-Borhaug, Chapter One, "War-culture and Sacrifice," *U.S.
      War-culture, Sacrifice and Salvation,* for additional investigation of the
      facets of war-culture's interpenetration with civil society.

50   Dower, 2017, 94.

51   Bill Arkin and Dana Priest, "A Hidden World, Growing Out of Control," *Washington Post,* July 19, 2010, http://projects.washingtonpost.com/ top-secret-america/articles/a-hidden-world-growing-beyond-control/ (accessed January 15, 2019.

52   Arkin and Priest, 2010, 4.

53   Atossa Araxia Abrahamian, "The Real Wall Isn't at the Border," *New York Times,* January 26, 2019, https://www.nytimes.com/2019/01/26/ opinion/sunday/border-wall-immigration-trump.html (accessed January 27, 2019). See also Ron Nixon, "U.S. to Collect Social Media Data on All Immigrants Entering the Country," *New York Times,* September 28, 2017, https://www.nytimes.com/2017/09/28/us/politics/immigrants-social- media-trump.html?module=inline (accessed January 27, 2019).

54   Arkin and Priest, 2010, 5.

55   Arkin and Priest, 2010, 6.

56   Dower, 2017, 95.

57   Ulrich Petersohn, "Privatising Securing: The Limits of Military Outsourcing," September, 2010. *CSS Analysis in Security Policy; ETH Zurich: Center for Security Studies.* http://www.css.ethz.ch/ (accessed January 17, 2019), 1.

58   Ulrich Petersohn, 2010, 2. Dower, 2017, 96.

59   William Hartung, "The Military-Industrial Complex Revisited: Shifting Patterns of Military Contracting in the Post-9/11 Period," *Costs of War,* Watson Institute: International and Public Affairs, Brown University, https://watson.brown.edu/costsofwar/files/cow/imce/papers/2011/The%20 Military-Industrial%20Complex%20Revisited.pdf (accessed January 17, 2019), 2.

60   Hartung, 2011, 7.

61   Hartung, 2011, 8.

62   Dower, 2017, 8.

63   "Summary of Findings," *Costs of War.* Watson Institute: International and Public Affairs, Brown University, https://watson.brown.edu/costsofwar/ papers/summary (accessed January 17, 2019).

64   "Summary of Findings," *Costs of War.*

65   Jonathan Shay, *Achilles in Vietnam: Combat Trauma and the Undoing of Character* (New York: Simon and Schuster, 1995).

66   Chris J. Antal, *Patient to prophet: Building adaptive capacity in veterans who suffer moral injury,* D. Min. Hartford Seminary, 2016 (ProQuest Dissertations and Theses Open, 2017; 166: 10673402), 7.

67   Duane Larson and Jeff Zust, *Care for the Sorrowing Soul: Healing Moral Injuries from Military Service and Implications for the Rest of Us* (Eugene, OR: Cascade Books, 2017), 62.

68   Bruce Allenby, "Respecting Moral Injury," in *War and Moral Injury: A Reader, eds.* Robert Emmet Meagher and Douglas A. Pryer (Eugene, OR: Cascade Books, 2018), 259–261.

69   Deane-Peter Baker, "Moral Ambiguity and Ethical Dilemma, 1915–2015," *Moral Injury: Unseen Wounds in an Age of Barbarism* (Sydney Australia: NewSouth Publishing, 2015), 98.

70   Baker, 2015, 105.

71   Baker, 2015, 105.

72   Shannon E. French and Anthony I. Jack, "Connecting Neuroethics and Military Ethics to Help Prevent Moral Injury," in *War and Moral Injury: A Reader*, eds. Robert Emmet Meagher and Douglas A. Pryer (Eugene, OR: Cascade Books, 2018), 270–279.

73   Stefan J. Malecek, "The Moral Inversion of War," in *War and Moral Injury: A Reader,* eds. Robert Emmet Meagher and Douglas A. Pryer (Eugene, OR: Cascade Books: 2018), 292–296.

74   Malecek, 2015, 300.

75   Dr. Martin Luther King, Jr., "Pilgrimage to Nonviolence," in *A Testament of Hope: The Essential Writings and Speeches of Martin Luther King, Jr.,* ed. James M. Washington (San Francisco: Harper, 1986), 39.

76   King, "Pilgrimage," 40.

77   Pete Kilner, "Leadership, War, and Moral Injury," in *War and Moral Injury: A Reader,* eds. Robert Emmet Meagher and Douglas A. Pryer (Eugene, OR: Cascade Books, 2018), 95–100.

78   Charles Pacello, "Moral Trauma and Nuclear War," *War and Moral Injury: A Reader*, 114–116.

79   Pacello, 2018, 115.

80   Eyal Press, "The Wounds of the Drone Warrior," *New York Times,* June 13, 2018, https://www.nytimes.com/2018/06/13/magazine/veterans-ptsd-drone-warrior-wounds.html (accessed January 23, 2019).

81   Eric Fair, *Consequence: A Memoir* (New York: Henry Holt and Co., 2016), 27.

82   Fair, 2016, 135.

83   Fair, 2016, 108.

84   Fair, 2016, 202.

85   Fair, 2016, 188.

86   Diane Feinstein, United States Senator, Senate Select Committee on Intelligence, *Committee Study of the Central Intelligence Agency's*

Detention and Interrogation Program. Released April 3, 2014. 11ff.
http://www.feinstein.senate.gov/public/index.cfm/senate-intelligence-
committee-study-on-cia-detention-and-interrogation-program (accessed
January 23, 2019). Also see Denton-Borhaug, "U.S. War-culture, the
post-9/11 'unlawful alien combatant,' and 'Peace in God's World,'" in
Lutheran Theology and Secular Law: The Work of the Modern State, eds.
Ron W. Duty and Marie Falinger (New York: Routledge, 2018), 101–114.
https://doi.org/10.4324/9781315276342-9

87   Feinstein, 2014, 11.

88   Feinstein, 2014, 1.

89   Jane Mayer, *The Dark Side: The Inside Story of How the War on Terror
Turned into a War on American Ideals* (New York: Doubleday, 2008), 31.
https://doi.org/10.1163/2468-1733_shafr_sim260040033. See also George
W. Bush, "Memorandum for the Vice President: Humane Treatment of
al Qaeda and Taliban Detainees," February 7, 2002, in *Torture Papers:
The Road to Abu Ghraib,* eds. Karen J. Greenberg, Joshua L. Dratel
(Cambridge: Cambridge University Press, 2005), 134–135. https://doi.
org/10.1017/cbo9780511511127

90   Feinstein, 2014, 11.

91   Flores, Reena Flores, "Trump Says Intelligence Officials Tell Him Torture
Works," *CBSNews.com.* January 29, 2017, http://www.cbsnews.com/news/
trump-says-intelligence-officials-tell-him-torture-works/ (accessed March
30, 2019). Also see David Wright, "Donald Trump Defends Torture:
'Nothing Should Be Taken Off the Table,'" *CNN.com..* February16, 2016,
http://www.cnn.com/2016/02/16/politics/donald-trump-waterboarding-
op-ed-usa-today-enhanced-interrogation-techniques-torture/ (accessed
March 30, 2019). And Connor Adam Sheets, "CIA Torture Report
Poll: Half of Americans Say Enhanced Interrogation Was 'Justified,'"
International Business Times, December 15, 2014, http://www.ibtimes.
com/cia-torture-report-poll-half-americans-say-enhanced-interrogation-was-
justified-1758576 (accessed March 30, 2019). Finally, see: Gershon Shafir,
Evrard Meade and William J. Aceves. *Routledge Critical Terrorism
Studies: Lessons and Legacies of the War on Terror: From moral
panic to permanent war* (New York: Routledge, 2013), 22. https://doi.
org/10.4324/9780203083987

92   Paul D. Shinkman, "Obama: 'Global War on Terror is Over,'" *U.S. News,*
May 23, 2013, https://www.usnews.com/news/articles/2013/05/23/
obama-global-war-on-terror-is-over (accessed November 28, 2020).

93   Matthew Beard, "Conceptual Distinctions," in *Moral Injury: Unseen
Wounds in an Age of Barbarism*, ed. Tom Frame (Sydney Australia:
NewSouth Publishing, 2015), 115.

94   Beard, 2015, 117–118.

95   Beard, 2015, 123.

96   Beard, 2015, 120–121.

97   Beard, 2015, 122.

98   Beard, 2015, 124.

99   Robert E. Meagher, "Hope Dies Last," *War and Moral Injury: A Reader*, eds. Robert Emmet Meagher and Douglas A. Pryer (Eugene, OR: Cascade Books, 2018), 318.

100   Duane Larson and Jeff Zust, 2017, 159.

101   Jonathan Shay, "Moral Leadership Prevents Moral Injury," *War and Moral Injury: A Reader,* eds. Robert Emmet Meagher and Douglas A. Pryer (Eugene, OR: Cascade Books, 2018), 304.

102   Shay, 2018, 303.

103   "Creating Peace: 2010 Social Statement of Conscience," *Unitarian Universalist Association*, https://www.uua.org/action/statements/creating-peace (accessed January 26, 2019).

104   Larson and Zust, 2017, 123.

105   Larson and Zust, 2017, 127.

106   Adam Brown, "The Trauma of 'Choiceless Choices': The Paradox of Judgement in Primo Levi's 'Grey Zone,'" in *Trauma, History, Philosophy (With Feature Essays by Agnes Heller and Gyorgy Markus)*, eds. Matthew Sharpe, Murray Noonan, and Jason Freddi (Newcastle, UK: Cambridge Scholars Publishing, 2007), 142–163, 149.

107   Massimo Giulinai, *Centaur in Auschwitz: Reflections on Primo Levi's Thinking* (Washington, D.C.: Lexington Books, 2003), 45. Quoted in Brown, 2007, 145.

108   Brown, 2007, 146.

109   Dominick LaCapra, "Approaching Limit Events: Siting Agamben," in *Witnessing the Disaster: Essays on Representation and the Holocaust*, eds. Michael F. Bernard-Donals and Richard R. Glejzer (Madison, WI: University of Wisconsin Press, 2003), 285 (https://doi.org/10.7202/014166ar), as quoted in Brown, 2007, 149–50.

110   Brown, 2007, 155.

111   Brown, 2007, 154.

112   Levi, "The Grey Zone," in *The Drowned and the Saved*, trans. Raymond Rosenthal (New York: Simon and Schuster, 1986), 37.

113   Levi, 39.

114   Levi, 32.

115   Brown, 2007, 162, quoting Inga Clendinnen, *Agamemnon's Kiss: Selected Essays* (Melbourne, Australia: Text Publishing, 2007), 2.

116   Levi, 41.

117 Levi, 41.

118 Levi, 35.

119 Robert E. Meagher, "Wounded Warriors, Wounded Nation: Closing the Gates of War," Lecture at Moravian College, Bethlehem PA, March 27, 2014.

120 I am grateful for Rev. Chris Antal's reminder of the story of Ted Westhusing, discussed in detail by Nancy Sherman in *The Untold War*, and the person to whom Bacevich dedicated his book, *Breach of Trust*, as an example of the impact of the isolation described here. See Nancy Sherman, *The Untold War: Inside the Hearts, Minds and Souls of our Soldiers*, Reprint Edition (New York: W.W. Norton & Co., 2011); and Andrew Bacevich, *Breach of Trust: How Americans Failed Their Soldiers and Their Country* (New York: Metropolitan Books, 2013).

121 Rita Nakashima Brock and Gabriella Lettini, *Soul Repair: Recovering from Moral Injury after War* (Boston, MA: Beacon Press, 2013) 101–102. https://doi.org/10.1177/0034637314541835h

122 Lieutenant Colonel Douglas A. Pryer, "Moral Injury and the American Service Member: What Leaders Don't Talk about when They Talk about War," in the "2014 Ethics Symposium Archives: 2014 Papers and Presentations," *Command and General Staff College Foundation, Inc.*, September 22, 2014, 78. https://www.cgscfoundation.org/events/ethics-symposium/ethics-symposium-archive-2014/, September 22, 2014 (accessed November 18, 2020).

123 Levi, 32.

Chapter 3

1 American Psychological Association, Boys and Men Guidelines Group, "APA guidelines for psychological practice with boys and men," *American Psychological Association*, 2018, https://www.apa.org/about/policy/boys-men-practice-guidelines.pdf (accessed November 30, 2020).

2 APA, 2020, 2–3.

3 APA, 2020, 1–4.

4 APA, 2020, 6.

5 APA, 2020, 19.

6 David French, "Grown Men Are the Solution, Not the Problem," *National Review*, January 7, 2019, www.nationalreview.com/2019/01/psychologists-criticize-traditional-masculinity/ (accessed November 30, 2020).

7　Johan Galtung, *Peace by Peaceful Means: Peace and Conflict, Development and Civilization* (Oslo: International Peace Institute and London: Sage Publications, 1996), 196. https://doi.org/10.7146/politica. v28i4.68086

8　See Galtung, 1996, Chapter One: "Peace Studies: An Epistemological Basis."

9　Galtung, 1996, 70, 71.

10　Galtung, 1996, 81.

11　Galtung, 1996, 90–94.

12　Bonnie Mann, *Sovereign Masculinity: Gender Lessons from the War on Terror* (New York: Oxford University Press, 2014), 69.

13　For a review of President Obama's rhetoric and policies regarding The Global War on Terror, see Trevor McCrisken, "Ten years on: Obama's war on terrorism in rhetoric and practice," *International Affairs* (Royal Institute of International Affairs 1944-) 87 (4) (July 2011): 781–801.

14　Mann, 2014, 69.

15　Mann, 2014, 63.

16　As quoted by Mann, 2014, 65.

17　Mann, 2014, 64.

18　Mann, 2014, 66.

19　*The Hurt Locker*, directed and produced by Kathryn Bigelow (2008; British Columbia: Voltage Pictures).

20　Mann, 2014, 51.

21　Mann, 2014, 53.

22　Mann, 2014, 56.

23　Mann, 2014, 116.

24　Mann, 2014, 122. Also see Judith Butler, "Precarious Life, Grievable Life," *Frames of War: When Is Life Grievable?*, Reprint Edition (Brooklyn: Verso, February 2, 2016), 14. https://doi.org/10.7227/r.15.1.16

25　Ben Wadham, "Violence in the military and Relations Among Men: Military Masculinities and 'Rape-Prone Cultures'," in *The Palgrave International Handbook of Gender and the Military*, eds. Rachel Woodman and Clare Duncanson, 1st Edition (London: Palgrave, June 27, 2017), 243. https://doi.org/10.1057/978-1-137-51677-0_15

26　Mann, 2014, 123.

27　Wadham, 2017, 243.

28　As recounted by Mann, 2014, 147–148. See Kayla Williams, *Love my Rifle More than You: Young and Female in the U.S. Army*, Reprint Edition (New York: W. W. Norton & Company, September 17, 2006), 214.

29   Wadham, 2017, 242.

30   Wadham, 2017, 246, 252.

31   Mann, 2014, 175.

32   Mann, 2014, 179.

33   *American Sniper*, directed by Clint Eastwood (2015; Warner Brothers). See the plot description from the *Internet Movie Database*. https://www. imdb.com/title/tdt2179136/. Chris Kyle, Scott McEwen, Jim DeFelice, *American Sniper: The Autobiography of the Most Lethal Sniper in U. S. Military History* (New York: HarperCollins, 2016).

34   Mann, 2014, 181.

35   Kevin Powers, "Separation," *Letter Composed During a Lull in the Fighting* (Boston, MA: Little, Brown and Co., 2014).

36   Wadham, 2017, 241–2.

37   Kathleen Barry, *Unmaking War, Remaking Men* (Santa Rosa: Phoenix Rising Press, 2011).

38   Barry, 2011, 12.

39   See Santanu Das, "'Dulce et Decorum Est', a close reading," *British Library: Discovering 20th Century Literature*. In 1917 English poet Wilfred Owen drew upon the Latin phrase for his poem with the same title, describing this belief as "the old Lie." https://www.bl.uk/20th-century-literature/articles/a-close-reading-of-dulce-et-decorum-est# (accessed January 7, 2021). Das writes, "'Dulce Et Decorum Est' is one of those primal moments in the history of not just English but world poetry when lyric form bears most fully the trauma of modern industrial warfare."

40   Chapter 5 takes this further, telling the story of the "Hometown Heroes" banners arrival in my own town, and front door. These widespread ritual commemorations consolidate sacrificial justifications of war-culture and war. As the local news described, "Just in time for Memorial Day weekend, when the service of those who have made the ultimate sacrifice defending America is honored, the Borough of Hellertown has hung nearly 50 Hometown Hero banners that salute its own." See Josh Popichak, "Hometown Hero Banners Flying High in Hellertown," *Saucon Source,* May 24, 2020, https://sauconsource.com/2020/05/24/hometown-hero-banners-flying-high-in-hellertown/ (accessed November 30, 2020).

41   "Most Stressful Jobs of 2017," *CareerCast,* careercast.com. https://www. careercast.com/jobs-rated/most-stressful-jobs-2017 (accessed February 22, 2019).

42   Barry, 2011, 16.

43   Toni Rico, media contact, "Media Advisory: Service women identify sexual assault, not deployment, as the number one factor that negatively affects their mental wellness," *Service Women's Action Network,*

November 10, 2017, https://www.servicewomen.org/press-releases/
media-advisory-service-women-identify-sexual-assault-not-deployment-
as-number-one-factor-that-negatively-affects-their-mental-wellness/
(accessed February 22, 2019).

44   Barry, 2011, 19, 20–21.

45   Barry, 2011, 30.

46   See Dave Grossman, *On Killing: The Psychological Cost of Learning to
Kill in War and Society* (Boston, MA: Little Brown and Co., 2009).

47   Barry, 2011, 30–31.

48   H. Patricia Hynes, "The Battlefield and the Barracks: Two War Fronts
for Women Soldiers," *Truthout,* five-part series, January 11–February
15, 2012. https://truthout.org/articles/why-do-soldiers-rape/1326306014/
(accessed November 30, 2020).

49   H. Patricia Hynes, "Battlefield and the Barracks: Why Do Soldiers Rape?
Truthout, January 18, 2012. https://truthout.org/articles/why-do-soldiers-
rape/1326306014/ (accessed November 30, 2020).

50   S.L.A. Marshall, *Men Against Fire: The Problem of Battle Command*
(Norman, Oklahoma: University of Oklahoma Press, 2000).

51   Barry, 2011, 32.

52   Barry, 2011, 33.

53   Denton-Borhaug, 2014, *U.S. War-culture, Sacrifice and Salvation* details
the "Army Experience Center," 35–36.

54   David Vine, "Militarized Masculinity," *Base Nation: How U.S. Military
Bases Abroad Harm America and the World* (New York: Metropolitan
Books, 2015), 180–191.

55   Vine, 2015, 181, 182.

56   French and Jack, "Connecting Neuroethics and Military Ethics to Help
Prevent Moral Injury," *War and Moral Injury: A Reader*, eds. Robert
Meagher and Douglas A. Pryer (Eugene, OR: Cascade Books, 2018), 277 ff.

57   Vine, 2015, 182.

58   "Interview: Why is there no end to sexual violence by U.S. Military
Personnel in Okinawa?" *The Mainichi: Japan's National Daily*,
September 15, 2016, https://mainichi.jp/english/articles/20160915/
p2a/00m/0na/017000c (accessed November 30, 2020).

59   Martin Castro, Chair, U.S. Commission on Civil Rights, "Sexual Assault
in the Military: 2013 Statutory Enforcement Report" (Washington,
D.C.: *U.S. Commission on Civil Rights,* Sept, 2013), https://www.hsdl.
org/?abstract&did=744910 (accessed January 7, 2021), 15.

60   Vine, 2015, 186. See H. Patricia Hynes, "The Battlefield and the
Barracks: Two War Fronts for Women Soldiers," *Truthout,* five-part

series, January 11–February 15, 2012, https://truthout.org/articles/why-do-soldiers-rape/1326306014/ (accessed November 30, 2020).

61   Claire Duncanson outlines the main themes of scholars with "anti-militarist feminist concerns." Two concerns are of special interest to this chapter: a) the military as an inherently hostile workplace for women, and b) militarism as a fundamentally anti-feminist system. According to Duncanson, the "anti-militarist feminist" perspective may slide into essentialism, and too narrowly define and describe the complexities of military cultures. At the same time, though women's entry into military service, especially combat roles, has been heralded as an advance by "right to fight" liberal feminists, anti-militarist feminist scholars are suspicious about the ways this supposed "gender-equality" furthers cultural, structural and direct forms of violence. Instead of legitimating military institutions through female participation, these scholars press for "the eradication of militarism in society." See Duncanson, "Anti-militarist Feminist Approaches to Researching Gender and the Military," *The Palgrave International Handbook of Gender and the Military*, eds. Rachel Woodward and Claire Duncanson (London: Palgrave, 2017), 50. https://doi.org/10.1057/978-1-137-51677-0_3

62   Denton-Borhaug, *U.S. War-culture, Sacrifice and Salvation.* To further explore the connection of sacrificial war-culture with U.S. nationalism, see Kelly Denton-Borhaug, "Is this America? Unfinished business with the U.S. national imaginary, religion and violence," *Dialog* 58, 2019, 30–38. https://doi.org/10.1111/dial.12451

63   Kelly Denton-Borhaug, "U.S. War-culture, the post-9/11 'unlawful alien combatant,' and 'Peace in God's World'" in *Lutheran Theology and Secular Law: The Work of the Modern State*, eds. Ron W. Duty and Marie Falinger (New York: Routledge, 2018) https://doi.org/10.4324/9781315276342-9. Also see Jane Mayer, *The Dark Side: The Inside Story of How the War on Terror Turned into a War on American Ideals*, Reprint Edition (Norwell, MA: Anchor, 2009), 31 ff. https://doi.org/10.1163/2468-1733_shafr_sim260040033

64   Martin M. Winkler, "*Dulce et decorum est pro patri mori?* Classical Literature in the War Film," *International Journal of the Classical Tradition,* Vol. 7 No. 2, Fall 2000, 177–214, 177–179.

65   For additional analysis of sacrificial war-culture, see Denton-Borhaug, 2011; also see Denton-Borhaug, "Sacrificial U.S. War-culture: Cognitive Dissonance, and the Absence of Self-Awareness." *Journal of Religion and Violence*, April 28, 2017. https://doi.org/10.5840/jrv201742538; Denton-Borhaug, "Resisting the sacred canopy over U.S. ways of war." *Political Theology*, 18 (3) (May 30, 2017): 206–218. https://doi.org/10.1179/1743171915y.0000000007

66   Leah Marianne Klett, "Veterans' Day 2015: History, Meaning and Bible Verse: Why Should Christians Celebrate This Holiday? *The Gospel Herald Society*, November 10, 2015. https://www.gospelherald.com/

articles/59639/20151110/veterans-day-2015-history-meaning-traditions-why-christians-celebrate-holiday.htm (accessed January 7, 2021).

67   For further analysis of sacrificial war-culture and Christian soteriology, see Denton-Borhaug, 2011, Chapter 4, "Rehabilitating Sacrifice?"

68   The articles and book already referenced in this chapter include additional analysis and examples.

69   See further analysis in Denton-Borhaug, 2011, with regard to theologian Jung Mo Sung, from whom I borrow the term, "transcendentalize."

70   See Denton-Borhaug, "Martyrdom Discourse in Contemporary U.S. War-culture," for further analysis of this political case study and the role of martyrdom in U.S. war-culture. *Wiley-Blackwell Companion to Christian Martyrdom*, ed. Paul Middleton (Hoboken, New Jersey: Wiley-Blackwell Publishing, 2020), 471–484. https://doi.org/10.1002/9781119100072.ch28

71   See "Dad of fallen Muslim soldier's powerful DNC speech (Khzir Khan full speech," YouTube.com, July 28, 2016. https://www.youtube.com/watch?v=Xzkkk-oJ6bo (accessed November 30, 2020). This moment later was mobilized for a "Stronger Together" campaign commercial for the 2016 Clinton campaign. See "Captain Khan/Hillary Clinton," YouTube.com, October 21, 2016, https://www.youtube.com/watch?v=WCqFCCgU1xk (accessed November 30, 2020).

72   Maggie Haberman and Richard A. Oppel, "Donald Trump Criticizes Muslim Family of Slain U.S. Soldier, Drawing Ire," *New York Times*, July 30, 2016, https://www.nytimes.com/2016/07/31/us/politics/donald-trump-khizr-khan-wife-ghazala.html (accessed November 30, 2020).

73   See "36 U.S. Code § 111. Gold Star Mother's Day," *Legal Information Institute*, Cornel Law School, https://www.law.cornell.edu/uscode/text/36/111 (accessed November 30, 2020). U.S. presidents issue "Presidential Proclamations" each year setting aside the last Sunday of September as "Gold Star Mother's Day." For example, see Barack Obama, "Presidential Proclamation – Gold Star Mother's and Family's Day, 2012," *The White House; President Barack Obama*, September 28, 2012, https://obamawhitehouse.archives.gov/the-press-office/2012/09/28/presidential-proclamation-gold-star-mothers-and-familys-day-2012 (accessed January 8, 2021).

74   "Gold Star Luminary Initiative," *MarineParents.com, Inc.,* Columbia, MO. http://luminaryinitiative.com/pledge-online.asp (accessed January 8, 2021).

75   "Valley Forge PA – Gold Stars Family Memorial Monument," *Hershel Woody Williams Medal of Honor Foundation*, September 21, 2014, http://hwwmohf.org/monument-projects.html (accessed January 8, 2021).

76   Vote.Vets.org, "VoteVets releases Gold Star Family Members letter to Trump, demand apology for all Gold Star Families," *VoteVets.org*, Aug 1,

2016, https://www.votevets.org/press/gold-star-letter (accessed January 8, 2021).

77   *Glory*, directed by Edward Zwick (1989; Tristar Pictures).

78   Catherine Albanese, *Sons of the Fathers: The Civil Religion of the American Revolution* (Philadelphia, PA: Temple University Press, 1976). https://doi.org/10.1086/ahr/82.5.1322

79   Butler, "Precarious Life, Grievable Life," *Frames of War: When Is Life Grievable?*

80   See further analysis of this case of military martyrdom in Denton-Borhaug, "Moral Injury and the U.S. War-culture Bible," *Moral Injury: A Guidebook to Understanding*, ed. Brad Kelle (New York: Lexington Books, 2020), 173–188. Also see Delores S. Williams, "Black Women's Surrogacy Experience," in *After Patriarchy: Feminist Transformations of the World Religions*, eds. Paula N. Cooey, William R. Eakin, Jay B. McDaniel (Maryknoll, NY: Orbis, 1991), 1–14. Williams writes, "Thus, to respond meaningfully to black women's historic experience of surrogacy-oppression, the theologian must show that redemption of humans can have nothing to do with any kind of surrogate role Jesus was reputed to have played in a bloody act that supposedly gained victory over sin and/or evil." (11). Also see Denton-Borhaug, *U.S. War-culture, Sacrifice and Salvation*, Chapter Four: "Rehabilitating Sacrifice?"

81   Joanna Dewey, "'Let Them Renounce Themselves and Take Up Their Cross': A Feminist Reading of Mark 8:34 in Mark's Social and Narrative World," in *A Feminist Companion to Mark*; *Feminist Companion to the New Testament and Early Christian Writings*, eds. Amy-Jill Levine and M. Blickerstaff (Sheffield, UK: Sheffield Academic, 2001), 23–36. https://doi.org/10.1177/01461079040340030201

82   James Crossley, "An Immodest Proposal for Biblical Studies," *Relegere: Studies in Religion and Reception* 2 no. 1 (2012): 153–77. https://doi.org/10.11157/rsrr2-1-515

83   Elisabeth Schüssler-Fiorenza, *In Memory of Her: A Feminist Reconstruction of Christian Origins*, 10th Edition. (Chestnut Ridge, NY: Herder and Herder, 1994). https://doi.org/10.1007/978-3-476-05728-0_20223-1

84   Liz Theoharis, *Always with Us? What Jesus Really Said about the Poor* (Grand Rapids, MI: Eerdmans, 2017). See *The Poor People's Campaign: A National Call for Moral Revival*, https://www.poorpeoplescampaign.org/ (accessed November 29, 2020).

85   I am grateful to Rev. Chris Antal for suggesting this particular language.

86   *Peace is Every Step: Meditation in Action: The Life and Work of Thich Nhat Hanh*, directed by Gaetano Kazuo Maida (1998; Festival Media), DVD. Chris J. Antal, *Patient to Prophet: Building Adaptive Capacity in*

Veterans who Suffer Moral Injury. DMin Dissertation, Hartford Seminary, March 2017.

87   Joseph M. Currier, Jacob K. Farnsworth, Kent D. Drescher, and Wesley H. McCormick, "Moral Injury and Resilience in the Military," in *Bulletproofing the Psyche: Preventing Mental Health Problems in Our Military and Veterans*, eds. Kate Hendricks Thomas and David L. Albright (Santa Barbara, CA: Praeger, 2018), 76–92.

88   Currier and Farnsworth, 2018, 79.

89   Currier and Farnsworth, 2018, 85.

90   Currier and Farnsworth, 2018, 86.

91   Currier and Farnsworth, 2018, 88.

92   Currier and Farnsworth, 2018, 91.

93   Currier and Farnsworth, 2018, 78,

94   Currier and Farnsworth, 2018, 80.

95   Currier and Farnsworth, 2018, 84–85.

96   Currier and Farnsworth, 2018, 85, 80.

97   Currier and Farnsworth, 2018, 80.

98   Currier and Farnsworth, 2018, 80.

99   Currier and Farnsworth, 2018, 86.

100   Currier and Farnsworth, 2018, 86.

101   Currier and Farnsworth, 2018, 86.

102   Currier and Farnsworth, 2018, 83.

103   Currier and Farnsworth, 2018, 83.

104   Currier and Farnsworth, 2018, 81.

105   Currier and Farnsworth, 2018, 76.

106   Currier and Farnsworth, 2018, 89.

107   Currier and Farnsworth, 2018, 88.

Chapter 4

1   Hannah Arendt, *Eichmann in Jerusalem: A Report on the Banality of Evil*, 1st Edition (New York: Penguin Classics, 2006).

2   *White Light, Black Rain*, directed by Stephen Okazaki (2007; HBO), DVD.

3   I am indebted to Tomoko Watanabe of ANT-Hiroshima for her coining of the phrase, "life under the mushroom cloud." See *ANT-Hiroshima*, https://

uri.org/who-we-are/cooperation-circle/ant-hiroshima (accessed April 16, 2019).

4   Yuki Miyamoto, "Unbearable Light/ness of the Bombing: Normalizing Violence and Banalizing the horror of atomic bomb experiences," *Critical Military Studies* 1 (2), July 2015, 116–130. https://doi.org/10.1080/23337 486.2015.1050268

5   Miyamoto, 2015, 121.

6   Miyamoto, 2015, 122.

7   Miyamoto, 2015, 122.

8   "Japan," *Atomic Heritage Foundation/National Museum of Nuclear Science and History*, https://www.atomicheritage.org/location/japan (accessed 06/22/2020).

9   "September 11 Terror Attacks Fast Facts," *CNN Library*, September 3, 2018. https://www.cnn.com/2013/07/27/us/september-11-anniversary-fast-facts/index.html (accessed April 15, 2019).

10   "Deadly WWII U.S. firebombing raids on Japanese cities largely ignored," Associated Press for the *Japan Times News*, March 10, 2015, https://www.japantimes.co.jp/news/2015/03/10/national/deadly-wwii-u-s-firebombing-raids-on-japanese-cities-largely-ignored/#.XLXp6JNKjOQ (accessed April 16, 2019).

11   Robert Lifton and Greg Mitchell, *Hiroshima in America* (New York: Harper Perennial, 1996).

12   William Mahedy uses the language of evil and moral outrage to describe Veterans' experience in Vietnam. See *Out of the Night* (Greyhound Books, 2005).

13   Truth Commission on Conscience in War to Protect and Honor Freedom of Conscience for Our Nation's Service Members. Commissioner. March 21–22, 2010. The Riverside Church, NY, New York.

14   Claudia Card, *The Atrocity Paradigm: A Theory of Evil* (New York: Oxford University Press, 2002). Further references and quotes from *The Atrocity Paradigm* cite the pages in the main text.

15   Johan Galtung, 1996, 197.

16   Chris J. Antal, Peter D. Yeomans, et al., "Transforming Veteran identity through community engagement: a chaplain–psychologist collaboration to address moral injury," *Journal of Humanistic Psychology* (April 29, 2019), 1–26. https://doi.org/10.1177/0022167819844071. Further page references to this article appear above in the text.

17   Joseph M. Currier, Jacob K. Farnsworth, Kent D. Drescher, and Wesley H. McCormick, "Moral Injury and Resilience in the Military," *Bulletproofing the Psyche: Preventing Mental Health Problems in Our Military and Veterans* (Santa Barbara, CA: Praeger, 2018), 88.

18   I first heard Andy speak during the Mental Health Summit at Crescenz
      VAMC. I was invited to provide the Spiritual Care Ground Rounds,
      immediately following the Summit. Denton-Borhaug, "Sacrifice and U.S.
      War-culture: Implications for Understanding Moral Injury," *Spiritual
      Grand Rounds*, Corporal Michael J. Crescenz Veterans Association
      Medical Center, September 27, 2018.

19   "Community Healing Ceremony," Sponsored by the Philadelphia
      Episcopal Diocese, St. Paul's Episcopal Church, Germantown, PA,
      November 11, 2018.

20   Chaplain Chris Antal, "Creating Welcoming Faith Communities for
      Veterans, and the Sacred Canopy over U.S. Ways of War," Clergy
      Training, Moravian Theological Seminary and Moravian College,
      Bethlehem, PA, March 21, 2019.

21   "About VA," *U.S. Department of Veterans Affairs*, https://www.va.gov/
      ABOUT_VA/index.asp (accessed December 5, 2020).

22   David L. Parsons, "Introduction," *Dangerous Grounds: Antiwar
      Coffeehouses and Military Dissent in the Vietnam Era* (Chapel Hill:
      University of North Carolina Press, 2017), 4–6.

23   Parsons, 2017, 65 ff.

24   John Lennon, "Imagine," *Songfacts*, https://www.songfacts.com/lyrics/
      john-lennon/imagine (accessed 04/25/2019).

25   Michael Yandell, featured in "Faith Communities, Veterans and Mental
      Health – Video #3 – 'Moral Injury,'" from Mental Health and Chaplaincy.
      (2017, February2). *A Place to Call Home* [Video]. U.S. Department of
      Veterans Affairs. https://www.mirecc.va.gov/mentalhealthandchaplaincy/
      community.asp (accessed December 5, 2020).

26   Hans Mohl, *Identity and the Sacred* (Oxford, UK: Basil Blackwell, 1976),
      5, 12.

27   Turse, Nick. *The Complex: How the Military Invades our Everyday Lives*
      (New York: Metropolitan, 2008).

28   Rev. Chris Antal, email to Denton-Borhaug, December 1, 2020. John
      Dower writes, "Since 1996, the Pentagon's proclaimed mission is to
      maintain 'full-spectrum dominance' in every domain (land, sea, air,
      space, and information) and, in practice, in every accessible part of the
      world. See Chapter One: "Measuring Violence," *The Violent American
      Century.*

29   Sam LaGrone, "Slogans that Sell the Service: A Brief History of U.S.
      Navy Television Ads after the End of the Draft," May 29, 2015, *USNI
      News*, https://news.usni.org/2015/05/29/slogans-that-sell-the-service-
      a-brief-history-of-u-s-navy-television-ads-after-the-end-of-the-draft
      (accessed December 4, 2020). LaGrone writes, "The Navy has long
      recognized the effectiveness of powerful visual images for attracting new
      recruits. Men who had not been drafted were often enticed to enlist by

the striking images found on ubiquitous posters as well as by the smartly uniformed personnel manning the recruiting booths."

30 See Corey Mead, *War Games: Video Games and the Future of Armed Conflict* (New York: Eamon Dolan/Houghton Mifflin Harcourt, 2017). Also see Hamza Shaban, "Playing War: How the Military Uses Video Games," *The Atlantic*, October 10, 2013. https://www.theatlantic.com/technology/archive/2013/10/playing-war-how-the-military-uses-video-games/280486/ (accessed December 4, 2020). With respect to the timeframe when Andy enlisted, Shaban writes, "The military offers funding and technical expertise to game and computer developers, and, in exchange, they give it proprietary technology and technical consulting … 1980's *Battlezone* and its successor, 1993's *Doom*, showed the potential for 3-D piloting, multiplayer networking, and virtual reality-based training. Through commercial gaming technology, the armed forces could adapt soldiers to the tactics of team fighting and trigger-fast decision making, or conjure tailor-made battle environments for them."

31 Chaplain Chris Antal, Clergy Training, Moravian Theological Seminary: "Creating Welcoming Faith Communities for Veterans, and the Sacred Canopy over U.S. Ways of War," Moravian College, March 21, 2019.

32 Chaplain Chris Antal, email to Denton-Borhaug, December 1, 2020.

33 Christine Pedersen, "I Followed My Father into the Marines. But It was Different for a Woman," *New York Times*, April 4, 2019, https://www.nytimes.com/2019/04/04/magazine/marine-corps-sexual-harassment.html (accessed April 30, 2019).

34 John Dower, *The Violent American Century: War and Terror Since WWII* (Chicago, IL: Haymarket Books, 2017), 84.

35 Marysia Zalewski, "What's the problem with the concept of military masculinities?" *Critical Military Studies* 3 (2) (April, 2017), 200–205. https://doi.org/10.1080/23337486.2017.1316480

36 Robert Meagher, *Killing from the Inside Out: Moral Injury and Just War* (Eugene, OR: Cascade Books, 2014).

37 Johan Galtung, *Peace by Peaceful Means: Peace and Conflict, Development and Civilization* (Oslo: PRIO, SAGE Publications Ltd, 1996). https://doi.org/10.7146/politica.v28i4.68086

38 See Judith Butler, *Frames of War: When is Life Grievable?* (New York: Verso, 2016).

39 Reuters, "Bowing to U.S. Demands, UN Waters Down Resolution on Sexual Violence in Conflict," *New York Times*, April 23, 2019, https://www.straitstimes.com/world/united-states/bowing-to-us-demands-un-waters-down-resolution-on-sexual-violence-in-conflict (accessed 11/11/2019).

40 Andrew Bacevich, *America's War for the Greater Middle East: A Military History* (New York: Random House, 2016). Meagher, 2014, 133.

41   Meagher, 2014, 141–142.

42   Meagher, 2014, 142. See also Tyler Boudreau, *Packing Inferno: The Unmaking of a Marine* (Port Townsend, Washington: Feral House, 2008), 165.

Chapter 5

1   Mike Baker, Jennifer Valentino-DeVries, Manny Fernandez and Michael LaForgia, "Three Words. 70 Cases. The Tragic History of 'I can't breathe,'" *New York Times*, June 20, 2020, https://www.nytimes.com/interactive/2020/06/28/us/i-cant-breathe-police-arrest.html (accessed December 20, 2020).

2   Sam Grant, Executive Director, *350MN.org*, https://mn350.org/how-we-work/ (accessed December 20, 2020).

3   Anne C. Mulkern, "Fast-moving California Fires Boosted by Climate Change," *Scientific American*, August 24, 2020, https://www.scientificamerican.com/article/fast-moving-california-wildfires-boosted-by-climate-change/#:~:text=Climate%20connection%20scrutinized,%2C%20while%20precipitation%20dropped%2030%25 (accessed December 20, 2020).

4   Vann R. Newkirk II, "Trump's EPA Concludes Environmental Racism is Real," *The Atlantic*, February 28, 2018, https://www.theatlantic.com/politics/archive/2018/02/the-trump-administration-finds-that-environmental-racism-is-real/554315/ (accessed December 20, 2020).

5   "Covid-19 Forecasts – Deaths," *Center for Disease Control and Prevention*, December 17, 2020, https://www.cdc.gov/coronavirus/2019-ncov/covid-data/forecasting-us.html (accessed December 20, 2020); "WHO Coronavirus Disease (Covid-19) Dashboard," *World Health Organization*, December 20, 2020, https://covid19.who.int/?gclid=Cj0KCQiAifz-BRDjARIsAEElyGIt0NEKzcOW7Wk9uphhgkKdShqCFtOhAJzplOMKLNv4tGcJRULHq70aAjluEALw_wcB (accessed December 20, 2020).

6   Neta C. Crawford, "United States Budgetary Costs and Obligations of Post-9/11 Wars through FY2020: $6.4 Trillion," *Costs of War*, Watson Institute: International and Public Affairs, Brown University, November 13, 2019, https://watson.brown.edu/costsofwar/papers/2019/united-states-budgetary-costs-and-obligations-post-911-wars-through-fy2020-64-trillion (accessed December 20, 2020).

7   See Josh Popichak, "Hometown Hero Banners Flying High in Hellertown," *Saucon Source*, May 24, 2020, https://sauconsource.com/2020/05/24/hometown-hero-banners-flying-high-in-hellertown/ (accessed November 30, 2020). Note how the the language of this article

repeats the sacrificial formulations that are so prevalent in U.S. war-culture. Memorial Day is "… a day to remember and honor the sacrifice of our uniformed men and women who've died in service to our nation." The Hometown Hero banner program was approved by the Hellertown Borough in 2019, and about 50 banners were purchased by businesses and individuals, and placed on utility poles. So far, one woman has been featured in the Hellertown collection.

8   See the most recent social teaching of the Catholic Church on just war. Pope Francis, *Fratelli Tutti*, Encyclical Letter, October 3, 2020, http://www.vatican.va/content/francesco/en/encyclicals/documents/papa-francesco_20201003_enciclica-fratelli-tutti.html (accessed December 20, 2020).

9   Angela Davis, interview by Amy Goodman, "Freedom Struggle: Angela Davis on Calls to Defund Police, Racism and Capitalism, and the 2020 Election," *Democracy Now.* DemocracyNow.org. September 7. 2020, https://www.democracynow.org/2020/9/7/freedom_struggle_angela_davis_on_calls (accessed December 20, 2020); Christine Amanpour, "Angela Davis: 'Devastating Consequences' if Barrett is Confirmed," *CNN*, CNN.com, October 13, 2020, https://www.cnn.com/videos/world/2020/10/13/angela-davis-scotus-amanpour-coronavirus.cnn (accessed December 20, 2020).

10   Goodman, "Freedom Struggle."

11   Brian Barrett, "The Pentagon's Hand-Me-Downs Helped Militarize Police. Here's How," *Wired*, June 17, 2020, https://www.wired.com/story/pentagon-hand-me-downs-militarize-police-1033-program/ (accessed December 20, 2020).

12   Barrett, 2020.

13   Barrett, 2020.

14   David Wenner, "Gun Sales surge in PA amid pandemic, news of protests and civil unrest," *Pennsylvania Real-Time News*, July 8, 2020, Pennlive.com, https://www.pennlive.com/news/2020/07/gun-sales-surge-in-pa-amid-pandemic-news-of-protests-and-civil-unrest.html (accessed December 20, 2020). On the issue of violence as saving, see Denton-Borhaug, *U.S. War-culture, Sacrifice and Salvation*, Chapter 3: "A Deadly Nexus: 'Necessity,' Christian Salvation and War-culture;" and Chapter 4: "Rehabilitating Sacrifice?"

15   See Timur Kuran, *Private Truths, Public Lies: The Social Consequences of Preference Falsification* (Boston, MA: Harvard University Press, 2007).

16   Ellen Knickmeyer, "Barrett deflects senators' questions on climate change," *AP News*, APNews.com, October 14, 2020, https://apnews.com/article/science-climate-climate-change-amy-coney-barrett-judiciary-7c901ed970c2e9bed1e14f28047c1022 (accessed December 20, 2020).

17   Cameron Jenkins, "Greta Thunberg mocks Barrett for not having 'views on climate change,'" *The Hill*, thehill.com, October 15, 2020, https://thehill.com/policy/energy-environment/521268-greta-thunberg-mocks-barrett-for-not-having-views-on-climate-change (accessed December 20, 2020).

18   Mike Pesca, "The Gist with Mike Pesca," *Slate*. Slate.com, https://slate.com/podcasts/the-gist (accessed December 20, 2020).

19   Sara Guaglione, "Slate's 'Gist' Podcast Celebrates 5 Years, Focuses on Promoting Episodes," *MediaPost*, May 13, 2019. Mediapost.com, https://www.mediapost.com/publications/article/335751/slates-gist-podcast-celebrates-5-years-focuses.html (accessed December 20, 2020).

20   Lori Galarreta, email to Kelly Denton-Borhaug, September 8, 2020.

21   Franco Ordoñez, "Trump Faces Fallout from Report He Calls Military, 'Suckers' and 'Losers,'" *National Public Radio*, September 4, 2020. NPR.org, https://www.npr.org/2020/09/04/909599762/trump-faces-fallout-from-report-he-calls-military-losers-and-suckers (accessed December 20, 2020); Mike Pesca, "The Gist: No Cause Bigger than Himself," *The Gist*. September 8, 2020. Slate.com/podcasts, https://slate.com/podcasts/the-gist/2020/09/trump-disdain-for-service (accessed December 20, 2020).

22   Pesca, 2020.

23   Kelly Denton-Borhaug, email to Lori Galarreta and Daniel Schroeder, September 8, 2020.

24   Daniel Schroeder, email to Kelly Denton-Borhaug and Lori Galarreta, September 9, 2020.

25   Mike Pesca, *The Gist*, interview with Kelly Denton-Borhaug, September 10, 2020.

26   Mike Pesca, *The Gist*, interview with Kelly Denton-Borhaug, September 10, 2020.

27   Mike Pesca, *The Gist*, interview with Kelly Denton-Borhaug, September 10, 2020.

28   Kelly Denton-Borhaug, email to Lori Galarreta and Daniel Shroeder, September 26, 2020.

29   Judith Butler, *The Force of Nonviolence* (New York: Verso, 2020).

30   Butler, 2020, 57.

31   Butler, 2020, 143.

32   Butler, 2020, 114.

33   Butler, 2020, 109.

34   Butler, 2020, 104.

35   Butler, 2020, 111.

36   Butler, 2020, 107.

37 "This American carnage stops right here," Trump proclaimed. Donald Trump, "The Inaugural Address," January 20, 2017, *The White House.gov*, https://www.whitehouse.gov/briefings-statements/the-inaugural-address/ (accessed December 20, 2020).

38 Butler, 2020, 138.

39 Butler, 2020, 198.

40 Butler, 2020, 199.

41 Butler, 2020, 198.

42 Butler, 2020, 107.

43 Butler, 2020, 109.

44 Butler, 2020, 138.

45 James A. DeVinney, Callie Crossley, "Bridge to Freedom," *Eyes on the Prize*, Episode 6, Min. 47–50 (1986; Blackside Production Co.), video. https://video-alexanderstreet-com.moravian.idm.oclc.org/watch/bridge-to-freedom-1965/details?context=channel:eyes-on-the-prize (accessed December 20, 2020).

46 Robert Jay Lifton, "The Climate Swerve," *The New York Times*, Aug. 23, 2014, http://nyti.ms/1mAySAC (accessed December 20, 20200; Also see: Lifton, *The Climate Swerve* (New York: The New Press, 2017). Lifton notes that "the term 'swerve' originated in the writing of Lucretius, the Roman poet and philosopher who lived during the first century BCE." Most recently drawn upon by humanist Stephen Greenblatt, the language and idea of "swerve" also appear in the writings of Jonathan Swift, James Joyce, Jacques Lacan and Simone de Beauvoir. "Climate Swerve: From Experience to Ideas," *The Climate Swerve*, 101–102.

47 Lifton, 2017, 103.

48 Lifton, 2014.

49 United Nations, "Nuclear-Weapon-Free-Zones," *United Nations Office for Disarmament Affairs*, https://www.un.org/disarmament/wmd/nuclear/nwfz/ (accessed December 20, 2020); "Treaty on the Prohibition of Nuclear Weapons," *United Nations Office for Disarmament Affairs*, https://www.un.org/disarmament/wmd/nuclear/tpnw/ (accessed December 20, 2020).

50 Lifton, "The Climate Swerve."

51 "Stranded assets" first was coined by The Carbon Tracker Initiative, through use of scientific data demonstrating that without "stranding" 70 to 80 percent of existing underground fossil fuels assets, the risk of "catastrophic effects on the human future" was at stake. Lifton, *The Climate Swerve*, 113.

52 Lifton, "The Climate Swerve." Also see Lifton, *The Climate Swerve*, 114–115.

53   Lifton, "The Climate Swerve."

54   Lifton, "The Climate Swerve."

55   Lifton, "The Climate Swerve."

56   U.S. Veterans Affairs sponsored a video series addressing these issues, including "Faith Communities, Veterans and Mental Health; Partners in Care; Trauma; Moral Injury; Belonging," Mental Health and Chaplaincy, *A Place to Call Home* [Video], U.S. Department of Veterans Affairs, February 2, 2017, https://www.mirecc.va.gov/mentalhealthandchaplaincy/community.asp (accessed December 20, 2020).

57   Rev. Chris Antal, "Military Moral Injury: How It Manifests and How to Work with It," *PA Society of Chaplains*, Fall 2020 Conference, Carlisle, PA, October 18–20, 2020.

58   *The Journal of Friends, Peace and Sanctuary*, Summer 2020, parabicnews@gmail.com.

59   Andy Wall, "Bees and Love," *The Journal of Friends, Peace and Sanctuary*, Summer 2020, parabicnews@gmail.com, 6.

60   Thich Nhat Hanh, "To Veterans," from *Love in Action: Writing on Nonviolent Social Change*, in *A Lifetime of Peace: Essential Writings by and about Thich Nhat Hanh*, ed. Jennifer Schwamm Willis (New York: Marlowe and Company, 2003), 124, 128.

61   "Military Moral Injury: How It Manifests and How to Work with It," *PA Society of Chaplains*, Fall 2020 Conference, October 18–20, 2020.

62   Lifton, "Climate Swerve."

63   Erica, Chenoweth, "The success of nonviolent civil resistance," November 4, 2013, TEDxBoulder, *TEDx Talks*, https://www.youtube.com/watch?v=YJSehRlU34w (accessed December 20, 2020). Also, Erica Chenoweth and Maria J. Stephan, *Why Civil Resistance Works: The Strategic Logic of Nonviolent Conflict* (New York: Columbia University Press, 2011).

64   Chenoweth, 2013. Also see Erica Chenoweth and Maria Stephan, 2011. Also see Gene Sharp, *There Are Realistic Alternatives* (Boston, MA: The Albert Einstein Institute, 2003).

65   Denton-Borhaug, "Moral Injury and the U.S. War-culture Bible," in *Moral Injury: A Guidebook for Understanding and Engagement*, ed. Brad E. Kelle (Lanham, MD: Lexington Books, 2020), 173–188.

66   Rev. Chris Antal, "Military Moral Injury: How It Manifests and How to Work with It," *PA Society of Chaplains*, Fall 2020 Conference, October 18–20, 2020.

67   Maria Pilar Aquino, "Religious Peacebuilding," in *Blackwell Companion to Religion and Violence*, ed. Andrew R. Murphy (Malden, MA: Blackwell Publishing, 2011): 568–593, 569–570. Also see Elisabeth

Schüssler-Fiorenza, *But She Said: Feminist Practices of Biblical Interpretation* (Boston, MA: Beacon Press, 1992) 8, 122–125. According to Schüssler-Fiorenza, "kyriarchal power operates not only along the axis of gender but also along those of race, class, culture, and religion ... [in] interlocking systems of oppression ... This 'politics of domination' refers to 'the ideological ground that they share, which is a belief in domination, and a belief in notions of superior and inferior.'" *But She Said*, 123.

68   Pilar Aquino, 2011, 570.

69   Caroline Randall Williams, "A Loving Chastisement for America," *New York Times*, November 8, 2020, https://www.nytimes.com/2020/11/07/opinion/sunday/trump-america-racism.html (accessed December 20, 2020).

70   Robert P. Jones, *White Too Long: The Legacy of White Supremacy in American Christianity* (New York: Simon and Schuster, 2020), 1.

71   Jones, 2020, 3.

72   Jones, 2020, 6.

73   Jones, 2020, 6.

74   Jones, 2020, 17.

75   See Celucien L. Joseph, "James Cone and the Crisis of American Theology," *Missionalia* 42 (2) (February 2019), 206 ff. https://doi.org/10.7832/46-2-309

76   Rev. Elizabeth Reed, conversation with author, November 15, 2020.

77   Jones, 2020, 24. See also *The Poor People's Campaign*, led by Drs. Samuel Barber and Liz Theoharis, a national movement for "moral revival" to address the intersecting crises of poverty, racism, militarism and climate justice in the United States. https://www.poorpeoplescampaign.org/ (accessed December 20, 2020).

78   I have witnessed this numerous times when attending Claude AnShin Thomas and Weibke KenShin Andersen's public lectures, most recently when they attended my zoom course to lecture in October, 2020. See the *Zaltho Foundation: Promoting Nonviolence, Awareness and Change*, https://zaltho.org/ (accessed December 20, 2020).

79   Claude AnShin Thomas, *The Zaltho Foundation*.

80   Jaqueline Shearer, Paul Stekler, dir., "The Promised Land (1967–68)," *Eyes on the Prize* (1990; Blackside Production company), TV series and video, https://www.pbs.org/wgbh/americanexperience/films/eyesontheprize/ (accessed December 20, 2020).

81   Tavis Smiley, *Death of a King: The Real Story of Dr. Martin Luther King's Final Year*, Reprint Edition (New York: Back Bay Books, 2016), 19–31, 243. Martin Luther King, "Beyond Vietnam," April 4, 1967, *Stanford University: The Martin Luther King Jr. Research and Education institute*, https://kinginstitute.stanford.edu/king-papers/documents/

beyond-vietnam (accessed December 20, 2020). Also see Tavis Smiley, "Q and A with Tavis Smiley," by Brian Lamb, *CSPAN*, September 25, 2014, https://www.c-span.org/video/?321711-1/qa-tavis-smiley (accessed December 20, 2020).

82   Tavis Smiley, 2016. Martin Luther King, "Beyond Vietnam," April 4, 1967. Also see "Q and A with Tavis Smiley," *CSPAN*, September 25, 2014.

83   King, 1967.

84   Andy Wall, 2020.

85   See the example of Bernie Sanders' attempt to create legislation for a 10% decrease in military spending in 2020: Joe Gould, "Progressive effort to cut defense fails twice in Congress," *DefenseNews*, July 22, 2020, https://www.defensenews.com/congress/2020/07/22/progressive-effort-to-cut-defense-fails-twice-in-congress/ (accessed December 2020).

86   Pilar Aquino's words quoted earlier in this chapter.

87   Pope Francis, *Fratelli Tutti*, Encyclical Letter (Rome: Libreria Editrice Vaticana, October 3, 2020). http://www.vatican.va/content/francesco/en/encyclicals/documents/papa-francesco_20201003_enciclica-fratelli-tutti.html (accessed December 20, 2020).

88   Robert Bellah, "Civil Religion in America," *Dædalus, Journal of the American Academy of Arts and Sciences*, from the issue entitled, "Religion in America," 96 (1) (Winter 1967): 1–21. Found in Robert N. Bellah, http://www.robertbellah.com/index.html (accessed December 22, 2020).

89   Bellah, 1967.

90   John Moore, "God, Guns, Trump Flag," *Getty*, in David Klepper and Matt O'Brien, "Tech Giants Lock Trump Accounts," *Associated Press, The Morning Call*, January 8, 2021. https://enewspaper.mcall.com/html5/desktop/production/default.aspx?&edid=4b8ec97f-0b86-449c-926e-6e0584f6ae67 (accessed January 12, 2021).

91   Paul Tillich, *Dynamics of Faith* (New York: Harper, 1957), 1, 40.

92   Fenit Nirappil, Julie Zauzmer, Rachel Chason, "'Black Lives Matter': In Large Yellow Letters, D.C. Mayor Sends Message to Trump," *Washington Post*, June 5, 2020, https://www.washingtonpost.com/local/dc-politics/bowser-black-lives-matter-street/2020/06/05/eb44ff4a-a733-11ea-bb20-ebf0921f3bbd_story.html.

93   Christopher Shorr, "Dictators 4 Dummies," *Touchstone Theater,* Bethlehem, PA, April, 2018 and October 2020, https://www.dictators4dummies.com/performances and http://www.touchstone.org/ (accessed December 22, 2020).

94   Patrisse Khan-Cullors and ashe bandele, *When They Call You a Terrorist: a Black Lives Matter Memoir* (St. New York: Martin's Press, 2018).

Students from Denison College began a community-based oral history project to gather the stories from activists involved in the 2016–17 Dakota Access Pipeline resistance movement, where "thousands of 'Water Protectors'" from around the world came in peace and prayer to "Stand with Standing Rock" against the Energy Transfer Partners Company." See *The Water Protector Community: Oral History Project*, https://waterprotectorscommunity.org/ (accessed December 22, 2020).

95 International Campaign to Abolish Nuclear Weapons, *Ican.org*, https://www.icanw.org/ (accessed December 22, 2020).

96 Michael Edison Hayden, Catherine Thorbecke and Evan Simon, "At Least 2,000 Veterans Arrive at Standing Rock to Protest Dakota Pipeline," *ABC News*, December 4, 2016, https://abcnews.go.com/US/2000-veterans-arrive-standing-rock-protest-dakota-pipeline/story?id=43964136 (accessed December 22, 2020).

97 Robert Polin and Heidi Garrett-Peltier, "Benefits of a Slimmer Pentagon," *The Nation*, May 28, 2012, 15–18.

98 Polin and Garrett-Peltier, 2012, 18.

99 "U.S. Military Bases Overseas: The Facts," *Overseas Base Realignment and Closure Coalition*, https://www.overseasbases.net/resources.html (accessed January 11, 2019).

100 For example, see Denton-Borhaug, "Jerryson's 'Exposure of Buddhism' and the Christian Religio-Cultural Legacy of Violence in U.S. War-Culture," in *Buddhist Violence and Religious Authority: A Tribute to the Work of Michael Jerryson*, eds. Margo Kitts and Mark Juergensmeyer (London: Equinox, 2021).

Bibliography

"36 U.S. Code § 111. Gold Star Mother's Day." *Legal Information Institute*, Cornel Law School. https://www.law.cornell.edu/uscode/text/36/111 (accessed November 30, 2020).

2014 Ethics Symposium Archives: 2014 Papers and Presentations, *Command and General Staff College Foundation, Inc.*, September 22, 2014. https://www.cgscfoundation.org/events/ethics-symposium/ethics-symposium-archive-2014/ (accessed November 28, 2020).

"About VA." *U.S. Department of Veterans Affairs.* https://www.va.gov/ABOUT_VA/index.asp (accessed December 5, 2020).

Abrahamian, Atossa Araxia. "The Real Wall Isn't at the Border." *New York Times*, January 26, 2019. https://www.nytimes.com/2019/01/26/opinion/sunday/border-wall-immigration-trump.html (accessed January 27, 2019.

Albanese, Catherine. *Sons of the Fathers: The Civil Religion of the American Revolution.* Philadelphia: Temple University Press, 1976.

Allenby, Bruce, "Respecting Moral Injury." In *War and Moral Injury: A Reader*, edited by Robert Emmet Meagher and Douglas A. Pryer, 259–261. Eugene, OR: Cascade Books, 2018.

American Psychological Association, Boys and Men Guidelines Group. "APA guidelines for psychological practice with boys and men." *American Psychological Association,* 2018. https://www.apa.org/about/policy/boys-men-practice-guidelines.pdf (accessed November 30, 2020).

"America's Navy: A Global Force for Good." *Youtube.com*, April 29, 2010. https://www.youtube.com/watch?v=bao2aPV9uUw (accessed November 28, 2020).

Antal, Chris J. & Kathy Winings, "Moral Injury, Soul Repair, and Creating a Place for Grace," *Religious Education* 110 (4) (2015): 382–394. DOI:10.1080/00344087.2015.1063962.

Antal, Chris J., *Patient to Prophet: Building Adaptive Capacity in Veterans Who Suffer Moral Injury.* D. Min. Hartford Seminary, 2017 (ProQuest Dissertations and Theses Open, 166: 10673402).

Antal, Chris J., Peter D. Yeomans, et al., "Transforming Veteran identity through community engagement: a chaplain-psychologist collaboration to address moral injury." *Journal of Humanistic Psychology* (April 29, 2019), 1–26. https://doi.org/10.1177/0022167819844071

ANT-Hiroshima. https://uri.org/who-we-are/cooperation-circle/ant-hiroshima (accessed April 16, 2019).

Aquino, Maria Pilar, "Religious Peacebuilding." In *Blackwell Companion to Religion and Violence*, edited by Andrew R. Murphy, 568–593. Malden, MA: Blackwell Publishing, 2011.

Arendt, Hannah. *Eichmann in Jerusalem: A Report on the Banality of Evil*, 1st Edition. New York: Penguin Classics, 2006.

Arkin, Bill and Dana Priest, "A Hidden World, Growing Out of Control." *Washington Post,* July 19, 2010, http://projects.washingtonpost.com/top-secret-america/articles/a-hidden-world-growing-beyond-control/ (accessed January 15, 2019).

Arkin, William, "My Departure Letter from NBC." *William M. Arkin Online*, January 4, 2019. https://williamaarkin.wordpress.com/2019/01/04/my-departure-letter-from-nbc/ (accessed January 7, 2019).

Bacevich, Andrew, *America's War for the Greater Middle East: A Military History.* New York: Random House, 2016.

Bacevich, Andrew, *Breach of Trust: How Americans Failed Their Soldiers and Their Country.* New York: Metropolitan Books, 2013.

Bacevich, Andrew, *Democracy Now.* By Amy Goodman. March 10, 2016. https://www.democracynow.org/2016/3/10/andrew_bacevich_why_is_no_candidate (accessed December 13, 2020).

Bacevich, Andrew, "Even If We Defeat the Islamic State, We'll Still Lose the Bigger War." *Washington Post*, October 3, 2014. https://www.washingtonpost.com/opinions/even-if-we- defeat-the-islamic-state-well-still-lose-the-bigger-war/2014/10/03/e8c0585e-4353-11e4-b47c-f5889e061e5f_story.html (accessed January 9, 2021).

Bacevich, Andrew, *The New American Militarism: How Americans are Seduced by War.* London: Oxford University Press, 2013.

Baker, Deanne-Peter, "Moral Ambiguity and Ethical Dilemma, 1915–2015." In *Moral Injury: Unseen Wounds in an Age of Barbarism*, 98–111. Sydney, Australia: NewSouth Publishing, 2015.

Bandura, Albert, *Moral Disengagement: How People Do Harm and Live with Themselves*. New York: Worth Publishers, 2016.

Baker, Mike, Jennifer Valentino-DeVries, Manny Fernandez and Michael LaForgia, "Three Words. 70 Cases. The Tragic History of 'I can't breathe.'" *New York Times*, June 20, 2020. https://www.nytimes.com/interactive/2020/06/28/us/i-cant-breathe-police-arrest.html (accessed December 20, 2020).

Bakotic, Kristen, "The Most Tested Among Us." *The White House: President Barack Obama.* November 11, 2014. https://obamawhitehouse.archives.gov/blog/2014/11/11/most-tested-among-us-vice-president-biden-pays-tribute-our-nations-veterans (accessed December 25, 2020).

Barrett, Brian, "The Pentagon's Hand-Me-Downs Helped Militarize Police. Here's How." *Wired*, June 17, 2020. https://www.wired.com/story/

pentagon-hand-me-downs-militarize-police-1033-program/ (accessed December 20, 2020).

Barry, Kathleen, *Unmaking War, Remaking Men*. Santa Rosa: Phoenix Rising Press, 2011.

Beard, Matthew, "Conceptual Distinctions." In *Moral Injury: Unseen Wounds in an Age of Barbarism*, edited by Tom Frame. Sydney Australia: NewSouth Publishing, 2015.

Bellah, Robert, "Civil Religion in America." *Dædalus, Journal of the American Academy of Arts and Sciences.* From the issue entitled, "Religion in America" 96 (1) (Winter 1967): 1–21. http://www.robertbellah.com/index.html (accessed December 22, 2020).

Berger, Peter, *The Sacred Canopy: Elements of a Sociological Theory of Religion.* New York: Anchor Books, 1967.

Bigelow, Kathryn, director and producer, *The Hurt Locker*, 2008. British Columbia: Voltage Pictures.

Blimes, Linda J. and Joseph El Stiglitz, *The Three Trillion Dollar War: The True Cost of the Iraq Conflict.* New York: W. W. Norton and Co., 2008.

Bottoms, Michael, "International Partners Attend Spiritual and Moral Resiliency Course." *United States Special Operations Command*, March 23, 2020, https://www.socom.mil/pages/International-partners-attend-Spiritual-and-Moral-Resiliency-course.aspx (accessed December 19, 2020).

Boudreau, Tyler, "The Morally Injured." *The Massachusetts Review*, 52 (3) (2011), 746–754.

Boudreau, Tyler, *Packing Inferno: The Unmaking of a Marine.* Port Townsend, Washington: Feral House, 2008.

Brock, Rita Natashima and Gabriella Lettini, *Soul Repair: Recovering from Moral Injury After War.* Boston, MA: Beacon Press, 2012.

Brown, Adam, "The Trauma of `Choiceless Choices': The Paradox of Judgement in Primo Levi's 'Grey Zone.'" In *Trauma, History, Philosophy (With Feature Essays by Agnes Heller and Gyorgy Markus).* Edited by Matthew Sharpe, Murray Noonan, and Jason Freddi, 142–163. Newcastle, UK: Cambridge Scholars Publishing, 2007.

Bush, George W., "Memorandum for the Vice President: Humane Treatment of al Qaeda and Taliban Detainees." February 7, 2002, in *Torture Papers: The Road to Abu Ghraib.* Edited by Karen J. Greenberg, Joshua L. Dratel, 134–135. Cambridge: Cambridge University Press, 2005.

Butler, Judith, *The Force of Nonviolence.* New York: Verso, 2020.

Butler, Judith, *Frames of War: When is Life Grievable?*, 1st Edition. New York: Verso, 2009.

"Captain Khan/Hillary Clinton." *Youtube.com,* October 21, 2016, https://www.youtube.com/watch?v=WCqFCCgU1xk (accessed November 30, 2020).

Card, Claudia., *The Atrocity Paradigm: A Theory of Evil.* New York: Oxford University Press, 2002.

Castro, Martin, Chair, U.S. Commission on Civil Rights, "Sexual Assault in the Military: 2013 Statutory Enforcement Report." Washington, D.C.: U.S. Commission on Civil Rights, September 2013. https://www.hsdl. org/?abstract&did=744910 (accessed January 7, 2021).

Childress, Sara, "How Baltimore's Police Policy Led to Freddie Gray." *Frontline: PBS.* August 10, 2016. https://www.pbs.org/wgbh/frontline/ article/how-baltimores-police-policy-led-to-freddie-gray/ (accessed December 25, 2020).

Chenoweth, Erica, "The success of nonviolent civil resistance." *TEDx Talks.* TEDxBoulder. November 4, 2013. https://www.youtube.com/ watch?v=YJSehRlU34w (accessed December 20, 2020).

Chenoweth, Erica and Maria J. Stephan, *Why Civil Resistance Works: The Strategic Logic of Nonviolent Conflict*. New York: Columbia University Press, 2011.

Clendinnen, Inga, *Agamemnon's Kiss: Selected Essays.* Melbourne, Australia: Text Publishing, 2007.

"Convention against Torture and Other Cruel, Inhuman or Degrading Treatment or Punishment." Article 1.1, *United Nations Treaty Collection.* New York, December 10, 1984. https://treaties.un.org/Pages/ViewDetails. aspx?src=IND&mtdsg_no=IV-9&chapter=4&lang=en (accessed December 13, 2020).

"Covid-19 Forecasts – Deaths." *Center for Disease Control and Prevention.* December 17, 2020. https://www.cdc.gov/coronavirus/2019-ncov/covid-data/ forecasting-us.html (accessed December 20, 2020).

Crawford, Neta C., "United States Budgetary Costs and Obligations of Post-9/11 Wars through FY2020: $6.4 Trillion." *Costs of War.* Watson Institute: International and Public Affairs, Brown University, November 13, 2019. https://watson.brown.edu/costsofwar/papers/2019/united-states-budgetary-costs-and-obligations-post-911-wars-through-fy2020-64-trillion (accessed December 20, 2020).

Currier, Joseph M., Jacob K. Farnsworth, Kent D. Drescher, and Wesley H. McCormick, "Moral Injury and Resilience in the Military." In *Bulletproofing the Psyche: Preventing Mental Health Problems in Our Military and Veterans.* Edited by Kate Hendricks Thomas and David L. Albright, 76–92. Santa Barbara, CA: Praeger, 2018.

"Creating Peace: 2010 Social Statement of Conscience." *Unitarian Universalist Association.* https://www.uua.org/action/statements/creating-peace (accessed 1/26/2019).

Crossley, James, "An Immodest Proposal for Biblical Studies." *Relegere: Studies in Religion and Reception* 2 (1) (2012): 153–77.

"Dad of fallen Muslim soldier's powerful DNC speech (Khzir Khan full speech.)" *Youtube.com*, July 28, 2016. https://www.youtube.com/watch?v=Xzkkk-oJ6bo (accessed November 30, 2020).

Das, Santanu, "*'Dulce et Decorum Est'*, a close reading." *British Library: Discovering 20th Century Literature*. https://www.bl.uk/20th-century-literature/articles/a-close-reading-of-dulce-et-decorum-est# (accessed January 7, 2021).

Davis, Angela, "Angela Davis: 'Devastating Consequences' if Barrett is Confirmed." By Christine Amanpour. *CNN.* CNN.com. October 13, 2020. https://www.cnn.com/videos/world/2020/10/13/angela-davis-scotus-amanpour-coronavirus.cnn (accessed December 20, 2020).

Davis, Angela, "Freedom Struggle: Angela Davis on Calls to Defund Police, Racism and Capitalism, and the 2020 Election." By Amy Goodman. *Democracy Now.* DemocracyNow.org. September 7, 2020. https://www.democracynow.org/2020/9/7/freedom_struggle_angela_davis_on_calls (accessed December 20, 2020).

"Deadly WWII U.S. firebombing raids on Japanese cities largely ignored." *Associated Press* for *The Japan Times News.* March 10, 2015, https://www.japantimes.co.jp/news/2015/03/10/national/deadly-wwii-u-s-firebombing-raids-on-japanese-cities-largely-ignored/#.XLXp6JNKjOQ (accessed 4/16/2019).

Denton-Borhaug, Kelly, "Is this America? Unfinished business with the U.S. national imaginary, religion and violence," *Dialog: A Journal of Theology* 58 (2019): 30–38. https://doi.org/10.1111/dial.12451

Denton-Borhaug, Kelly, "Jerryson's 'Exposure of Buddhism' and the Christian Religio-Cultural Legacy of Violence in U.S. War-Culture." In *Buddhist Violence and Religious Authority: A Tribute to the Work of Michael Jerryson*. Edited by Margo Kitts and Mark Juergensmeyer, 103–112. London: Equinox, 2021.

Denton-Borhaug, Kelly, "'Like Acid Seeping into Your Soul'; Religio-cultural Violence in Moral Injury," In *Exploring Moral Injury in Sacred Texts.* Edited by Joseph McDonald, 111–134. London: Jessica Kingsley Publishers, 2017.

Denton-Borhaug, Kelly, "Martyrdom Discourse in Contemporary U.S. War-culture." In *Wiley-Blackwell Companion to Christian Martyrdom.* Edited by Paul Middleton, 471–484. Hoboken, New Jersey: Wiley-Blackwell Publishing, 2020.

Denton-Borhaug, Kelly, "Moral Injury and the U.S. War-culture Bible," In *Moral Injury: A Guidebook to Understanding.* Edited by Brad Kelle, 173–188. New York: Lexington Books, 2020.

Denton-Borhaug, Kelly, "A Theological Response to Torture and Democracy." *Dialog: A Journal of Theology* 47 (3) (fall 2008), 217–227. https://doi.org/10.1111/j.1540-6385.2008.00402.x

Denton-Borhaug, Kelly. "Resisting the sacred canopy over U.S. ways of war." *Political Theology* 18 (3) (May 30, 2017), 206–218. https://doi.org/10.117 9/1743171915y.0000000007

Denton-Borhaug, Kelly, "Sacrificial U.S. War-culture: Cognitive Dissonance, and the Absence of Self-Awareness." *Journal of Religion and Violence* 5 (1) (April 28, 2017), 5–26. https://doi.org/10.5840/jrv201742538

Denton-Borhaug, Kelly, "U.S. War-culture and the Political Economy of the United States." *Word and World* 34 (4) (fall 2014): 376-377.

Denton-Borhaug, Kelly, "U.S. War-culture, the post-9/11 'unlawful alien combatant,' and 'Peace in God's World.'" In *Lutheran Theology and Secular Law: The Work of the Modern State.* Edited by Ron W. Duty and Marie Falinger, 101–114. New York: Routledge, 2018.

Denton-Borhaug, Kelly, *U.S. War-culture, Sacrifice and Salvation*, 1st Edition. London: Equinox, 2011. New York: Routledge, 2014.

DeVinney, James A., Callie Crossley, director, "Bridge to Freedom." *Eyes on the Prize.* Episode 6. 1986; Blackside Production Co. Video. https://video-alexanderstreet-com.moravian.idm.oclc.org/watch/bridge-to-freedom-1965/details?context=channel:eyes-on-the-prize (accessed December 20, 2020).

Dewey, Joanna, "'Let Them Renounce Themselves and Take Up Their Cross': A Feminist Reading of Mark 8:34 in Mark's Social and Narrative World." In *A Feminist Companion to Mark*; *Feminist Companion to the New Testament and Early Christian Writings.* Edited by Amy-Jill Levine and M. Blickerstaff, 23–36. Sheffield: Sheffield Academic, 2001.

"Disabled Veterans Memorial Underway Near the National Mall." *Associated Press,* July 23, 2014. https://wjla.com/features/veterans/disabled-veterans-memorial-underway-near-the-national-mall-105344 (accessed December 13, 2020).

Dower, John, *The Violent American Century: War and Terror Since WWI.* Chicago, IL: Haymarket Books, 2017.

Duncanson, Claire, "Anti-militarist Feminist Approaches to Researching Gender and the Military." In *The Palgrave International Handbook of Gender and the Military.* Edited by Rachel Woodward and Claire Duncanson, 39–58. London: Palgrave, 2017.

Eastwood, Clint, director, *American Sniper*, 2015. Warner Brothers. See the Independent Movie Database, *Imdb.com.* https://www.imdb.com/title/tt2179136/ (accessed January 13, 2021).

Emmerich, Roland, director, *Independence Day, Resurgence*, 2016. Twentieth Century Fox. See the Independent Movie Database, *Imdb.com.* https://www.imdb.com/title/tt1628841/ (accessed January 13, 2019.

Fair, Eric, *Consequence: A Memoir.* New York: Henry Holt and Co., 2016.

Fair, Eric, "The U.S. must open the book on the use of torture to move forward." *The Washington Post,* April 11, 2014.

"Federal Budget Tipsheet: Pentagon Spending." *National Priorities Project.* https://www.nationalpriorities.org/guides/tipsheet-pentagon-spending/ (accessed January 6, 2021).

Feinstein, Diane, United States Senator; Senate Select Committee on Intelligence. *Committee Study of the Central Intelligence Agency's Detention and Interrogation Program.* Released April 3, 2014. http://www. feinstein.senate.gov/public/index.cfm/senate-intelligence-committee-study-on-cia-detention-and-interrogation-program (accessed January 23, 2019).

Flores, Reena, "Trump Says Intelligence Officials Tell Him Torture Works." *CBSNews.com.* January 29, 2017. http://www.cbsnews.com/news/trump-says-intelligence-officials-tell-him-torture-works/ (accessed March 30, 2019).

Fountain, Ben, *Billy Lynn's Halftime Walk*. New York: Ecco, 2012.

Francis, Holy Father (Pope), *Fratelli Tutti:* Encyclical Letter. October 3, 2020. http://www.vatican.va/content/francesco/en/encyclicals/documents/papa-francesco_20201003_enciclica-fratelli-tutti.html (accessed December 20, 2020).

French, David, "Grown Men Are the Solution, Not the Problem." *National Review*, January 7, 2019. www.nationalreview.com/2019/01/psychologists-criticize-traditional-masculinity/ (accessed November 30, 2020).

French, Shannon E. and Anthony I. Jack, "Connecting Neuroethics and Military Ethics to Help Prevent Moral Injury." In *War and Moral Injury: A Reader*, edited by Robert Emmet Meagher and Douglas A. Pryer, 270–279. Eugene, OR: Cascade Books, 2018.

Gates, Tucker, writer, *House of Cards,* Season Three: Chapter 30, February 1, 2013. Media Rights Capital and Panic Pictures. Television.

Galtung, Johan, "Cultural Violence." *Journal of Peace Research* 27 (3) (August 1990), 291–305.

Galtung, Johan, *Peace by Peaceful Means: Peace and Conflict, Development and Civilization.* Oslo: International Peace Institute and London: Sage Publications, 1996.

Giulinai, Massimo, *Centaur in Auschwitz: Reflections on Primo Levi's Thinking.* Washington, D.C.: Lexington Books, 2003.

"Gold Star Luminary Initiative." *MarineParents.com, Inc.,* Columbia, MO. http://luminaryinitiative.com/pledge-online.asp (accessed January 8, 2021).

Gould, Joe, "Progressive effort to cut defense fails twice in congress." *DefenseNews*, July 22, 2020. https://www.defensenews.com/congress/2020/07/22/progressive-effort-to-cut-defense-fails-twice-in-congress/ (accessed December 20, 2020).

Grant, Sam, Executive Director, *350MN.org*. https://mn350.org/how-we-work/ (accessed December 20, 2020).

Griffin, Brandon J., Natalie Purcell, Kristine Burkman, Brett T. Litz, Craig J. Bryan, Martha Schmitz, Claudia Villierme, Jessica Walsh, and Shira Maguen, "Moral Injury: An Integrative Review." *Journal of Traumatic Stress* 32 (3) (June 2019): 350–362. https://doi.org/10.1002/jts.22362

Grossman, Dave, *On Killing: The Psychological Cost of Learning to Kill in War and Society.* Boston, MA: Little, Brown and Co., 2009.

Guaglione, Sara, "Slate's 'Gist' Podcast Celebrates 5 Years, Focuses on Promoting Episodes." *MediaPost.* Mediapost.com., May 13, 2019. https://www.mediapost.com/publications/article/335751/slates-gist-podcast-celebrates-5-years-focuses.html (accessed December 20, 2020).

Haberman, Maggie and Richard A. Oppel, "Donald Trump Criticizes Muslim Family of Slain U.S. Soldier, Drawing Ire." *New York Times,* July 30, 2016. https://www.nytimes.com/2016/07/31/us/politics/donald-trump-khizr-khan-wife-ghazala.html (accessed November 30, 2020).

Hanh, Thich Nhat, "To Veterans." From *Love in Action: Writing on Nonviolent Social Change.* In *A Lifetime of Peace: Essential Writings by and about Thich Nhat Hanh.* Edited by Jennifer Schwamm Willis, 123–132. New York: Marlowe and Company, 2003.

Hartung, William, "The Military-Industrial Complex Revisited: Shifting Patterns of Military Contracting in the Post-9/11 Period." *Costs of War.* Watson Institute: International and Public Affairs, Brown University. https://watson.brown.edu/costsofwar/files/cow/imce/papers/2011/The%20Military-Industrial%20Complex%20Revisited.pdf. (accessed January 17, 2019).

Hauerwas, Stanley, *War and the American Difference: Theological Reflections on Violence and National Identity.* Grand Rapids, MI: Baker, 2011.

Hayden, Michael Edison, Catherine Thorbecke and Evan Simon, "At Least 2,000 Veterans Arrive at Standing Rock to Protest Dakota Pipeline." ABC News, December 4, 2016. https://abcnews.go.com/US/2000-veterans-arrive-standing-rock-protest-dakota-pipeline/story?id=43964136 (accessed December 22, 2020).

Hermann, Peter and John Woodrow Cox, "A Freddy Gray Primer: Who was he, How did he die, Why is there so much anger?" *The Washington Post,* April 28, 2015. https://www.washingtonpost.com/news/local/wp/2015/04/28/a-freddie-gray-primer-who-was-he-how-did-he-why-is-there-so-much-anger/ (accessed December 25, 2020).

Hynes, H. Patricia, "The Battlefield and the Barracks: Two War Fronts for Women Soldiers." *Truthout.* Five-part series, January 11–February 15, 2012. https://truthout.org/articles/why-do-soldiers-rape/1326306014/ (accessed November 30, 2020).

Hynes, H. Patricia, "Battlefield and the Barracks: Why Do Soldiers Rape?" *Truthout,* January 18, 2012. https://truthout.org/articles/why-do-soldiers-rape/1326306014/ (accessed November 30, 2020).

International Campaign to Abolish Nuclear Weapons. *Ican.org*, https://www. icanw.org/ (accessed December 22, 2020).

"Interview: Why is there no end to sexual violence by U.S. Military Personnel in Okinawa?" *The Mainichi: Japan's National Daily*, September 15, 2016. https://mainichi.jp/english/articles/20160915/p2a/00m/0na/017000c (accessed November 30, 2020).

Isaacs, Arnold R., "Moral Injury and America's endless conflicts." *Salon.com.,* December 8, 2018. https://www.salon.com/2019/12/08/moral-injury-and-americas-endless-conflicts_partner/ (accessed December 19, 2020).

"Japan," *Atomic Heritage Foundation/National Museum of Nuclear Science and History.* https://www.atomicheritage.org/location/japan (accessed June 22, 2020).

Jenkins, Cameron, "Greta Thunberg mocks Barrett for not having ,'views on climate change.'" *The Hill*. thehill.com., October 15, 2020. https://thehill. com/policy/energy-environment/521268-greta-thunberg-mocks-barrett-for-not-having-views-on-climate-change (accessed December 20, 2020).

Johnson, Chalmers, *The Sorrows of Empire: Militarism, Secrecy and the End of the Republic.* Blackstone Audio Inc., 2007.

Jonas, T. C., Wayne B., Colonel Francis O'Connor, Patricia Deuster, Colonel Christian Macedonia, Eds. "Total Force Fitness for the 21st Century: A New Paradigm." *Military Medicine* 175 (August Supplement, 2010).

Jones, Ann. *They Were Soldiers: How the Wounded Return from America's Wars – The Untold Story*. Chicago: Haymarket Books, 2013.

Jones, Robert P., *White Too Long: The Legacy of White Supremacy in American Christianity.* New York: Simon and Schuster, 2020.

Joseph, Celucien L., "James Cone and the Crisis of American Theology." *Missionalia* 42 (2) (February 2019), 197–221. https://doi. org/10.7832/46-2-309

Joseph, Simon J., *The Nonviolent Messiah: Jesus, Q, and the Enochic Tradition*. Minneapolis: Fortress Press, 2014.

Juster, Susan, *Sacred Violence in Early America*. Philadelphia: University of Pennsylvania Press, 2016.

Khan-Cullors, Patrisse and ashe bandele, *When They Call You a Terrorist: A Black Lives Matter Memoir.* New York: St. Martin's Press, 2018.

Kean, Chair Thomas H., "The 9/11 Commission Report." *National Commission on Terrorist Attacks Upon the United States,* August 21, 2004. https://9-11commission.gov/report/ (accessed December 13, 2020).

Kilner, Pete, "Leadership, War, and Moral Injury." In *War and Moral Injury: A Reader.* Edited by Robert Emmet Meagher and Douglas A. Pryer, 95–100. Eugene, OR: Cascade Books, 2018.

King, Martin Luther Jr., "Beyond Vietnam: A Call to Conscience." Riverside Church, New York, April 4, 1967. *Stanford University, The Martin Luther King Jr., Education and Research Institute.* https://kinginstitute.stanford.edu/king-papers/documents/beyond-vietnam (accessed December 13, 2020).

King, Martin Luther Jr., "Pilgrimage to Nonviolence." In *A Testament of Hope: The Essential Writings and Speeches of Martin Luther King, Jr.* Edited by James M. Washington, 35–40. San Francisco: Harper, 1986.

Kinghorn, Warren, "Combat Trauma and Moral Fragmentation: A Theological Account of Moral Injury," *Journal of the Society of Christian Ethics* 32 (2) (2012): 57–74. https://doi.org/10.1353/sce.2012.0041

Klett, Leah Marianne, "Veterans' Day 2015: History, Meaning and Bible Verse: Why Should Christians Celebrate This Holiday? *The Gospel Herald Society*, November 10, 2015. https://www.gospelherald.com/articles/59639/20151110/veterans-day-2015-history-meaning-traditions-why-christians-celebrate-holiday.htm (accessed January 7, 2021).

Knickmeyer, Ellen., "Barrett deflects senators' questions on climate change" *AP News.* APNews.com., October 14, 2020. https://apnews.com/article/science-climate-climate-change-amy-coney-barrett-judiciary-7c901ed970c2e9bed1e14f28047c1022 (accessed December 20, 2020).

Koistinen, Paul A. C., *State of War: The Political Economy of American Warfare, 1945–2011.* Lawrence, KS: University of Kansas Press, 2012.

Kuran, Timur, *Private Truths, Public Lies: The Social Consequences of Preference Falsification.* Boston, MA: Harvard University Press, 2007.

Kyle, Chris, Scott McEwen, Jim DeFelice, *American Sniper: The Autobiography of the Most Lethal Sniper in U. S. Military History*. New York: HarperCollins, 2016.

LaCapra, Dominick, "Approaching Limit Events: Siting Agamben." In *Witnessing the Disaster: Essays on Representation and the Holocaust.* Edited by Michael F. Bernard-Donals and Richard R. Glejzer, 262–304. Madison, WI: University of Wisconsin Press, 2003.

LaGrone, Sam, "Slogans that Sell the Service: A Brief History of U.S. Navy Television Ads after the End of the Draft." *USNI News,* May 29, 2015. https://news.usni.org/2015/05/29/slogans-that-sell-the-service-a-brief-history-of-u-s-navy-television-ads-after-the-end-of-the-draft (accessed December 4, 2020).

Larson, Duane and Jeff Zust, *Care for the Sorrowing Soul: Healing Moral Injuries from Military Service and Implications for the Rest of Us.* Eugene, OR: Cascade Books, 2017.

Lederer, Edith M., "US urges countries to withdraw from US nuke ban treaty." *Associated Press*, October 21, 2020. https://apnews.com/article/nuclear-weapons-disarmament-latin-america-united-nations-gun-politics-4f109626a1cdd6db10560550aa1bb491 (accessed December 23, 2020)

Lennon, John, "Imagine." *Songfacts*. https://www.songfacts.com/lyrics/john-lennon/imagine (accessed April 25, 2019).

Lifton, Robert Jay, "The Climate Swerve." *The New York Times*, August 23, 2014. http://nyti.ms/1mAySAC (accessed December 20, 2020).

Lifton, Robert Jay, *The Climate Swerve*. New York: The New Press, 2017.

Lifton, Robert Jay and Greg Mitchell, *Hiroshima in America*. New York: Harper Perennial, 1996.

Lilley, Kevin, "Army's New Recruitment Drive: Sign up, maybe fight aliens." *Army Times,* May 18, 2016. https://www.armytimes.com/off-duty/movies-video-games/2016/05/18/army-s-new-recruitment-drive-sign-up-maybe-fight-aliens/ (accessed January 13, 2019).

Lindorff, Dave, "The Pentagon's Massive Accounting Fraud Exposed," *The Nation,* November 27, 2018, https://www.thenation.com/article/pentagon-audit-budget-fraud/ (accessed January 9, 2019).

Litz, Brett T., Nathan, Stein, Eileen Delaney, Leslie Lebowitz, William P. Nash, Caroline Silva, Shira Maguen, "Moral injury and moral repair in war veterans: A preliminary model and intervention strategy," *Clinical Psychology Review* 29 (2009): 695–706. https://doi.org/10.1016/j.cpr.2009.07.003

Lutz, Catherine, "Making War at Home in the United States: Militarization and the Current Crisis." *American Anthropologist* 104 (3) (September 2002).

Mahedy, William, *Out of the Night*. Greyhound Books, 2005.

"The Main Exporters and Importers of Major Arms, 2015–2019," *SIPRI Yearbook 2020: Armaments, Disarmament and International Security: Summary,* 13. Oxford: Oxford University Press, 2020. https://www.sipri.org/yearbook/2020 (accessed January 10, 2021).

Maida, Gaetano Kazuo, director, *Peace is Every Step: Meditation in Action: The Life and Work of Thich Nhat Hanh*, 1998. Festival Media. DVD.

Malecek, Stefan J., "The Moral Inversion of War." In *War and Moral Injury: A Reader.* Edited by Robert Emmet Meagher and Douglas A. Pryer, 292–296. Eugene, OR: Cascade Books, 2018.

Mann, Bonnie, *Sovereign Masculinity: Gender Lessons from the War on Terror.* New York: Oxford University Press, 2014.

Marlantes, Karl, *What it is Like to Go to War*. New York: Grove Press, 2012.

Marshall, S.L.A., *Men Against Fire: The Problem of Battle Command.* Norman, OK: University of Oklahoma Press, 2000.

Martin, David. "Building a Monument to Wounded Warriors." *CBS News: Sunday Morning*, September 28, 2014. https://www.cbsnews.com/news/building-a-monument-to-wounded-warriors/ (accessed December 13, 2020).

Mayer, Jane, *The Dark Side: The Inside Story of How the War on Terror Turned into a War on American Ideals.* New York: Doubleday, 2008.

Mazzarino, Andrea, Marcia C. Inhorn, and Catherine Lutz, "Introduction: The Health Consequences of War." In *War and Public Health.* Edited by Catherine Lutz and Andrea Mazzarino, 1–37. New York: New York University Press, 2019.

McCloskey, Megan, "Combat Stress as 'Moral Injury' Offends Marines." *Stars and Stripes*, April 18, 2011, https://www.stripes.com/blogs/stripes-central/stripes-central-1.8040/combat-stress-as-moral-injury-offends-marines-1.142177 (accessed December 13, 2020).

McCrisken, Trevor, "Ten years on: Obama's war on terrorism in rhetoric and practice." *International Affairs* 87 (4) (July 2011), 781–801. https://doi.org/10.1111/j.1468-2346.2011.01004.x

Mead, Corey, *War Games: Video Games and the Future of Armed Conflict.* New York: Eamon Dolan/Houghton Mifflin Harcourt, 2017.

Meagher, Robert E., "Wounded Warriors, Wounded Nation: Closing the Gates of War." Lecture at Moravian College, Bethlehem, PA, March 27, 2014.

Meagher, Robert E., "Hope Dies Last." In *War and Moral Injury: A Reader.* Edited by Robert Emmet Meagher and Douglas A. Pryer, 317–328. Eugene, OR: Cascade Books, 2018.

Meagher, Robert E., *Killing from the Inside Out: Moral Injury and Just War.* Eugene, OR, Cascade Books, 2014.

Mehta, Aaron, "Here's what the Pentagon's first-ever audit found," *Defense News,* November 16, 2018, https://www.defensenews.com/pentagon/2018/11/15/heres-what-the-pentagons-first-ever-audit-found/ (accessed January 9, 2019).

"The Militarized Budget 2020." *National Priorities Project*, https://www.nationalpriorities.org/analysis/2020/militarized-budget-2020/ (accessed January 7, 2021).

Miyamoto, Yuki, "Unbearable Light/ness of the Bombing: Normalizing Violence and Banalizing the horror of atomic bomb experiences." *Critical Military Studies* 1 (2) (July 2015), 116–130. https://doi.org/10.1080/23337486.2015.1050268

"Military Expenditure." *The Stockholm International Peace Research Institute Yearbook 2020.* Sipri.org. https://www.sipri.org/yearbook/2020 (accessed January 6, 2021).

Mohl, Hans, *Identity and the Sacred.* Oxford, UK: Basil Blackwell, 1976.

"Most Stressful Jobs of 2017." *CareerCast.* careercast.com. https://www.careercast.com/jobs-rated/most-stressful-jobs-2017 (accessed February 22, 2019).

Moore, John, "God, Guns, Trump Flag." *Getty.* In David Klepper and Matt O'Brien, "Tech Giants Lock Trump Accounts." *Associated Press, The Morning Call,* January 8, 2021. https://enewspaper.mcall.com/html5/

desktop/production/default.aspx?&edid=4b8ec97f-0b86-449c-926e-6e0584f6ae67 (accessed January 12, 2021).

Morris, Ian, *War! What Is It Good For? Conflict and the Progress of Civilization From Primates To Robots.* New York: Straus and Giroux, 2014.

Mulkern, Anne C., "Fast-moving California Fires Boosted by Climate Change," *Scientific American,* August 24, 2020. https://www.scientificamerican. com/article/fast-moving-california-wildfires-boosted-by-climate-change/#:~:text=Climate%20connection%20scrutinized,%2C%20 while%20precipitation%20dropped%2030%25 (accessed December 20, 2020).

Nash, William P., Brett T. Litz, "Moral Injury: A Mechanism for War-Related Psychological Trauma in Military Family Members." *Clinical Child Family Psychological Review* 16 (4) (2013), 365–375. https://doi. org/10.1007/s10567-013-0146-y

Nash, William P. "Commentary on the Special Issue on Moral Injury: Unpacking Two Models For Understanding Moral Injury." *Journal of Traumatic Stress* 32 (3) (June 2019), 465–470. https://doi.org/10.1002/ jts.22409

Nash, Captain William P., Teresa L. Marino Carper, Mary Alice Mills, Teresa Au, Abigail Goldsmith, Brett T. Litz, "Psychometric Evaluation of the Moral Injury Events Scale." *Military Medicine* 178 (6) (June 2013): 646–652.

Newkirk II, Vann R., "Trump's EPA Concludes Environmental Racism is Real." *The Atlantic.* February 28, 2018, https://www.theatlantic.com/politics/ archive/2018/02/the-trump-administration-finds-that-environmental-racism-is-real/554315/ (accessed December 20, 2020).

Newman, Andrew, "Treaty of Shakamaxon." *Encyclopedia of Greater Philadelphia.* https://philadelphiaencyclopedia.org/archive/treaty-of-shackamaxon-2/ (accessed January 6, 2021).

Nirappil, Fenit, Julie Zauzmer, Rachel Chason, "'Black Lives Matter': In Large Yellow Letters, D.C. Mayor Sends Message to Trump." *Washington Post.* June 5, 2020, https://www.washingtonpost.com/local/dc-politics/ bowser-black-lives-matter-street/2020/06/05/eb44ff4a-a733-11ea-bb20-ebf0921f3bbd_story.html (accessed December 20, 2020).

Nixon, Ron, "U.S. to Collect Social Media Data on All Immigrants Entering the Country." *New York Times,* September 28, 2017, https://www. nytimes.com/2017/09/28/us/politics/immigrants-social-media-trump. html?module=inline (accessed January 27, 2019).

Novotney, Amy, "Stopping suicide in the military." *Monitor on Psychology* 51 (1) (January 2020). http://www.apa.org/monitor/2020/01/ce-corner-suicide (accessed December 12, 2020).

Obama, Barack, "Remarks by the President and the First Lady on the End of the War in Iraq." *The White House: President Barack Obama,* Fort Bragg, North Carolina, December 14, 2011. https://obamawhitehouse.archives.gov/the-press-office/2011/12/14/remarks-president-and-first-lady-end-war-iraq (accessed December 13, 2020).

Obama, Barack, "Presidential Proclamation – Gold Star Mother's and Family's Day, 2012." *The White House; President Barack Obama*, September 28, 2012. https://obamawhitehouse.archives.gov/the-press-office/2012/09/28/presidential-proclamation-gold-star-mothers-and-familys-day-2012 (accessed January 8, 2021).

Ostrach, Bayla and Merrill Singer, "Syndemics of War: Malnutrition-Infectious Disease Interactions and Unintended Health Consequences of Intentional Health Policies," *Annals of Anthropological Practice* 36 (2) (2013), 257–273. https://doi.org/10.1111/napa.12003

Owen, Wilfred, "Dulce et Decorum est." *The War Poetry Website.* https://www.warpoetry.uk/ (accessed December 13, 2020).

Okazaki, Stephen, director, *White Light Black Rain.* 2007; HBO. DVD.

Ordoñez, Franco, "Trump Faces Fallout from Report He Calls Military, 'Suckers' and 'Losers.'" *National Public Radio.* NPR.org. September 4, 2020. https://www.npr.org/2020/09/04/909599762/trump-faces-fallout-from-report-he-calls-military-losers-and-suckers (accessed December 20, 2020).

Pacello, Charles, "Moral Trauma and Nuclear War." In *War and Moral Injury: A Reader.* Edited by Robert Emmet Meagher and Douglas A. Pryer, 114–116. Eugene, OR: Cascade Books, 2018.

Parsons, David L., "Introduction," *Dangerous Grounds: Antiwar Coffeehouses and Military Dissent in the Vietnam Era.* Chapel Hill: University of North Carolina Press, 2017.

Pedersen, Christine, "I Followed My Father into the Marines. But It was Different for a Woman." *New York Times*, April 4, 2019. https://www.nytimes.com/2019/04/04/magazine/marine-corps-sexual-harassment.html (accessed April 30, 2019).

Penn State Blue Band Military Halftime Show. *Youtube.com.* October 3, 2015. https://www.youtube.com/watch?v=kwa94MI5Vc8 (accessed December 13, 2020).

Penn, William, "First Letter to the Delaware Indians," In *Nonviolence in America: A Documentary History.* Eds. Staughton Lynd and Alice Lynd. Maryville, NY: Orbis, 1995.

Personnel Processing (In-Out-, Soldier Readiness, and Deployment Cycle). Army Regulation 600–8–101, Headquarters Department of the Army Washington, DC, February 19, 2015.

Pesca, Mike, "The Gist with Mike Pesca." *Slate.* Slate.com, https://slate.com/podcasts/the-gist (accessed December 20, 2020).

Pesca, Mike, "The Gist: No Cause Bigger than Himself." *The Gist.* Slate.com/ podcasts. September 8, 2020. https://slate.com/podcasts/the-gist/2020/09/ trump-disdain-for-service (accessed December 20, 2020).

Petersohn, Ulrich, "Privatising Securing: The Limits of Military Outsourcing." *CSS Analysis in Security Policy; ETH Zurich: Center for Security Studies,* September, 2010. http://www.css.ethz.ch/ (accessed January 17, 2019).

Pilisuk, Mark with Jeinnifer Achord Rountree, *Who Benefits From Global Violence and War: Uncovering a Destructive System.* Westport, Connecticut: Praeger Security International, 2008.

Pollin, Robert and Heidi Garrett-Peltier, "Benefits of a Slimmer Pentagon." *The Nation,* May, 2012, 15–18. https://www.peri.umass.edu/publication/ item/747-benefits-of-a-slimmer-pentagon (accessed December 13, 2020).

Pollin, Robert and Heidi Garrett-Peltier, "The U.S. Employment Effects of Military and Domestic Spending Priorities: 2011 Update." *PERI Political Economy Research Institute.* Amherst: University of Massachusetts, 2012.

The Poor People's Campaign: A National Call for Moral Revival. https://www. poorpeoplescampaign.org/ (accessed November 29, 2020).

Popichak, Josh, "Hometown Hero Banners Flying High in Hellertown." *Saucon Source,* May 24, 2020. https://sauconsource.com/2020/05/24/hometown- hero-banners-flying-high-in-hellertown/ (accessed November 30, 2020).

Powers, Kevin, "Separation," *Letter Composed During a Lull in the Fighting.* Boston, MA: Little, Brown and Co., 2014.

Powers, Kevin, *The Yellow Birds.* New York: Back Bay Books, 2011.

Press, Eyal, "The Wounds of the Drone Warrior." *New York Times,* June 13, 2018. https://www.nytimes.com/2018/06/13/magazine/veterans-ptsd-drone- warrior-wounds.html (accessed January 23, 2019).

Pryer, Lieutenant Colonel Douglas A., "Moral Injury and the American Service Member: What Leaders Don't Talk about when They Talk about War," in the 2014 Ethics Symposium Archives: 2014 Papers and Presentations, *Command and General Staff College Foundation, Inc.,* September 22, 2014, 78. https://www.cgscfoundation.org/events/ethics-symposium/ethics- symposium-archive-2014/ (accessed November 28, 2020).

Ramsay, Nancy J., "Moral Injury as Loss and Grief with Attention to Ritual Resources for Care." *Pastoral Psychology* 68 (1) (2019), 107–25. https:// doi.org/10.1007/s11089-018-0854-9

Rejali, Darius, *Torture and Democracy.* Princeton: Princeton University Press, 2007.

Reuters, "Bowing to U.S. Demands, UN Waters Down Resolution on Sexual Violence in Conflict." *New York Times.* April 23, 2019. https://www. straitstimes.com/world/united-states/bowing-to-us-demands-un-waters- down-resolution-on-sexual-violence-in-conflict (accessed 11/11/2019).

Rico, Toni, media contact, "Media Advisory: Service women identify sexual assault, not deployment, as the number one factor that negatively affects their mental wellness." *Service Women's Action Network,* November 10, 2017. https://www.servicewomen.org/press-releases/media-advisory-service-women-identify-sexual-assault-not-deployment-as-number-one-factor-that-negatively-affects-their-mental-wellness/ (accessed 2/22/2019).

Samet, Elizabeth, "Can an American Soldier Ever Die in Vain." *Foreign Policy*, May 9, 2014, https://foreignpolicy.com/2014/05/09/can-an-american-soldier-ever-die-in-vain/ (accessed November 4, 2019).

Saul, Jack, "An Audio Experience: Exploring the Costs of War." *International Trauma Studies Program and Windmill Factory.* Debut in 2019 at UNFINISHED festival at the National Museum of Art of Romania. https://www.moralinjuriesofwar.org/about (accessed December 13, 2020).

Schüssler-Fiorenza, Elisabeth, *But She Said: Feminist Practices of Biblical Interpretation.* Boston, MA: Beacon Press, 1992.

Schüssler-Fiorenza, Elisabeth, *In Memory of Her: A Feminist Reconstruction of Christian Origins*, 10th Edition. Chestnut Ridge, NY: Herder and Herder, 1994.

"Sept. 11 Terror Attacks Fast Facts," *CNN Library*, September 3, 2018. https://www.cnn.com/2013/07/27/us/september-11-anniversary-fast-facts/index.html (accessed 4/15, 2019).

Shaban, Hamza, "Playing War: How the Military Uses Video Games." *The Atlantic,* October 10, 2013. https://www.theatlantic.com/technology/archive/2013/10/playing-war-how-the-military-uses-video-games/280486/ (accessed December 4, 2020).

Shafir, Gershon Evrard Meade and William J. Aceves, *Routledge Critical Terrorism Studies: Lessons and Legacies of the War on Terror: From Moral Panic to Permanent War.* New York: Routledge, 2013.

Sharp, Gene, *There Are Realistic Alternatives.* Boston, MA: The Albert Einstein Institute, 2003.

Shay, Jonathan, *Achilles in Vietnam: Combat Trauma and the Undoing of Character*. New York: Atheneum, 1994.

Shay, Jonathan, "Moral Leadership Prevents Moral Injury." In *War and Moral Injury: A Reader.* Edited by Robert Emmet Meagher and Douglas A. Pryer, 301–306. Eugene, OR: Cascade Books, 2018.

Shay, Jonathan, "The Trials of Homecoming: Odysseus Returns from Iraq/Afghanistan." *Smith College Studies in Social Work,* 79 (2009): 286–298.

Shearer, Jaqueline and Paul Stekler, director, *Eyes on the Prize.* "The Promised Land (1967–68)." 1990; Blackside Production company. TV series and video. https://www.pbs.org/wgbh/americanexperience/films/eyesontheprize/ (accessed December 20, 2020).

Sheets, Connor Adams, "CIA Torture Report Poll: Half of Americans Say Enhanced Interrogation Was 'Justified.'" *International Business Times*, December 15, 2014. http://www.ibtimes.com/cia-torture-report-poll-half-americans-say-enhanced-interrogation-was-justified-1758576 (accessed March 30, 2019).

Sherman, Nancy, *The Untold War: Inside the Hearts, Minds and Souls of our Soldiers*, Reprint Edition. New York: W. W. Norton & Co., 2011.

Shinkman, Paul D., "Obama: 'Global War on Terror is Over.'" *U.S. News*, May 23, 2013. https://www.usnews.com/news/articles/2013/05/23/obama-global-war-on-terror-is-over (accessed November 28, 2020).

Shorr, Christopher, "Dictators 4 Dummies." *Touchstone Theater.* Bethlehem, PA, April 2018 and October 2020. https://www.dictators4dummies.com/performances and http://www.touchstone.org/ (accessed December 22, 2020).

Sisk, Richard, "Alarming VA Report Totals Decade of Veteran Suicides." *Military.com*, September 23, 2019. https://www.military.com/daily-news/2019/09/23/alarming-va-report-totals- decade-veteran-suicides.html (accessed October 8, 2019).

Smiley, Tavis, *Death of a King: The Real Story of Dr. Martin Luther King's Final Year.* New York: Back Bay Books, 2016. Reprint Ed. Smiley, Tavis. "Q and A with Tavis Smiley." By Brian Lamb. *CSPAN.* September 25, 2014. https://www.c-span.org/video/?321711-1/qa-tavis-smiley (accessed December 20, 2020).

Sobrino, Jon, *Where is God? Earthquake, Terrorism, Barbarity and Hope.* New York: Orbis Books, 2004.

"Summary of Findings." *Costs of War.* Watson Institute: International and Public Affairs, Brown University. https://watson.brown.edu/costsofwar/papers/summary (accessed January 17, 2019).

Theoharis, Liz, *Always with Us? What Jesus Really Said about the Poor.* Grand Rapids, MI: Eerdmans, 2017.

Thomas, Claude AnShin, *At Hell's Gate: A Soldier's Journey From War to Peace.* Boston, MA: Shambhala, 2004.

Tick, Edward, *War and the Soul: Healing Our Nation's Veterans from Post-traumatic Stress Disorder.* Wheaton, IL: Quest Books, 2005.

Tillich, Paul, *Dynamics of Faith.* New York: Harper, 1957.

Turse, Nick. "One Down, Who Knows How Many to Go?" *Tomgram: TomDispatch.com.* January 8, 2019. https://www.tomdispatch.com/post/176513/tomgram:_nick_turse,_one_down,_who_knows_how_many_to_go/ (accessed November 28, 2020).

Turse, Nick, "Will U.S. 'successes' lead to more Iraqi military failure?" *Middle East Eye*, January 22, 2016. https://www.middleeasteye.net/big-story/

will-us-successes-lead-more-iraqi-military-failures (accessed December 13, 2020).

Turse, Nick, *The Complex: How the Military Invades Our Everyday Lives.* New York: Metropolitan Books, 2008.

United Nations, "Nuclear-Weapon-Free-Zones." *United Nations Office for Disarmament Affairs.* https://www.un.org/disarmament/wmd/nuclear/nwfz/ (accessed December 20, 2020).

United Nations, "Treaty on the Prohibition of Nuclear Weapons." *United Nations Office for Disarmament Affairs.* https://www.un.org/disarmament/wmd/nuclear/tpnw/ (accessed December 20, 2020).

"U.S. Army Earth Space Defense Recruitment." *Youtube.com,* May 15, 2016. https://www.youtube.com/watch?v=Uzkp1m1wmMk (accessed January 13, 2019).

"U.S. Military Bases Overseas: The Facts." *Overseas Base Alignment and Closure Coalition,* https://www.overseasbases.net/. (accessed January 11, 2019).

U.S. Veterans Affairs, sponsor, "Faith Communities, Veterans and Mental Health; Partners in Care; Trauma; Moral Injury; Belonging," Mental Health and Chaplaincy. *A Place to Call Home.* U.S. Department of Veterans Affairs, February 2, 2017. Video. https://www.mirecc.va.gov/mentalhealthandchaplaincy/community.asp (accessed December 20, 2020).

"Valley Forge PA – Gold Stars Family Memorial Monument." *Hershel Woody Williams Medal of Honor Foundation,* September 21, 2014. http://hwwmohf.org/monument-projects.html (accessed January 8, 2021).

Vine, David, *Base Nation: How U.S. Military Bases Abroad Harm America and the World.* New York: Metropolitan Books, 2015.

VoteVets.org, "VoteVets releases Gold Star Family Members letter to Trump, demand apology for all Gold Star Families." *VoteVets.org,* August 1, 2016. https://www.votevets.org/press/gold-star-letter (accessed January 8, 2021).

Wadham, Ben, "Violence in the military and Relations Among Men: Military Masculinities and 'Rape-Prone Cultures'." In *The Palgrave International Handbook of Gender and the Military,* 1st Edition. Edited by Rachel Woodman and Clare Duncanson, 241–256. London: Palgrave, June 27, 2017.

Wall, Andy, "Bees and Love." *The Journal of Friends, Peace and Sanctuary.* Summer 2020. parabicnews@gmail.com.

The Water Protector Community: Oral History Project. https://waterprotectorscommunity.org/ (accessed December 22, 2020).

Wenner, David, "Gun Sales surge in PA amid pandemic, news of protests and civil unrest." *Pennsylvania Real-Time News.* Pennlive.com, July 8, 2020. https://www.pennlive.com/news/2020/07/gun-sales-surge-in-pa-amid-pandemic-news-of-protests-and-civil-unrest.html (accessed December 20, 2020).

"WHO Coronavirus Disease (Covid-19) Dashboard." *World Health Organization,* December 20, 2020. https://covid19.who.int/?gclid=Cj0KCQiAifz-BRDjARIsAEElyGIt0NEKzcOW7Wk9uphhgk KdShqCFtOhAJzplOMKLNv4tGcJRULHq70aAjluEALw_wcB (accessed December 20, 2020).

Williams, Caroline Randall, "A Loving Chastisement for America." *New York Times,* November 8, 2020. https://www.nytimes.com/2020/11/07/opinion/sunday/trump-america-racism.html (accessed December 20, 2020).

Williams, Delores S., "Black Women's Surrogacy Experience." In *After Patriarchy: Feminist Transformations of the World Religions.* Edited by Paula N. Cooey, William R. Eakin, Jay B. McDaniel, 1–14. Maryknoll, NY: Orbis, 1991.

Williams, Kayla, *Love my Rifle More than You: Young and Female in the U.S. Army*, Reprint Edition. New York: W. W. Norton & Company, September 17, 2006.

Wisco, Blair E., Brian P. Marx, Casey L. May, Brenda Martini, John H. Krystal, Steven M. Southwick, Robert H. Pietrzak, "Moral injury in U.S. combat veterans: Results from the national health and resilience in veterans study." *Depression and Anxiety* 34 (4) (April 2017), 340–347. https://doi.org/10.1002/da.22614 (accessed January 6, 2021).

Wood, David, "Moral Injury: Healing—Can We Treat Moral Wounds?" *The Huffington Post,* March 20, 2014. http://projects.huffingtonpost.com/moral-injury/healing (accessed January 6, 2021).

Wood, David, "The Grunts: Damned if They Kill, Damned if They Don't." *Huffington Post*, March 18, 2014. http://pach.org/from-the-media/the-grunts-damned-if-they-kill-damned-if-they-dont (accessed January 6, 2021).

Wright, David, "Donald Trump Defends Torture: 'Nothing Should Be Taken Off the Table.'" *CNN.com.* February 16, 2016. http://www.cnn.com/2016/02/16/politics/donald-trump-waterboarding-op-ed-usa-today-enhanced-interrogation-techniques-torture/ (accessed March 30, 2020).

Yandell, Michael, in "Faith Communities, Veterans and Mental Health – Video #3 – 'Moral Injury.'" From Mental Health and Chaplaincy. *A Place to Call Home,* February 2, 2017. Video. U.S. Department of Veteran Affairs. https://www.mirecc.va.gov/mentalhealthandchaplaincy/community.asp (accessed December 5, 2020).

Zalewski, Marysia, "What's the problem with the concept of military masculinities?" *Critical Military Studies* 3 (2) (April, 2017), 200–205. https://doi.org/10.1080/23337486.2017.1316480

Zaltho Foundation: Promoting Nonviolence, Awareness and Change. https://zaltho.org/ (accessed December 20, 2020).

Zwick, Edward, director, *Glory*, 1989, Tristar Pictures.

Index